You Can, Through Christ

You Have Purpose

Lexi Hermes

You Can, Through Christ

Published in Maryville, Tennessee by Beautifully Designed For More
www.beautifullydesignedformore.com
First Edition

ISBN: 9798824754629

Religion/Christian Life/ Spiritual Growth

Senior copyeditor/Interior Design and Typeset: Aimee Larsen @
www.aimeelarsen.com
Cover Design: Kalley Dietz
Cover Image: Provided by Author & Photostock
Printed in the United States of America

CONTENTS

Forward

If you've spent any time with little ones, it's likely that you've played the "why" game. Toddlers are infamous for their curiosity and persistence to learn everything about the world around them. Why is the sky blue? Why do we wear pajamas to bed? Why can't I touch that? Why does Daddy go to work? It is endless! Parents can only hope the phase will end soon, right? Not exactly, as we enter adolescence and ultimately adulthood, the questions only deepen. Why do I exist? What does my future hold? Do I matter? Unfortunately, if we don't have a trusted source of truth to turn to, we often let the world and people around us answer these questions for us. The hurt, shame, and trials that life can bring inevitably shape what we think about ourselves and unveils our purpose, or lack thereof. I recall too many memories of a diagnosis, a broken relationship, a poor grade, or social media post that led me to the conclusion that I must have no worth or value as a person. How could my life have a purpose amidst the pain I'm experiencing?

You Can Through Christ uses the truth of Scripture to answer the deepest questions of our heart and reveal the beauty of a new life that Christ bought for you. Each life on earth has purpose. When that reality sinks into our soul, it changes what's possible. God intended so much more for our lives than the comfortable routines we've grown accustomed to. He went to the depths of all pain and darkness to make a way for us to experience His love, glory, and righteousness! Through a relationship with Him, we can do anything! Our lives are utterly transformed when we come to know Emmanuel, "God with us."

Lexi is a dear friend of mine with passion and boldness I've never encountered before. She is on a mission to share the gospel of truth with everyone around her and lives a life that genuinely looks different because of the joy and hope that Christ brings to her soul. That's not to say that she doesn't experience pain, disappointment, or suffering, but when all is lost, she opens her Bible, pours out her heart to the Savior of the world, and trusts that His plan and purpose is sovereign and good. There will be times when we don't feel happy, but we have the truth of Romans 5:10, 2 Timothy 1:9 and Philippians 4:13 to rest in.

This book is a labor of love, one that began long before Lexi even knew it was a book! I am honored to introduce *You Can Through Christ,* and I pray that its words may change the way you view the world around you and the purpose you've been called to in a life with Christ.

-Karissa Kunze

Introduction

Are you questioning your exact purpose in life? You are in the right place. Now, you may be wondering, "how do *you* know my exact purpose, *you* don't even know me?" Well, God knows you, and you are not reading this book by accident. You are about to make an investment, not only for today, but for eternity. He made you, and He does not make mistakes. More importantly, everything He designs has an intentional purpose. This book is full of advice, motivation, and direction you can be sure of, not because it's advice from me, but it's from the One who made you and knows you the best. I have hoped and prayed that God led me to share with you exactly what He wants you to know. *Disclaimer: I need this book as much as you do.* If this advice was given solely from me, I would fail you without a doubt, but when it's from Him and His Word directly, it will never fail. He has been my best friend since I was little, and I believe Jesus has put this on my heart since that time. I have saved countless scripture, advice, and heart-to-heart talks from a journal I have had since I was 8. I called it "My Book of Inspiration," which I thought should now be made public. I strongly want my family, friends, patients, teammates, players, and even strangers I come across to know the truth and be able to live it. Once I finally read through my Bible, I knew it was time. I continue to learn more and fall more in love with Him every day. He has put so many different roles and obligations on my life, and I know He has done the same for you. We have so many responsibilities, and even though we are always kept busy with this crazy life, there is one thing I have learned: spending time with God is vital. It is the purpose of our lives, and once we give Him the time of all our passions and relationships, He provides the way to let them flourish more than we can on our own. I am excited this book will show you the purpose we are looking for: purpose for this life, and purpose for the one to come. This is a love that will give you the courage and confidence to do all things through Him who strengthens you...starting now.

Purpose of Our Lives

"I can do all things through Christ who gives me strength." Philippians 4:13

I can live my *salvation, purpose, and his grace* through Christ who strengthens me.

The theme of the book is based upon scripture, specifically Philippians 4:13, "I can do all things through Christ who strengthens me." We always want to keep scripture in context. Here, Paul is telling the church at Philippi that no matter the circumstances, he has learned contentment through Christ who gives him strength. Even though you should keep this verse in context, I want us to remember and keep the theme that anything and everything is possible with God.

Created for a Purpose

You are reading this right now. Where did you come from? Why are you here? What is your purpose? God created everything out of nothing, the Heavens and the earth. He created us and our spirit, as well as the animals out of dust. (See Revelation 10:6, Psalm 33:6, Genesis 2:7, Genesis 2:19 and Zechariah 12:1)

"He spreads out the northern skies over empty space; he suspends the earth over nothing. He wraps up the waters in his clouds, yet the clouds do not burst under their weight. He covers the face of the full moon, spreading his clouds over it. He marks out the horizon on the face of the waters for a boundary between light and darkness." -Job 26:7-10.

"And these are but the outer fringe of his works." -Job 26:14.

"By faith we understand that the universe was formed at God's command, so that what is seen was not made out of what was visible." -Hebrews 11:3.

"This is what the Lord says, he who appoints the sun to shine by day, who decrees the moon and stars to shine by night, who stirs up the sea so that its waves roar- the Lord Almighty is his name." -Jeremiah 31:35.

Have you ever thought about where you come from? Why you are here? Did you know you not only have a Creator, but the Creator is faithful? (See Psalm 146:6, Job 38: 28-29, Psalm 147:17-18 and Isaiah 48:12-13).

The earth is beautiful and cannot be recreated. It was originally designed, and the earth is only the outer fringe of the His works, just like you! He designed you through His wisdom. He put thought into creating you, it was not random or accidental. (See Psalm 104:24-25).

He wanted to make you, before the beginning of time.

How do you picture God? Do you picture Him as a dad, pointing to a picture on His fridge telling others about how proud He is of His child, and how much He loves you? Can you fathom the Creator of the universe cares for you and thinks about you even though, in the millions of people who have lived on this earth, you are one soul? (See Psalm 144:3-4).

Everyone feels inadequate at times. Even David, who was a man after God's own heart, asked God, "who is he that the Creator has brought him this far?" -2 Samuel 7:18. Do you understand that there are more stars than grains of sand, and this was all created out of love for us from God? How can we think creation was an accident? How can we think God isn't behind all science? How can we not praise and worship such a mighty and loving God?

When some people think of religion, they think of an angry higher-being who punishes you when you do wrong. Maybe it is punishment from when you were younger or life's challenges that makes you think religion is punishment, or maybe you have had a negative experience with a Christian in your life. Despite our experience, the beauty that is God wants you to run to Him first when you mess up, but maybe you assume that a God who is perfect could never find joy in someone who is imperfect. That is not the case of our Father. Maybe you didn't have the best experiences with your parents, if so, then I hope this scripture encourages you. "Though my father and mother forsake me, the Lord will receive me." -Psalm 27:10. You may have had an abusive parent, or just not the best relationship with your parents. Even if you have a great relationship with your parents, they are still human and cannot completely satisfy the role God has as our Father. God designed our parents to give us just a glimpse of what the eternal relationship with Him looks like. Even then, we as humans can mess that up too, but God always gets it right- gets it perfect.

For some, when we disobey our parents, we receive correction whether through punishment or guidance. Even when people read the Old Testament about how angry God would get when the Israelites rebelled, He always forgave and tried to help them. His anger was always justified, and He always pursued the Israelites hearts until Christ came to complete His justice and His grace in one act on the cross. An example, God sent venomous snakes to attack the Israelites as punishment for their ways; however, when they repented, God sent a bronze snake and put it on a pole so all who believed in its power and looked upon it would live, their lives saved (Numbers 21:6-9). Even though their actions deserved punishment and death, God made a way. Just like Christ, when we look upon Him at the cross and believe, we are also saved. Side note: today, the snake and pole together are the world-known medical signs!

Like a child that belongs to his or her earthly Father, we belong to God. "Know that the Lord is God. It is he who made us, and we are his; we are his people, the sheep of his pasture." -Psalm 100:3 (Psalm 119:73, Psalm 22:9-10, Isaiah 49:1 and Deuteronomy 32:6). We belong to Him, but more than that, He delights in us. (See Genesis 1:31).

You exist because the idea of you made God so incredibly happy. This is also good to keep in mind when thinking of others. No one would be here if the idea of them existing did not make God jump for joy, which is how love for others develops. God longs for His creation. (See Job 14:15-17).

"Before I formed you in the womb I knew you, before you were born, I set you apart; I appointed you as a prophet to the nations." -Jeremiah 1:5.

"I want you to know, brothers and sisters, that the gospel I preached is not of human origin. I did not receive it from any man, nor was I taught it; rather, I received it by revelation from Jesus Christ. For you have heard of my previous way of life in Judaism, how intensely I persecuted the church of God and tried to destroy it. I was advancing in Judaism beyond many of my own age among my people and was extremely zealous for the traditions of my fathers. But when God, who set me apart from my mother's womb and called me by His grace, was pleased to reveal His Son in me so that I might preach Him among the Gentiles, my immediate response was not to consult any human being." -Galatians 1:11-16.

Even Paul, who persecuted the church, was set apart from the time he was in his mother's womb to preach the gospel; not of human origin, God purposefully gave him the ability to share it with others. Whether your parents planned to have a child or not, God planned you specifically. Which leads me to ask, do you feel unsatisfied? No matter who you are, I am going to say the answer is "yes". How can I be so sure? We were not made for this world. God created us, put us here for a temporary time, and is going to want us back. The only One who can satisfy you is God. We should be thankful for the world; it is beautiful even though it can't satisfy, as it was created by God and leads us right to him. "My soul faints with longing for your salvation, but I have put my hope in your word." -Psalm 119:81.

As we have all experienced, everyone lets us down at some point: our spouse, family, friends, people that you think could never do such a thing. The truth is, they are human beings. People are an amazing part of our lives whom God designed for us to have a relationship with; however, they can never fulfill us. The only way you can know who you are, is to understand who God is and what He has done for you. We always think we will be happy if we achieve that accomplishment, become that athlete, get that one outfit, use this type of make-up, travel to this one place, buy this one house, lose so much weight, workout out this many times, get that one job, earn that one degree, date that one person, be more famous, get married, or have kids. We wonder why when we accomplish these things, we are still unsatisfied and always want more. When someone is married, they want a better job. Someone with a great job desire to be married. As people, we are experts on how to obsess over what we do not have- thinking those missing pieces are the key to our contentment! This is simply not true; when most people acquire what they were longing for, they continue to think of what they want next. Our call is to be God's and to be used by Him to help others. Life is not about finding yourself; it is about discovering who God made you to be.

"Do not put your trust in princes, who cannot save, in human beings, who cannot save." -Psalm 146:3.

"Those who trust in themselves are fools, but those who walk in wisdom are kept safe" -Proverbs 28:26.

Truth time. If you put your hope in anything I mentioned above, what you trust in is fragile. (See Job 8:12-14). What does that mean? You will only be let down. Whether you believe it or not, there is a life after this one, and only that life can satisfy you. His name is our heart's desire. Our soul longs for Him, whether morning or night. (See Isaiah 26:8-9, Psalm 42:1-2 and Psalm 63:1). You were made by God, for God and for more than this temporary earth. Until you realize this, you will always be longing for more. The only way to be satisfied, while here, is to realize you will eventually reach "there." Jesus says He is all you need to be satisfied. "Then Jesus declared, I am the bread of life. Whoever comes to me will never go hungry, and whoever believes in me will never be thirsty." -John 6:35-38 (John 4:14, Psalm 107:8-9 and John 6:47-51). When we trust Jesus, we are not doing nothing. Trusting Him means doing what He says. There is nothing we can do to obtain salvation; He has already done it all! However, we can obey what He says while we are here on earth, as He allows you this trust and draws you in.

"In their hearts, humans plan their course, but the Lord establishes their steps." -Proverbs 16:9 (Proverbs 20:24). It is great to have dreams and desires, if we allow God to change them as needed for our good and His glory. There are many great self-help books, but if you haven't noticed, it is hard to accomplish what is in them on your own. We also make New Year's resolutions and wonder why, by February, we do not have the same motivation or power. Only God has the power to change your life. Only Jesus makes things new! Without Him, there will be no difference. Who are we to say that today or tomorrow, we will do this or that? "Why, you do not know what will happen tomorrow. What is your life? You are a mist that appears for a little while and then vanishes. Instead, you ought to say, if it is the Lord's will, I will do this or that." -James 4:13-15.

We only have a brief window here on Earth. Before we live out our day-to-day lives, it is wise to consult God first, since He is all-knowing and all caring. Isn't it comforting to ask and inquire of someone who already knows your tomorrow?

We live as if we are going to live forever; we are not. Satan wants you to think you have all this time, but you don't. Satan has blinded the minds of unbelievers, which is why they do not see the light of the glory of Christ, the image of God. (See 2 Corinthians 4:4, Matthew 13:1-23, Mark 4:1-20 and Luke 8:5-15). When you die, if you do not have Christ, the curtains will rise on everything you thought you knew, and you will see how much more there is.

The Bible Reveals the Purpose

The Word of God is the divinely inspired Holy Bible. Divinely inspired means God intervened with the authors to inspire their words in accordance with His will, thus breathing life and His Spirit into the Bible. Understanding that when you accept the Word of God, you realize it is not a human word, but the Word of God which is at work in those who believe (See 1 Thessalonians 2:13).

We know the Bible is accurate and valid because of its content, history, context, reliable sources, and because the message has remained unchanged from the beginning of time. It is easy to be a skeptic because, like many others, you feel you need to see something to believe it.

I know it seems crazy to believe a story like Jonah eaten by a big fish, but what is even more of a miracle, and real to me, is how my selfish heart has been changed by this Book. Even though following God does not guarantee we get everything we want, or that everything goes perfect, it is impossible to follow God your entire life and not see miracles, my changed heart is one of them. "You performed signs and wonders in Egypt and have continued them to this day, in Israel and among all mankind, and have gained the renown that is still yours." -Jeremiah 32:20 (Daniel 4:2-3).

The Bible is directly from God, and we know God is all-knowing and infallible. Not to mention that He gave us His Word because He loves us! It is for us! "All scripture is God-breathed and is useful for teaching, rebuking, correcting and training in righteousness, so that the servant of God may be thoroughly equipped for every good work." -2 Timothy 3:16-17.

God has equipped us to be able to share the gospel. I get nervous or fearful sometimes, then I realize we are equipped because God literally lives inside us as the Holy Spirit. I was nervous because I had the false impression that I had to defend God or His Word, or explain it perfectly, but His Word is power in and of itself. It doesn't need to be defended but proclaimed. I used to get nervous thinking I had to explain scripture to others. Why would I try if I do not understand it all completely myself? Then I realized it doesn't need to be explained. It is the complete Word of God speaking to each one of us; it has its fullness.

"For the Word of God is living and active and sharper than any two-edged sword and piercing as far as the division of soul and spirit, of both joints and marrow, and able to judge the thoughts and intentions of the heart. And there is no creature hidden from His sight, but all things are open and laid bare to the eyes of Him with whom we have to do." -Hebrews 4:12-13.

"Every word of God is tested; He is a shield to those who take refuge in Him. Do not add to His words or He will reprove you, and you will be proved a liar." -Proverbs 30:5-6. Did you know the Bible has a 100% batting average? Every single prophecy has been fulfilled; none has failed. Due to a perfect batting average, we never have to fear striking out because scripture is our proof; the very Word of God is our evidence.

"For he vigorously refuted his Jewish opponents in public debate, proving from the Scriptures that Jesus was the Messiah." -Acts 18:28.

"God is not human, that he should lie, not a human being, that he should change his mind. Does he speak and then not act? Does he promise and not fulfill?" -Numbers 23:19 (1 Samuel 15:29). "In the hope of eternal life, which God, who does not lie, promised before the beginning of time." -Titus 1:2. If I ever read something I am not sure about in the Bible, I know I am wrong. I am fallible- God is not. We also have the prophetic message as something completely reliable, and you will do well to pay attention to it.

"We also have the prophetic message as something completely reliable, and you will do well to pay attention to it, as to a light shining in a dark place, until the day dawns and the morning star rises in your hearts. Above all, you must understand that no prophecy of Scripture came about by the prophet's own interpretation of things. For prophecy never had its origin in the human will, but prophets, though human, spoke from God as they were carried along by the Holy Spirit." - 2 Peter 1:19-21.

The Bible is broken up into books and chapters, and every author has the same message; the Dead Sea Scrolls confirm the original words. The Dead Sea Scrolls are 12 copies of the Bible discovered by a shepherd and archaeologists from Jerusalem in caves of the Qumran community where David fled from Saul.

Archaeology confirms the Bible's history is accurate, such as finding the wheels with certain spokes in the Red Sea. Many secular texts have the same events recorded as the Bible. Many have argued the Bible is unable to be understood, but even though we will always be learning, I do not think God gave us His Word with the intent that we wouldn't understand anything from it. That is why we must keep studying, as you will always learn something new! Do you realize how blessed we are to have the Bible? Not everyone had this bound, translated Bible like we do today. We get the whole story! Matthew 1:1-16 and Luke 3:23-38 shows a list of the genealogy of Jesus the Messiah. The amazing thing about His genealogy is, along with the geography and measurements of the buildings, it can be matched with secular historical accounts to prove these people existed. Just as promised, "This is the genealogy of Jesus the Messiah the son of David, the son of Abraham." - Matthew 1:1.

"My faithful love will be with him, and through my name, his horn will be exalted. I will set his hand over the sea, his right hand over the rivers. He will call out to me, 'You are my Father, my God, the Rock my Savior.' And I will appoint him to be my firstborn, the most exalted of the kings of the earth. I will maintain my love to him forever, and my covenant with him will never fail. I will establish his line forever, his throne as long as the Heavens endure. If his sons forsake my law and do not follow my statutes, if they violate my decrees and fail to keep my commands, I will punish their sin with the rod, their iniquity with flogging; but I will not take my love from him, nor will I ever betray my faithfulness. I will not violate my covenant or alter what my lips have uttered. Once for all, I have sworn by my holiness—and I will not lie to David—that his line will continue forever and his throne endure before me like the sun; it will be established forever like the moon, the faithful witness in the sky." -Psalm 89:24-37 (1 Chronicles 17:11-13).

This is just the beginning of the prophesy, that God is going to bring our salvation through David by bringing Jesus through his bloodline. Solomon and other kings through this line are unfaithful to God in the end; however, God says because of David's faithfulness these mistakes and the rebellion toward Him will not stop salvation from coming. God doesn't promise He will not punish His offspring who do not follow Him, but He promises to continue to be faithful through His line no matter what they chose.

If you think the Bible is contradicting, make sure you are always looking at the context of who is being spoken to, why, the situation, and using dispensation. (2 Timothy 2:15). Dispensation is looking at the different promises God makes before and after He sends Jesus via the Old and New Testament to bring us salvation.

The Old Testament was written in Hebrew, and the New Testament was written in Greek, which eventually lead to the translations of our English Bibles. However, if you read any translation, you see the same message is being brought across. The more you read scripture, talk about the Bible, and listen to God, the more it will all make sense. Despite thousands of years between its creation and now, the message is always the same.

It is all about falling in love with His Word, which is ultimately Him! You will have stability in your life, no matter your circumstances when you are firmly rooted in His Word. You will know where to turn in times of trouble. "But whose delight is in the law of the Lord, and who meditates on his law, day and night. That person is like a tree planted by streams of water, which yields its fruit in season and whose leaf does not wither- whatever they do prosper." -Psalms 1:2-3 (Psalm 19:7 and Psalm 119:97). The proof of the Bible is your stability when rooted in the Word.

"In the beginning was the word, the word was with God and was God. Through him everything was made. In him is life, and the light of all mankind, and darkness has not overcome it." -John 1:1-5 (Revelation 19:13-16). God, Jesus, the Holy Spirit and the words in the Bible were here in the beginning but made their appearances to the Earth at different times.

"Now this is eternal life: that they know you, the only true God, and Jesus Christ, whom you have sent. I have brought you glory on earth by finishing the work you gave me to do. And now, Father, glorify me in your presence with the glory I had with you before the world began." -John 17:3-5.

God's Word is Him directly talking to us. "The Word became flesh and made his dwelling among us. We have seen his glory, the glory of the one and only Son, who came from the Father, full of grace and truth" -John 1:14.

Transactional or Relational

In the Old Testament, God mandated a transactional form of forgiveness where there was a specific and different sacrifice for each type of sin. Jesus was the sacrifice to take away that transactional form of "religion" and introduce the relational form of forgiveness. God is not pleased with rams, or first born for the sin of our souls. He requires we act justly, love mercy and walk humbly with Him. (See Micah 6:7-8). He does not delight in sacrifice or burnt offerings, but the sacrifice of a broken spirit and contrite heart. (See Psalm 51:16-17). Praising God in song and with thanksgiving will please him more than ox. The Lord hears the needy. (See Psalm 69:30-33).

"This is an illustration for the present time, indicating that the gifts and sacrifices being offered were not able to clear the conscience of the worshiper. They are only a matter of food and drink and various ceremonial washings- external regulations applying until the time of the new order. But when Christ came as high priest of the good things that are now already here, He went through the greater and more perfect tabernacle that is not made with human hands is not a part of this creation. He did not enter by means of the blood of goats and calves; but he entered the Most Holy Place once for all by his own blood, thus obtaining eternal redemption. The blood of goats and bulls and the ashes of a heifer sprinkled on those who are ceremonially unclean sanctify them so that they are outwardly clean. How much more, then, will the blood of Christ, who through the eternal Spirit offered himself unblemished to God, cleanse our consciences from acts that lead to death, so that we may serve the living God! For this reason, Christ is the mediator of a new covenant, that those who are called may receive the promised eternal inheritance- now that he has died as a ransom to set them free from the sins committed under the first covenant." -Hebrews 9:9-15.

Even though works do not lead to salvation, they matter. We don't do more by trying harder but by falling in love with Jesus!

Not one of the good promises of the Lord our God has failed. Everyone has been fulfilled. (See Joshua 23:14, Joshua 21:44-45 and 2 Chronicles 6:10). "But I the

Lord will speak what I will, and it shall be fulfilled without delay." -Ezekiel 12:25. Not only does God keep His promises, but His promises are fulfilled in His perfect timing. "The Lord has done what he planned; he has fulfilled his word, which he decreed long ago." -Lamentations 2:17. Not only does He fulfill these promises in his perfect timing, but He will carry out His plans, which are always good. "This is the disciple who testifies to these things and who wrote them down. We know that his testimony is true. Jesus did many other things as well. If every one of them were written down, I suppose that even the whole world would not have room for the books that would be written." -John 21:24-25 (Psalm 40:5). God has done more for us than we realize, but if every miracle were recorded in the Bible, the world wouldn't have room for His power!

The Bible is one love story line from beginning to end of God's redemptive plan to save us through Jesus. Even though people wrote the book physically, the Holy Spirit, acting through them, is why there is no error. The Bible can answer any question you have, even if sometimes the answer is to simply trust Him. The questions people feel cannot be answered can be left at the cross instead of leading to disbelief. It answers why there is so much brokenness today from the fall of humanity, to what will happen in our own lives when we act in certain ways.

Many people wonder how we can know other books and religions are not accurate, or a part of the Bible. The answer is they contradict the Bible. It is impossible for all religions to be "correct" because they contradict each other as well. Most religions are trying to help us find a god, but Jesus said, "He is God coming here to save *you*." -Luke 19:10. There is one God- the Trinity- three in one. If you read, believing the God of the universe wrote the Book, you will not find one contradiction.

Ever since the beginning of time, people were contesting God. "Then you call on the name of your god, and I will call on the name of the Lord. The god who answers by fire- he is God." -1 Kings 18:24. "Baal, answer us!" they shouted. But there was no response; no one answered. And they danced around the altar they had made." -1 Kings 18:26.

"At the time of sacrifice, the prophet Elijah stepped forward and prayed: "Lord, the God of Abraham, Isaac and Israel, let it be known today that you are God in Israel and that I am your servant and have done all these things at your command. Answer me, Lord, answer me, so these people will know that you, Lord, are God, and that you are turning their hearts back again." Then the fire of the Lord fell and burned up the sacrifice, the wood, the stones and the soil, and also licked up the water in the trench. When all the people saw this, they fell prostrate and cried, "The Lord- he is God! The Lord- he is God!" -1 Kings 18:36-39.

God continues to prove Himself repeatedly. God never gave up on Israel even when they were in exile. He sent the prophets Ezra, Nehemiah, and Zerubbabel to continue to pursue His people and turn them back from destroying their lives. What is even more fascinating is how God takes people who do not consult Him but changes their hearts in order to help his people. "...the Lord moved the heart of Cyrus king of Persia to make a proclamation throughout his realm and also to put it in writing..." -Ezra 1:1.

As Christians, we have the same evidence as atheists. We see the same exact world, but we interpret differently how everything came to be. For example, look at the flood of Noah. Why can't all the fossils be from the flood? Why are there sea remains on top of mountains and in deserts? Another example is evolution from an animal perspective. Why can't it be God who created animals that can adapt over time? Whether you believe in evolution from an ape to a human perspective, or just that a loving God created us, neither have been physically witnessed, and both take "faith," in the sense of believing without seeing. Show God's love to those who do not feel the same as you and have confidence you have the ultimate truth. It is obvious there is a Mastermind behind our creation who also loves, has a purpose, and has a will. I'm a hand therapist. I love science, but I also love the "why" behind the science of who created the human body. Your DNA is too specifically designed to be an accident.

People often will think I have it all together, and that is why I am a Christ-follower, and why I go to church. I am here to tell everyone, in fact, it is the complete opposite. I am broken in every way, and in need of a Savior more than I can express in words. I need and have the awesome opportunity to have a church family to love who hold me accountable. My brokenness is beyond fixing. I can't do it on my own. I need a Savior; we all do! His name is Jesus.

"Just as Moses lifted up the snake in the wilderness, so the Son of Man must be lifted up, that everyone who believes may have eternal life in him. For God so loved the world that he gave His only begotten Son, that whoever believes in Him should not perish, but have everlasting life." -John 3:14-16 (Luke 1:77-79 and Revelation 1:4-6).

Many stop here, but I want to read you the rest.

"For God did not send His son to condemn the world, but to save the world through Him. Whoever believes in Him is not condemned, but whoever does not believe stands condemned already because they have not believed in the name of God's one and only Son. This is the verdict: Light has come into the world, but people loved darkness instead of light because their deeds were evil. Everyone who does evil hates the light and will not come into the light for fear that their deeds will be exposed. But whoever lives by the truth comes into the light, so that it may be seen plainly that what they have done has been done in the sight of God." -John 3:17-21.

The God who created everything loves you! Jesus plus nothing. Not Jesus plus good works. Jesus alone.

"…know that a person is not justified by the works of the law, but by faith in Jesus Christ. So, we too, have put our faith in Christ Jesus that we may be justified by faith in Christ and not by the works of the law, because by the works of the law no one will be justified." -Galatians 2:16.

This completely takes the burden off us when we fail and sin, but what He did ignites, in us, a response of love and wanting to obey. Wanting to do right or the fear of getting caught will never be enough to change your heart and motivate you to do good. God so loved us; He sent Jesus to die for us and to give us everlasting life. Jesus didn't come to condemn us but to condemn Satan and save us. We were already condemned before Christ came for our sin. It is so tempting to want to hide our brokenness when we are exposed to the light; we are so scared of rejection. The beauty is, once you admit your brokenness, God accepts you regardless and helps you repair. If you deny your brokenness, you are denying the truth and only hurting yourself.

"For the Lord is righteous, he loves justice; the upright will see his face."

-Psalm 11:7 (Psalm 89:13-14 and Psalm 97:2). Justice is the foundation of God's throne as seen in the Psalms. "But the Lord is the true God; he is the living God, the eternal King. When He is angry, the earth trembles; the nations cannot endure His wrath." -Jeremiah 10:10.

"Tell them this: 'These gods, who did not make the Heavens and the earth, will perish from the earth and from under the Heavens. But God made the earth by his power; he founded the world by his wisdom and stretched out the Heavens by his understanding. When he thunders, the waters in the Heavens roar; he makes clouds rise from the ends of the earth. He sends lightning with the rain and brings out the wind from his storehouses." -Jeremiah 10:11-13 (Jeremiah 50:15-16 and Psalm 90:11).

"Learn to do what is right; seek justice. Defend the oppressed. Take up the cause of the fatherless; plead the case of the widow." -Isaiah 1:17 (Isaiah 56:1 and Jeremiah 5:28-29). "For I, the Lord, love justice; I hate robbery and wrongdoing. In my faithfulness, I will reward my people and make an everlasting covenant with them." -Isaiah 61:8. Amos 5:14-15 says God wants us to seek good so He may be with us and maintain justice in the courts. God is just. Could you imagine a referee or umpire who does not abide by the rules of the game or a judge who does not uphold the law? God wants us to practice justice while we are here on earth, helping the fatherless, the widows and keeping justice in our court systems. This justice is why God sent His only son to die for us. Therefore, He had to suffer. God upholds justice but wants to show mercy.

God is so Holy and just, no sin is allowed into Heaven; that's why it is perfect. Therefore, just like in a court or in our justice system, there needs to be a consequence for wrongdoings. "For the wages of sin is death, but the gift of God is eternal life in Christ Jesus our Lord." -Romans 6:23. "But because they served them in the presence of their idols and made the people of Israel fall into sin, therefore I have sworn with uplifted hand that they must bear the consequences of their sin, declares the Sovereign Lord." -Ezekiel 44:12. The only thing is, the consequence of our sin is death- eternal separation from God, since when we sin, we are ultimately choosing to be separated from God's way. This is the definition of sin. Sin is what separates us from God, but He loves us so much, He could not stand to be separated from us.

"But your iniquities have separated you from God; your sins have hidden His face from you, so that He will not hear. For your hands are stained with blood, your fingers with guilt. Your lips have spoken falsely, and your tongue mutters wicked things. No one calls for justice; no one pleads a case with integrity. They rely on empty arguments, they utter lies; they conceive trouble and give birth to evil." -Isaiah 59:2-4.

He needed to break the separation, the ultimate love story.

"Therefore, just as sin entered the world through one man, and death through sin, and in this way, death came to all people, because all sinned." -Romans 5:12 (Romans 5:18-19 and 1 Corinthians 15:22).

"This righteousness is given through faith in Jesus Christ to all who believe. There is no difference between Jew and Gentile, for all have sinned and fall short of the glory of God, and all are justified freely by his grace through the redemption that came by Christ Jesus. God presented Christ as a sacrifice of atonement, through the shedding of his blood—to be received by faith. He did this to demonstrate his righteousness, because in his forbearance he had left the sins committed beforehand unpunished." -Romans 3:22-25 (Hebrews 2:17).

"If you, Lord, kept record of sins, Lord, who could stand? But with you there is forgiveness, so that we can, with reverence, serve you." -Psalm 130:3-4.

"But I will pass judgment on you because you say, "I have not sinned" - Jeremiah 2:35. "Indeed, there is no one on earth who is righteous, no one who does what is right and never sins." -Ecclesiastes 7:20 (Proverbs 20:9, 1 Kings 8:46 and 2 Chronicles 6:36). "...every inclination of the human heart is evil from childhood." Genesis 8:21. We have no good in us; anything good is reflected from God. According to some research I came across while studying for the psych portion of my certified hand therapy exam, people believe the world is good, and comprehensible, and they themselves are worthy and effective. Trauma shatters this image, and forces people to see a new image. (Janoff-Bulman, Shattered Assumptions: Towards a New Psychology of Trauma, 1992). All of us experience trauma at some point in our lives, and what do we do with this new image?

22

"Surely I was sinful at birth, sinful from the time my mother conceived me." -Psalm 51:5. "But they do not realize that I remember all their evil deeds. Their sins engulf them; they are always before me." -Hosea 7:2. God has seen every single wrong you have ever done, and He loves you anyways.

"This is the message we have heard from him and declare to you: God is light; in him there is no darkness at all. If we claim to have fellowship with him and yet walk in the darkness, we lie and do not live out the truth. But if we walk in the light, as he is in the light, we have fellowship with one another, and the blood of Jesus, his Son, purifies us from all sin. If we claim to be without sin, we deceive ourselves and the truth is not in us. If we confess our sins, he is faithful and just and will forgive us our sins and purify us from all unrighteousness. If we claim we have not sinned, we make him out to be a liar and his word is not in us." -1 John 1:5-10.

Every single one of us has done wrong. The issue is, our definition of what is wrong is skewed since we have eaten from the tree giving us our own opinion, not the truth. When we are the judge, we judge ourselves inaccurately.

"Fools find no pleasure in understanding but delight in airing their own opinions." -Proverbs 18:2. To be honest, my opinion does not matter and neither does yours *when it comes to God's authoritative Word*. Take your opinion and compare it to God's Word. I know when people are gratifying the flesh, sometimes they do not realize what they are doing is evil because their own opinion has convinced them otherwise. When God says something is a sin, we like to have another opinion. When you are in Christ, even when you do not understand, your opinion doesn't matter anymore if it contradicts with His.

If you do not think you have done wrong, what if I told you anything we do that is not from faith is a sin? "But whoever has doubts is condemned if they eat, because their eating is not from faith; and everything that does not come from faith is sin." -Romans 14:23. Or even if you do anything without consulting or seeking the Lord first? "He did evil because he had not set his heart on seeking the Lord." -2 Chronicles 12:14. I am not sure about you, but the fact that having any doubts, or doing anything without faith are sins makes me realize how far gone I am. I would think I have no hope, but good news is here! I am not telling you this to make you feel bad, but I want you to see the reality of our condition and realize much more how loved you are.

The Beginning of Sin

Sin has been here since the beginning. "In the middle of the garden were the tree of life and the tree of the knowledge of good and evil." -Genesis 2:9.

"The Lord God took the man and put him in the Garden of Eden to work it and take care of it. And the Lord God commanded the man, "you are free to eat from any tree in the garden; but you must not eat from the tree of the knowledge of good and evil, for when you eat from it, you will certainly die." -Genesis 2:15-17.

"'You will not certainly die,' the serpent said to the woman." -Genesis 3:4. "...she took some and ate it. She also gave some to her husband, who was with her, and he ate it" -Genesis 3:6. What is it about us that makes us want to do something when told we can't? What happened when we ate the fruit of the knowledge of good and evil? We began having our own opinions and wanting our own way, as opposed to following God our Creator, who knows us better than we know ourselves. God is so upset we listened to Satan. "And I will put enmity between you and the woman, and between your offspring and hers; he will crush your head, and you will strike his heel." -Genesis 3:15. This is a reference to Jesus being crucified as striking the heel, but Satan's head was crushed when He overcame death. We have rule over Satan.

Even though, right away, God is saying in the end there will be victory, it doesn't mean we do not have pain from rebellion from Him in our day-to-day lives until we are with Him. "...until you return to the ground, since from it you were taken; for dust you are and to dust you will return." -Genesis 3:19. "And the Lord God said, "The man has now become like one of us, knowing good and evil. He must not be allowed to reach out his hand and take also from the Tree of Life and eat and live

24

forever." -Genesis 3:22. "As at Adam, they have broken the covenant; they were unfaithful to me there." -Hosea 6:7. If Adam and Eve had eaten from the Tree of Life after sinning, they would have lived eternally separated from God in our sinful condition, and God loves us too much to let that happen. The second they ate of the Tree; they were spiritually dead; the process of aging and death had begun. God hates sin because He loves us. Sin destroys us and pulls us away from Him. God did not make us die; we chose death when we chose of the fruit. You may be thinking "Why should I suffer because of what Adam and Eve did?" We would have made the same decision as them. Yet, He does not hate us for causing our sin. God loves us more than we can imagine but hates sin because it separates us from Him. He wanted us to be with Him so badly, He sent His only son, Himself, to die, in order to take the punishment, we deserve. God always seeks to restore His creation, which is why we have not been destroyed. He refuses to abandon His workmanship to the point of giving everything to Him, his Son. He could have sent us to Hell right after Adam and Eve sinned, but He didn't.

Why Hell? Hell exists because love means you have the choice to say yes or no. God is saying if you choose to be apart from me for eternity, I will not force you to be with me. God's holiness and justice demand a Hell. Think of someone who has wronged you. Think of the worst possible circumstance, someone murdering a child or rape. Don't you think there needs to be consequences? Jesus' death was the price paid. His horrible death shows how terrible our sin is. Hell exists to defeat evil. Satan will be thrown there in the end, into the lake of fire. The question is not, "is there life after death?" The question is, "what are you choosing today?"

Luke 16:19-31 talks about two men, one who was sent in torment to Hades, and Lazarus in Heaven with Abraham. From Hades, the man asks for pity from Abraham to have Lazarus cool his tongue from the agony of the fire. Abraham said that a great chasm separates those who want to go from here, so you cannot and vice versa. The man in Hades then asked if Lazarus could go back to earth to warn his brothers. Abraham said, if they will not listen to Moses and the Prophets, they won't be convinced even if someone rises from the dead. I want to point out, in this circumstance, the rich man was not in Hell because of his wealth and the poor man was not in Heaven just because he was poor. There is nothing "righteous" about being poor, and nothing evil in God blessing you with money from the work of your hands if it was not gained deceitfully. Think about it. If people get angry at people who are well off, then we give the poor more and they are well off, then continue to be angry at them when they are provided for? It was a matter of heart. The next thing I want you to notice is that once you are in Heaven or Hell, you cannot reverse your decision. You may be thinking, "I would not choose Hell!" Our loving Father would never send anyone to Hell. It is a conscious decision to not be with Him for eternity that He is honoring. He wants to save you and wants you in paradise forever with Him!

Jesus Our Savior

"He grew up before him like a tender shoot, and like a root out of dry ground. He has no beauty or majesty to attract us to him, nothing in his appearance that we should desire him. He was despised and rejected by mankind, a man of suffering, and familiar with pain. Like one from whom people hide their faces he was despised, and we held him in low esteem. Surely, he took up our pain and bore our suffering, yet we considered him punished by God, stricken him, and afflicted. But He was pierced for our transgressions, He was crushed for our iniquities; the punishment that brought us peace was Him, and by his wounds we are healed. We all, like sheep, have gone astray, each of us has turned to our own way; and the Lord has laid on him the iniquity of us all. He was oppressed and afflicted, yet he did not open his mouth; he was led like a lamb to the slaughter, and as a sheep before its shearers is silent, so he did not open his mouth. By oppression and judgment, he was taken away. Yet who of his generation protested? For he was cut off from the land of the living; for the transgression of my people, he was punished. He was assigned a grave with the wicked, and with the rich in his death, though he had done no violence, nor was any deceit in his mouth." -Isaiah 53:2-9.

Jesus cares so much about your suffering, He decided to put it on Himself. People, including myself, shout out and say, "God, you do not know what I am going through. You do not know how much this hurts. You do not understand." God sending Jesus Himself is proof God understands suffering. God is not indifferent to suffering. "He himself bore our sins" in his body on the cross, so that we might die to sins and live for righteousness; 'by his wounds you have been healed.'" For "you were like sheep going astray," but now you have returned to the Shepherd and

Overseer of your souls." -1 Peter 2:24-25. When Jesus died for us, all our sins were nailed to that cross with Him, to satisfy the wrath God has toward sin. However, we must confess our sin.

"Then I acknowledged my sin to you and did not cover up my iniquity, I said, "I will confess my transgressions to the Lord." And you forgave the guilt of my sin." -Psalm 32:5. "Whoever conceals their sin does not prosper, but the one who confesses and renounces them finds mercy." -Proverbs 28:13.

We often think God is upset with us, but remember, once we have Jesus, God's wrath is all placed at the cross where our sin was hung. When we have Christ, God sees His son in us! We do not deserve grace, but man does God desire to pour it on us! Life is not fair. We deserve condemnation. Now, all our shortcomings have a purpose instead of condemnation. The fact that we are forgiven does not lessen how terrible sin is but shows how much more powerful God's grace is! Since we have been justified through faith, we have peace with God because of what Jesus did (Romans 5:1). Jesus can completely save those who come to God through Him, because He always intercedes as a high priest who truly meets our needs, set apart from sinners above the Heavens. Unlike the other high priests, He does not need to offer a sacrifice every day, for He was the sacrifice once and for all of our sins past, present and future. He is made perfect forever. (Hebrews 7:25-28 and Romans 8:33-34). I think many teach about God well, but just incompletely, making the view of ourselves incomplete as well. We want to fit God into our lives, instead of realizing that He is both the very reason we have life, and the very purpose of life.

"You killed the author of life, but God raised him from the dead. We are witnesses of this." Acts 3:15.

"But what does it say? "The word is near you; it is in your mouth and in your heart," that is, the message concerning faith that we proclaim: If you declare with your mouth, "Jesus is Lord," and believe in your heart that God raised him from the dead, you will be saved. For it is with your heart that you believe and are justified, and it is with your mouth that you profess your faith and are saved. As Scripture says, "Anyone who believes in him will never be put to shame." For there is no difference between Jew and Gentile—the same Lord is Lord of all and richly blesses all who call on him, for, "Everyone who calls on the name of the Lord will be saved." -Romans 10:8-13 (Joel 2:32 and Romans 1:16).

"For what I received I passed on to you as of first importance: that Christ died for our sins according to the Scriptures, that he was buried, that he was raised on the third day according to the Scriptures, and that he appeared to Cephas, and then to the Twelve. After that, he appeared to more than five hundred of the brothers and sisters at the same time, most of whom are still living, though some have fallen asleep. Then he appeared to James, then to all the apostles, and last of all he appeared to me also, as to one abnormally born. For I am the least of the apostles and do not even deserve to be called an apostle, because I persecuted the church of God. But by the grace of God, I am what I am, and his grace to me was not without effect. No, I worked harder than all of them-yet not I, but the grace of God that was with me." -1 Corinthians 15:3-10.

"We are going up to Jerusalem, and the Son of Man will be delivered over to the chief priests and the teachers of the law. They will condemn him to death and will hand him over to the Gentiles to be mocked and flogged and crucified. On the third day he will be raised to life!" -Matthew 20:18-19 (Mark 10:33-34 and Luke 18:31-33).

"Jesus completed the word of God. "Then he said to Thomas, 'Put your finger here; see my hands. Reach out your hand and put it into my side. Stop doubting and believe'." Thomas said to him, "My Lord and my God!" Then Jesus told him, "Because you have seen me, you have believed; blessed are those who have not seen and yet have believed." -John 20:27-29. He is talking about us here!

You may be wondering what a relationship with the Creator of the universe looks like? How easy would it be to love someone with your whole being if you heard they died in order to save you for eternity after they had nails in their hands, a crown of thorns on their head and were spit on in shame? I want to mention having a relationship with Jesus is just that, a relationship. I have many people come to me, frustrated they did not experience the "BAM" of God coming to them in a burning bush the one time they went to church. To get to know God is talking with Him daily, reading your Bible, getting into His house (church), and both listening and talking to others that are in Him. When we think of being "proud of" someone, we usually mean we appreciate or admire them. When we truly know God, we will be naturally humbled. Not that God is "proud", but by who he is, we can't help but be humble. He says when you delight in yourself, and not in the praise, you have reached the peak of pride. Many have also come to me saying they do not feel good enough to come to Christ. Waiting to come to God until you are good enough is like waiting until you are healthy to go to the Doctor! We will never be good enough, but that is the beauty of who God is! He wants us to come as we are. Before you know it, Jesus will be your best friend, and talking to Him will be your favorite time of the day.

Salvation Through Faith

How can we be saved? We are all unclean, and any righteous acts we do are filthy rags. (See Isaiah 64:5-6). "Where, then, is boasting? It is excluded. Because of what law? The law that requires works? No, because of the law that requires faith. For we maintain that a person is justified by faith apart from the works of the law. Or is God the God of Jews only? Is he not the God of Gentiles too? Yes, of Gentiles too, since there is only one God, who will justify the circumcised by faith and the uncircumcised through that same faith. Do we, then, nullify the law by this faith? Not at all! Rather, we uphold the law." -Romans 3:27-31. "It was not through the law that Abraham and his offspring received the promise that he would be heir of the world, but through the righteousness that comes by faith. For if those who depend on the law are heirs, faith means nothing and the promise is worthless, because the law brings wrath. And where there is no law there is no transgression." -Romans 4:13-15. "The law was brought in so that the trespass might increase. But where sin increased, grace increased all the more, so that, just as sin reigned in death, so also grace might reign through righteousness to bring eternal life through Jesus Christ our Lord." -Romans 5:20-21. The whole point of the law was to recognize our faults and how much we need a Savior. "Now we know that whatever the law says, it says to those who are under the law, so that every mouth may be silenced and the whole world held accountable to God. Therefore no one will be declared righteous in God's sight by the works of the law; rather, through the law we become conscious of our sin." -Romans 3:19-20. He knew we would never be able to keep the law. One of my best friends Karissa once said, "I want to be remembered for how I showed grace," and I felt like my heart softened, and realized I want the same goal.

Now what about those before the coming of Christ? They still had to believe in a Savior to come from God. "What does Scripture say? Abraham believed God, and it was credited to him as righteousness. Now to the one who works, wages are not credited as a gift, but as an obligation. However, to the one who does not work but trusts God who justifies the ungodly, their faith is credited as righteousness. David says the same thing when he speaks of the blessedness of the one to whom God credits righteousness apart from works: "Blessed are those whose transgressions are forgiven, whose sins are covered. Blessed is the one whose sin the Lord will never count against them." -Romans 4:3-8 (Luke 10:7-8). "Under what circumstances was it credited? Was it after he was circumcised, or before? It was not after, but before!" -Romans 4:10. "Yet he did not waver through unbelief regarding the promise of God but was strengthened in his faith and gave glory to God, being fully persuaded that God had power to do what he had promised. Therefore, "it was credited to him as righteousness." The words "it was credited to him" were written not for him alone, but also for us, to whom God will credit righteousness—for us who believe in him who raised Jesus our Lord from the dead. He was delivered over to death for our sins and was raised to life for our justification." -Romans 4:20-25 (Romans 4:13-16). If people say to me, they do not understand or experience God's power, I ask if they are getting in the Word; the answer is no.

"But my people would not listen to me; Israel would not submit to me. So, I gave them over to their stubborn hearts to follow their own devices. If my people would only listen to me, if Israel would only follow my ways." -Psalm 81:11-13 (2 Kings 17:13-14). He has nothing but grace for every wrong you have ever done, and nothing but pure purpose for your life! He wants to take away your guilt of all sins. He has given us the gift of salvation but just like when we receive gifts, they need to be opened. We have not earned this gift, but it has been given to us through the cross. Love does not force a relationship, but man does God invite you with wide, open, and unconditional loving arms! With salvation, your sins are forgiven, your life has purpose, and you have a forever home in Heaven! He won't break down the doors of your heart, but He will never stop knocking. Jesus wants to embrace you home as his child. What are you waiting for? Christianity is the only religion where you do not get to Heaven through works, but by grace alone. Come and join the family!

God's Commands

God gives us specific commands through His Word not to restrict us, but to protect us and ultimately to help us thrive. You can find the 10 great commands in Exodus 20:2-17.

I am the Lord your God, you shall have no gods before me for He is a jealous God punishing children's generations down the line whose parents hate me but showing love to a thousand generations of those who love me and keep my commandments, do not misuse the name of God, remember the Sabbath day by keeping it holy. Six days you shall labor and do all your work, but the seventh day is a Sabbath to the Lord your God. On it you shall not do any work, neither you, nor your son or daughter, nor your male or female servant, nor your animals, nor any foreigner residing in your towns for He blessed this day and declares it holy (also see Jeremiah 17:22-24), honor your father and your mother to live long in the land God is giving you, you shall not murder, shall not commit adultery, shall not steal, shall not give false testimony against your neighbor, shall not covet your neighbor or anything that belongs to your neighbor. (See Exodus 20:2-17 and Exodus 34:6-7).

God says he will also testify against sorcerers, adulterers, perjurers, those who defraud laborers of their wages, those who oppress the widows and the fatherless, and deprive the foreigners among you of justice, but do not fear Him. (See Malachi 3:5). "Parents are not to be put to death for their children, nor children put to death for their parents; each will die for their own sin." -2 Kings 14:6. This is the new rule over punishment of children for their parents' sins.

What you eat does not defile you any longer like it did in the Old Testament. What defiles is from within; if, in the heart, evil thoughts come such as sexual immorality, theft, murder, adultery, greed, malice, deceit, lewdness, envy, slander, arrogance, and folly. (See Mark 7:18-23). "For whoever keeps the whole law and yet stumbles in one point, he has become guilty of all. For He who said, "Do not commit adultery," also said, "Do not commit murder." Now if you do not commit adultery, but do commit murder, you have become a transgressor of the law." -James 2:10-11. Many try to say there are different levels of sin, but God says if even one part of a law is broken, we are guilty of breaking all of it. It took one sin to separate Adam and Eve, and ultimately us from God.

What does it mean to keep the Sabbath day holy?

"Going on from that place, he went into their synagogue, and a man with a shriveled hand was there. Looking for a reason to bring charges against Jesus, they asked him, "Is it lawful to heal on the Sabbath?" He said to them, "If any of you has a sheep and it falls into a pit on the Sabbath, will you not take hold of it and lift it out? How much more valuable is a person than a sheep! Therefore, it is lawful to do good on the Sabbath." Then he said to the man, "Stretch out your hand." So, he stretched it out and it was completely restored, just as sound as the other. But the Pharisees went out and plotted how they might kill Jesus." -Matthew 12:9-14 (Mark 3:1-5, Luke 6:5-10, Luke 13:15-17 and Mark 2:23-24).

God's rule to keep the Sabbath still stands firm today; however, Jesus had to give this example because we missed the point of his heart and purpose behind keeping this date holy.

"Then he said to them, "The Sabbath was made for man, not man for the Sabbath. So, the Son of Man is Lord even of the Sabbath." -Mark 2:27-28 (2 Chronicles 36:21, John 5:2-9, Luke 14:1-5 and John 5:16-18). I am biased to the hand story, but if you look at the reference verses, He does this for the blind, paralyzed and those with edema. God made the Sabbath to give us rest. What we do not understand is it is a gift to us, not meant to burden us and make us unproductive. God wants us productive; however, He gave us an example of rest when He made creation, wanting us to follow and do the same.

In Acts 1:12, the apostles take a Sabbath day walk. "If you keep your feet from breaking the Sabbath and from doing as you please on my holy day, if you call the Sabbath a delight and the Lord's holy day honorable, and if you honor it by not going your own way and not doing as you please or speaking idle words, then you will find your joy in the Lord, and I will cause you to ride in triumph on the heights of the land and to feast on the inheritance of your father Jacob. For the mouth of the Lord has spoken." -Isaiah 58:13-14 (Isaiah 56:2 and Isaiah 56:4-7). God's heart behind the Sabbath is to see where your heart is with Him.

Jesus is Constant, Jesus is Freedom

Many have been saying that times have changed. The only problem with that statement is Scripture says, "Jesus Christ is the same yesterday, today and forever. Do not be carried away by all kinds of strange teachings. It is good for our hearts to be strengthened by grace, not by eating ceremonial foods, which is of no benefit to those who do so." -Hebrews 13:8-9. There is a change in dispensation, or exemption from the rule, which is the concept of how God handles each of the generations before Christ and after, but God Himself, His plan since the beginning of time and his purposes have not changed. Since He created us, He knows from the beginning what is best for us. "Jesus is 'the stone you builders rejected, which has become the cornerstone.' Salvation is found in no one else, for there is no other name under Heaven given to mankind by which we must be saved." -Acts 4:11-12 (Matthew 21:42, Mark 12:10-11 and Psalm 118:22-24). Jesus is the stumbling block because we need to put our pride aside and admit we need a Savior.

Live as if someone died for you because Jesus did! He did this knowing every wrong you have ever done. You are fully known, and fully loved flaws and all, how freeing! When I was in graduate school, I was with my friend Naomi in a study session with our professor for our scientific inquiry statistic research class. Long story short, our professor was going over a long math equation and ended up saying the answer would be two zeroes instead of just one. My friend Naomi said, "Shouldn't it not matter if the answer is two zeroes as compared to just zero?" The professor jokingly responded with, "Why do you matter?" Her response, "I matter to Jesus!" The next lecture, our professors first slide read, "You matter to Jesus, no matter what the answer is to any equation in life." My whole life, I have often believed what others thought about me was true. The way my friend responded with confidence woke me up to know that Jesus says what the truth is. Satan wants us to believe all the lies people tell us. He wants us to believe we do not matter, we are not good enough, we are not athletic enough, we are not pretty enough, or talented enough, and the list goes on! He is a liar, and we need to respond to any discouragement he brings with Jesus' truth, "I can do all things through Christ who strengthens me." -Philippians 4:13. This same friend was the one who told me as I was crying during our final's week, "Will this affect your eternal salvation?" What a good question to ask anytime we are stressed in life.

Jesus, God, came into the world during a hard time when Caesar Augustus had a census taken of the entire Roman world. (See Luke 2:1-2).

"In the sixth month of Elizabeth's pregnancy, God sent the angel Gabriel to Nazareth, a town in Galilee, to a virgin pledged to be married to a man named Joseph, a descendant of David. The virgin's name was Mary. The angel went to her and said, "Greetings, you who are highly favored! The Lord is with you." Mary was greatly troubled at his words and wondered what kind of greeting this might be. But the angel said to her, "Do not be afraid, Mary; you have found favor with God. You will conceive and give birth to a son, and you are to call him Jesus. He will be great and will be called the Son of the Most High. The Lord God will give him the throne of his father David, and he will reign over Jacob's descendants forever; his Kingdom will never end." "How will this be," Mary asked the angel, "since I am a virgin?" The angel answered, "The Holy Spirit will come on you, and the power of the Most High will overshadow you. So, the holy one to be born will be called the Son of God. Even Elizabeth your relative is going to have a child in her old age, and she, who was said to be unable to conceive, is in her sixth month. For no word from God will ever fail." -Luke 1:26-37 (Matthew 1:18, Matthew 1:21-23, Isaiah 7:14, Luke 2:20-21 and Matthew 1:16).

"All this took place to fulfill what the Lord had said through the prophet. The virgin will conceive and give birth to a son, and they will call him Immanuel" (which means "God with us)." -Matthew 1:22-23.

"While they were there, the time came for the baby to be born, and she gave birth to her firstborn, a son. She wrapped him in cloths and placed him in a manger, because there was no guest room available for them. And there were shepherds living out in the fields nearby, keeping watch over their flocks at night. An angel of the Lord appeared to them, and the glory of the Lord shone around them, and they were terrified. But the angel said to them, "Do not be afraid. I bring you good news that will cause great joy for all of the people. Today in the town of David a Savior has been born to you; he is the Messiah, the Lord." -Luke 2:6-14 (Luke 2:3-6 and 1 Samuel 20:6).

Once Jesus was born in Bethlehem in Judea, the Magi from the east came to Jerusalem asking King Herod where the king of the Jews was, since they saw the star and wanted to worship him. King Herod called the chief priests and teachers of the law, asking where the Messiah was supposed to be born. They quoted this scripture from the book of Micha, "But you, Bethlehem Ephrathah, through you are small among the clans of Judah, out of you will come for me one who will be ruler over Israel, whose origins are from of old, from ancient times." -Micah 5:2. King Herod asked the Magi when the star had appeared, and asked them to find the child, and tell him where he was so he could "worship" him too, when truly he wanted to kill him. The star was right over Jesus, and they were overjoyed. They worshiped there, giving him gold, frankincense, and myrrh. The Magi were warned in a dream not to go back to Herod, so they returned by a different route. An angel then appeared to Joseph in a dream and told him to escape to Egypt because Herod was coming to kill Jesus. They stayed in Egypt until Herod died which fulfilled the prophesy, "Out of Egypt I called my son." -Matthew 2:1-15 (Hosea 11:1). However, Archelaus, King Herod's son, was now reigning in Judea. Warned in a dream, they went to Galilee and lived in a town called Nazareth fulfilling the prophesy, "he would be called a Nazarene." People questioned, "How can anything good come out of Nazareth?" -Matthew 2:22-23. Again, proof that God, Jesus, was able to come from a town that nothing good was supposed to come out of. God chose to come in the humblest way possible, while His power was still on full display in every aspect of Jesus' life.

"Coming up to them at that very moment, she gave thanks to God and spoke about the child to all who were looking forward to the redemption of Jerusalem." -Luke 2:38. "When Joseph and Mary had done everything required by the Law of the Lord, they returned to Galilee to their own town of Nazareth. And the child grew and became strong; he was filled with wisdom, and the grace of God was on him." -Luke 2:39-40.

"When the Pharisees saw this, they asked his disciples, "Why does your teacher eat with tax collectors and sinners?" On hearing this, Jesus said, "It is not the healthy who need a doctor, but the sick. But go and learn what this means: 'I desire mercy, not sacrifice.' For I have not come to call the righteous, but sinners." -Matthew 9:11-13 (Mark 2:14-17 and Luke 5:27-32). We are all sick and in need of a

Savior, and Jesus is the Doctor! He will eat with any of us, because he loves us. I love the example of Zacchaeus, the wealthy chief tax collector, who climbed a sycamore tree to see Jesus. Jesus told him to come down because he was going to stay at his house. "All the people saw this and began to mutter, He has gone to be the guest of a sinner." -Luke 19:7. Jesus came to seek and to save the lost.

God can give us the same mind set if we ask him to. Wanting to spend time with others regardless of their "status."

"Suppose one of you has a hundred sheep and loses one of them. Doesn't he leave the ninety-nine in the open country and go after the lost sheep until he finds it? And when he finds it, he joyfully puts it on his shoulders and goes home. Then he calls his friends and neighbors together and says, 'Rejoice with me; I have found my lost sheep.' I tell you that in the same way there will be more rejoicing in heaven over one sinner who repents than over ninety-nine righteous persons who do not need to repent. Or suppose a woman has ten silver coins and loses one. Doesn't she light a lamp, sweep the house and search carefully until she finds it? And when she finds it, she calls her friends and neighbors together and says, 'Rejoice with me; I have found my lost coin.' In the same way, I tell you, there is rejoicing in the presence of the angels of God over one sinner who repents." -Luke 15:4-10. God loves you as if you are the only person in the world. God has a heart for sinners, us. He would risk it all, sacrifice it all, just like He did, even if he had to do it for only you and not the entire world. What does it mean to repent? It means realizing we are not walking in the right way, and changing our direction in the way we are walking.

Jesus then tells the story about a man with two sons, one who ran away and wasted part of his father's wealth, and the other who stayed. Many know this story as the prodigal son. When a famine came, the son returned home planning to tell his Father he had sinned against both Heaven and him. He was no longer worthy to be called his son, and he would like to be one of his servants. His father ran when he saw him, threw his arms around him, and kissed him with compassion. As the son was apologizing, his father asked for his servants to bring the best robe, ring, sandals, and fattened calf to eat for a feast to celebrate. The older son heard the music and dancing and became angry. He told his father all these years he had obeyed, yet he was never given even a goat to celebrate with his friends, but when his younger brother squandered his wealth with prostitutes, we celebrate?! The father responded saying everything he owns is his older sons, so he is rewarded already, but his brother was dead and now alive, lost and now found! (See Luke 15:11-32 and Matthew 18:11-14). "I will search for the lost and bring back the strays. I will bind up the injured and strengthen the weak, but the sleek and the strong I will destroy. I will shepherd the flock with justice." -Ezekiel 34:16. You can come run home to God no matter what you have done or what state you are in. He accepts you with open arms! Many see God as looking down on us because of the wrong we have done, and even though He does hate our sin, He loves you individually more than you can imagine. He is a Father who rejoices and wants us to come to Him when we repent of our wrongs. I understand in the story of the prodigal son, it is easy to get angry with what seems like injustice. Shouldn't the son who left and spent all his dad's inheritance be disciplined, and the son who stayed home and worked the right way for his father have the party? Do not be fooled. The dad said all he had was his son's, so his son did have access to his father's love, but the father rejoiced out of love for the rebellious son that repented and came home. The son who stayed was not perfect, he had also done wrong, and was prideful, thinking differently. We show grace and understand the Father's love when we realize we are all prodigals.

"Truly I tell you, people can be forgiven all their sins and every slander they utter." -Mark 3:28. "Whoever is not with me is against me, and whoever does not gather with me scatters." -Matthew 12:30 (Luke 11:23). Many try to be "lukewarm", and you can't. Jesus is clear; you are either for Him or against Him. This does not mean we can't all express Jesus differently as he has beautifully designed each of us to have different personalities in doing so. However, in your heart, He needs to know you either trust Him as your Lord and Savior or you do not. "...If you do not stand firm in your faith, you will not stand firm at all." -Isaiah 7:9.

"Whoever listens to you listens to me; whoever rejects you rejects me; but whoever rejects me rejects him who sent me." -Luke 10:16. Going back to being lukewarm, you either must decide Jesus is the Son of God and God Himself as He claims, or that He is a man who was the ultimate liar. You really cannot just claim Him to be a good man or teacher. Everything He taught referred to Him as being God, having the power to heal and forgive sins. "But what about you?" He asked. "Who do you say I am?" Simon Peter answered, "You are the Messiah, the

Son of the living God." -Matthew 16:15-16 (Matthew 16:17, Mark 16:13-14 Mark 8:29, Luke 9:20, Matthew 12:41-42 and Luke 11:30-32). Even though Jesus was given into the hands of the elders, chief priests, and teachers of the law, we are ultimately the ones who killed Him as Scripture says, "He was given into the hands of men." (See Mark 9:31-32, Matthew 17:22-23, Matthew 16:21, Mark 8:31 and Luke 9:22). The disciples didn't understand and were afraid to ask Him about it.

Jesus tells us plainly who He is. He never keeps us guessing and is confident because He knows exactly where He came from and where He is going. The woman said, "I know that Messiah (called Christ) is coming. When He comes, He will explain everything to us. Then Jesus declared, "I, the one speaking to you—I am He." -John 4:25-26. "The Jews who were there gathered around him, saying, "How long will you keep us in suspense? If you are the Messiah, tell us plainly. Jesus answered, "I did tell you, but you do not believe. The works I do in my Father's name testify about me..." -John 10:24-25 (John 10:14-15, Luke 5:20-26, Matthew 9:2-8, Mark 2:6-12, Mark 14:61-64, Matthew 26:67-68 and Luke 22:63-65). "In spite of all this, they kept on sinning; in spite of His wonders, they did not believe." -Psalm 78:32.

"The Lord their God will save His people on that day as a shepherd saves his flock. They will sparkle in His land like jewels in a crown. How attractive and beautiful they will be! Grain will make the young men thrive, and new wine the young women." -Zechariah 9:16-17. "They took palm branches and went out to meet him, shouting, "Hosanna!" "Blessed is he who comes in the name of the Lord!" "Blessed is the king of Israel!" Jesus found a young donkey and sat on it, as it is written: "Do not be afraid, Daughter Zion; see, your King is coming, seated on a donkey's colt." -John 12:13-15 (Zechariah 9:9, Matthew 21:2-5, Matthew 21:8-9, Mark 11:8-10 and Luke 19:30-38). Jesus came to save us, and we are His jewels. Our King comes. Humbly, He comes and conquers!

"Then Satan entered Judas, called Iscariot, one of the Twelve. And Judas went to the chief priests and the officers of the temple guard and discussed with them how he might betray Jesus. They were delighted and agreed to give him money. He consented, and watched for an opportunity to hand Jesus over to them when no crowd was present." -Luke 22:3-6 (John 13:2). While they were reclining at the table eating, he said, "Truly I tell you, one of you will betray me- one who is eating with me." -Mark 14:18 (John 13:26).

"Do you think I cannot call on my Father, and he will at once put at my disposal more than twelve legions of angels? But how then would the Scriptures be fulfilled that say it must happen in this way?" -Matthew 26:53-54. I want you to understand, God did not sacrifice His Son, Jesus willingly was sacrificed while being God, His very self, choosing to die in our place. God is trying to save you; He is not up in Heaven waiting to place his wrath on you.

Now we can see that you know all things and that you do not even need to have anyone ask you questions. This makes us believe that you came from God." "Do you now believe?" Jesus replied. "A time is coming and in fact has come when you will be scattered, each to your own home. You will leave me all alone. Yet I am not alone, for my Father is with me." -John 16:30-32 (Mark 14:50). "At my first defense, no one came to my support, but everyone deserted me. May it not be held against them. But the Lord stood at my side and gave me strength, so that through me the message might be fully proclaimed, and all the Gentiles might hear it. And I was delivered from the lion's mouth. The Lord will rescue me from every evil attack and will bring me safely to his Heavenly kingdom. To him be glory for ever and ever. Amen." -2 Timothy 4:16-18.

Even if everyone in your life abandons or leaves, God will never leave, and He is enough to give you strength. We are never, ever alone! I love how Jesus says this. God is always with us. I tease my mom when really, I look up to how she does this. She never, ever says she is alone. One time I asked her where she was, and she said Taco Bell. I said I was sorry she was alone there, and her response was, "I'm at Taco Bell with Jesus." I had to laugh, but at the same time realize she was right. I can't imagine how Jesus must have felt to have his closest friends desert Him, and to be humiliated and crucified even when he did nothing wrong. These verses remind us that even if everyone in our life abandons us, we always have Him, and He knows the feeling.

"No one ever spoke the way this man does," the guards replied. "You mean he has deceived you also?" the Pharisees retorted. "Have any of the rulers or of the Pharisees believed in Him? No! But this mob that knows nothing of the law-there is a curse on them." Nicodemus, who had gone to Jesus earlier and who was one of their own numbers, asked, "Does our law condemn a man without first hearting him to find out what he has been doing?" They replied, "Are you from Galilee too? Look into it, and you will find that a prophet does not come out of Galilee." -John 7:46-52. "The chief priests and the whole Sanhedrin were looking for evidence against Jesus so that they could put him to death, but they did not find any. Many testified falsely against him, but their statements did not agree." -Mark 14:55-56. "So again, Pilate asked him, "Aren't you going to answer? See how many things they are accusing you of." But Jesus still made no reply, and Pilate was amazed." -Mark 15:4-5 (Mark 15:6-9, Mark 15:12-15, Matthew 27:15, Matthew 27:22-26, Matthew 27:20 and Matthew 27:18-19). Jesus knew His identity was in God and was confident in that. The chief priests and whole Sanhedrin could not find any, any, evidence against Him and yet when Pilate asked Him to answer, He was silent in His strength and confidence of His identity. Also, even more importantly, out of love for what Jesus knew He had to do for us.

"The Jewish leaders insisted, we have a law, and according to that law he must die, because he claimed to be the Son of God." When Pilate heard this, he was even more afraid, and he went back inside the palace, "Where do you come from?" he asked Jesus, but Jesus gave him no answer. "Do you refuse to speak to me?" Pilate said. "Don't you realize I have power either to free you or to crucify you?" Jesus answered, "You would have no power over me if it were not given to you from above. Therefore, the one who handed me over to you is guilty of a greater sin." From then on, Pilate tried to set Jesus free, but the Jewish leaders kept shouting, "If you let this man go, you are no friend of Caesar. Anyone who claims to be a king opposes Caesar." -John 19:7-12 (John 19:4-6, Mark 14:61-64, Matthew 26:67-68 and Luke 22:63-65).

Since they could not find evidence to have Jesus crucified, they accused him of blasphemy for claiming that He is God, even though Jesus was telling the truth. When Jesus answered Pilate, He was making a point that even though it was all the people's evil ultimately leading Him to be crucified, it had to happen for our sins to be forgiven. He referenced that Pilate only had the power and was allowed to do what he was about to do because of God. Again, Pilate gave into the peer pressure of being accused that he was no friend of Caesar's if he let Jesus go free. He cared more about human approval than God's.

The chief priests handed Jesus over out of self-interest, stirring up the crowd to have Barabbas released. Pilate said, "You gave me this man as if he was starting rebellion. Neither I nor Herod have found basis for your charges against Him to deserve death." I want to remind us here that, yet again, there is no basis to crucify Jesus, yet the chief priests, out of their pride, stirred up the crowd, having them shout to release Barabbas, a murderer, instead. Wanting to release Jesus, Pilate appealed to them again, but they kept shouting, "Crucify him! Crucify him!" He said, "Why? What crime has this man committed? But with loud shouts they yelled to crucify. They had no reason. Pilate granted their demand out of fear of the crowd. He released the man who had been thrown into prison for insurrection and murder, the one they asked for, and surrendered Jesus to their will. (See Mark 15:10-17). Could you imagine how Barabbas felt, being released as a murderer in place of an innocent man? That is exactly how we should all feel. Jesus not only took Barabbas's place, but every one of ours.

"Then the governor's soldiers took Jesus into the Praetorium and gathered the whole company of soldiers around him. They stripped him and put a scarlet robe on him, and then twisted together a crown of thorns and set it on his head. They put a staff in his right hand. Then they knelt in front of him and mocked him. "Hail, king of the Jews!" they said. They spit on him and took the staff and struck him on the head again and again. After they mocked him, they took off the robe and put his own clothes on him. Then they led him away to crucify him." -Matthew 27:27-31 (John 19:1-3).

Jesus left Heaven, his throne of perfection, for this painful, sin-tainted world. If you ever think God does not love you or does not care, please just remember this, if anything, the cross is proof God loves you.

"The two other men, both criminals, were also led out with him to be executed. When they came to the place called the Skull, they crucified him there, along with the criminals-one on his right, and other on his left. Jesus said, "Father forgive them, for they do not know what they are doing." And they divided up his clothes by casting lots. The people stood watching, and the rulers even sneered at him. They said, "He saved others; let him save himself if he is God's Messiah, the Chosen One." The soldiers also came up and mocked him. They offered him wine vinegar and said, "If you are the king of the Jews, save yourself." There was a written notice above him, which read: This is the King of the Jews. One of the criminals who hung their hurled insults at him: "Aren't you the Messiah? Save yourself and us!" But the other criminal rebuked him. "Don't you fear God," he said, "since you are under the same sentence? We are punished justly, for we are getting what our deeds deserve. But this man has done nothing wrong." Then he said, "Jesus, remember me when you come into your kingdom." Jesus answered him, "Truly I tell you, today you will be with me in paradise." It was now about noon, and darkness came over the whole land until three in the afternoon, for the sun stopped shining. And the curtain of the temple was torn in two. Jesus called out with a loud voice, "Father, into your hands I commit my spirit." When he had said this, he breathed his last." -Luke 23:32-45 (Luke 23:46-47, John 19:15-24, Psalm 22:18, Matthew 27:32-37 and Matthew 27:38-44).

Jesus is the definition of humility. Could you imagine being in agonizing pain on the cross and, as God, having those words yelled at you, "Oh, if you are really God, save yourself?!" When He could have! He wasn't there to save Himself. He only hung there for the very people yelling at Him. He hung there for you and me. Even while on His way to the worst death imaginable, He has the love and strength to say the words, "Father, forgive them, they know not what they are doing!" (See Luke 23:34). This is the definition of true love. I also love how one criminal finds God right before He dies, and Jesus tells him that same day he will be with Him in paradise. It is never too late for anyone!

"From noon until three in the afternoon darkness came over all the land. About three in the afternoon Jesus cried out in a loud voice, "Eli, Eli, lemasabachthani?" (which means "My God, my God, why have you forsaken me?"). When some of those standing there heard this, they said, "He's calling Elijah." Immediately one of them ran and got a sponge. He filled it with wine vinegar, put it on a staff, and offered it to Jesus to drink. The rest said, "Now leave him alone. Let's see if Elijah comes to save him." And when Jesus had cried out again in a loud voice, he gave up his spirit. At that moment the curtain of the temple was torn in two from top to bottom. The earth shook, the rocks split, and the tombs broke open. The bodies many holy people who had died were raised to life. They came out of the tombs after Jesus' resurrection and went into the holy city and appeared to many people. When the centurion and those with him who were guarding Jesus saw the earthquake and all that had happened, they were terrified, and exclaimed, "Surely he was the Son of God!" -Matthew 27:45-54 (Mark 15:16-39 and Mark 14:65).

For that split second, God's wrath had to go onto Jesus as He carried the weight of everything, we have done wrong, every single one of us, referring to the term sin. Remember we sin not only when we do wrong, but when we fail to do right. I do not know about you, but I am covered, drowning in sin without Christ. The significance of the temple curtain being torn in two was that the veil separated the "Holy of Holies" in the place of the temple. Only the highest rank priest could go in. Now, Jesus physically tore the veil giving all of us direct access to God ourselves.

"...and to the disciple, "Here is your mother." From that time on, this disciple took her into his home. Later, knowing that everything had now been finished, and so that Scripture would be fulfilled. Jesus said, "I am thirsty." A jar of wine vinegar was there, so they soaked a sponge in it, put the sponge on a stalk of the hyssop plant, and lifted it to Jesus' lips. When he had received the drink, Jesus said, "It is finished." With that, he bowed his head and gave up his spirit." -John 19:27-30 (John 18:36-40, Matthew 12:40 and John 18:19-23).

Even up until the very end, Jesus made sure His family was taken care of. When Jesus said it was finished, He meant it. If we place our faith and salvation in what He did at the cross that day, we do not have to keep picking up our own crosses every single day. We get to live in His love and power as new creations because, It. Is. Finished. No more trying, working, or pleasing. Once we fall in love with Jesus knowing He finished it, for you, you will have such enthusiasm and passion to serve Him that it will flow out of you.

"But when they came to Jesus and found that he was already dead, they did not break his legs. Instead, one of the soldiers pierced Jesus' side with a spear, bringing a sudden flow of blood and water. The man who saw it has given testimony, and his testimony is true. He knows that he tells the truth, and he testifies so that you also may believe. These things happened so that the scripture would be fulfilled: "Not one of his bones will be broken," and, as another scripture says, "They will look on the one they have pierced." -John 19:33-37 (Psalm 34:20).

Jesus was the perfect, spotless lamb, and for that to happen, not one of his bones could be broken as was prophesied hundreds of years prior. Proof once again that the Bible is infallible. Some claim they saw Jesus rise from the dead because He never really died. I ask you now, do you understand what a Roman crucifixion was? Next question, do you think anyone ever survived a Roman crucifixion?

"Early on the first day of the week, while it was still dark, Mary Magdalene went to the tomb and saw that the stone had been removed from the entrance." - John 20:1. Mary's first reaction was to think the worst. Jesus' body has been stolen. "...and saw two angels in white, seated where Jesus' body had been, one at the head and the other at the foot." -John 20:12. After the sabbath, at dawn on the first day of the week, Mary Magdalene and the other Mary went to look at the tomb. There was a violent earthquake, for an angel of the Lord came down from heaven and, going to the tomb, rolled back the stone and sat on it. His appearance was like lightning, and his clothes were white as snow. The guards were so afraid of him that they shook and became like dead men. The angel said to the women, "Do not be afraid, for I know that you are looking for Jesus, who was crucified. He is not here; he has risen, just as he said. Come and see the place where he lay. Then go quickly and tell his disciples: "He has risen from the dead and is going ahead of you into Galilee. There you will see him.' Now I have told you." -Matthew 28:1-7 (Matthew 28:8-10, Mark 16:4-7 and Luke 24:1-4).

Jesus also comforts them. "He asked her, "Woman why are you crying? Who is it you are looking for?" Thinking he was the gardener, she said, "Sir, if you have carried him away, tell me where you have put him, and I will get him." Jesus said to her, "Mary." She turned toward him and cried out in Aramaic, "Rabboni!" (which means "Teacher"). -John 20:15-16 (John 14 and John 20:17-19). Jesus has risen from the dead! You see, the gospels do not contradict one another, but complement each other so we get the entire story. If we were all at a crime scene, I might notice certain details while others might have noticed other details, but together we get the whole picture.

"In their fright the women bowed down their faces to the ground, but the men said to them, "Why do you look for the living among the dead? He is not here; he has risen! Remember how he told you, while he was still with you in Galilee: 'The son of Man must be delivered over to the hands of sinners, be crucified and on

44

the third day be raised again." -Luke 24:5-7. The next day, the one after Preparation Day, the chief priests and the Pharisees went to Pilate. "Sir," they said, "we remember that while he was still alive that deceiver said, 'After three days I will rise again.' Otherwise, his disciples may come and steal the body and tell the people that he has been raised from the dead. This last deception will be worse than the first." "Take a guard," Pilate answered. "Go, make the tomb as secure as you know how." So, they went and made the tomb secure by putting a seal on the stone and posting the guard." -Matthew 27:62-66. "When the chief priests had met with the elders and devised a plan, they gave the soldiers a large sum of money, telling them, "You are to say, 'His disciples came during the night and stole him away while we were asleep.' If this report gets back to the governor, we will satisfy him and keep you out of trouble." So, the soldiers took the money and did as they were instructed. And this story has been widely circulated among the Jews to this very day." -Matthew 28:12-15.

The chief priests and Pharisees knew what they were doing was wrong. They did everything they could to hide the truth from both those at the current time, and from you today that Jesus had risen. Believe the truth.

When they came back from the tomb, they told the disciples who did not believe because their words seemed to them like nonsense. (See Luke 24:9-11 and Luke 24:12-37). Even after Jesus rose from the dead, (and told His disciples it was going to happen ahead of time) they still did not believe. "He said to Thomas, "Put your finger here; see my hands. Reach out your hand and put it into my side. Stop doubting and believe." Jesus told him, "Because you have seen me, you have believed; blessed are those who have not seen and yet have believed." -John 20:27 29. (John 20:20 and Acts 1:3). I feel bad for Thomas, as he is popularly known as "doubting Thomas" even when all the disciples did not believe it initially. Jesus is saying, blessed are those who have not seen and have believed, referring to us!

"And He said to them, "Why are you troubled, and why do doubts arise in your hearts? "See My hands and My feet, that it is I Myself; touch Me and see, for a spirit does not have flesh and bones as you see that I have." And when He had said this, He showed them His hands and His feet. While they still could not believe it because of their joy and amazement, He said to them, "Have you anything here to eat?" They gave Him a piece of a broiled fish; and He took it and ate it before them.

Now He said to them, "These are My words which I spoke to you while I was still with you, that all things which are written about Me in the Law of Moses and the Prophets, and the Psalms must be fulfilled." Then He opened their minds to understand the Scriptures, and He said to them, "Thus it is written, that the Christ would suffer and rise again from the dead the third day, and that repentance for forgiveness of sins would be proclaimed in His name to all the nations, beginning from Jerusalem." -Luke 24:38-47 (Luke 24:48-52).

Jesus is alive today, this very day. He is waiting for you to accept His free gift of salvation. He has been spoken of and written about since the beginning, came to be here on earth, is now in Heaven, and at the same time omnipresent here, right now.

"Philip found Nathanael and told him, "We have found the one Moses wrote about in the Law, and about whom the prophets also wrote—Jesus of Nazareth, the son of Joseph." -John 1:45. "The next day John saw Jesus coming toward him and said, "Look, the Lamb of God, who takes away the sin of the world! This is the one I meant when I said, 'A man who comes after me has surpassed me because he was before me.' -John 1:29-30 (1 John 2:1-2).

Jesus prays for his disciples and us to be one, just as Him and the Father are one. He prays we are in Him as He has given us His glory, so people will believe God sent Him and even more loves them just as God loved Him, and then we can be in complete unity. Jesus prays anyone in Him will be where He is and see His glory He was given because the Father loves Him before the creation of the world. Though the world does not know God, they know Jesus making Him known to us so the love God has for Jesus can be in us and Christ with us. (See John 17:20-26 and John 17:11).

"Jesus answered, "I am the way and the truth and the life. No one comes to the Father except through me. If you really know me, you will know my Father as well. From now on, you do know him and have seen him." -John 14:6-7 (John 10:9 and John 14:9-11). If I had not come and spoken to them, they would not be guilty of sin; but now they have no excuse for their sin. Whoever hates me hates my Father as well. If I had not done among them the works no one else did, they would not be guilty of sin. But this is to fulfill what is written in their Law: 'They hated me without reason." -John 15:22-25.

Jesus said He is the light of the world, if you follow Him, you will never walk in darkness, but have the light of life. The Pharisees challenged him saying if you appear as your own witness, your testimony is not valid. Jesus said I know where I come from and where I am going. You judge by human standards. My decisions and judgments are true because I stand with the Father who sent me. He is my witness. (See John 8:12-18, John 8:19, John 12:44-50, 1 John 2:23 and John 9:5). The confidence! I cannot emphasize it enough, because Jesus is saying we can have this same confidence that I know I need more of. Can you just see and hear how confident Jesus is here? He knows who He is and declares it with confidence. If you are not confident, this world is going to push you in every direction telling you who you are. I have experienced it. I have my own moments where I do not tend to declare and remember who I am, I believe the lies of who others say I am. We have all heard them. "You can't. You are worthless. You are not pretty enough. You are not good enough. You're not a good enough athlete. You're not a good friend, husband, wife, sibling, son, daughter." We have all heard the world's opinions. You are who God says you are. We need this confidence and self-esteem not only to help ourselves, but others! How can we serve when we do not know who we are?

We do not physically see Christ, but we see him because He lives as He is in the Father and in us. (See John 14:19-20 and John 14:16-20).

"All this I have spoken while still with you. But the Advocate, the Holy Spirit, whom the Father will send in my name, will teach you all things and will remind you of everything I have said to you." -John 14:25-26 (John 16:14, John 14:27, John 15:26, John 16:8-11 and Acts 1:6-11). I used to struggle with what Jesus meant when He said it is better that the Advocate comes, but then realized when Jesus was here, He was fully human and God, still meaning He was only in one place at one time. In the Holy Spirit, He can be in each one of us who invite Him in.

"Fellow Israelites, listen to this: Jesus of Nazareth was a man accredited by God to you by miracles, wonders and signs, which God did among you through him, as you yourselves know. This man was handed over to you by God's deliberate plan and foreknowledge; and you, with the help of wicked men, put him to death by nailing him to the cross. But God raised him from the dead, freeing him from the agony of death, because it was impossible for death to keep its hold on him. David said about him: "'I saw the Lord always before me. Because he is at my right hand, I will not be shaken. Therefore, my heart is glad, and my tongue rejoices; my body also will rest in hope, because you will not abandon me to the realm of the dead, you will not let your holy one see decay. You have made known to me the paths of life; you will fill me with joy in your presence.' "Fellow Israelites, I can tell you confidently that the patriarch David died and was buried, and his tomb is here to this day. But he was a prophet and knew that God had promised him on oath that he would place one of his descendants on his throne. Seeing what was to come, he spoke of the resurrection of the Messiah, that he was not abandoned to the realm of the dead, nor did his body see decay. God has raised this Jesus to life, and we are all witnesses to it. Exalted to the right hand of God, he has received from the Father the promised Holy Spirit and has poured out what you now see and hear. For David did not ascend to heaven, and yet he said, "'The Lord said to my Lord: Sit at my right hand until I make your enemies a footstool at your feet. Therefore, let all Israel be assured of this: God has made this Jesus, who you crucified, both Lord and Messiah." -Acts 2:22-36 (Psalm 16:8-11 and Psalm 110:1). Even though wicked men nailed him to the cross, it was always God's plan to save us, Jesus' plan, as they are one. Jesus was raised from the dead and overcame death for us, to forgive us our sins. He is seated at the right hand of God, and we now have the Holy Spirit poured out to us when we believe in Jesus as our Lord and Savior.

Sin always starts in the mind or as a temptation, so we need to catch it early to not conceive birth to such evil. This takes confession to one another, prayer immediately to God for help and control of our mind, shifting our focus. Reminder: we are not free to sin, we now have the freedom to not sin.

"Since the children have flesh and blood, he too shared in their humanity so that by his death he might break the power of him who holds the power of death—that is, the devil— and free those who all their lives were held in slavery by their fear of death." -Hebrews 2:14-15. Jesus became fully man and was still fully God to share in our humanity. No one can say He does not understand what we are going through.

"Since you died with Christ to the elemental spiritual forces of this world, why, as though you still belonged to the world, do you submit to its rules: "Do not handle! Do not taste! Do not touch!'"? These rules, which have to do with things that are all destined to perish with use, are based on merely human commands and teachings." -Colossians 2:20-22.

There are many worldly, man-made rules talking about not being able to eat certain foods, etc. Jesus said these are no longer law.

"Now the Lord is the Spirit, and where the Spirit of the Lord is, there is freedom. And we all, who with unveiled faces contemplate the Lord's glory, are being transformed into his image with ever-increasing glory, which comes from the Lord, who is the Spirit." -2 Corinthians 3:17-18.

We have freedom in Christ.

"What then? Shall we sin because we are not under the law but under grace? By no means! Don't you know that when you offer yourselves to someone as obedient slaves, you are slaves of the one you obey—whether you are slaves to sin, which leads to death, or to obedience, which leads to righteousness? But thanks be to God that, though you used to be slaves to sin, you have come to obey from your heart the pattern of teaching that has now claimed your allegiance. You have been set free from sin and have become slaves to righteousness. I am using an example from everyday life because of your human limitations. Just as you used to offer yourselves as slaves to impurity and to ever-increasing wickedness, so now offer yourselves as slaves to righteousness leading to holiness. When you were slaves to sin, you were free from the control of righteousness. What benefit did you reap at that time from the things you are now ashamed of? Those things result in death! But now that you have been set free from sin and have become slaves of God, the benefit you reap leads to holiness, and the result is eternal life." -Romans 6:15-22 (Galatians 5:1, Galatians 5:13, 1 Peter 2:16, Hebrews 10:26-27 and Ezekiel 18:4).

Some people think "Oh, I can sin whenever I would like because Jesus covers it." Jesus does forgive us of every sin, but once you realize the sacrifice and love He went through to do it, sin begins to repel you. Jesus gave you freedom to say *no* to sin, because of His grace. There are no benefits to sin. Initially, the enemy may have you deceived there are, but in truth, the result is always death- whether eternally, relationally, or in circumstances in our lives.

"To the Jews who had believed him, Jesus said, "If you hold to my teaching, you are really my disciples. Then you will know the truth, and the truth will set you free." They answered him, "We are Abraham's descendants and have never been slaves of anyone. How can you say that we shall be set free?" Jesus replied, "Very truly I tell you, everyone who sins is a slave to sin. Now a slave has no permanent place in the family, but a son belongs to it forever. So, if the Son sets you free, you will be free indeed." -John 8:31-36 (John 8:37-42).

You are set free! How do we get enslaved to sin? Even as believers? From my experience, once I commit it once, I feel convicted. The more I ignore the conviction, the more I "quiet" the voice of the Holy Spirit, leading to enslavement. The good news is even if you get to this point as I have, who the Son sets free is free indeed! Jesus can always set you free if you ask Him and make the effort to remove what you are enslaved to from your life.

"These people are springs without water and mists driven by a storm. Blackest darkness is reserved for them. For they mouth empty, boastful words and, by appealing to the lustful desires of the flesh, they entice people who are just escaping from those who live in error. They promise them freedom, while they themselves are slaves of depravity—for "people are slaves to whatever has mastered them." -2 Peter 2:17-19.

If you are a slave to sin without Jesus to set you free, you are in for trouble. It is easy for people living in sin to look "free" in a sense. I know I have struggled throughout my life thinking sin looks more fun, thinking someone else has more freedom. Every time I have left Jesus' commands and have run to this sin, I found myself a slave. People living in sin will not admit this to you, but I will. People living in sin feel better when others join them, as then they are not living in enslavement alone. I promise you, living in the freedom of Christ is the freest you will ever be.

"What shall we say, then? Shall we go on sinning so that grace may increase? By no means! We are those who have died to sin; how can we live in it any longer? Or don't you know that all of us who were baptized into Christ Jesus were baptized into his death? We were therefore buried with him through baptism into death in order that, just as Christ was raised from the dead through the glory of the Father, we too may live a new life." -Romans 6:1-4.

Some people may say, "The more I sin, the more grace abounds, maybe I should sin more!" You are dead to sin; you will not want to run to it anymore! There is a difference between the fact that as believers we will without a doubt fall into sin as opposed to us purposefully desiring it and running toward it.

"For if we have been united with him in a death like his, we will certainly also be united with him in a resurrection like his. For we know that our old self was crucified with him so that the body ruled by sin might be done away with, that we should no longer be slaves to sin— because anyone who has died has been set free from sin. Now if we died with Christ, we believe that we will also live with him. For we know that since Christ was raised from the dead, he cannot die again; death no longer has mastery over him. The death he died, he died to sin once for all; but the life he lives, he lives to God. In the same way, count yourselves dead to sin but alive to God in Christ Jesus. Therefore, do not let sin reign in your mortal body so that you obey its evil desires. Do not offer any part of yourself to sin as an instrument of wickedness, but rather offer yourselves to God as those who have been brought from death to life; and offer every part of yourself to him as an instrument of righteousness. For sin shall no longer be your master, because you are not under the law, but under grace." -Romans 6:5-14 (Acts 10:38-40 and 1 Peter 3:18).

How can we continue to chase sin, when we are dead to it and alive in Christ?! The truth shares that we have the conscious choice to either offer ourselves as a slave to sin or a slave to Christ. I know our connotation of slavery is rightfully distorted due to it turning into abuse to those of a different race, which is absolutely heart shattering. Back in biblical times, slavery was a form of people to work and receive good care. Once people were done with their contract of being a slave, they could leave their master, however many times they would leave in poverty. They had a relationship with their master and trusted them to take care of them. Jesus wants to take care of you under His grace to give you complete freedom.

The ultimate tragedy for someone determined to believe the Bible is not true and God does not exist, is their isolation from a sense of hope or purpose. However, the beauty is they have a purpose, His purpose, whether they know it or not. I know I cannot force someone to believe because only God can change hearts. I pray you know your purpose, starting now.

Life is Short, Heaven is Not

What you do every single day matters more than you realize. "Teach us to number our days, that we may gain a heart of wisdom." -Psalm 90:12.

"Be very careful, then, how you live—not as unwise but as wise, making the most of every opportunity, because the days are evil. Therefore, do not be foolish, but understand what the Lord's will is. Do not get drunk on wine, which leads to debauchery. Instead, be filled with the Spirit, speaking to one another with psalms, hymns, and songs from the Spirit. Sing and make music from your heart to the Lord, always giving thanks to God the Father for everything, in the name of our Lord Jesus Christ." -Ephesians 5:15-20.

"What I mean, brothers and sisters, is that the time is short..." -1 Corinthians 7:29. "...For this world in its present form is passing away." -1 Corinthians 7:31. Tell your family, friends, and spouse how much you love them. Spend more time with Jesus. Put your heart and soul into your job knowing you have purpose and are helping God's people. Compete in sports, help in ministry, learn an instrument, listen to others, write a letter, go hiking, dance in public, go the extra mile. Even though our souls were made to live forever, we are only in this broken world for so long. "For my days vanish like smoke; my bones burn like glowing embers." -Psalm 102:3. "My days are like the evening shadow; I wither away like grass." -Psalm 102:11. Life seems to get shorter the older we get. Guys, Jesus is enough. Even if nothing else good were to happen to us the rest of our lives, He gave everything so in the end, we will be living in glory with Him forever. Live with joy, and most importantly never forget, you have purpose, and your exact days are numbered. You can either use this to incite fear or give you peace knowing you cannot change the amount of time God has allotted for you to fulfill the purposes He has planned for you. "A person's days are determined; you have decreed the number of his months and have set limits he cannot exceed." -Job 14:5.

God Our Idol

"But when you saw that Nahash king of the Ammonites was moving against you, you said to me, 'No, we want a king to rule over us'—even though the Lord your God was your king. Now here is the king you have chosen, the one you asked for; see, the Lord has set a king over you. If you fear the Lord and serve and obey him and do not rebel against his commands, and if both you and the king who reigns over you follow the Lord your God—good! But if you do not obey the Lord, and if you rebel against his commands, his hand will be against you, as it was against your ancestors." -1 Samuel 12:12-15 (Deuteronomy 28:13-15, 1 Samuel 8:6-9 and 1 Samuel 8:19-22).

"...You praised the gods of silver and gold, of bronze, iron, wood and stone, which cannot see or hear or understand..." -Daniel 5:23 (Isaiah 44:19, Isaiah 45:20, Revelation 9:20, Psalm 106:20 and 2 Kings 19:18-19). Why would we go anywhere other than to the Lord who sees us, hears us, and understands exactly what we are going through. Our phones, jobs, homes, clothes, and even other people do not always hear us, see us or understand. God created relationships with others and throughout this book I will emphasize more than anything loving others as yourself, but they are not meant to be idols.

"...I have been grieved by their adulterous hearts..." -Ezekiel 6:9. God is a jealous God and longs for you to worship Him because he loves you. When we have other idols in our lives, honestly, He sees it as if we are committing adultery in front of Him. "Do any of the worthless idols of the nation bring rain? Do the skies themselves send down showers? No, it is you, Lord our God. Therefore, our hope is in you, for you are the one who does all this." -Jeremiah 14:22. Idols do not have the power God has to transform our lives. I honestly feel silly even comparing God to an idol, because there is no comparison to our God. "The Lord replied, "When the Egyptians, the Amorites, the Ammonites, the Philistines, the Sidonians, the Amalekites and the Moanites oppressed you and you cried to me for help, did I not save you from their hands? But you have forsaken me and served other gods, so I will no longer save you. Go and cry out to the gods you have chosen. Let them save you when you are in trouble!" -Judges 10:11-14 (Deuteronomy 26:6-9). I take this as a warning, that if you choose with your free will to put your hope in idols, God is saying let's see if they will save you in your time of trouble. "They lift their shoulders and carry it; they set it up in its place, and there it stands. From that spot it cannot move. Even though someone cries out to it, it cannot answer; it cannot save them from their troubles." -Isaiah 46:7 (Samuel 12:21).

Saul and Solomon are examples of leaders and kings who suffered from idolatry in a way that may not have seemed as obvious as the Israelites. For Solomon, it was his wealth, many wives, and his political agenda. In Saul's case, his security lay in his throne making it his idol. Because of this, Saul was seeking the arrogance of his own heart as opposed to God's commands and heart. "But now your kingdom will not endure; the Lord has sought out a man after his own heart and appointed him ruler of his people, because you have not kept the Lord's command." -1 Samuel 13:14. "For rebellion is like the sin of divination and arrogance like the evil of idolatry. Because you have rejected the word of the Lord, he has rejected you as king." -1 Samuel 15:23. A shepherd boy named David was the man God is talking about that sought his own heart and because of this, God blessed him. "The Philistine commanders continued to go out to battle, and as often as they did, David met with more success than the rest of Saul's officers, and his name became well known." -1 Samuel 18:30. Even though Solomon was David's son and he disobeyed God's commands, God honored the heart of David and kept his promises.

"...his heart was not fully devoted to the Lord his God, as the heart of David his forefather had been. Nevertheless, for David's sake the Lord his God gave him a lamp in Jerusalem by raising up a son to succeed him and by making Jerusalem strong. For David had done what is right in the eyes of the Lord and had not failed to keep any of the Lord's commands all the days of his life- except in the case of Uriah the Hittite." -1 Kings 15:3-5.

We have made it clear nothing is to take precedence before God, but what does it look like when God is the center of our life?

"Give praise to the Lord, proclaim his name; make known among the nations what he has done. Sing to him, sing praise to him; tell of all his wonderful acts. Glory in his holy name; let the hearts of those who seek the Lord rejoice. Look to the Lord and his strength; seek his face always. Remember the wonders he has done, his miracles, and the judgments he pronounced, you his servants, the descendants of Israel, his chosen ones, the children of Jacob. He is the Lord our God; his judgments are in all the earth."-1 Chronicles 16:8-14 (1 Chronicles 12:22).

Summary of Old Testament

"...Blessed be your glorious name exalted above all. You alone are the Lord. You made the Heavens and all their starry hosts, the earth and all that is on it. You give life to everything, and the multitudes of Heaven worship you. You are the Lord God, who chose Abram and brought him out of Ur of the Chaldeans and named him Abraham. You found his heart faithful to you, and you made a covenant with him to give to his descendants the land of the Canaanites, Hittites, Amorites, Perizzites, Jebusites and Girgashites. You have kept your promise because you are righteous. You saw the suffering of our ancestors in Egypt; you heard their cry at the Red Sea. You sent signs and wonders against Pharaoh, against all his officials and all the people of his land, for you knew how arrogantly the Egyptians treated them. You made a name for yourself, which remains to this day. You divided the sea so that they passed through it on dry ground, but you hurled their pursuers into the depths, like a stone into mighty waters. By day you led them with a pillar of cloud, and by night with a pillar of fire to give them light on the way they were to take. You came down on Mount Sinai from Heaven; you spoke to them from heaven. You gave them regulations and laws that were just and right, and decrees and commands that are good. You made known to them your holy Sabbath and gave them commands, decrees, and laws through your servant Moses. In their hunger you gave them bread from heaven and in their thirst, you brought them water from the rock; you told them to go in and take possession of the land you had sworn with uplifted hand to give them. But they, our ancestors, became arrogant and stiff-necked, and they did not obey your commands. They refused to listen and failed to remember the miracles you performed among them. They became stiff-necked and, in their rebellion, appointed a leader in order to return to their slavery. But you are a forgiving God, gracious and compassionate, slow to anger and abounding in love. Therefore, you did not desert them, even when they cast for themselves an image of a calf and said, 'This is your god, who brought you up out of Egypt,' or when they committed awful blasphemies. Because of your great compassion you did not abandon them in the wilderness. By day the pillar of cloud did not fail to guide them on their path, nor the pillar of fire by night to shine on the way they were to take. You gave your good Spirit to instruct them. You did not withhold your manna from their mouths, and you gave them water for their thirst. For forty years you sustained and instructed them in the wilderness; they lacked nothing, their clothes did not wear out nor did their feet become swollen. "You gave them kingdoms and nations allotting to them even the remotest frontiers. They took over the country of Sihon king of Heshbon and the country of Og king of Bashan. You made their children as numerous as the stars in the sky, and you brought them into the land that you told their parents to enter and possess. Their children took possession of the land. You subdued before them the Canaanites, who lived in the land; you gave the Canaanites into their hands, along with their kings and the peoples of the land, to deal with them as they pleased. They captured fortified cities and fertile land; they took possession of houses filled with all kinds of good things, wells already dug, vineyards, olive groves and fruit trees in abundance. They ate to the full and were well-nourished; they reveled in your great goodness. You gave the Canaanites into their hands. They took possession of good things, water, houses and food in your goodness. But they were disobedient and rebelled against you; they turned their backs on your law. They killed your prophets, who warned them to turn them back to you; they committed awful blasphemies. So, you delivered them into the hands of their enemies, who oppressed them. But when they were oppressed, they cried out to you. From Heaven, you heard them, and in your great compassion you gave them deliverers, who rescued them from the hand of their enemies. But as soon as they were at rest, they again did what was evil in your sight. Then you abandoned them to the hands of their enemies so that they ruled over them. And when they cried out to you again, you hear from heaven, and in your compassion, you delivered them time after time. You warned them to turn them back to your law, but they became arrogant and disobeyed your commands. They sinned against your ordinances, of which you said, 'The person who obeys them will live by them. "Stubbornly they turned their backs on you, became stiff-necked and refused to listen. For many years you were patient with them. By your Spirit, you warned them through your prophets. Yet they paid no attention, so you gave them into the hands of the neighboring peoples. But in your great mercy you did not put an end to them or abandon them, for you are a gracious and merciful God. "Now therefore, our God, the great God, mighty and awesome, who keeps his covenant of love, do not let all this hardship seem trifling in your eyes-the hardship that has come on us, on our kings and leaders, on our priests and prophets, on our ancestors and all your people, from the days of the kings of Assyria until today. In all that has happened to us, you have remained righteous; you have acted faithfully, while we acted wickedly. Our kings, our leaders, our priests, and our ancestors did not follow your law; they did not pay attention to your commands or the statues you warned them to keep. Even while they were in their kingdom, enjoying your great goodness to them in the spacious and fertile land you gave them, they did not serve you or turn from their evil ways. "But see, we are slaves today, slaves in the land you gave our ancestors so they could eat its fruit and the other good things it produces." - Nehemiah 9:5-35 (Jeremiah 7:22-26 and 2 Kings 19:18-19).

Fearing God to Rest in Him

"No one is like you, Lord; you are great, and your name is mighty in power." - Jeremiah 10:6 (Psalm 24:8). "Immediately, because Herod did not give praise to God, an angel of the Lord struck him down, and he was eaten by worms and died." -Acts 12:23. "He will be the sure foundation for your times, a rich store of salvation and wisdom and knowledge; the fear of the Lord is the key to this treasure." -Isaiah 33:6. Isaiah saw the Lord, high and exalted, seated on a throne; and the train of his robe filled the temple. Above him were seraphim and they were calling to one another:

...Holy, holy, holy is the Lord Almighty; the whole earth is full of his glory." At the sound of their voices the doorposts and thresholds shook, and the temple was filled with smoke. "Woe to me!" I cried. "I am ruined! For I am a man of unclean lips, and I live among a people of unclean lips, and my eyes have seen the King, the Lord Almighty." Then one of the seraphim flew to me with a live coal in his hand, which he had taken with tongs from the alter. With it he touched my mouth and said, "See, this has touched your lips; your guilt is taken away and your sin atoned for." -Isaiah 6:1-7.

"His lightning lights up the world; the earth sees and trembles. The mountains melt like wax before the Lord, before the Lord of all the earth. The Heavens proclaim his righteousness, and all peoples see his glory." -Psalm 97:4-6 (Isaiah 2:10, Psalm 114:7-8 and Nahum 1:5). The beauty is once you fear God, you have nothing else to fear! You realize this God who has this power is on your side. I just never want us to underestimate the might of our Lord.

"Surely, his salvation is near to those who fear him, that his glory may dwell in our land." -Psalm 85:9 (Luke 1:50 and Proverbs 14:27). Once we begin to fear God, you understand who He is. "…for those who fear him lack nothing." -Psalm 34:9. "The angel of the Lord encamps around those who fear him, and he delivers them." -Psalm 34:7. God takes care of those who fear Him, they lack nothing. "Let all the earth fear the Lord; let all the people of the world revere him. For he spoke, and it came to be he commanded, and it stood firm." -Psalm 33:8-9 (Isaiah 8:13 and Proverbs 14:27). How can we not fear our God, a God who literally simply speaks and the world, the universe and even "we" came to be with but a breath?

"Who, then, are those who fear the Lord? He will instruct them in the ways they should choose. They will spend their days in prosperity, and their descendants will inherit the land. The Lord confides in those who fear him; he makes his covenant known to them. My eyes are ever on the Lord, for only he will release my feet from the snare." -Psalm 25:12-15.

Once we fear God, He begins to instruct us in the ways He wants us to go, as His plans are always good even if there is suffering along the way. It is not that the suffering is good, but we know we never suffer in vain. "Now all has been heard; here is the conclusion of the matter: Fear God and keep his commandments, for this is the duty of all mankind. For God will bring every deed into judgment, including every hidden thing, whether good or evil." -Ecclesiastes 12:13-14 (Ecclesiastes 3:17). The duty, our duty, our purpose, is to fear God and keep his commandments. "I will make an everlasting covenant with them: I will inspire them to fear me, so that they will never turn away from me." -Jeremiah 32:40. The beautiful thing is once we fear God, we have nothing to fear as the All Mighty, the One and Only, the most Powerful is encamped around us. "…A scroll of remembrance was written in his presence concerning those who feared the Lord and honored his name." -Malachi 3:16. "The fear of the Lord leads to life; then one rests content, untouched by trouble." -Proverbs 19:23. "The fear of the Lord adds length to life, but the years of the wicked are cut short." -Proverbs 10:27.

What is the definition of fearing God?

"God understands the way of it, and he alone knows where it dwells, for he views the ends of the earth and sees everything under the Heavens. When he established the force of the wind and measured out the waters, when he made a decree for the rain and a path for the thunderstorm, then he looked at wisdom and appraised it; he confirmed it and tested it. And he said to the human race, "The fear of the Lord-that is wisdom, and to shun evil is understanding." -Job 28:23-28. Fear of the Lord is wisdom and to shun evil is understanding.

"As far as the east is from the west, so far has he removed our transgressions from us. As a father has compassion for his children, so the Lord has compassion on those who fear him; for he knows how we are formed, he remembers that we are dust. The life of mortals is like grass, they flourish like a flower of the field; the wind blows over it and it is gone, and its place remembers it no more. But from everlasting to everlasting the Lord's love is with their children's children- with those who keep his covenant and remember to obey his precepts. The Lord has established his throne in heaven, and his kingdom rules overall. Praise the Lord, you his angels, you mighty ones who do his bidding, who obey his word. Praise the Lord, all his heavenly hosts, you his servants who do his will. Praise the Lord, all his works everywhere in his dominion." -Psalm 103:12-22 (Psalm 117:1-2).

We are His children when we fear Him, leading Him to have compassion for us as a Father would. I have had times in my life when I would get frustrated that God was in a sense "using" me as a pawn either in someone else's life to do His will even if it hurt me, or even a pawn in my own life to go through a particular situation, bringing me pain in order to do His will. Then my friend Karissa said, "You are not a pawn, you are His child!"

"For to us a child is born, to us a son is given, and the government will be on his shoulders. And he will be called Wonderful Counselor, Mighty God, Everlasting Father, Prince of Peace. Of the greatness of his government and peace there will be no end. He will reign on David's throne and over his kingdom, establishing and upholding it with justice and righteousness from that time on and forever. The zeal of the Lord Almighty will accomplish this." -Isaiah 9:6-7 (Jeremiah 23:5-6 and Jeremiah 33:14-16).

What a relief! I, like many others, can get so overwhelmed during election time as to who will be in office. I think we are to care and vote; however, realize that the government Jesus established when he came will have no end. He rules as a Wonderful Counselor, Mighty God, Everlasting Father and Prince of Peace. Talk about the perfect candidate. He came through King David's line as prophesied many times, and David was even told by God himself. The zeal of God has accomplished this, which means his great enthusiasm!

"Do you not know? Have you not heard? Has it not been told you from the beginning? Have you not understood since the earth was founded? He sits enthroned above the circle of the earth, and its people are like grasshoppers. He stretches out the Heavens like a canopy, and spreads them out like a tent to live in. He brings princes to naught and reduces the rulers of this world to nothing. No sooner are they planted, no sooner are they sown, no sooner do they take root in the ground, than he blows on them and they wither, and a whirlwind sweep them away like chaff. "To whom will you compare me? Or who is my equal?" says the Holy One. Lift up your eyes and look to the Heavens: Who created all these? He who brings out the starry host one by one and calls forth each of them by name. Because of his great power and mighty strength, not one of them is missing. Why do you complain, Jacob? Why do you say, Israel, "My way is hidden from the Lord; my cause is disregarded by my God"? Do you not know? Have you not heard? The Lord is the everlasting God, the Creator of the ends of the earth. He will not grow tired or weary, and his understanding no one can fathom. He gives strength to the weary and increases the power of the weak. Even youths grow tired and weary, and young men stumble and fall." -Isaiah 40:21-30 (Luke 1:49, Psalm 93:4 and Isaiah 46:5).

Convicting. Picture that- to Him we are like small grasshoppers, a stretch of His hand gives us life and a place to live, who can we compare Him to?! He knows every star by name. Then he asks, "Why do you complain?" His response after He asks this question, helps me when I complain. He reminds us he does not grow weary and His power increases in us when we are weak.

I love the story of Joseph. His brothers sold him into slavery out of their jealousy, leading him to a whole slew of other problems such as him being falsely accused of sleeping with his master's wife, him ending up in prison, however God used every single circumstance that people meant him for evil, and he tells us God used it for good, ultimately making him the ruler over Egypt and reconciling with his family when a drought in Israel causes his family to travel to Egypt for food. It also said God gave him wisdom. Many times, I like to take credit for the studying I do, but honestly any wisdom we have comes from the Lord. Joseph had no idea as he sat in a ditch, assuming he was going to die that God was using his brothers' evil intentions for Joseph to save many as ruler over Egypt. God's hand was completely over both Joseph's life, and the life of Moses. Moses purposefully learned the way of the Egyptians, as God knew he was going to use this to help him save his people, the Israelites. Moses killed an Egyptian out of rage for mistreating an Israelite, which led him to flee. God uses all people, even those who have murdered. God then used Moses to lead the Israelites out of slavery, part the Red Sea, and take His people into the promised land. The Israelites, even while seeing the miracle God had done, and how He provided in the wilderness for 40 years, refused to obey. We need to understand there is no way possible the Israelites could have been freed from the power of the Egyptians in their own strength against one of the strongest empires of that time. God is the only explanation and deserved their praise. Then as Moses was spending time with God on Mount Sinai to receive the Ten commandments, the people became impatient and asked Aaron, Moses' brother, to make a calf as an idol. They worshiped the calf, along with the sun, moon and stars. Then Joshua had faith the Lord would provide and led him and Caleb to the promised land. Then David was seen as a man after the Lord's own heart, and even though he wanted to build the temple for God, his son Solomon ended up building it. God talks about how the people of the current generation were just as stiff-necked as their ancestors who killed the prophets who foretold the coming of Jesus. The Holy Spirit has been around since the beginning like God, and Jesus, and people have been resisting them since. (See Acts 13:20-39).

God must have been so hurt because His own people did not want Him as King anymore, and on top of this, He knew it would hurt them to not have Him as King. Once Saul was appointed, he did not follow God. God thought David was after His own heart and told Saul if he did not turn from his ways, David was going to be appointed. Because of David's faithfulness, God said Jesus was going to come through his line. The Pharisees, even though they condemned Jesus, by doing so, God used the hate in their hearts to fulfill His purpose and promise to bring Jesus as the Messiah. Everyone who believes in Christ is set free from sin. The law and routine sacrifices were not sufficient to bring justification.

Now then, why do you try to test God by putting on the necks of Gentiles a yoke that neither we nor our ancestors have been able to bear? No! We believe it is through the grace of our Lord Jesus that we are saved, just as they are." -Acts 15:10-11 (Acts 15:5-9, Romans 11:1, Acts 11:18, Romans 1:5-6). "And he is not served by human hands, as if he needed anything. Rather, he himself gives everyone life and breath and everything else. From one man he made all the nations, that they should inhabit the whole earth; and he marked out their appointed times in history and the boundaries of their lands. God did this so that they would seek him and perhaps reach out for him and find him, though he is not far from any one of us. 'For in him we live and move and have our being.' As some of your own poets have said, 'We are his offspring.' -Acts 17:25-28. "The day is yours, and yours is also the night; you established the sun and moon. It was you who set all the boundaries of the earth; you made both summer and winter." -Psalm 74:16-17.

The people of Jewish heritage held so tightly to being God's chosen people and could not understand that Jesus had broken the walls and chains, allowing both Jews and gentiles to be saved. The people of Jewish heritage at this time continued to hold a "perfect" standard to the gentiles that they could not even hold themselves. God does not need anything from you, and simply loves and wants you to love Him. You have breath today because God is purposefully giving it to you. He made this world for and through Jesus. He is literally our source of life that allows us to have our being.

"The gospel was promised through the prophets in the Holy Scriptures regarding his Son, who as to his earthly life who was a descendent of David and who through the Spirit of holiness was appointed the Son of God in power by his resurrection from the dead: Jesus Christ our Lord." -Romans 1:2-4.

"But because of your stubbornness and your unrepentant heart, you are storing up wrath against yourself for the day of God's wrath, when his righteous judgment will be revealed. God "will repay each person according to what they have done." To those who by persistence in doing good seek glory, honor and immortality, he will give eternal life. But for those who are self-seeking and who reject the truth and follow evil, there will be wrath and anger." -Romans 2:5-8 (Ezekiel 22:31, Revelation 2:23, Revelation 3:10, Jeremiah 11:20 and Psalm 7:9).

I am not sure about you, but to be repaid for everything I have ever done is beyond scary to think about. We can be assured and grateful once we place our faith in Jesus, this wrath is no longer on us. God does not desire to place wrath on us but wants each of us to be saved resulting in the sacrifice of his own Son, which Jesus willingly agreed to. God is also just, and our sin deserves punishment, which Jesus took for us when we trust in Him.

"He testifies to what He has seen and heard, but no one accepts His testimony. Whoever has accepted it has certified that God is truthful. For the One whom God has sent speaks the words of God, for God gives the Spirit without limit. The Father loves the Son and has placed everything in His hands. Whoever believes in the Son has eternal life, but whoever rejects the Son will not see life, for God's wrath remains on them." -John 3:32-36.

When we accept Jesus, we are telling God our creator we trust Him. Everything Jesus says shows who God is and his character. He is the only way to Heaven.

"But God demonstrates his own love for us in this: While we were still sinners, Christ died for us. Since we have now been justified by his blood, how much more shall we be saved from God's wrath through him! For if, while we were God's enemies, we were reconciled to him through the death of his Son, how much more, having been reconciled, shall we be saved through his life! Not only is this so, but we also boast in God through our Lord Jesus Christ, through whom we have now received reconciliation." -Romans 5:8-11.

We are justified through the blood of Christ. Before Jesus, we are considered enemies to God and against Him whether you realize it or not. We are saved and our relationship with God since the fall at the beginning is reconciled. We have peace with God! God wants to draw you near to him, as his wrath has been placed on his Son to be taken away from you. He loves you that much.

"Therefore, there is now no condemnation for those who are in Christ Jesus, because through Christ Jesus the law of the Spirit who gives life has set you free from the law of sin and death. For what the law was powerless to do because it was weakened by the flesh, God did by sending his own Son in the likeness of sinful flesh to be a sin offering. And so, he condemned sin in the flesh, in order that the righteous requirement of the law might be fully met in us, who do not live according to the flesh but according to the Spirit." -Romans 8:1-4.

Giving rules, laws, and regulations, even though they are good, were not powerful enough to change hearts. Only the radical love of Christ could.

"It is written: "I believed; therefore, I have spoken." Since we have that same spirit of faith, we also believe and therefore speak, because we know that the one who raised the Lord Jesus from the dead will also raise us with Jesus and present us with you to himself." -2 Corinthians 4:13-14. We have the Holy Spirit living inside of us and have the power to speak the truth in love. We can have confidence we will be raised on the last day. Jesus is now our advocate, presenting us now as clean.

"Do not think that I have come to abolish the Law or the Prophets; I have not come to abolish them but to fulfill them. For truly I tell you, until Heaven and earth disappear, not the smallest letter, not the least stroke of a pen, will by any means disappear from the Law until everything is accomplished. Therefore, anyone who sets aside one of the least of these commands and teaches others accordingly will be called least in the kingdom of Heaven, but whoever practices and teaches these commands will be called great in the kingdom of Heaven. For I tell you that unless your righteousness surpasses that of the Pharisees and the teachers of the law, you will certainly not enter the kingdom of Heaven." -Matthew 5:17-20 (Matthew 24:35, Mark 13:31, Luke 21:33, Hebrews 7:18-19, John 1:17 and Luke 16:17).

Many separate the Old and New Testament, saying the Old is no longer important because Jesus in a sense "got rid of it" when He came. This is not true. Jesus *fulfilled* the law when He came. He is saying here the old is just as important as the new, they are all a part of the entire story of the world and creation. He was the fulfillment. Also, when He talks about having to be completely righteous to get into Heaven, the standard He is saying is not possible on our own. We can only be declared righteous by placing our trust in Him for our salvation.

If you believed Moses, you would believe me, for he wrote about me. But since you do not believe what he wrote, how are you going to believe what I say?" -John 5:46-47. Jesus was frustrated with the Pharisees who were the religious leaders at the time, because they clung so heavily on the scriptures and what Moses had to say, but not Jesus who fulfilled everything they believed. "What shall we say, then? Is the law sinful? Certainly not! Nevertheless, I would not have known what sin was had it not been for the law. For I would not have known what coveting really was if the law had not said, "You shall not covet." -Romans 7:7. Emphasis needs to be placed on the fact the law is good, not bad. However, the law exposes our sin, showing how evil we are. The law helps us understand why we need a Savior, it does not create us to be bad, simply exposes that we desperately need Him.

We are born into slavery by the spiritual force of the world but at the right time God sent His Son, born under the law, born of a virgin to redeem those under the law so we can be adopted. God sent the Spirit of Jesus in our hearts so we can call out "Abba, Father." We are no longer slaves but God's children, and co-heirs with Christ when we share in his sufferings in order to share in his glory. (See Galatians 4:3-7, Corinthians 1:9 and Romans 8:16-17). It is crazy to think about God's plan to have us be co-heirs with Christ when the new Heaven and new Earth are created. He freed us of slavery from the enemy, Satan, who has a grip on you if you are not in Christ, whether you believe it or not. When a child is adopted, they are chosen! God adopts us into His family as a chosen child.

"We know that the whole creation has been groaning as in the pains of childbirth right up to the present time. Not only so, but we ourselves, who have the first fruits of the Spirit, groan inwardly as we wait eagerly for our adoption to sonship, the redemption of our bodies. For in this hope, we were saved. But hope that is seen is no hope at all. Who hopes for what they already have? But if we hope for what we do not yet have, we wait for it patiently." -Romans 8:22-25 (Romans 8:21).

When women have a baby, their pains and contractions increase as the baby gets closer to arrival. Even though creation has been groaning since sin entered the world, the pain will continue to increase, as each day that passes is another day closer to Christ's return. Due to the natural disasters, decay in the world, animals suffering and us as people suffering, anyone can see that creation is just waiting to be restored. Every single one of us has an imperfect body. As an athlete and someone who enjoys working out, it can slow the process of decay but never stop it. We also all know people in very good shape who still have health concerns. Working in health care, I can tell you almost every single human being does, even if they are unaware of them at this moment. Regardless of this, we have hope. Hope that one day when we are in Heaven our brokenness physically, emotionally, and spiritually will all be restored.

"The earth is defiled by its people; they have disobeyed the laws, violated the statutes and broken the everlasting covenant. Therefore, a curse consumes the earth; its people must bear their guilt. Therefore, earth's inhabitants are burned up, and very few are left." -Isaiah 24:5-6. "In the streets they cry out for wine; all joy turns to gloom; all joyful sounds are banished from the earth. The city is left in ruins, its gate is battered to pieces. So will it be on the earth and among the nations, as when an olive tree is beaten, or as when gleanings are left after the grape harvest." -Isaiah 24:11-13. The world is broken. It was created good and beautiful, but now, in our sinful desires, a curse has now been placed on the earth. The beauty is God can make beauty from the brokenness. It is all over the Bible, and He continues to do so today!

"For those who are led by the Spirit of God are the children of God." -Romans 8:14 (2 Corinthians 6:18 and John 1:9-13). When you accept Jesus as your Savior, you literally have Him living inside of you! You are claimed as God's child and can have confidence in this. "But whoever loves God is known by God." -1 Corinthians 8:3. If you love God, you can bet he is a part of every aspect of your life, even the small details. "See what great love the Father has lavished on us, that we should be called children of God! And that is what we are! The reason the world does not know us is that it did not know him." -1 John 3:1.

"For none of us lives for ourselves alone, and none of us dies for ourselves alone. If we live, we live for the Lord; and if we die, we die for the Lord. So, whether we live or die, we belong to the Lord. For this very reason, Christ died and returned to life so that he might be the Lord of both the dead and the living." -Romans 14:7-9. You were not created for yourself, but you were created for God. Your life is not your own. For this reason, God has taken it on Himself to save his fallen creation. Honestly, think how much pressure it relieves you of to think your life belongs to God. You can have confidence He is going to counsel you and help you if He is choosing to have your life belong to Him.

"Therefore, God exalted Jesus to the highest place and gave him the name above every name, that at the name of Jesus every knee should bow, in heaven and on earth and under the earth, and every tongue acknowledge that Jesus Christ is Lord, to the glory of God the Father." -Philippians 2:9-11 (Romans 14:11-12, Isaiah 45:23-24, Isaiah 52:10, Revelation 15:3-4, Revelation 1:7-8, Mark 13:26-27, Matthew 24:29-30, Luke 21:27-28, 1 Thessalonians 4:15-18, Revelation 10:7 and Micah 5:3-5). Even if you do not believe in Christ now, one day you will. I want you to have Him as your Lord and Savior before it is too late. The Bible says that every single person will bow, and every tongue will confess, He is Lord.

Jesus was crucified, we received the spirit and God performs miracles when we believe this and not by works of the law. You cannot start by Spirit, and finish by flesh. Abraham "believed God, and it was credited to him as righteousness." Those who have faith are children of Abraham. Scripture foresaw that God would justify the Gentiles by faith and announced the gospel in advance to Abraham: "All nations will be blessed through you." So those who rely on faith are blessed along with Abraham, the man of faith. God's Word did not fail. Not all physical descendants of Israel and Abraham are who God considers Israel. (See Galatians 3:1-9 and Romans 9:6-8). Israel is singled out as the nation of God's inheritance. You are saved by faith alone and cannot try to work to complete what Jesus has completed already. Many people wonder how others in the Old Testament received salvation, and it was the same in the sense of having faith in God for salvation presenting us as righteous before Him. Even though many are not Jewish by heritage, we are considered children of Abraham through our faith, as God foresaw and planned for this at the creation of the world. It is all a part of the redemption plan. "What then shall we say? Is God unjust? Not at all!" -Romans 9:14. God is completely just in saving those of Jewish heritage and gentiles when they place their faith in Him, as

God looks at the heart.

Anyone who tries to move Jerusalem will injure themselves. (See 1 Kings 8:53, Zechariah 12:3, Deuteronomy 33:29 and Psalm 33:12). Israel is God's chosen Country. To this day, it stands fulfilling the promise and prophecy. We need to support Israel as a country and encourage others to do the same.

"Your father Abraham rejoiced at the thought of seeing my day; he saw it and was glad." "You are not yet fifty years old," they said to him, "and you have seen Abraham!" "Very truly I tell you," Jesus answered, "before Abraham was born, I am!" -John 8:56-58 (John 8:59). The Pharisees could not see that Jesus was the fulfillment of the promise God made through Abraham. "I will make you into a great nation, and I will bless you; I will make your name great, and you will be a blessing. I will bless those who bless you, and whoever curses you I will curse; and all peoples on earth will be blessed through you." -Genesis 12:2-3 (Numbers 10:29, Numbers 23:21-23 and Numbers 23:23).

"God made him who had no sin to be sin for us, so that in him we might become the righteousness of God." -2 Corinthians 5:21 (1 Peter 3:18, Galatians 3:13-14 and Romans 1:17). Jesus became the curse of sin for us, making us righteous. He, who had no sin, became all our sin to make us righteous before God. Life is not fair guys, but not in the way we think. We think it is not fair because it is hard, when really it is not fair that God saved us. "But since you excel in everything—in faith, in speech, in knowledge, in complete earnestness and in love, we have kindled in you—see that you also excel in this grace of giving. I am not commanding you, but I want to test the sincerity of your love by comparing it with the earnestness of others. For you know the grace of our Lord Jesus Christ, that though he was rich, yet for your sake he became poor, so that you through his poverty might become rich." -2 Corinthians 8:7-9. He left His throne of glory and became poor, so we may become rich in Spirit, to excel in faith, speech, knowledge, and earnestness, being zealous for Him, being full of His love to give gracefully. These are all qualities the Spirit can give when we ask of Him. Remember, it may not look like we are excelling in these areas from our tainted standard or thoughts, but God is faithful and will guide us by His Holy Spirit.

We are Abraham's seed through faith. "What if he did this to make the riches of His glory known to the objects of his mercy, whom he prepared in advance for glory— even us, whom he also called, not only from the Jews but also from the Gentiles? As he says in Hosea: "I will call them 'my people' who are not my people; and I will call her 'my loved one' who is not my loved one." -Romans 9:23-25 (Hosea 2:23). God knew in advance and His plan all along was to save gentiles as well as the Jewish heritage. "So, in Christ Jesus you are all children of God through faith, for all of you who were baptized into Christ have clothed yourselves with Christ. There is neither Jew nor Gentile, neither slave nor free, nor is there male and female, for you are all one in Christ Jesus. If you belong to Christ, then you are Abraham's seed, and heirs according to the promise." -Galatians 3:26-29 (Ephesians 3:6). In Christ we are no longer differentiated by race, gender, ethnicity but at the core of our soul one in him.

"You who are trying to be justified by the law have been alienated from Christ; you have fallen away from grace." -Galatians 5:4. Stop working to receive grace. It is pointless. We are justified only by grace, and our works come from our love for Christ and desire to follow his laws out of pure love.

"So, I say, walk by the Spirit, and you will not gratify the desires of the flesh. For the flesh desires what is contrary to the Spirit, and the Spirit what is contrary to the flesh. They are in conflict with each other, so that you are not to do whatever you want. But if you are led by the Spirit, you are not under the law. The acts of the flesh are obvious: sexual immorality, impurity and debauchery; idolatry and witchcraft; hatred, discord, jealousy, fits of rage, selfish ambition, dissensions, factions and envy; drunkenness, orgies, and the like. I warn you, as I did before, that those who live like this will not inherit the kingdom of God." -Galatians 5:16-21 (Romans 3:13-18).

Deuteronomy 18:10-11 says not to consult the dead. We follow the spirit, not when we are so focused on avoiding sin, but when we focus on Jesus, sin begins to repel us. Why does God give us these rules? To protect us, out of his love for us. He made us and knew what was best. We are not under bondage of these. We are free in Christ to follow him, avoid the trouble, have fun in life in the freedom he has given us, and we now have the power to follow Him!

"Praise be to the God and Father of our Lord Jesus Christ, who has blessed us in the Heavenly realms with every spiritual blessing in Christ. For he chose us in him before the creation of the world to be holy and blameless in his sight. In love he predestined us for adoption to sonship through Jesus Christ, in accordance with his pleasure and will— to the praise of his glorious grace, which he has freely given us in the One he loves. In him we have redemption through his blood, the forgiveness of sins, in accordance with the riches of God's grace that he lavished on us. With all wisdom and understanding, he made known to us the mystery of his will according to his good pleasure, which he purposed in Christ, to be put into effect when the times reach their fulfillment—to bring unity to all things in Heaven and on earth under Christ. In him we were also chosen, having been predestined according to the plan of him who works out everything in conformity with the purpose of his will, in order that we, who were the first to put our hope in Christ, might be for the praise of his glory. And you also were included in Christ when you heard the message of truth, the gospel of your salvation. When you believed, you were marked in him with a seal, the promised Holy Spirit, who is a deposit guaranteeing our inheritance until the redemption of those who are God's possession—to the praise of his glory." -Ephesians 1:3-14 (Romans 8:29-30).

We are His. You were thought of to be created before the creation of the world! Think about that! He gives us wisdom. He gives us grace. When it says we are "predestined" it does not mean God chose some and not others. God desires all to be saved, however some will deny Him. Please join the family! We have a seal placed over us when we have the Holy Spirit, and even though we may not always listen to the Holy Spirit as we should, I am a firm believer you cannot "lose" the Holy Spirit. Once you see truth, you cannot "unsee" truth. "He provided redemption for his people; he ordained his covenant forever- holy and awesome is his name." -Psalm 111:9. "Being confident of this; that he who began a good work in you will carry it on to completion until the day of Christ Jesus." -Philippians 1:6.

"The beginning of wisdom is this: Get wisdom. Though it costs all you have, get understanding. Cherish her, and she will exalt you; embrace her, and she will honor you. She will give you garland to grace your head and present you with a glorious crown. Listen, my son, accept what I say, and the years of your life will be many. I instruct you in the way of wisdom and lead you along straight paths. When you walk, your steps will not be hampered; when you run, you will not stumble. Hold on to instruction, do not let it go; guard it well, for it is your life. Do not set foot on the path of the wicked or walk in the way of evildoers." -Proverbs 4:7-14 (Proverbs 4:18).

If you pursue wisdom, wisdom will honor you. If you want to run the race, hold onto God's instruction, as it is your life.

"The fruit of the righteous is the tree of life, and the one who is wise saves lives." -Proverbs 11:30. "The one who gets wisdom loves life; the one who cherishes understanding will soon prosper." -Proverbs 19:8. "Wisdom makes one wise person more powerful than ten rulers in a city." -Ecclesiastes 7:19. Many would say strength is the key to victory, but the Bible seems to feel it is wisdom and influence. Wisdom gives life, saves lives, helps you prosper and makes you more powerful than ten rulers in a city by influencing others. Who is wise? What is wisdom considered? Fear of the Lord. This means that it does not matter your profession, even though it is wise to continue to learn within your profession, but many of the disciples and apostles other than Luke the Doctor, and Matthew and Judas, the accountants, were not educated, yet people were amazed by their wisdom. "Since they have rejected the word of the Lord, what kind of wisdom do they have?" -Jeremiah 8:9. "The teaching of the wise is a fountain of life, turning a person from the snares of death." -Proverbs 13:14.

"Blessed are those who find wisdom, those who gain understanding, for she is more profitable than silver and yields better returns than gold. She is more precious than rubies; nothing you desire can compare with her. Long life is in her right hand; in her left hand are riches and honor. Her ways are pleasant ways, and all her paths are peace. She is a tree of life to those who take hold of her; those who hold her fast will be blessed. By wisdom the Lord laid the earth's foundations, by understanding he set the Heavens in place; by his knowledge the watery depths were divided, and the clouds let drop the dew. My son, do not let wisdom and understanding out of your sight, preserve sound judgment and discretion; they will be life for you, an ornament to grace your neck." -Proverbs 3:13-22.

Wisdom brings life and peace rooted from God. Wisdom, just like love, flows from God. By wisdom He created the universe, which is why people cannot separate science as if it were apart from God. God created physics, chemistry, math, anatomy and physiology, so when people claim they believe in science over God, it is not possible because by wisdom even your very nature has been formed, including ever part of the brain giving you the ability to read this book.

"In every matter of wisdom and understanding about which the king questioned them, he found them ten times better than all the magicians and enchanters in his whole kingdom." -Daniel 1:20. "This made the king so angry and furious that he ordered the execution of all the wise men of Babylon. So, the decree was issued to put the wise men to death, and men were sent to look for Daniel and his friends to put them to death." -Daniel 2:12-13. "Some of the wise will stumble, so that they may be refined, purified and made spotless until the time of the end, for it will come at the appointed time." -Daniel 11:35.

"...but you do not believe. The works I do in my Father's name testify about me, but you do not believe because you are not my sheep. My sheep listen to my voice; I know them, and they follow me. I give them eternal life, and they shall never perish; no one will snatch them out of my hand. My Father, who has given them to me, is greater than all; no one can snatch them out of my Father's hand. I and the Father are one." -John 10:25-30.

The fact that we cannot be snatched out of His hand is another truth I hold onto, that we cannot lose our salvation once saved. The more time we spend with God and in His word, the more you recognize His voice. "I am the good shepherd. The good shepherd lays down his life for the sheep." -John 10:11. His sheep listen to his voice as he calls them by name, leading ahead of them, and they will run from a stranger's voice (See John 10:3-5). You are a new creation, and nothing can snatch you out of the Father's hand. "Grace to all who love our Lord Jesus Christ with an undying love." -Ephesians 6:24. "Undying" love, it cannot be lost.

"Let no one take you captive through deceptive philosophy which is on human tradition and the spiritual forces of the word instead of Christ. In Christ is fullness, He is head over every power and authority who circumcises, not performed by human hands, allowing us to put off the flesh. We are buried with Him, baptized with Him and raised with Him through faith. We were dead in our sins, God made us alive in Christ, forgiving us of our sins. He disarms the authorities and cancels our legal indebtedness which condemns us, nailing it to the cross." -Colossians 2:8-15 (Romans 2:29).

Do not follow or believe something when it comes to faith or God if it is only based on tradition, whether in a church, your family, friends, etc., but make sure it is in the word of God. "You have let go of the commands of God and are holding on to human traditions." And he continued, "You have a fine way of setting aside the commands of God in order to observe your own traditions!" -Mark 7:8-9. Jesus nailed our sins to the cross, ultimately having Satan humiliated publicly. "...the prince of this world now stands condemned." -John 16:11 (John 12:31). I think after Satan had taken down all of God's previous men...Abraham, Noah, Moses, Sampson, David, Solomon, Elijah, etc. he thought he would have no problem taking care of Jesus through Judas. Satan, I am sure, thought he won, as his plan succeeded and he saw Jesus on that cross, alone, scorned and what looked for a moment like forsaken. I cannot imagine how he felt, seeing Jesus rise from the dead, overcoming the very battle he thought he won. It is the same today. When we fail or mess up, Satan will make us believe he won and we "disappointed" God, when really God is an expert at taking our messes and using them for his good and glory.

"God is just: He will pay back trouble to those who trouble you and give relief to you who are troubled, and to us as well. This will happen when the Lord Jesus is revealed from Heaven in blazing fire with his powerful angels. He will punish those who do not know God and do not obey the gospel of our Lord Jesus. They will be punished with everlasting destruction and shut out from the presence of the Lord and from the glory of his might on the day he comes to be glorified in his holy people and to be marveled at among all those who have believed. This includes you, because you believed our testimony to you." -2 Thessalonians 1:6-10 (2 Chronicles 12:6 and Deuteronomy 7:10).

I do not like to tell people these types of truths, but I also did not create the truth and it needs to be shared; regardless of if you are aware of it or not, it is true. Naturally, we like to think those who have wronged us are being punished; it makes us giddy! The only problem is, each one of us has wronged someone else, and I am sure that person is hoping we get the "pay back" too. The consequences for not having Christ are real, as God is just and must punish sin, even though he does not want to. We get a glimpse into the consequences in His Word.

"Here is a trustworthy saying that deserves full acceptance: Christ Jesus came into the world to save sinners—of whom I am the worst. But for that very reason I was shown mercy so that in me, the worst of sinners, Christ Jesus might display his immense patience as an example for those who would believe in him and receive eternal life. Now to the King eternal, immortal, invisible, the only God, be honor and glory for ever and ever. Amen." -1 Timothy 1:15-17.

Think you are not good enough? Think other people are either better or worse than you? We are all the worst as far as the justice system goes. We have all broken every law.

"At one time we too were foolish, disobedient, deceived and enslaved by all kinds of passions and pleasures. We lived in malice and envy, being hated and hating one another. But when the kindness and love of God our Savior appeared, he saved us, not because of righteous things we had done, but because of his mercy. He saved us through the washing of rebirth and renewal by the Holy Spirit, whom he poured out on us generously through Jesus Christ our Savior, so that, having been justified by his grace, we might become heirs having the hope of eternal life. This is a trustworthy saying. And I want you to stress these things, so that those who have trusted in God may be careful to devote themselves to doing what is good. These things are excellent and profitable for everyone." - Titus 3:3-8.

We are no longer slaves to sin. It does not help to think about the sin and say to yourself "I can't do that." Instead, continue to fall in love and draw closer to Jesus and sin will begin to naturally repel you. Will we be perfect? Of course not, but I can guarantee you will sin "less" and not enjoy it as much as you used to.

"How shall we escape if we ignore so great a salvation? This salvation, which was first announced by the Lord, was confirmed to us by those who heard him. God also testified to it by signs, wonders and various miracles, and by gifts of the Holy Spirit distributed according to his will." -Hebrews 2:3-4. "In bringing many sons and daughters to glory, it was fitting that God, for whom and through whom everything exists, should make the pioneer of their salvation perfect through what he suffered." -Hebrews 2:10. We all belong to God. He is the reason anything or anyone exists. He took responsibility to save us through His suffering, the suffering of His son.

"The sanctuary that is a copy and shadow of what is in Heaven. This is why Moses was warned when he was about to build the tabernacle: "See to it that you make everything according to the pattern shown you on the mountain." But in fact, the ministry Jesus has received is as superior to theirs as the covenant of which he is mediator is superior to the old one, since the new covenant is established on better promises. For if there had been nothing wrong with that first covenant, no place would have been sought for another. But God found fault with the people and said: "The days are coming, declares the Lord, when I will make a new covenant with the people of Israel and with the people of Judah. It will not be like the covenant I made with their ancestors when I took them by the hand to lead them out of Egypt, because they did not remain faithful to my covenant, and I turned away from them, declares the Lord. This is the covenant I will establish with the people of Israel after that time, declares the Lord. I will put my laws in their minds and write them on their hearts. I will be their God, and they will be my people. No longer will they teach their neighbor, or say to one another, 'Know the Lord,' because they will all know me, from the least of them to the greatest. For I will forgive their wickedness and will remember their sins no more." -Hebrews 8:5-12 (Jeremiah 31:34 and Psalm 130:7-8).

"In fact, the law requires that nearly everything be cleansed with blood, and without the shedding of blood there is no forgiveness." -Hebrews 9:22. For in the first covenant, people continued to turn from God. This second covenant through Jesus has us follow the law from our hearts. There cannot be forgiveness without the shedding of blood, which is where Jesus took our place.

"For Christ did not enter a sanctuary made with human hands that was only a copy of the true one; he entered Heaven itself, now to appear for us in God's presence. Nor did he enter Heaven to offer himself again and again, the way the high priest enters the Most Holy Place every year with blood that is not his own. Otherwise, Christ would have had to suffer many times since the creation of the world. But he has appeared once for all at the culmination of the ages to do away with sin by the sacrifice of himself. Just as people are destined to die once, and after that to face judgment, ^{so} Christ was sacrificed once to take away the sins of many; and he will appear a second time, not to bear sin, but to bring salvation to those who are waiting for him." -Hebrews 9:24-28.

Jesus was the sacrifice once and for all which is why he had to be crucified and be raised from the dead only once. The high priest before Jesus came would have to sacrifice for sins every year as one was not sufficient. Jesus is sufficient to forgive sins past, present and future. He is the only chance you have of being saved in this life. There are no second chances after we die. People will talk about Hell almost being temporary, but then one would have to ask, "Then what was the point of Jesus coming to die if we were all going to be saved anyway?" Jesus did not have to come and die if we were all just going to be saved regardless. The entire point of Jesus' crucifixion is that we can be made right with God through faith now, in order to be seen as righteous to enter Heaven once we die through Jesus' blood. If God is going to just save everyone without them calling on His Son, what is the point of continuing to allow all this suffering? He is waiting for people to come to repentance as he desires all to be saved. If he was just going to save us all regardless of faith, why did he not just make us perfect to begin with? Without free will or even giving us the option to choose sin. This is because God wanted us to choose to be with him forever. What is the point of going and making disciples as Jesus commands in the great commission if everyone is going to be saved anyways? Scripture is clear about Heaven and Hell, and that each one of us is going to one or the other. Our only hope to Heaven and to escape the lake of fire is placing our faith in Jesus before we die. He can save you, just ask!

"The law is only a shadow of the good things that are coming-not the realities themselves. For this reason, it can never, by the same sacrifices repeated endlessly year after year, make perfect those who draw near to worship. Otherwise, would they not have stopped being offered? For the worshipers would have been cleansed once for all and would no longer have felt guilty for their sins. But those sacrifices are an annual reminder of sins. It is impossible for the blood of bulls and goats to take away sins. Therefore, when Christ came into the world, he said: "Sacrifice and offering you did not desire, but a body you prepared for me; with burnt offerings and sin offerings you were not pleased. Then I said, 'Here I am-it is written about me in the scroll- I have come to do your will, my God.'" First, he said,

"Sacrifices and offerings, burnt offerings and sin offerings you did not desire, nor were you pleased with them" – though they were offered in accordance with the law. Then he said, "Here I am, I have come to do your will." He sets aside the first to establish the second. And by that will, we have been made holy through the sacrifice of the body of Jesus Christ once for all. Day after day every priest stands and performs his religious duties; again, and again he offers the same sacrifices, which can never take away sins. But when this priest had offered for all time one sacrifice for sins, he sat down at the right hand of God, and since that time he waits for his enemies to be made his footstool. For by one sacrifice, he has made perfect forever those who are being made holy. The Holy Spirit also testifies to us about this. First, he says: "This is the covenant I will make with them after that time, says the Lord. I will put my laws in their hearts, and I will write them on their minds." Then he adds: "Their sins and lawless acts I will remember no more." And where these have been forgiven, sacrifice for sin is no longer necessary." -Hebrews 10:1-18 (Colossians 2:17).

"By faith Abel brought God a better offering than Cain did. By faith he was commended as righteous when God spoke well of his offerings. And by faith Abel still speaks, even though he is dead." -Hebrews 11:4. Satan wanted Abel dead to try and discontinue the offspring of Adam, Abraham, and eventually leading to the Messiah. "Then Pharaoh gave this order to all his people: "Every Hebrew boy that is born you must throw into the Nile but let every girl live." -Exodus 1:22 (Exodus 1:16). Many times, through the kings it came down to one to continue the line. If people aren't born, Satan thinks this will stop God. An example of this is when Herod tried to kill Jesus and all the baby boys two years and under. In today's world, an example would be abortion. "You believe that there is one God. Good! Even the demons believe that—and shudder." -James 2:19 (Luke 4:33-35 and Matthew 9:32-34). In Luke 4:33-37 and Matthew 9:32-34, the demon shouts he knows who Jesus is, but Jesus rebukes him having complete power and authority. In Mark 5:15 Jesus commands a legion of demons to come out of a man. That is 6,000 demons in one person who Jesus had authority over!

"Praise be to the God and Father of our Lord Jesus Christ! In his great mercy he has given us new birth into a living hope through the resurrection of Jesus Christ from the dead, and into an inheritance that can never perish, spoil or fade.

This inheritance is kept in heaven for you…" -1 Peter 1:3-4.

"For you know that it was not with perishable things such as silver or gold that you were redeemed from the empty way of life handed down to you from your ancestors, but with the precious blood of Christ, a lamb without blemish or defect. He was chosen before the creation of the world but was revealed in these last times for your sake. Through him you believe in God, who raised him from the dead and glorified him, and so your faith and hope are in God." -1 Peter 1:18-21.

"Every day you are to provide a year-old lamb without defect for a burnt offering to the Lord; morning by morning you shall provide it." -Ezekiel 46:13. Jesus was the lamb without defect.

"…and this water symbolizes baptism that now saves you also-not the removal of dirt from the body but the pledge of a clear conscience toward God. It saves you by the resurrection of Jesus Christ, who has gone into heaven and is at God's right hand- with angels, authorities, and powers in submission to him." -1 Peter 3:21-22 (1 Peter 3:19-20). Physical water baptism does not save you as opposed to popular belief. Paul says in the Bible it is so important, and once you become a believer it is your way of proclaiming and telling the world you are made new, however I do not want you to be confused as only baptism of the spirit saves you.

"For if God did not spare angels when they sinned, but sent them to hell, putting them in chains of darkness to be held for judgement; if he did not spare the ancient world when he brought the flood on its ungodly people, but protected Noah, a preacher of righteousness, and seven others; if he condemned the cities of Sodom and Gomorrah by burning them to ashes, and made them an example of what is going to happen to the ungodly; and if he rescued Lot, a righteous man, who was distressed by the depraved conduct of the lawless (for the righteous man, living among them day after day, was tormented in his righteous soul by the lawless deeds he saw and heart)- If this is so, then the Lord knows how to rescue the godly from trials and to hold the unrighteous for punishment on the day of judgement. This is especially true of those who follow the corrupt desire of the flesh and despise authority." -2 Peter 2:4-10 (Jude 1:5-9, Matthew 13:37-43, Matthew 13:47-52, Matthew 13:30, Matthew 18:7-9, Mark 9:43-48, Jude 1:14-16 and Psalm 9:17).

Matthew 7:21-23 are scary verses saying some will say they knew Jesus when they first get to Heaven, saying they acted in his name, but he will say he never knew them. Guys, Hell is real. I did not make it up; it is uncomfortable to talk about, but I would not be loving you if I did not tell you. The truth says Satan and even some of the angels who rebelled against God and became demons will be there. Please choose to be with God.

Jesus spoke to them again in parables, saying: "The kingdom of heaven is like a king who prepared a wedding banquet for his son." -Matthew 22:1-2 (Matthew 7:13-14, Revelation 19:6-8 and Revelation 16:7-9). "Anyone whose name was not found written in the book of life was thrown into the lake of fire." -Revelation 20:15 (Revelation 11-14, Revelation 21:8, Revelation 14:9-10 and 2 Chronicles 18:18). "They will wage war against the Lamb, but the Lamb will triumph over them because he is Lord of lords and King of kings—and with Him will be his called, chosen and faithful followers." -Revelation 17:14 (Revelation 19:19-21). "...the two of them were thrown alive into the fiery lake of burning sulfur." -Revelation 19:20 (Revelation 6:17). You are invited to God's party in Heaven. If you are not in the book of life, the consequence is Hell, the lake of fire. Please accept his invitation today! "Nothing impure will ever enter it, nor will anyone who does what is shameful or deceitful, but only those whose names are written in the Lamb's book of life." -Revelation 21:27 (Revelation 3:5).

"The Lord is not slow in keeping his promise, as some understand slowness. Instead, he is patient with you, not wanting anyone to perish, but everyone to come to repentance." -2 Peter 3:9 (1 Timothy 2:3-4). The reason Jesus has not returned yet, part of His grace, is His postponement of judgment on the world right now. God wants to save every single individual, and Jesus has not returned yet to rapture the current believers because He is being patient to let as many come to Him as possible because He loves us. When you are a believer in Christ, the Holy Spirit dwells in you, and in other believers making us all one team. Jesus is going to come back in victory. God is being patient because He wants everyone to willingly join His team. We must choose now before it is too late. Once He is revealed, your choice will have already been made. Whether you realize it or not, you are making a choice now, and this choice will simply be revealed when we die or when Christ returns. God wants you to choose Him, He loves you!

"For my Father's will is that everyone who looks to the Son and believes in Him shall have eternal life, and I will raise them up at the last day." -John 6:40. "Like water spilled on the ground, which cannot be recovered, so we must die. But that is not what God desires; rather, he devises ways so that a banished person does not remain banished from him." -2 Samuel 14:14. God has an act for wanting to save those who are lost, which is every single one of us. "For I take no pleasure in the death of anyone, declares the Sovereign Lord. Repent and live!" -Ezekiel 18:32 (Ezekiel 33:11).

"I have listened attentively, but they do not say what is right. None of them repent of their wickedness saying, "What have I done?" Each pursues their own course like a horse charging into battle." -Jeremiah 8:6. God hears us and wants us to turn from our rebellion of Him. "Yet the Lord longs to be gracious to you; therefore, he will rise up to show you compassion. For the Lord is a God of justice. Blessed are all who wait for Him! People of Zion, who live in Jerusalem, you will weep no more. How gracious he will be when you cry for help! As soon as he hears, he will answer you." -Isaiah 30:18-19 (Psalm 50:6). God desires to pour grace on you! It is the opposite of what most picture. Most picture God wanting to punish any and every one He can, when He is wanting us to come to Him, confess our sin, trust in His Son and pour out His grace! "If someone who is righteous disobeys, that person's former righteousness will count for nothing. And if someone who is wicked repents, that person's former wickedness will not bring condemnation." -Ezekiel 33:12.

"And if I say to a wicked person, 'You will surely die,' but they then turn away from their sin and do what is just and right— if they give back what they took in pledge for a loan, return what they have stolen, follow the decrees that give life, and do no evil—that person will surely live; they will not die. None of the sins that person has committed will be remembered against them. They have done what is just and right; they will surely live." -Ezekiel 33:14-16.

"If a righteous person turns from their righteousness and does evil, they will die for it. And if a wicked person turns away from their wickedness and does what is just and right, they will live by doing so." -Ezekiel 33:18-20 (1 Samuel 2:10).

People will say where is this second coming of Jesus. Everything is the same as it was since the beginning, but they have forgotten the work God has done since then. Even then the world was destroyed by the flood of Noah. The present Heavens and earth will be destroyed by fire for the day of judgment. (See 2 Peter 3:4-7). Let's not lose hope, as we know the day will come when we least expect it! Earth is where the enemy and his demons were before we were created. God created us to overcome the enemy! Satan was a beautiful angel, and yet God is using us (who were not created with as much power as Satan), to overcome Satan by God's power when we trust in Him!

"Whoever believes in the Son of God accepts this testimony. Whoever does not believe God has made him out to be a liar, because they have not believed the testimony God has given about his Son. And this is the testimony: God has given us eternal life, and this life is in his Son. Whoever has the Son has life; whoever does not have the Son of God does not have life." -1 John 5:10-12.

If we deny Jesus is Lord, we are calling God a liar.

"Here I am! I stand at the door and knock. If anyone hears my voice and opens the door, I will come in and eat with that person, and they with me. To the one who is victorious, I will give the right to sit with me on my throne, just as I was victorious and sat down with my Father on his throne." -Revelation 3:20-21. Jesus is knocking on the door of your heart; all you must do is answer! Plagues will happen, and mankind continues to not repent, worships demons and idols, continues to kill, performs magic arts, sexual immorality, and steal (See Revelation 9:20-21). In these last days, people will continue to stray further from God and His ways, but with Him there is always hope, starting with how He can use you. "Come now, let us settle the matter," says the Lord. "Though your sins are like scarlet, they shall be as white as snow; though they are red as crimson, they shall be like wool." -Isaiah 1:18.

"Look, I am coming soon! My reward is with me, and I will give to each person according to what they have done. I am the Alpha and the Omega, the First and the Last, the Beginning and the End. "Blessed are those who wash their robes, that they may have the right to the tree of life and may go through the gates into the city. Outside are the dogs, those who practice magic arts, the sexually immoral, the murderers, the idolaters and everyone who loves and practices falsehood. "I, Jesus, have sent my angel to give you this testimony for the churches. I am the Root and the Offspring of David, and the bright Morning Star." The Spirit and the bride say, "Come!" And let the one who hears say, "Come!" Let the one who is thirsty come; and let the one who wishes take the free gift of the water of life. I warn everyone who hears the words of the prophecy of this scroll: If anyone adds anything to them, God will add to that person the plagues described in this scroll. And if anyone takes words away from this scroll of prophecy, God will take away from that person any share in the tree of life and in the Holy City, which are described in this scroll. He who testifies to these things says, "Yes, I am coming soon." Amen. Come, Lord Jesus." -Revelation 22:12-20 (Isaiah 48:12-13).

Every single day that passes is another day closer to Jesus' return, no matter when you are reading this. The tree of life, the one that we were never able to grasp, the one in the beginning that held the fruit that ultimately led to our death, that very same tree of knowledge of good and evil we will finally have hold of, but not in a broken state. We will be in a perfect state because Christ will have made us perfect. This is the mic drop of the Bible, the final words.

Where you spend your time and money shows where your priorities and deepest desires are, not just for now but for eternity. How many distractions would you get rid of if you really believed there is a Heaven or Hell for yourself, friends, and family. We are all sinners, and you are either saved by the grace of Christ or in need of it. You cannot live until you know what's worth dying for, confident of where you are going and why you are here. Christ's love compels us. One died for all so those who live no longer live for themselves but for Jesus. (See 2 Corinthians 5:14-15).

"If you love me, keep my commands." -John 14:15 (John 14:12 and Nehemiah 1:5). Sometimes when we are discerning God's will, we do not realize that his will is to obey what he commands out of love. "He replied, "Blessed rather are those who hear the word of God and obey it." -Luke 11:28. "…but keep my commands in your heart, for they will prolong your life for many years and bring you peace and prosperity." -Proverbs 3:1-2 (Proverbs 19:16 and Deuteronomy 30:16). "Why do you call me, 'Lord, Lord,' and do not do what I say? As for everyone who comes to me and hears my words and puts them into practice, I will show you what they are like. They are like a man building a house, who dug down deep and laid the foundation on rock. When a flood came, the torrent struck that house but could not shake it, because it was well built. But the one who hears my words and does not put them into practice is like a man who built a house on the ground without a foundation. The moment the torrent struck that house, it collapsed, and its destruction was complete." -Luke 6:46-49 (Matthew 7:24-27). We obey out of love, not obligation.

"As the Father has loved me, so have I loved you. Now remain in my love. If you keep my commands, you will remain in my love, just as I have kept my Father's commands and remain in his love. I have told you this so that my joy may be in you and that your joy may be complete." -John 15:9-11. "Lord, the God of Israel, there is no God like you in Heaven or on earth- you who keep your covenant of love with your servants who continue wholeheartedly in your way." -2 Chronicles 6:14. No one has ever obeyed God wholeheartedly and regretted it.

"Everyone who sins breaks the law; in fact, sin is lawlessness. But you know that he appeared so that he might take away our sins. And in Him is no sin. No one who lives in Him keeps on sinning. No one who continues to sin has either seen Him or known Him. Dear children, do not let anyone lead you astray. The one who does what is right is righteous, just as he is righteous. The one who does what is sinful is of the devil, because the devil has been sinning from the beginning. The reason the Son of God appeared was to destroy the devil's work. No one who is born of God will continue to sin, because God's seed remains in them; they cannot go on sinning, because they have been born of God. This is how we know who the children of God are and who the children of the devil are: Anyone who does not do what is right is not God's child, nor is anyone who does not love their brother and sister." -1 John 3:4-10.

Jesus came to defeat Satan and his schemes. "We know that we have come to know Him if we keep his commands. Whoever says, "I know Him," but does not do what He commands is a liar, and the truth is not in that person. But if anyone obeys his word, love for God is truly made complete in them. This is how we know we are in Him: Whoever claims to live in Him must live as Jesus did." -1 John 2:3-6.

There is a distinct difference in a believer who desires to keep the commands of God and love others. We will not be perfect, but I believe you will notice a difference. Someone with Jesus in their life may fall into sin but will not run toward the sin. When a believer sins, they confess their sin to God, get back up and want to make it right. Someone who does not believe will not have this desire.

"To the pure, all things are pure, but to those who are corrupted and do not believe, nothing is pure. In fact, both their minds and consciences are corrupted. They claim to know God, but by their actions they deny Him. They are detestable, disobedient, and unfit for doing anything good." -Titus 1:15-16.

Our minds are so powerful, more than we realize.

"For it is not those who hear the law who are righteous in God's sight, but it is those who obey the law who will be declared righteous." -Romans 2:13. Jesus is who makes us righteous. We can desire to hear and learn the law but when we have Him, we desire to not just hear but to obey.

"Whoever has my commands and keeps them is the one who loves me. The one who loves me will be loved by my Father, and I too will love them and show myself to them." -John 14:21 (1 John 5:3).

"Jesus replied, "Anyone who loves me will obey my teaching. My Father will love them, and we will come to them and make our home with them. Anyone who does not love me will not obey my teaching. These words you hear are not my own; they belong to the Father who sent me." -John 14:23-24.

When we love Jesus, we accept and follow His teaching. The proof of our love is not that we work to obtain the proof, but the proof comes flowing out of us and our love for Him. "Know therefore that the Lord your God is God; he is the faithful God, keeping his covenant of love to a thousand generations of those who love Him and keep his commandments." -Deuteronomy 7:9. When you follow the Lord, He is faithful.

Sin is not freedom, it is destruction. "Evildoers are snared by their own sin, but the righteous shout for joy and are glad." -Proverbs 29:6. "The wicked draw the sword and bend the bow to bring down the poor and needy, to slay those whose ways are upright. But their swords will pierce their own hearts, and their bows will be broken." -Psalm 37:14-15. Powerful. The sin we commit that we think is going to prosper us, benefit us, satisfy us, or flat out looks fun at the time will literally pierce our very life if we are not careful.

"Whoever is pregnant with evil conceives troubles and gives birth to disillusionment. Whoever digs a hole and scoops it out falls into the pit they have made. The trouble they cause recoils on their own heads. I will give thanks to the Lord because of his righteousness; I will sing the praises of the name of the Lord Most High." -Psalm 7:14-17.

Conflict & Forgiveness

"I can do all things through Christ who strengthens me." Philippians 4:13

I can *forgive* through Christ who strengthens me.

"Get rid of all bitterness, rage and anger, brawling, and slander, along with every form of malice. Be kind and compassionate to one another, forgiving each other, just as in Christ God forgave you." -Ephesians 4:31-32 (1 Peter 3:8, Zechariah 7:8-9 and Colossians 3:13). Forgiveness is a choice. Easier said than done, but what makes it a little easier is thinking of the wrong we have done, that God has chosen to forgive. We are guilty, but because of grace, we are clean. The least we can do is do the same for others. Forgiveness sets you free of bitterness. We can forgive because we are forgiven and know what it feels like. What helps me to be more patient with others is remembering who the enemy is and remembering I do not deserve forgiveness myself. The enemy is Satan, not each other. God loves you, but we need to remember He loves the person who hurt you. Jesus gets upset when others hurt us, except He reminds us that we too, have hurt others in the same way. Therefore, He had to die. He wanted justice to be served for all our sins, while bringing us together in unity. Once you realize how much tolerance God has for you, your tolerance will begin to grow for others.

"Rend your heart and not your garments. Return to the Lord your God, for he is gracious and compassionate, slow to anger and abounding in love, and he relents from sending calamity." -Joel 2:13 (Psalm 103:8, Psalm 86:15 and Psalm

145:9). Many people fear going to God or returning to Him, thinking that He may be angry. God desires your heart and is slow to anger, seeing you as His child, not wanting to send punishment if you return to Him. God will not turn his face from us if we return to Him. (See 2 Chronicles 30:9).

God has compassion on everything He has made. If we seek Him, He will always turn His face toward us. He wants your heart, nothing more or less. Saul was delivered into David's hands, but David refused to kill him because he belonged to God. (See 1 Samuel 24:10). "When a man finds his enemy, does he let him get away unharmed? May the Lord reward you well for the way you treated me today. I know you will surely be king, and that the kingdom of Israel will be established in your hands." -1 Samuel 24:19-20. Saul was trying to kill David, and finally David had his chance for revenge. He relented, realizing Saul is God's. We too, need to realize God has created everyone, keeping us from the revenge we desire. Matthew 18:32-35 says, "Then the master called the servant in. 'You wicked servant, 'he said, 'I canceled all that debt of yours because you begged me to. Shouldn't you have had mercy on your fellow servant just as I had on you?' In anger his master handed him over to the jailers to be tortured, until he should pay back all he owed. This is how my heavenly Father will treat each of you unless you forgive your brother or sister from your heart."

 You may feel you have done no wrong and have never had bitterness against anyone, but according to this next verse you are only deceiving yourself. "For you know in your heart that many times you yourself have cursed others." -Ecclesiastes 7:22 (Ecclesiastes 10:20). We all have done wrong at some point. It is easy to fall into the trap of gossip, but be aware, Solomon warns us in Ecclesiastes that you never know who is listening when you gossip, and they will share what you say. Above all, "Do not seek revenge or bear a grudge against anyone among your people but love your neighbor as yourself. I am the Lord." -Leviticus 19:18 (Matthew 10:12, 3 and John 1:5). It's hard to get annoyed with others when you love them. It's super easy to get annoyed with people if there is no love. Even if someone treats you horribly, it helps me to remember they are an image bearer of our God, just as we are. We are not their judge; God is and when we gossip about others, we are putting ourselves above someone else.

There is no better feeling than being around someone who knows you messed up, who knows everything about you, yet forgives you unconditionally. Who are we supposed to mimic? Jesus. Who is full of grace more than anyone? Jesus! He cuts you slack all the time. It's time we start cutting others slack too. "May the Lord show mercy to the household of Onesiphorus, because he often refreshed me and was not ashamed of my chains. On the contrary, when he was in Rome, he searched hard for me until he found me." -2 Timothy 1:16-17.

One of the ultimate ways you can glorify God in any relationship is how you show grace. Grace is what draws people to the love of Christ. I once had someone tell me she wanted to know Jesus just by the way I released bitterness. Is it easy? No, and you cannot do it on your own. Only through God's power which He will give to you, because it is what He calls us to do. When I hold someone's wrong against them, it destroys me and makes me so bitter. When I forgive, it is so freeing.

"I will give you a new heart and put a new spirit in you; I will remove from you your heart of stone and give you a heart of flesh. And I will put my Spirit in you and move you to follow my decrees and be careful to keep my laws." -Ezekiel 36:26-27.

Only God can shatter our heart of stone and give us a heart of flesh toward others who have deeply hurt us.

"Then you will call, and the Lord will answer; you will cry for help, and he will say: Here am I. If you do away with the yoke of oppression, with the pointing finger and malicious talk, and if you spend yourselves on behalf of the hungry and satisfy the needs of the oppressed, then your light will rise in the darkness, and your night will become like the noonday." -Isaiah 58:9-10.

Accountability. No pointing fingers when you mess up. This is something we all need when we have conflict or confrontation with others. Most do not like conflict, but there is a way to handle it.

"When tempted, no one should say, "God is tempting me." For God cannot be tempted, by evil, nor does he tempt anyone; but each person is tempted when they are dragged away by their own evil desire and enticed." -James 1:13-14.

God always gives us a way out when we are tempted to act out in our anger. Others cannot make us sin aka, no one can "make you mad" (even though it seems like it!), and God cannot make us sin when in confrontation. Never say "you made me mad." You are giving them power they do not have over you. Only you can let yourself get angry.

"Therefore, each of you must put off falsehood and speak truthfully to your neighbor, for we are all members of one body. "In your anger do not sin": Do not let the sun go down while you are still angry, and do not give the devil a foothold." - Ephesians 4:25-27.

The good ole' saying "don't go to bed angry" is a verse in the Bible! You are giving Satan a foothold in your relationships if you go to bed angry. Many may think that by giving a situation time, it just goes away, when they are just harvesting and pushing down bitterness that will eventually come to the surface. I am not saying to react quickly instead of going to bed in your anger. Sometimes we do need time to cool down, but immediately pray and ask how God would want you to handle your anger in that moment and pray for how He would like you to feel toward that individual. It is not easy. I have been there and have made the wrong decisions, which is why I am telling you this so you can make the right ones and can go forward. I get particularly angry when people either slander Jesus, or in a heated sport game or match. I have gotten physically angry during sport games, particularly with basketball (if you know you know!) and have pushed girls back. Let me tell you, it only led to me getting a bloody lip and fouled out of the game.

Having patience when you are angry helps you to make the best decision. We all get angry, as it is a normal human emotion. Jesus was angry, but it is how we handle our anger with the fruit of the spirit, self- control.

"In the temple courts he found people selling cattle, sheep and doves, and others sitting at tables exchanging money. So, he made a whip out of cords, and drove all from the temple courts, both sheep and cattle; he scattered the coins of the money changers and overturned their tables. To those who sold doves he said, "Get these out of here! Stop turning my Father's house into a market!" His disciples remembered that it is written: "Zeal for your house will consume me." The

Jews then responded to him, "What sign can you show us to prove your authority to do all this?" Jesus answered them, "Destroy this temple, and I will raise it again in three days." They replied, "It has taken forty-six years to build this temple, and you are going to raise it in three days?" But the temple he had spoken of was his body. After he was raised from the dead, his disciples recalled what he had said. Then they believed the scripture and the words that Jesus had spoken. Now while he was in Jerusalem at the Passover Festival, many people saw the signs he was performing and believed in his name. But Jesus would not entrust himself to them, for he knew all people. He did not need any testimony about mankind, for he knew what was in each person. (See John 2:14-25).

Jesus was rightfully angry. Naturally, Him being God, His anger is justified. Did Jesus ever sin? No. It shows feeling anger is not a sin; however, how we handle our anger can lead to sin.

When you are angry, pray. It will be the most challenging thing you do at first, but once it becomes a habit, you will learn self-control. Even if it is super short and under your breath. God will show you what to do! "Like a city whose walls are broken through is a person who lacks self-control." -Proverbs 25:28.

If you let your anger get the best of you, you are only hurting yourself. "Through patience a ruler can be persuaded, and a gentle tongue can break a bone." -Proverbs 25:15. Admit to the Lord you need self-control with your anger and watch Him work. God does not expect us to know what to do all the time or how to handle every confrontation, but He does expect you to ask Him.

"The quiet words of the wise are more to be heeded than the shouts of a ruler of fools." -Ecclesiastes 9:17. "Like a maniac shooting flaming arrows of death is one who deceives their neighbor and says, "I was only joking!" -Proverbs 26:18-19. Many will say a joke out of anger or being passive aggressive, but here God is saying this only brings hurt. "Fools give full vent to their rage, but the wise bring calm in the end." -Proverbs 29:11. "A hot-tempered person stirs up conflict, but one who is patient calms a quarrel." -Proverbs 15:18. Patience is the key to calming tension when it builds. "An angry person stirs up conflict, and a hot-tempered person commits many sins." -Proverbs 29:22. In natural human fashion, we tend to let our anger lead to sin unlike Jesus did. Therefore, God warns against harvesting and living in anger as a lifestyle as opposed to the natural human emotion we get. Also, when you are wrong, admit it, and be honest if you were only seeking after your own interest. You will feel rage, but do not give in to the impulses it brings. If you are patient, you can calm others during the anger.

"My dear brothers and sisters, take note of this: Everyone should be quick to listen, slow to speak and slow to become angry, because human anger does not produce the righteousness that God desires. Therefore, get rid of all moral filth and the evil that is so prevalent and humbly accept the word planted in you, which can save you. Do not merely listen to the word and be so deceived yourselves. Do what it says." -James 1:19-22.

When Jesus is angry, He is also God, meaning His ways are perfect. This can mean that when we are angry, if we are following Jesus, we may not produce the same justice with our anger as others. Instead, we are to be quick to listen, slow to speak, and slow to become angry. How can we control our anger? In graduate school for Occupational Therapy, I learned we have two parts of our brain responsible for our emotions, the amygdala and the limbic system. God created our brain and would not give us commands if they were out of our control. "But whoever looks intently into the perfect law that gives freedom and continues in it—not forgetting what they have heard but doing it—they will be blessed in what they do." -James 1:25.

"To answer before listening- that is folly and shame." -Proverbs 18:13. I especially find this difficult to keep quiet when I feel I am being blamed for something I did not do or feel the need to defend myself. What helps me to be quick to listen and slow to anger is remembering Jesus was crucified for a crime he never committed. Always listen first, and then respond. Also, it is about how you respond. "A gentle answer turns away wrath, but a harsh word stirs up anger." -Proverbs 15:1. Tone makes all the difference. Most of the time in a confrontation, it is not what you say, but how you say it. Say what you need to with truth and in a gentle tone. When we are upset, think how much angrier you get when others continue to shout at you. Now, think when someone responds with love and gentleness? Your walls come down!

I had a patient who would always come in so angry, and even though it was very tempting to talk back in the same tone to him, I would ask how he was feeling throughout the session in a cheerful voice. At the end of every session, he would apologize for being so angry, every single time. It calms people when they know you love and care for them. My mom works at the front desk of a clinic and once had a patient so angry about a bill he had received. Come to find out, it was someone she knew, and once he realized it was my mom, his entire demeanor changed. Relationship can change others' demeanor, and you can build relationship during confrontation with God's help.

Now you may be saying, "Lexi, you don't understand how bad this individual has hurt me." Remember, when you forgive you are not justifying the actions of your oppressor. You are simply making sure you do not become your own enemy, full of bitterness, and leaving the judgment in the hands of your Father, remembering you too deserve punishment and have sinned. Someone is also saying to God about you, "God, you do not understand how much this individual has hurt me." People need to be forgiven because of what Christ has done for every single one of us, not because our sin deserves it. This is called grace, which leads to love.

"Whoever is patient has great understanding, but one who is quick-tempered displays folly." -Proverbs 14:29. Patience develops wisdom. Wisdom leads to understanding. "The one who has knowledge uses words with restraint, and whoever has understanding is even-tempered." -Proverbs 17:27. Once you recognize your own shortcomings, it helps you stay even keel with others. When we are prideful and think we are better, we tend to look down and become more easily angered.

"Don't have anything to do with foolish and stupid arguments, because you know they produce quarrels. And the Lord's servant must not be quarrelsome but must be kind to everyone, able to teach, not resentful. Opponents must be gently instructed, in the hope that God will grant them repentance leading them to a knowledge of the truth, and that they will come to their senses and escape from the trap of the devil, who has taken them captive to do his will." -2 Timothy 2:23-26.

"An unfriendly person pursues selfish ends and against all sound judgment starts quarrels." -Proverbs 18:1. When we are friendly, you are in the pursuit of the best interest of others! The opposite of this is trying to start quarrels with others. Do not try to make conflict. Naturally it will happen and there is a way to handle it, but do not go searching for it. God tells us to be kind to everyone, even in conflict where it is necessary something is addressed. Being open to being taught and gently instructing you on how to handle conflict is key. We are to look at people who are fighting us on matters of faith as lost sheep, not the enemy. We are to help them, knowing the devil has tricked them, and we lead them to God's way.

I understand there are times when you may feel people are just flat out not healthy to be around. It is not from God when we isolate or cut anyone from our lives, because if that were the case, we should be cut out of His for all we have done.

"All this is from God who reconciled us to himself through Christ and gave us ministry of reconciliation: that God was reconciling the world to himself in Christ, not counting people's sins against them. And he has committed to us the message of reconciliation." -2 Corinthians 5:18-19.

However, I have come to find that reconciliation takes two. If the other party refuses to reconcile, do not continue in their quarrels, and instead pray for them. This is the best way to still love them from afar. Even if you have good intentions, it does not give you the authority to play God. I have learned this. I continued to long after people, desiring to be reconciled because I felt that is what Jesus wanted me to do, but they were not interested. This is where I need to give Him control. Maybe you've already been in multiple confrontations and now are wondering how to reconcile. I love and have used this nifty trick, "A gift given in secret soothes anger, and a bribe concealed in the cloak pacifies great wrath." -Proverbs 21:14.

The perfect example of how God calls us to treat our enemies, forgive them and how reconciliation should be handled from our end, is the story of Joseph. "Then Joseph said to his brothers, 'Come close to me.' When they had done so, he said, 'I am your brother, the one you sold into Egypt! And now, do not be distressed and do not be angry with yourselves for selling me here, because it was to save lives that God sent me ahead of you.'" -Genesis 45:4-5. I love how Joseph's first response when he sees his brothers is to tell them to not be angry with themselves, to save them of the guilt and shame I am sure they immediately felt. "So then, it was not you who sent me here, but God. He made me father to Pharaoh, lord of his entire household, and ruler of all Egypt." -Genesis 45:8. He recognized even though their intentions were evil, God had a master plan behind the chaos. Even though God did not cause the chaos, He foreknew everything his brothers were going to devise and was able to make Joseph ruler of all Egypt. How incredible! "Then he threw his arms around his brother Benjamin and wept, and Benjamin embraced him, weeping. And he kissed all his brothers and wept over them. Afterward his brothers talked with him." -Genesis 45:14-15. Then, Joseph gave them food and money. Joseph was thrown into a pit by his brothers who were jealous of him and tried to kill him. He was then sold in slavery to the Israelites by his brothers. In slavery, his master ranked him high in position, but his master's wife wanted to sleep with him. Joseph said no, but she lied and told her husband, Joseph's master, that Joseph tried to sleep with her! Joseph was then thrown into prison, where he helped prisoners, and God blessed him. He was forgotten until, finally, Pharaoh had a dream only Joseph could interpret. Joseph was then made ruler of all Egypt.

How would you respond to your family in need who literally tried to kill you and sold you into slavery? If you were then granted the highest power in all of Egypt, would you say justice is needed and your brothers should be killed? Joseph not only forgave his brothers, but he *reconciled* with them. Embraced them, fed them, provided financially for them, wept over them and kissed them! This can *only* be done through God. Joseph could love and fulfill Christ's ministry of reconciliation because He saw God at work in every aspect of his life. Though his brothers meant it for evil, God used it for good. Joseph was so confident in who he was, knew he also had faults and most importantly knew God could heal relationships that seemed impossible to be healed, let alone made new. When I was eight years old, I wrote about 9/11, and how we need to forgive those behind the tragedy who crashed planes into the Twin Towers. Only with God's power could an eight-year-old write that; it was not from me.

"Blessed are the merciful, for they will be shown mercy." -Matthew 5:7. How do you do it when someone has hurt you? I am not talking about little mess ups. I'm talking the deep, cut to the soul, hurt that tears you apart.

"Do not judge, or you too will be judged. For in the same way, you judge others, you will be judged, and with the measure you use, it will be measured to you. "Why do you look at the speck of sawdust in your brother's eye and pay no attention to the plank in your own eye? How can you say to your brother, 'Let me take the speck out of your eye,' when all the time there is a plank in your own eye? You hypocrite, first take the plank out of your own eye, and then you will see clearly to remove the speck from your brother's eye." -Matthew 7:1-5.

We are all hypocrites. Every sin you are mad at your brother for committing, you have committed. Behind every sin, you can find the pride that has caused issues in every relationship. We all want justice and grace for ourselves, but not to others. We like to think of our intentions and justify what we do, but we only see the actions of others and assume the worst, causing division. We all have pride. Most can admit they have other sin problems, but it is so hard to admit we have a pride problem. That is pride in and of itself!

Pride is at the core of why people will not admit and accept Christ as their Savior, because pride makes them believe they do not need a Savior in the first place. "because judgment without mercy will be shown to anyone who has not been merciful. Mercy triumphs over judgment." -James 2:13. The funny thing is, you cannot even pass judgment on those passing judgment. Read that again. Make sense? If you judge someone for passing judgment on you, you are doing the very thing you are upset with them for. Mind blown.

"You, therefore, have no excuse, you who pass judgment on someone else, for at whatever point you judge another, you are condemning yourself, because you who pass judgment do the same things. Now we know that God's judgment against those who do such things is based on truth. So, when you, a mere human being, pass judgment on them and yet do the same things, do you think you will escape God's judgment? Or do you show contempt for the riches of his kindness, forbearance, and patience, not realizing that God's kindness is intended to lead you to repentance?" -Romans 2:1-4.

Furthermore, "There is only one Lawgiver and Judge, the one who is able to save and destroy. But you—who are you to judge your neighbor?" -James 4:12.

Now let's define what it means to judge. It is to judge as if you are condemning an individual. God is the Highest Judge, and we are not to condemn others. However, we are called to "admonish" the sin of others in the sense of holding the accountable out of love. Also, God's Word says we are allowed to help our brother with their speck if we remove the plank in our own eye (See Matthew 7:4) Once you humble yourself to the point of realizing you have a "plank" in your own eye, the way you help your brother remove their speck will be done with such love and gentleness. You can disagree with someone and not judge them. Speak the truth to others, without condemnation. One of my favorite pastors Sid Like once said, "If someone is falling asleep at the steering wheel in your car would you "correct" them? Absolutely!" How seriously do you take sin and how much do you love the person driving?

"These are the things you are to do: Speak the truth to each other and render true and sound judgment in your courts; do not plot evil against each other, and do not love to swear falsely. I hate all this,' declares the Lord." -Zechariah 8:16-17.

As human beings, it is almost impossible for us to live our life without constant "judgments." We judge where we are on the road when we drive, we judge how close we are to the flame during a bonfire; do you see where I am going with this?

I remember when I was in school, everyone warned me about my teacher. I pre-judged, and she ended up being one of my favorite teachers of all time. You can miss out on some incredible relationships if you judge someone before you even know them! I cannot begin to tell you how upsetting it is once you get to know someone you pre-judged and end up loving them. You feel so guilty and wish you would have been able to be friends or closer with them sooner. This leads me to discuss envy. There have been times I was jealous with envy when my friends found other friends. The funny thing is, I can honestly tell you that every single time I grew to treasure the added relationships with the new friends brought into my life! My fears were always about losing my current friend, when God was just trying to add another beautiful relationship into my life.

"This, then, is how you ought to regard us: as servants of Christ and as those entrusted with the mysteries God has revealed. Now it is required that those who have been given a trust must prove faithful. I care very little if I am judged by you or by any human court; indeed, I do not even judge myself. My conscience is clear, but that does not make me innocent. It is the Lord who judges me. Therefore, judge nothing before the appointed time; wait until the Lord comes. He will bring to light what is hidden in darkness and will expose the motives of the heart. At that time each will receive their praise from God." -1 Corinthians 4:1-5.

We need to pray God creates in us a clean and pure heart (See Psalm 51:10). As far as "condemnation" with judging, Paul doesn't even condemn himself because he knows it would be taking God's authority away from Him which is wrong. Guilt will eat at us when we do wrong but take comfort in knowing God doesn't want us to condemn ourselves. Guilt is a "symptom" that there is something wrong in our lives we should remove, so it is good it is there initially. Once we ask God to remove what is causing the guilt, we do not need to live in it anymore.

Every person handles confrontation differently, and this is where we need to pray how to approach everyone. (See Titus 1:12-14), the Cretans had to be rebuked sharply, out of love because they were lying, evil, and lazy in order to restore them back to faith and away from myths. 1 Corinthians 5:9-13 talks about if we just chose to not associate with anyone who is immoral, greedy, idolaters, swindlers or the sexually immoral, we literally would have to leave the world, and we have all committed these sins as well. Instead, He tells us to warn our brothers and sisters in Christ to protect them and hold them accountable, where God will handle those in the world as we continue to reach out in love.

"If your brother or sister sins, go and point out their fault, just between the two of you. If they listen to you, you have won them over. But if they will not listen, take one or two others along, so that 'every matter may be established by the testimony of two or three witnesses.' If they still refuse to listen, tell it to the church; and if they refuse to listen even to the church, treat them as you would a pagan or a tax collector. 'Truly I tell you, whatever you bind on earth will be bound in Heaven, and whatever you loose on earth will be loosed in Heaven.'" -Matthew 18:15-18.

We receive exact instructions on how to handle conflict and confrontation. I love how the initial response is not to gossip about the individual to someone else, but instead to go directly to the source. Instead of gossiping to another, go directly to

God in prayer for them. Your heart will be softened and only He can do that when someone has truly hurt you. God will help you progress from there.

Now the question is, what do you do to the individual who hurt you if you cannot show revenge and are supposed to forgive? What does this look like? "You have heard that it was said, 'Eye for eye, and tooth for tooth.' But I tell you, do not resist an evil person. If anyone slaps you on the right cheek, turn to them the other cheek also. And if anyone wants to sue you and take your shirt, hand over your coat as well. If anyone forces you to go one mile, go with them two miles. Give to the one who asks you and do turn away from the one who wants to borrow from you. You have heard that it was said, 'Love your neighbor and hate your enemy.' But I tell you, love your enemies and pray for those who persecute you, that you may be children of your Father in Heaven. He causes the sun to rise on the evil and the good and sends rain on the righteous and the unrighteous." -Matthew 5:38-45.

When we love our enemies, we are doing the very essence of what God does to us. Before we became a friend of God, our sin made us an enemy to Him, yet He chose to pursue us to have a personal relationship with us, loving us anyways. God is love in very nature, and we show others who He is when we love them. "I will heal their waywardness and love them freely, for my anger has turned away from them." -Hosea 14:4.

"If you love those who love you, what credit is that to you? Even sinners love those who love them. And if you do good to those who are good to you, what credit is that to you? Even sinners do that. And if you lend to those from whom you expect repayment, what credit is that to you? Even sinners lend to sinners, expecting to be repaid in full. But love your enemies, do good to them, and lend to them without expecting to get anything back. Then your reward will be great, and you will be children of the Most High, because he is kind to the ungrateful and wicked. Be merciful, just as your Father is merciful." -Luke 6:32-36. We are supposed to reflect our Father who is merciful.

"If you love those who love you, what reward will you get? Are not even the tax collectors doing that? And if you greet only your own people, what are you doing more than others? Do not even pagans do that? Be perfect, therefore, as your Heavenly Father is perfect." -Matthew 5:46-48.

Is God asking us to be complete pushovers here? Absolutely not! Do you understand how powerful it is to love your enemies?! Do you understand the Cross was the most powerful act in history and from a worldly view it looked like Jesus was being a "pushover?" Yet, who conquered death three days later? God is just! Understand this. If you love your enemies so much that you take care of them when they persecute you, how much more is God going to bless you? "Do not repay evil with evil or insult with insult. On the contrary, repay evil with blessing, because to this you were called so that you may inherit a blessing." -1 Peter 3:9. Praying for your enemies is extremely difficult, but from personal experience it is freeing, leaving you with peace and bringing a love for them that cannot be explained. God changes your heart. God created this, and I believe for a purpose.

"And one of them struck the servant of the high priest, cutting off his right ear. But Jesus answered, 'No more of this!' And he touched the man's ear and healed him. Then Jesus said to the chief priests, the officers of the temple guard, and the elders, who had come for him, 'Am I leading a rebellion, that you have come with swords and clubs? Every day I was with you in the temple courts, and you did not lay a hand on me. But this is your hour—when darkness reigns.'" -Luke 22:50-53.

Jesus healed the very people trying to arrest Him. He is the perfect example of how we are to treat others, even our enemies. Jesus never hurt or attacked anyone, yet they were so offended and threatened by his righteousness and love, that they came at Him with weapons.

"The Lord will fight for you; you need only to be still." -Exodus 14:14. Did God have the Israelites kill the Egyptians? No. Did God take care of the Israelites when they chased them into the red sea? Absolutely.

"And he passed in front of Moses, proclaiming, 'The Lord, the Lord, the compassionate and gracious God, slow to anger, abounding in love and faithfulness, maintaining love to thousands, and forgiving wickedness, rebellion, and sin. Yet he does not leave the guilty unpunished; he punishes the children and their children for sin of the parents to be the third and fourth generation.'" -Exodus 34:6-7.

This verse reminds us that He does not leave the guilty unpunished. In order to humble ourselves, we need to remember that *every single one of us is guilty*. We get so excited to see justice served for others, but not ourselves. This is why we are to seek God's justice, realizing we deserve it too, and realizing His grace is more. What a hard balance, huh? Between justice and grace? If you struggle with this, my advice is to pray. Pray God shows you how to lovingly call others out in a way that is humble, realizing you deserve the same punishment.

"Lord our God, you answered them; you were to Israel a forgiving God, though you punished their misdeeds." -Psalm 99:8. "When the Lord heard them, he was furious; his fire broke out against Jacob, and his wrath rose against Israel, for they did not believe in God or trust in his deliverance. Yet he gave a command to the skies above and opened the doors of the Heavens; he rained down manna for the people to eat, he gave them the grain of Heaven. Human beings ate the bread of angels; he sent them all the food they could eat." -Psalm 78:21-25.

"'Therefore, wait for me,' declares the Lord, 'for the day I will stand up to testify. I have decided to assemble the nations, to gather the kingdoms and to our out my wrath on them – all my fierce anger. The whole world will be consumed by the fire of my jealous anger.'" -Zephaniah 3:8.

"You, Lord, showed favor to your land; you restored the fortunes of Jacob. You forgave the iniquity of your people and covered all their sins. You set aside all your wrath and turned from your fierce anger." -Psalm 85:1-3.

"You, Lord, are forgiving and good, abounding in love to all who call to you." -Psalm 86:5. Without Jesus, we are God's enemy and God's wrath remains on our *sin*. Remember, God created us and desires you.

God is a strong defense attorney. "You, Lord, took up my case; you redeemed my life. Lord, you have seen the wrong done to me. Uphold my cause!" -Lamentations 3:58-59. I trust him to fight my battles more than myself if I do what He says, and He will do it on his time. "You have wearied the Lord with your words. 'How have we wearied him?' you ask. By saying, 'All who do evil are good in the eyes of the Lord, and he is pleased with them' or 'Where is the God of justice?'" -Malachi 2:17. "'Shall I leave their innocent blood unavenged? No, I will not. The Lord dwells in

Zion!'" -Joel 3:21. In Psalm 5:14, God avenges the blood of his servants. He is justified when He judges, "Say among the nations, 'The Lord reigns.' The world is firmly established, it cannot be moved; he will judge the peoples with equity." -Psalm 96:10. God detests letting the guilty go unpunished and condemning the innocent. (See Proverbs 17:15). "Do not show partiality in judging; hear both small and great alike. Do not be afraid of anyone, for judgment belongs to God. Bring me any case too hard for you, and I will hear it." -Deuteronomy 1:17.

"These also are sayings of the wise: To show partiality in judging is not good: Whoever says to the guilty, 'You are innocent,' will be cursed by peoples and denounced by nations. But it will go well with those who convict the guilty, and rich blessings will come on them." -Proverbs 24:23-25. "When the sentence for a crime is not quickly carried out, people's hearts are filled with schemes to do wrong." -Ecclesiastes 8:11. Showing grace does not mean pretending the other party who may have sinned against you did nothing wrong. That will only hurt them as well, since sin destroys us from its consequences spiritually as much as it does physically when played out in our lives and relationships. It is ok to *lovingly* point out why you are hurt and why you feel you were wronged to make the other aware. This is a skill that takes a lot of prayer in which how to approach others and the timing of how to do it.

"The Lord is a jealous and avenging God; the Lord take vengeance and is filled with wrath. The Lord takes vengeance on his foes and vents his wrath against his enemies. The Lord is slow to anger but great in power; the Lord will not leave the guilty unpunished. His way is in the whirlwind and the storm, and clouds are the dust of his feet." -Nahum 1:2-3. "For he guards the course of the just and protects the way of his faithful ones. Then you will understand what is right and just and fair—every good path. For wisdom will enter your heart, and knowledge will be pleasant to your soul." -Proverbs 2:8-10.

"You exalted me above my foes; from a violent man you rescued me. Therefore, I will praise you, Lord, among the nations; I will sing the praises of your name. He gives his king great victories; he shows unfailing kindness to his anointed, to David and his descendants forever." -2 Samuel 22:49-51. God's justice should lead us to praise, and His grace should lead us to never stop!

Can you imagine being whipped, beaten, spit at, abandoned, and mocked when you are the Creator, God of the universe, and still have the heart to say, "Forgive them Father." This is our example. This is our God. This is *not* weakness, but the definition of strength covered in the absolute, unconditional, selfless love that God calls us to have for others. "I offered my back to those who beat me, my cheeks to those who pulled out my beard; I did not hide my face from mocking and spitting. Because the Sovereign Lord helps me, I will not be disgraced. Therefore, have I set my face like flint, and I know I will not be put to shame." -Isaiah 50:6-7. Think about Jesus himself. No one was less deserving of a death sentence. The perfect lamb who had done no wrong was crucified for what we have done wrong. What leaves me even more in awe is how He responded to those crucifying Him. "Jesus said, 'Father forgive them, for they do not know what they are doing.' And they divided up his clothes by casting lots." -Luke 23:34. Um, excuse me?! What?! These were your words while you were being whipped, beaten, and starved, with a crown of thorns on your head, right before You were nailed to a cross to die? "Forgive them." This is our Savior and example. He knows forgiveness will free us, regardless of how we feel.

"Do not repay anyone evil for evil. Be careful to do what is right in the eyes of everyone. If it is possible, as far as it depends on you, live at peace with everyone. Do not take revenge, my dear friends, but leave room for God's wrath, for it is written: "It is mine to avenge; I will repay," says the Lord. On the contrary: "If your enemy is hungry, feed him; if he is thirsty, give him something to drink. In doing this, you will heap burning coals on his head." Do not be overcome by evil but overcome evil with good." -Romans 12:17-21.

"How good and pleasant it is when God's people live together in unity!" -Psalm 133:1. "Blessed are the peacemakers, for they will be called children of God." -Matthew 5:9. "Now we ask you, brothers and sisters, to acknowledge those who work hard among you, who care for you in the Lord and who admonish you. Hold them in the highest regard in love because of their work. Live in peace with each other." -1 Thessalonians 5:12-13.

But Lexi, how many times should I forgive someone?!

"Then Peter came to Jesus and asked, 'Lord, how many times shall I forgive my brother or sister who sins against me? Up to seven times?' Jesus answered, 'I tell you, not seven times, but seventy-seven times.'" -Matthew 18:21-2.

So, I know what you are thinking. If someone wrongs me 77 times, I should forgive them? The answer is...yes. And get ready for it. Not only should you forgive your prosecutor, but you should also pray for them. Pray for them and pray God blesses them! God is not justifying their actions. His point is you are not the judge; He is. Our view of what is "just" is so skewed, and His view is perfect. Let me put it this way: if I was allowed to be the judge, I probably wouldn't be here today, because someone I hurt might say they wish wrath on me......see where I am going with this?

Luke 7:37-39 says a sinful woman wept at Jesus' feet wiping them with her hair, kissing them and pouring perfume on them.

"When the Pharisee who had invited him saw this, he said to himself, 'If this man were a prophet, he would know who is touching him and what kind of woman she is—that she is a sinner.' Jesus answered him, 'Simon, I have something to tell you.' 'Tell me, teacher,' he said. 'Two people owed money to a certain moneylender. One owed him five hundred denarii, and the other fifty. Neither of them had the money to pay him back, so he forgave the debts of both. Now which of them will love him more' Simon replied, 'I suppose the one who had the bigger debt forgiven.' 'You have judged correctly,' Jesus said." -Luke 7:39-43.

"Therefore, I tell you, her many sins have been forgiven—as her great love has shown. But whoever has been forgiven little loves little." -Luke 7:47. We can forgive much because we are forgiven much! We can love others unconditionally, even when they wrong us because we know how much we are forgiven. Then our love naturally pours out from us. It can be exhausting to be like the Pharisees, believing you need to be "good enough" to get to God. You may be thinking that this woman had more sins than you can imagine. The catch is, we are just as sinful. We tend to forget or justify our own sins, but always remember the sins of others. It doesn't have to be this way. We can rejoice like the sinful woman, knowing the many, *many* sins we committed since we were little are *all* wiped clean.

I am not saying you should take all criticism to heart or accept it as truth by any means. When I am criticized, I try to pray and ask God if the criticism is true and should I take it into consideration, or is the individual purposely trying to put me down because of their insecurities? Thank the individual for helping you be better. Pray for discernment, as well as for the heart of the individual who has criticized you. God can use others criticism to make you more like Jesus. When you respond to others, it should be in a way that glorifies God. "Then I can answer anyone who taunts me, for I trust in your word." -Psalm 119:42. When you pray for others, God changes your heart toward them. Pray and ask God if what someone says has truth, or if it is only meant to hurt you.

Usually when we have conflict with someone or we are angry with them, it leads us to want to gossip. I can tell you from personal experience, when I gossip, I only become angrier with the person and am filled with more bitterness. When I pray for the person instead and consult others not to gossip but to genuinely seek guidance, it has a much better outcome. You know you are asking advice from the right people when instead of gossiping with you, they want you to pray for the individual and truly help you see your own flaws in the matter.

"A gossip betrays a confidence, but a trustworthy person keeps a secret." -Proverbs 11:13. "The Lord detests lying lips, but he delights in people who are trustworthy." -Proverbs 12:22. I wish this would have been plastered on my mirror in middle school, high school, college and now! Gossip is a sin that seems to "innocently" creep into our lives, but it is so destructive. We each know this because we have all been hurt by gossip before. "Those who guard their lips preserve their lives, but those who speak rashly will come to ruin." -Proverbs 13:3. I try to picture it as if my family member, friend, co-worker or teammate was standing right next to me. Is what I am saying trying to benefit them, or would they be hurt? "Whoever would foster love covers over an offense, but whoever repeats the matter separates close friends." -Proverbs 17:9. "Whoever loves life and desires to see many good days, keep your tongue from evil and your lips from telling lies. Turn from evil and do good; seek peace and pursue it." -Psalm 34:12-14 (1 Peter 3:11 and 1 Thessalonians 4:10-12).

"Keep your mouth free of perversity; keep corrupt talk far from your lips. Let your eyes look straight ahead; fix your gaze directly before you. Give careful thought to the paths for your feet and be steadfast in all your ways. Do not turn to the right or the left; keep your foot from evil." -Proverbs 4:24-27.

If you say everything that's on your mind knowing it will be hurtful, that is not truthful, but cold. Alternatively, being dishonest or shallow by not meaning what you say is not love either. The best approach is to speak the truth in love.

"Fools show their annoyance at once, but the prudent overlook an insult." - Proverbs 12:16. Once, after my college volleyball season was over, I went to a Zumba class. A year later, I went to the same place at the same time, but everyone was wearing jeans and backwards hats with the same Jason Derulo song playing over and over. I went with it, and at the end, the instructor told me I made the team. I was so embarrassed, thinking "What team, I'm in Zumba?!" Turns out, I was at hip hop dance try outs. I could have let the embarrassment get to me, but I was able to get a laugh out of it instead.

"A person's wisdom yields patience; it is to one's glory to overlook an offense." -Proverbs 19:11. When we try to look past the insult's others give us and think of their purpose, insecurity or hurt as the reason they are saying it, it changes our perspective and consequently how we react. It helps us to be empathetic when it doesn't seem we should be. I have even had situations where people have simply tried to give me constructive criticism that may have seemed like an insult at the time.

"Listen to advice and accept discipline, and at the end you will be counted among the wise. Many are the plans in a person's heart, but it is the LORD's purpose that prevails." -Proverbs 19:20-21.

You also never know who is watching. I received an artifact in graduate school for accepting criticism and using the discipline given to me by my professors to help me become a better therapist. I was shocked and did not even realize anyone was paying attention. Continue to pray God uses others' insults and discipline to help you grow, and if they are simply saying something untrue to hurt you, pray for the discernment that you do not take it as truth, but instead that God helps to soften that person's heart. As an athlete, I would take insults and use it as motivational fire to work harder to glorify God. He can use it for good for you and that individual, if you let Him.

Many times, when we commit a sin, sincerely repent, we are confused as to why the consequences of our sin are still happening to us. A specific situation comes up in my life when I was in 8th grade. I was in a relationship, and another boy in my class began emailing me inappropriate messages even though I was in a relationship. Even though I did not have feelings for this individual, I emailed him back to "fit in" and I did not even understand the content of the messages. I was fully aware what I was doing was wrong, however. Once the boy I was in a relationship with and my friends found out, they cut me out of their lives, as well as the rest of my grade. They could not believe "Lexi" could ever do such a thing. I felt horrible and guilt flooded my life. "Because of your wrath there is no health in my body; there is no soundness in my bones because of my sin. My guilt has overwhelmed me like a burden too heavy to bear." -Psalm 38:3-4. I prayed for God to forgive me, the boy I was in the relationship with to forgive me, my friends to forgive me and ultimately my grade to forgive me. Even though I know God had forgiven me, it did not stop the aftermath of all the hurt and wounded relationships. This may sound like an innocent story of a girl in grade school making a small mistake but looking back it was one of the most depressing periods of my life. However, if God had given less severe consequences to that 14-year-old girl, I would not be as terrified as I am today of being unfaithful in my marriage. If Satan tries to put the idea of flirting or thinking about other guys in my mind, I instantly turn my thoughts away and feel the hurt again. "Now instead, you ought to forgive and comfort him, so that he will not be overwhelmed by excessive sorrow." -2 Corinthians 2:7. I have asked others for forgiveness only to be told they do not accept it. It is the most sorrowful feeling and makes you feel worthless; however, it does not define you. God says you are forgiven, and even though it is never easy when someone denies you their forgiveness, you have the freedom to move forward knowing the Almighty says otherwise.

This brings up the saying, once a cheater always a cheater. This is not fact or biblical. You are reading someone who was once a cheater, and claiming this common saying is true would ultimately dismiss the truth that Jesus changes hearts. "Because of the Lord's great love, we are not consumed, for his compassion never fails. They are new every morning; great is your faithfulness." -Lamentations 3:22-23.

"The teachers of the law and the Pharisees brought in a woman caught in adultery. They made her stand before the group and said to Jesus, 'Teacher, this woman was caught in the act of adultery. In the Law Moses commanded us to stone such women. Now what do you say?' They were using this question as a trap, in order to have a basis for accusing him. But Jesus bent down and started to write on the ground with his finger. When they kept on questioning him, he straightened up and said to them, 'Let any one of you who is without sin be the first to throw a stone at her.' Again, he stooped down and wrote on the ground. At this, those who heard began to go away one at a time, the older ones first, until only Jesus was left, with the woman still standing there. Jesus straightened up and asked her, 'Woman, where are they? Has no one condemned you?' 'No one, sir,' she said. 'Then neither do I condemn you,' Jesus declared. 'Go now and leave your life of sin.' -John 8:3-11.

Jesus welcomes you with open arms as you are, but He loves you too much to leave you there. He embraces you with your brokenness, but from that moment on begins to clean it. It's not about perfection, but it's about increasing your consistency. Instead of fixing your mind and eyes on the sin, fix them on Christ and loving Him. It naturally makes you want to move from sin, instead of when we just focus on "not sinning," When you first play a sport, you may find it tiring and very confusing. However, the more you play, get to know your teammates, and get in shape, the game becomes fun, and you can compete!

"But the wisdom that comes from Heaven is first of all pure; then peace-loving, considerate, submissive, full of mercy and good fruit, impartial and sincere. Peacemakers who sow in peace reap a harvest of righteousness." -James 3:17-18.

If you're full of God's peace, it is hard for things to tick you off. Oh, it still happens, but not as often and not with the same intensity producing lack of control. One time we were about to pull into a parking space, and someone cut us off. My mom goes, "That's ok, God wanted them to have that spot." Excuse me, what? How could you be at peace about that?! However, her response showed me it is possible for me, and you! Peace isn't pretending like everything is ok and the world is great. We have peace because we rest in God's righteousness knowing justice will ultimately prevail, but His grace still triumphs over all!

Anxiety & Addiction

"I can do all things through Christ who strengthens me." -Philippians 4:13.

I can overcome *anxiety, depression, loneliness and addictions* through Christ who strengthens me.

"'For I know the plans I have for you,' declares the Lord, 'plans to prosper you and not to harm you, plans to give you hope and a future. Then you will call on me and come and pray to me, and I will listen to you.'" -Jeremiah 29:11-12.

God cares more about your life than you do. What if I told you His will for your life not only includes the big events, but He also cares about every detail such as your grocery shopping, cleaning, etc. Many like to quote this verse, but have you read the second part? He says to complete this promise, you must call on Him in prayer. Call on Him and pray. He will listen.

"Can you fathom the mysteries of God? Can you probe the limits of the Almighty? They are higher than the Heavens above- what can you do? They are deeper than the depths below- what can you know? Their measure is longer than the earth and wider than the sea." -Job 11:7-9. "Do you send the lightning bolts on their way? Do they report to you, 'Here we are'?" -Job 38:35. This scripture humbles us and gives us peace.

"Who has gone up to Heaven and come down? Whose hands have gathered up the wind? Who has wrapped up the waters in a cloak? Who has established all the ends of the earth? What is his name, and what is the name of his son? Surely you know!" -Proverbs 30:4.

When you feel anxious, remember how in control God is.

"The Mighty One, God, the Lord, speaks and summons the earth from the rising of the sun to where it sets." -Psalm 50:1. We will never understand what He is doing, but our peace in the mist of anxiety and depression does not come from understanding, but trusting in the One who created us, loves us, and is in complete control of our lives.

"Cast all your anxiety on Him, because he cares for you." -1 Peter 5:7. How do you cast your anxiety on Him? Through prayer. "Cast your cares on the Lord and he will sustain you; he will never let the righteous be shaken." -Psalm 55:22. God would not command us to do this if it were not possible with His help. I have learned to train myself over the years, but I still catch myself getting caught up in the "what ifs." It is so easy to create an entire situation, an entire life inside your head incorporating all your fears, jealousies, and anxieties. When I notice my mind wandering, and Satan seems to be in control, I stop and tell God exactly what I am feeling and why. I then continue to ask Him to take away and calm my fear, anxieties, and jealousies.

"For seven days they celebrated with joy the Festival of Unleavened Bread, because the Lord had filled them with joy by changing the attitude of the king of Assyria so that he assisted them in the work on the house of God, the God of Israel." -Ezra 6:22. God has the power to change attitudes, including ours when we think there is no hope! "Lord my God, I called to you for help, and you healed me." -Psalm 30:2. We can also underestimate how powerful showing someone else joy can change their attitude or give them joy. I would always wave at people who I walked by in high school. One guy, years later, said it made him feel like he was noticed and had a purpose.

Depression is very complex and can have multiple causes. One cause can be trauma, even if we are unaware of the trauma through suppression or regression of our own anger, or if the trauma in our life was not mourned or dealt with in a healthy manner. Depression can be caused because sin looks good at first, but we are always disappointed because it does not bring us fulfillment. When we are in a dark place, it is a sign we could be in a situation or somewhere God does not intend us to be.

"I cannot carry all these people by myself; the burden is too heavy for me. If this is how you are going to treat me, please go ahead and kill me- if I have found favor in your eyes-and do not let me face my own ruin." -Numbers 11:14-15.

Moses was exhausted from caring for the rebellious Israelites. Guess who else feels exhausted during the week? All of us. It's crazy how stimulated we are all the time. We must constantly respond: Facebook, Twitter, Instagram, TikTok, texts, emails, calls, Snapchat, our job, family, friends, and all the people we interact with day to day. Everything demands our attention. I truly do not think we were designed to be stimulated every second of every day. You need rest, and you need to give God control of your schedule to aide in the prevention of anxiety and depression. Even God, the One who created you, rested!

"By the seventh day God had finished the work he had been doing; so on the seventh day he rested from all his work. Then God blessed the seventh day and made it holy, because on it he rested from all the work of creating that he had done." -Genesis 2:2-3.

Moses was able to use Joshua in order to relieve some of his responsibility which helped to cure his depression.

Job was another. Job said "Oh, that I might have my request, that God would grant what I hope for, that God would be willing to crush me, to let loose his hand and cut off my life!" -Job 6:8-9. He was experiencing every pain and grief in life you could imagine, and none was His fault. It was when he stopped seeing a purpose and questioning God's character and goodness that he wanted his life cut off. Elijah was another. "Elijah was afraid and ran for his life. When he came to Beersheba in Judah, he left his servant there." -1 Kings 19:3.

"...prayed that he might die. "I have had enough Lord," he said.

'Take my life; I am no better than my ancestors.' Then he lay down under the bush and fell asleep. All at once an angel touched him and said, 'Get up and eat.' He looked around, and there by his head was some bread baked over hot coals, and a jar of water. He ate and drank and then lay down again. Strengthened by that food, he traveled forty days and forty nights until he reached Horeb, the mountain of God". Elijah was anxious and fearful. "And the word of the Lord came to him: 'What are you doing here, Elijah?'" -1 Kings 19:4-9.

God did not need Elijah to tell him what was happening as He knows all. Instead, He asked Elijah to return to civilization to provide comfort. We should also do that with others who are depressed. Being there for someone is more important than words. Take it from someone who has experienced; I've worked with patients who suffered from depression and anxiety and had loved ones who were clinically depressed or anxious. Most of the time, your presence is needed more than your words.

Jonah 1:1-4 says the Lord told Jonah to go to the great city of Nineveh and preach against its wickedness. Jonah ran away from the Lord and headed for Tarshish on a ship when a violent storm arose threatening to destroy the ship. Jonah 1:15-17 says they threw Jonah overboard and the storm grew calm and then the men on the ship feared the Lord. A huge fish swallowed Jonah and he was in the belly for three days and nights.

"From inside the fish Jonah prayed to the Lord his God. He said: "In my distress I called to the Lord, and he answered me. From deep in the realm of the dead I called for help, and you listened to my cry. You hurled me into the depths, into the very heart of the seas, and the currents swirled about me; all your waves and breakers swept over me. I said, 'I have been banished from your sight; yet I will look again toward your holy temple.' The engulfing waters threatened me, the deep surrounded me; seaweed was wrapped around my head. To the roots of the mountains, I sank down; the earth beneath barred me in forever. But you, Lord my God, brought my life up from the pit. "When my life was ebbing away, I remembered you, Lord, and my prayer rose to you, to your holy temple. "Those who cling to worthless idols turn away from God's love for them. But I, with shouts of grateful praise, will sacrifice to you. What I have vowed I will make good. I will say, 'Salvation comes from the Lord.'" And the Lord commanded the fish, and it vomited Jonah onto dry land." -Jonah 2:1-10 (Joshua 24:14).

"Then the word of the Lord came to Jonah a second time: 'Go to the great city of Ninevah and proclaim to it the message I give you.' Jonah obeyed the word of the Lord and went to Nineveh." -Jonah 3:1-3. "The Ninevites believed God." - Jonah 3:5. "When God saw what they did and how they turned from their evil ways, he relented and did not bring on them the destruction he had threatened." -Jonah 3:10 (Matthew 12:41). "But to Jonah this seemed very wrong, and he became angry. He prayed to the Lord, 'Isn't this what I said, Lord, when I was still at home? That is what I tried to forestall by fleeing to Tarshish. I knew that you are a gracious and compassionate God, slow to anger and abounding in love, a God who relents from sending calamity. Now Lord, take away my life, for it is better for me to die than to live.' But the Lord replied, 'Is it right for you to be angry?'" -Jonah 4:2-4 (Jonah 4:5-9). "But the Lord said, 'You have been concerned about this plant, though you did not tend it or make it grow. It sprang up overnight and died overnight.'" -Jonah 4:10.

Jonah was literally running from God's plan for him to preach to Nineveh out of stubbornness and anger. Jonah was upset God was so gracious to Nineveh when he felt they deserved condemnation. Sometimes depression can come from suppressed anger that is not dealt with appropriately, stemming from his lack of grace. He also knew how wicked the city was and did not want to go even though

God would take care of Him. The cause of His depression was intentionally running from God's will for His life. The beauty of this story is even though Jonah was rebellious to God's plan, God would not let him get away that easy. Jonah was swallowed by a large fish until Jonah prayed, turning from his ways and praising God. Once Jonah saw the purpose God had for where he was sending him, he complied and was no longer depressed (even though he was still unhappy with God's grace).

"Early in the morning, all the chief priests and the elders of the people made their plans how to have Jesus executed. So, they bound him, led him away and handed him over to Pilate the governor. When Judas, who had betrayed him, saw that Jesus was condemned, he was seized with remorse and returned the thirty pieces of silver to the chief priests and the elders. 'I have sinned,' he said, 'for I have betrayed innocent blood.' 'What is that to us?' they replied. 'That's your responsibility.' So, Judas threw the money into the temple and left. Then he went away and hanged himself." -Matthew 27:1-5.

"Then what was spoken by Jeremiah the prophet was fulfilled: They took the thirty pieces of silver, the price set on him by the people of Israel, and they used them to buy the potter's field, as the Lord commanded me." -Matthew 27:9-10.

Judas was repenting to men and not Christ, causing his depression out of guilt and lack of forgiveness from these men. Guilt can eat us alive if we do not give it to God and live in his free grace and forgiveness. "When Ahithophel saw that his advice had not been followed, he saddled his donkey and set out for his house in his hometown. He put his house in order and then hanged himself. So, he died and was buried in his father's tomb." -2 Samuel 17:23. Ahithophel was relying on approval of others to fulfill him instead of God. If we rely on men for our forgiveness, we may never get it leading us into depression. When we rely on Christ for our forgiveness, His blood washes us every time.

"I took you from the ends of the earth, from its farthest corners I called you. I said, 'You are my servant'; I have chosen you and have not rejected you." -Isaiah 41:9. If you ever think for a second God does not see you or will not use you, he sees from the farthest corners of the earth.

"You have searched me, Lord, and you know me. You know when I sit and when I rise; you perceive my thoughts from afar. You discern my going out and my lying down; you are familiar with all my ways. Before a word is on my tongue you, Lord, know it completely. You hem me in behind and before, and you lay your hand upon me. Such knowledge is too wonderful for me, too lofty for me to attain. Where can I go from your Spirit? Where can I flee from your presence? If I go up to the Heavens, you are there; if I make my bed in the depths, you are there. If I rise on the wings of the dawn, if I settle on the far side of the sea, even there your hand will guide me, your right hand will hold me fast. If I say, 'Surely the darkness will hide me and the light become night around me,' even the darkness will not be dark to you; the night will shine like the day, for darkness is as light to you. For you created my inmost being you knit me together in my mother's womb. I praise you because I am fearfully and wonderfully made; your works are wonderful; I know that full well. My frame was not hidden from you when I was made in the secret place, when I was woven together in the depths of the earth. Your eyes saw my unformed body; all the days ordained for me were written in your book before one of them came to be." -Psalm 139:1-16.

"But will God really dwell on earth with humans? The heavens, even the highest heavens, cannot contain you. How much less this temple I have built!" -2 Chronicles 6:18. God knew every single detail about you before you were born, before the beginning of time and before we even understood what time is. Everything from how you look, your personality and when in time you were to be placed, who you are to meet, who your parents are, who is to be in your life, all of it because He loves you. Ask anyone who has had a miscarriage, life is a true miracle, and this is not a cliché. The fact that you were a successful birth should be enough proof God hand-picked you to be in this world in his perfect timing.

"Consider it pure joy, my brothers and sisters, whenever you face trials of many kinds, because you know that the testing of your faith produces perseverance. Let perseverance finish its work so that you may be mature and complete, not lacking anything." -James 1:2-4.

"In all this you greatly rejoice, though now for a little while you may have had to suffer grief in all kinds of trials. These have come so that the proven genuineness of your faith – of greater worth than gold, which perishes even though refined by fire- may result in praise, glory and honor when Jesus Christ is revealed. Though you have not seen him, you love him; and even though you do not see him now, you believe in him and are filled with an inexpressible and glorious joy, for you are receiving the end result of your faith, the salvation of your souls." -1 Peter 1:6-9.

"Now faith is confidence in what we hope for and assurance about what we do not see." -Hebrews 11:1. Your faith means more to God than gold. Your faith is the purpose of your life. For so long I have held so tightly to thinking, "as long as I have faith, my struggles and troubles will be minimal." I have been so angry at the pain of the trials, at some points refusing to mature in my faith and not wanting the refining. I have learned I can truly rejoice in my struggle through life until I get to Heaven, knowing that God has a purpose for everything we face. Even though I cannot see Him or how He is working, I am genuinely filled with the inexpressible joy of truth through my love for Him, which cannot change no matter what happens in this life.

"Not only so, but we also glory in our sufferings, because we know that suffering produces perseverance; perseverance, character; and character, hope. And hope does not put us to shame, because God's love has been poured out into our hearts through the Holy Spirit, who has been given to us. You see, at just the right time, when we were still powerless, Christ died for the ungodly." -Romans 5:3-6.

You may have a diagnosis of depression or anxiety that you cannot shake. If you have a personal relationship with Christ, you are just as incredible of a Jesus follower as someone who does not have these diagnoses. Instead of being glorified without suffering, Jesus says we are to be glorified *in* our sufferings, and many of us know the suffering that can come from being diagnosed with anxiety and depression. We live in a broken, tough world and unfortunately, just like experiencing diabetes, cancer, or a fracture as a believer, having Christ also does not make us immune to psychological diagnoses. However, He is right there next to us as our Savior, whether it is help from the church, others who love us in our lives, counseling, or medication to help with chemical imbalances of the brain. He can use this to still glorify Him if we let Him.

Would you believe God wants us to rejoice when we have difficulties? Not for the difficulties that are caused by sin, but *within* the difficulty. Sounds crazy, I know. It is so easy to feel anxious when we are challenged, but God is telling us our challenges are going to help us grow. When my great-grandpa Joe found out he had cancer, he said "isn't it a joy?" "They will have no fear of bad news; their hearts are steadfast, trusting in the Lord. Their hearts are secure; they will have no fear." - Psalms 112:7 (Zechariah 10:12). There is security in Christ. We cannot let fear stop us. Our mission here is too important. When I get bad news, I usually cry, or get angry. It's good to be honest with yourself and God, to just let it out. Then I realized, the clock is ticking. Life is short. Yes, it is ok to be upset but we have too much to accomplish, too much of a purpose here to stay down. When I am down, the best way to distract myself is help others.

I have made it a habit to go to the Lord in prayer immediately whenever I receive bad news. No news is ever a surprise to God. He knows, and even better He cares! He hurts with you and is there to help. The good news is this...

"And he who searches our hearts knows the mind of the Spirit, because the Spirit intercedes for God's people in accordance with the will of God. And we know that in all things, God works for the good of those who love him, who have been called according to His purpose." -Romans 8:27-28.

Even though our thoughts of good may not be aligned with His in the moment, we will be glad in the end He had His way. My dad was an incredible commodities trader on the Board of Trade growing up and was blessed tremendously by his work and labor. 30 years in, God had other plans and brought him back to his hometown with a career change. Initially, our family was devastated. Shortly after our move, we found out my grandma had cancer, my great grandpa passed, and my grandpa's death followed. As hard as this was for us, God's fingerprints and perfect timing were over the entire situation. With his career change, my dad was able to help my grandparents before they passed. This tragic event that still brought our family a lot of pain, was the closure needed due to God's direction.

God is doing more right now than you realize, than I realize. I would rather be in the will of God, than have no troubles. If you have a personal relationship with Jesus and love Him, He will work this out for your good. When we are steadfast in God, we stand firm in Him regardless of our circumstances.

"Surely the righteous will never be shaken; they will be remembered forever. They will have no fear of bad news; their hearts are steadfast, trusting in the Lord. Their hearts are secure, they will have no fear; in the end they will look in triumph on their foes." -Psalm 112:6-8.

"And the God of all grace, who called you to his eternal glory in Christ, after you have suffered a little while, will himself restore you and make you strong, firm and steadfast." -1 Peter 5:10. Your suffering will not last. This is a promise.

"For it is God who works in you to will and to act in order to fulfill his good purpose." -Philippians 2:13. God works in you to prepare and equip you to complete His purpose for your life, a part of His story.

"However, as it is written: 'What no eye has seen, what no ear has heard, and what no human mind has conceived'—the things God has prepared for those who love him— these are the things God has revealed to us by his Spirit. The Spirit searches all things, even the deep things of God." -1 Corinthians 2:9-10.

"To the angel of the church in Philadelphia write: These are the words of him who is holy and true, who holds the key of David. What he opens no one can shut, and what he shuts no one can open." -Revelation 3:7.

I am a firm believer God has a sovereign will, even though we have free will. The only way every single one of His prophesies and promises can come to life through the Bible is the fact that God is in control, even though He does not desire us to sin, and we still do. We have free will, but it is limited. God has the best for you.

"When they heard this, they raised their voices together in prayer to God. 'Sovereign Lord,' they said, 'you made the Heavens and the earth and the sea, and everything in them. You spoke by the Holy Spirit through the mouth of your servant, our father David: "Why do the nations rage and the peoples plot in vain? The kings of the earth rise up and the ruler's band together against the Lord and against his anointed one." Indeed, Herod and Pontius Pilate met together with the Gentiles and the people of Israel in this city to conspire against your holy servant Jesus, whom you anointed. They did what your power and will had decided beforehand should happen. Now, Lord, consider their threats and enable your servants to speak your word with great boldness. Stretch out your hand to heal and perform signs and wonders through the name of your holy servant Jesus.' After they prayed, the place where they were meeting was shaken. And they were all filled with the Holy Spirit and spoke the word of God boldly." -Acts 4:24-31.

What will never cease to amaze me is the fact that God decided, before creating the world, His will and plan. He knew exactly how Jesus was going to die, even though Herod, Pontius Pilate, the Pharisees, Chief Priests and entire Sanhedrin thought killing Christ was their act, nothing was out of God's control. God used the evil in their hearts that He foreknew and used it for His glory and good. We can use this information to scare us, or to encourage us to be bold knowing God already has our back. He already knows your next move, mistake, success, and effort before we do. He can, and will work it out for His glory, which when you see the truth, will desire as well.

"Trouble pursues the sinner, but the righteous are rewarded with good things." -Proverbs 13:21 (Proverbs 14:14). We do not always know what God is up to, but we can know it is something good. This is a promise from our God saying He can turn any situation for good, even when we cannot see a way. I am fully convinced that God has designed life in a way that even though He desires for us not to sin, out of His love for us before He created life, He knew every single mistake or wrong turn we were going to take. He is so powerful that He can make use of our worst mistakes and decisions for good. It is not difficult for God, as it is for us when we attempt to be anxious and worry about every angle, direction or circumstance in our lives. God has already accounted for every wrong turn we could make. When we love God, we are a part of His family, and let me tell you, our God takes care of His children. "And a voice from Heaven said, "This is my Son, whom I love; with him I am well pleased." -Matthew 3:17 (Matthew 17:5, Mark 1:11, Mark 9:7, Luke 3:22, Luke 9:35 and 2 Peter 1:16-18). Your choices are also not stronger than God's purposes, and He will use every choice you make for the ultimate good when you love Him. God sees your heart above all else and rewards those who work diligently. "The least of you will become a thousand, the smallest a mighty nation. I am the Lord; in its time I will do this swiftly." -Isaiah 60:22.

When we worry, we are telling God we do not believe all His promises in the Bible. We are telling God we don't trust Him. "Blessed is the one who perseveres under trial because, having stood the test, that person will receive the crown of life that the Lord has promised to those who love him." -James 1:12. "You need to persevere so that when you have done the will of God, you will receive what he has promised." -Hebrews 10:36. How relieving it is to trust in a God who turns our mistakes into a perfect plan because He Himself makes no mistakes. "Praise be to the Lord, who has given rest to his people Israel just as he promised. Not one word has failed of all the good promises he gave through his servant Moses." -1 Kings 8:56. In 1948, Israel was formed again and yet, we are still here! This had to happen before His return. However, the Jews were still scattered as predicted and Jerusalem is the number one issue for the world today.

"Now God had caused the official to show favor and compassion to Daniel." -Daniel 1:9.

"In the first year of Cyrus king of Persia, in order to fulfill the word of the Lord spoken by Jeremiah, the Lord moved the heart of Cyrus king of Persia to make a proclamation throughout his realm and also to put in writing: This is what Cyrus king of Persia says: 'The Lord, the God of Heaven, has given me all the kingdoms of the earth and he has appointed me to build a temple for him at Jerusalem in Judah. Any of his people among you may go up to Jerusalem in Judah and build the temple of the Lord, the God of Israel, the God who is in Jerusalem, and may their God be with them.'" -Ezra 1:1-3.

"So, the Lord stirred up the spirit of Zerubbabel son of Shealtiel, governor of Judah, and the spirit of Joshua son of Jozadak, the high priest, and the spirit of the whole remnant of the people. They came and began to work on the house of the Lord Almighty, their God." -Haggai 1:14. Take comfort in this. God uses the hearts of those who do not believe in Him, for His ultimate purpose, and if you are a child of God, this includes you! Here we see examples of unbelievers God moved in order to help his people. This is how powerful our God is. He uses those who do not even believe in Him!

"In peace I will lie down and sleep, for you alone, Lord, make me dwell in safety." -Psalm 4:8 (Proverbs 18:10 and Psalm 27:5). "I will listen to what God the Lord says, he promises peace to his people, his faithful servants- but let them not turn to folly." -Psalm 85:8. God wants you to sleep well. You know why? Peace comes from knowing you are not in control, and that it is a good thing! He has everything under control. No matter what, we will always have uncertainty to some degree in our lives. Whether it is in our own lives, or uncertainties for someone we love. However, you know, in the end, God has your best interest in mind. This right here is what helps me sleep at night. It is ok to be upset, but I want you to always remember the end of your story. For it is the best ending.

"Therefore, we do not lose heart. Though outwardly we are wasting away, yet inwardly we are being renewed day by day. For our light and momentary troubles are achieving for an eternal glory that far outweighs them all. So, we fix our eyes not on what is seen, but on what is unseen, since what is seen is temporary, but what is unseen is eternal." -2 Corinthians 4:16-18.

Ready to let out a big sigh of relief? Every trouble you are facing right now, no matter how big or small, is momentary. *Momentary.* Do you understand what momentary means? For a moment! In the scheme of life, this is short, eternity is long. It does not make the pain we feel any less but makes the hope and joy we can feel in the pain that much more! What is seen, what you feel today is temporary. What is unseen is eternal.

"Do not love the world or anything in the world. If anyone loves the world, love for the Father is not in them. For everything in the world—the lust of the flesh, the lust of the eyes, and the pride of life—comes not from the Father but from the world. The world and its desires pass away, but whoever does the will of God lives forever." -1 John 2:15-17.

This life, the world and our bodies are temporary, and we were made for more. "It is better to go to a house of mourning than to go to a house of feasting, for death is the destiny of everyone; the living should take this to heart." -Ecclesiastes 7:2. This is why God commands us to fix our eyes on eternity. Eternity includes other people as well, which is why we are to love them as Christ loves them, but not conform to the sinful ways of the world.

"We must pay the most careful attention, therefore, to what we have heard, so that we do not drift away." -Hebrews 2:1.

"Since then, you have been raised with Christ, set your hearts on things above, where Christ is, seated at the right hand of God. Set your minds on things above, not on earthly things. For you died, and your life is now hidden with Christ in God. When Christ, who is your life, appears, then you also will appear with him in glory." -Colossians 3:1-4.

"Pay attention." "Set your heart." Following God is active participation. God's power is what allows us to actively participate, but out of His love for you, He still chooses not to force you to do these things.

Do you feel like your best years are behind you? Do you have regrets about certain times of your life and how you have spent it? Maybe regrets about your entire life? Heaven and eternity will be the best, so you can take a big breath and have peace knowing no matter how great life gets, your best moments are yet to come! "Say to him, 'Be careful, keep calm and don't be afraid. Do not lose heart because of these two smoldering stubs of firewood – because of the fierce anger of Rezin and Aram and of the son of Remaliah." -Isaiah 7:4. Do not lose heart! Or in other words, do not lose passion! Life will continue to knock us down while we are here. "Therefore, since through God's mercy we have this ministry, we do not lose heart." -2 Corinthians 4:1.

"For I am already being poured out like a drink offering, and the time for my departure is near. I have fought the good fight, I have finished the race, I have kept the faith. Now there is in store for me the crown of righteousness, which the Lord, the righteous Judge, will award to me on that day- and not only to me, but also to all who have longed for his appearing." -2 Timothy 4:6-8.

"For the Lord watches over the way of the righteous, but the way of the wicked leads to destruction." -Psalm 1:6. We can have peace knowing God watches over us.

"From Heaven you pronounced judgment, and the land feared and was quiet- when you, God, rose up to judge, to save all the afflicted of the land." -Psalm 76:8-9.

Not only does He watch over us, but He blesses the righteous surrounding them with His favor.

"Then you will go on your way in safety, and your foot will not stumble. When you lie down, you will not be afraid; when you lie down, your sleep will be sweet. Have no fear of sudden disaster or of the ruin that overtakes the wicked, for the Lord will be at your side and will keep your foot from being snared." -Proverbs 3:23-26.

We never have to be anxious or afraid because regardless of what we go through, God keeps His promise of protection.

"Look at the birds in the air; they do not sow or reap or store away in barns, and yet your Heavenly Father feeds them. Are you not much more valuable than they." -Matthew 6:26 (Luke 12:22-24).

If God takes care of His birds, He says people are of more value than animals. He promises He will take care of you.

"...you of little faith? So do not worry, saying, 'What shall we eat?' or 'What shall we drink?' or 'What shall we wear?' For the pagans run after all these things, and your Heavenly Father knows that you need them. But seek first his kingdom and his righteousness, and all these things will be given to you as well." -Matthew 6:30-33 (Matthew 6:28-29 and Luke 12:27-31).

God's provision generally comes with God's instruction. He says to not be like the pagans, or those who do not have a personal relationship with God and fret your life over running after these things. He says to seek first His kingdom, then, all these things will be provided for you regardless of your circumstance.

"'How can I set this before a hundred men?' his servant answered. But Elisha answered, 'Give it to the people to eat. For the Lord says: "They will eat and have some left over."' Then he set it before them, and they ate and had some left over, according to the word of the Lord." -2 Kings 4:43-44.

God knows what you need before you ask Him. If He is taking care of nature, how much more will be taken care of for you, created in His own image who He loves and adores? God not only provides, but He has a trend of doing abundantly more than we can think or ask for.

If Jesus himself tells us not to worry, then we know we have the power not to do so! It is extremely (let me emphasize extremely) difficult not to do, but God would not give us a command if we did not have the power to do so with Him. This comes with controlling our minds. This takes practice. Just like we exercise our bodies, our minds need the same practice. We need to choose whether to keep our thoughts on Jesus, or our worries. I have verbally said to myself "stop" when worries or irrational thoughts creep into my mind and prayed. "Lord, capture my thoughts." "You will keep in perfect peace those whose minds are steadfast, because they trust in You." -Isaiah 26:3. As an athlete, I know my reaction time has improved since childhood from practicing over the years. It is the same with practicing being in the Word of God. It improves our ability to obey and control our minds, and changes how we respond when God calls us to do something we do not want to do. The more we practice and obey, the quicker our reaction time.

As an occupational therapist and certified hand therapist, I have been taught that when we have traumatic flash backs, we get anxiety and avoid the situation. Research shows it is best to approach these situations head on. Jesus wants to replace your worries and anxiousness with confidence and faith in Him. He wants to help you with depression or even take it away. When I worry the most, it is usually when I am most focused on myself. What am I going to do? Am I going to get everything done I need to? Am I good enough? Athletic enough? Pretty enough? You will have peace when your focus is on God and others. Change your thought process to, "what is God doing in my life?" Tell yourself, "I am good enough because God says I am." Instead of asking God how this will work out, tell Him how excited you are to see how He makes everything work out! Confidence is key. When we are confident in God, it leads us to humility, not pride. God lifts those who are bowed down to Him.

"The Lord sets prisoners free, the Lord gives sight to the blind, the Lord lifts up those who are bowed down, the Lord loves the righteous. The Lord watches over the foreigner and sustains the fatherless and the widow, but he frustrates the ways of the wicked." -Psalm 146:8-9.

"The tempter came to him and said, "If you are the Son of God, tell these stones to become bread." Jesus answered, "It is written: 'Man shall not live on bread alone, but on every word that comes from the mouth of God.'" Then the devil took him to the holy city and had him stand on the highest point of the temple. "If you are the Son of God," he said, "throw yourself down. For it is written: "'He will command his angels concerning you, and they will lift you up in their hands, so that you will not strike your foot against a stone.'" Jesus answered him, "It is also written: 'Do not put the Lord your God to the test.'" Again, the devil took him to a very high mountain and showed him all the kingdoms of the world and their splendor. "All this I will give you," he said, "if you will bow down and worship me." Jesus said to him, "Away from me, Satan! For it is written: 'Worship the Lord your God and serve him only.'" Then the devil left him, and angels came and attended him." -Matthew 4:3-11 (Luke 4:2-13).

Combat Satan's sinister lies with the truth of scripture just as Jesus did, and He will flee! "Because He himself suffered when He was tempted, He is able to help those who are being tempted." -Hebrews 2:18. Jesus left this throne and experienced the same temptations we do, so we can never say He doesn't understand.

"Do not be anxious about anything, but in every situation, by prayer and petition, with thanksgiving, present your requests to God. And the peace of God, which transcends all understanding, will guard your hearts and your minds in Christ Jesus." -Philippians 4:6-7. Paul wrote this as he was waiting to know if he was going to get executed in prison. The world does not have this peace because it doesn't know it. You can't find it from someone else's advice or the world. If you don't pray, the problem lingers. You can have perfect peace when your mind is fixed on Him. I know this, I am not perfect at it, but have experienced this peace in difficult circumstances. You have a choice every time you face hardship to complain or pray. We all experience more pain and anxiousness than needed when we do not give everything to God in prayer. It does not matter your age; we fall into Satan's trap of worry. Since I was little, my parents told me that the only way they can calm their worries about us is by praying for us to stay in the hands of God, for we are His, not theirs. As a parent, I can't imagine how hard that must be! Worry is trying to take God's duty and control away when it was never ours to begin with. God is directly linking anxiousness and prayer. The more you pray, the less anxious you will be. He is promising prayer is the answer. "Be careful, or your hearts will be weighed down with carousing, drunkenness and the anxieties of life, and that day will close on you suddenly like a trap. For it will come on all those who live on the face of the whole earth. Be always on the watch and pray that you may be able to escape all that is about to happen, and that you may be able to stand before the Son of Man." -Luke 21:34-36. Anxiety is a trap. It seems God continues to tell us the antidote to worry is prayer.

The second a worry creeps into my mind, I pray and tell God about it. I tell Him first as I am not strong enough to handle what is happening on my own. I then tell Him I do not want to worry. I begin to feel His peace, even when the problems are still happening, as this does not mean they go away. I know it is possible because I have experienced it. I also know it is possible because God tells us not to worry, and God would never force anything on us. He has said we should give our worries to Him. Just like practicing for a sport to get better, I am constantly practicing in my prayer life and guarding my mind. This does not mean pray and do nothing. It means giving the situation to God and pray on how to proceed forward; this is taking action. Sometimes God will lead you to act, and other times He will lead you to be still. Both are still an action. Practice builds habits. If you just wait until you feel like praying, you may never pray.

Use the community God gives you. For me, that is my family, friends, and loved ones who have been there and continue to be there for me through my worries and struggles. God gave a support system of people to you to help you, because He knows we cannot do it alone. Isolation causes depression. Build your community. You may be thinking, "Lexi, I have tried everything. Nothing is working." I want to remind you that worrying, and self-doubt are habits, and from personal experience with these, habits take a while to break. *Grant yourself grace.* Jesus shows it to us every second of every day! Busy, stress, worry and even joy are all choices we make every day no matter what we are going through. Being busy and not having time for God will create anxiousness. We tend to try to squeeze God in, but this should remind you of when they gave blemished sacrifices in the Old Testament. Did God accept the blemished sacrifices? No. He wants your best, and best does not mean perfection, but your full attention, no matter your scars. He wants your attention because He loves you!

We need to choose to love the way we look. Read that again. It is a choice. There is not one of us who can deny unhappiness with some part of how we look, and I believe this is because the enemy wants to criticize God's incredible, wonderful, and beautiful creations. I have the most beautiful family, friends, therapists, trainers, teammates, coaches, patients and even strangers who sometimes criticize the way they look. It breaks my heart when others can't see the beauty in how they are made. In my mind, I think just how beautiful or handsome they are, or how perfect their weight is. I wish they could see the same. I realize then that I do the same thing to myself that they are doing. It does not matter about your weight or how you look as you will never be happy with how you look until you choose to be. I have met the healthiest people who think they are overweight or bloated. I am all for health, exercise, sports, and nutrition to take care of yourself, but be happy today. Even when you are healthier you can always do better. Continue to strive but be content in the present. Do not give up!

Nothing is harder than facing depression and anxiety. Guys, I have been through both to the point of serious panic attacks where I ended up in the ER telling them something was physically wrong with me only to hear everything looked normal. For me, it was situational. I'm telling you all of this because I have been there with you and have experienced it. I am not saying this to undermine the seriousness of these situations, but to emphasize the power of Jesus to give you hope! This could be with the help of medications, counseling or seeing a therapist. I was on medication for a temporary period. If you are trusting Jesus through the entire process, He will not leave you.

"To grasp how wide and long and high and deep is the love of Christ, and to know this love that surpasses knowledge- that you may be filled to the measure of all the fullness of God. Now to him who is able to do immeasurably more than all we ask or imagine, according to his power that is at work within us, to him be glory in the church and in Christ Jesus throughout all generations, for ever and ever! Amen." -Ephesians 3:18-21.

"To him who is able to keep you from stumbling and to present you before his glorious presence without fault and with great joy." -Jude 1:24. This verse is proof no matter what you are struggling with, whether anxiety, depression, PTSD or bipolar, God can do more than you can imagine.

"You, dear children, are from God and have overcome them, because the one who is in you is greater than the one who is in the world." -1 John 4:4. No matter what your struggle is physically, psychologically, socially, financially, emotionally, or spiritually, it is overcome through God. Greater is the one who is in you than He who is in the world. Not that having Him in you changes all your circumstances and removes you from the hardships, but I can say with confidence no matter what you face in this world He is enough, and you have already overcome, because He lives in you.

"I remember my affliction and my wandering, the bitterness and the gall. I well remember them, and my soul is downcast within me. Yet this I call to mind and therefore I have hope: Because of the LORD's great love we are not consumed, for his compassions never fail. They are new every morning; great is your faithfulness." -Lamentations 3:19-23.

When you are dwelling on the past, your hardships and the pain, your soul will be downcast. I can promise you. Yet, Jeremiah says he calls to mind hope. Understand this mentality did not just come. He had to *call it to mind*. He remembered the Lord's great love, compassions, and faithfulness. Jeremiah went through extreme persecution, not facing anything you could excuse for him not feeling downcast within his soul. He was alone.

"'On the day when I act,' says the Lord Almighty, 'they will be my treasured possession. I will spare them, just as a father has compassion and spares his son who serves him. And you will again see the distinction between the righteous and the wicked, between those who serve God and those who do not.'" -Malachi 3:17-18.

There is an obvious distinction between those who suffer with anxiety, depression, and mental health who have the Lord and those who do not. Following the Lord does not mean we will not suffer through these; however, we will suffer with hope, which means we can suffer *well*. What does it mean to suffer well?

There are times I have been angry with God, thinking He was putting me through hurtful or tough circumstances just to test me. I always would come back to the realization God is on our side and hurts with you because you are His child. Jeremiah is saying to focus on God's faithfulness to cure your downcast soul which is so easy to come on us in such a broken world. "For he does not willingly bring affliction or grief to anyone." -Lamentations 3:33. I need this verse. God does not willingly bring grief, but he is so powerful he uses our grief and afflictions. "I am the Lord, the God of all mankind. Is anything too hard for me?" -Jeremiah 32:27.

"Come to me, all you who are weary and burdened, and I will give you rest. Take my yoke upon you and learn from me, for I am gentle and humble in heart, and you will find rest for your souls. For my yoke is easy and my burden is light." -Matthew 11:28-30.

The yoke was a wooden piece that was placed on the back of animals to carry or pull whatever was needed. Jesus says to come to Him when we are weary and burdened from our sin and the tiredness of life. He says to learn from Him, following His heart of humility, ultimately finding rest for our souls. People in darkness have seen a great light, increasing their joy. He shattered the burden of their yoke, the bar across their shoulders, the oppressor (Isaiah 9:2-5). Jesus wants to share your burdens and take away your stress.

"Praise be to the Lord, to God our Savior, who daily bears our burdens. Our God is a God who saves; from the Sovereign Lord comes escape from death." -Psalm 68:19-20 (Psalm 81:6-7). *Daily* bears our burdens. Our God saves us from death, He saves us daily from our burdens. How does He bear them? He shares them with us, He brings others into our lives to bear them, and He has the power to either change our situation or use our situation. Whatever He chooses, is best. When struggling with anxiousness, lay it on Him first thing in the morning and last thing at the end of the day. We try to bear our burdens when we were never meant to.

"Those who hope in the Lord will renew their strength. They will soar on wings like eagles, they will run and not grow weary, they will walk and not be faint." -Isaiah 40:31. God renews our strength when it feels like it is gone or running low. God renews our strength when we can't go on emotionally or physically exhausted, too beaten down by others, this life or when the enemy attacks. We will soar. We will run and not grow weary and walk without feeling faint. We are human and will get tired, but when you have the Holy Spirit inside of you as your motivation and passion, it springs in you new energy to soar that you would never gain from someone else, a certain situation or from a self-help book.

"Kings will be your foster fathers, and their queens your nursing mothers. They will bow down before you with their faces to the ground; they will lick the dust at your feet. Then you will know that I am the Lord; those who hope in me will not be disappointed." -Isaiah 49:23. God will never let you down. He will never disappoint you. Unfortunately, no matter how close you are with someone, at some point and at some time you will be disappointed. When you have Jesus, it is nice to know you are relying on a foundation that can't disappoint.

"My people have been lost sheep; their shepherds have led them astray and caused them to roam on the mountains. They wandered over mountain and hill and forgot their own resting place." -Jeremiah 50:6. We try to find rest in every other area of our life. People try to find rest in meditation, yoga, self-care, relationships, family and there is nothing wrong with these, however they are not our resting place. Jesus is. We are led astray in life by others who promise we can have things not of God, and those distractions always leave us more exhausted.

"Then, because so many people were coming and going that they did not even have a chance to eat, he said to them, 'Come with me by yourselves to a quiet place and get some rest.'" -Mark 6:31. Jesus is waiting for us to rest in him. We go to Facebook, Instagram, our phones, and others for contentment, but will not find the rest our souls need. These areas of our life are not "evil", but they need to come second to Christ, who is the peace provider in our lives. There is something powerful about going somewhere quiet to be with God, whether that is a room, outside or out on a dock.

"He says, 'Be still and know that I am God; I will be exalted among the nations, I will be exalted in the earth,'" is great in the New International Version but I also love the New American Standard Bible Version which says, "Cease striving and know that I am God." -Psalm 46:10. In other words let go and let God. Part of being still is trusting in God's will and plan. He has our best outcome in mind. He will make a purpose for every circumstance in our lives. Anxiety wastes time. We all have a huge list of why we should be anxious, but do you trust your Heavenly Father? "He says, 'Be still, and know that I am God; I will be exalted among the nations, I will be exalted in the earth.'" -Psalm 46:10. He wants us to be still so we can acknowledge He is in control. He wants us to be still, because only then can we come to Him with everything going on and confront our sin and the hardships we face to find healing. If we simply live our busy lives, you may think time "heals," but God heals. We have all had deep hurts, even if we just ignore it and time passes, it is still there. We need to give it to God, and in order to do that, we need to give Him time and modify our busy schedules for that personal time with Him.

"The Lord works out everything to its proper end- even the wicked for a day of disaster." -Proverbs 16:4. If we worry, we are telling God we do not trust Him. We are telling Him that He does not want to take care of us or cannot take care of us. We know this is not true! Many people do not understand how to find God's will. Sometimes we must trust and obey. You went to work today, maybe worked out, ate healthy, but did not contemplate if it was God's will. I am not saying these things aren't God's will, but sometimes when it feels too hard, we don't want to really listen. We use the excuse that since we don't actually hear God's verbal voice, we can't know His will.

"Trust in the Lord with all your heart and lean not on your own understanding; in all your ways acknowledge Him and He will set your path straight." -Proverbs 3:5-6. The Bible says not to lean on your own understanding because there is so much, we cannot understand from our perspective. God sees the start of creation to the end; He sees things about yourself you can't even see and He sees the bigger purpose. This doesn't mean we go through life without guidance but taking His hand to guide us when we can't see the next step.

"They will neither hunger nor thirst, nor will the desert heat or the sun beat down on them. He who has compassion on them will guide them and lead them beside springs of water." -Isaiah 49:10. You can trust God's hand in guiding you while you can't see because He has compassion on you and will only guide you where He wants you. If you are blind, of course you would only follow someone you trust. This means building a relationship with Jesus, knowing His character and His heart for you, and trusting Him as He guides you. I used to feel so strongly that I didn't trust God, because I pictured Him more as a Father constantly taking me to the next trial and giving me heartache to test my faith, instead of trusting His goodness and His desire for goodness for me. Those thoughts affected my decisions. I love to be challenged. Love it. Probably comes with me being an athlete, but I always wanted to know how I could be better. It was the same with my job as an occupational and certified hand therapist. I want to know what I can do to get better to better help my patients. God has the perfect way of guiding us to challenge us to reach our potential, not to hurt us. Also, within this guidance, He takes us on roads to grow our relationship with Him.

Through my heartache, the hardest thing I had to face was imagining the person I love with someone else. I would immediately get so mad at God, questioning why He would lead me to an area or decision that would cause me such pain. Then I would think God does not want me to feel that pain any more than I do, and immediately felt at peace with Him in a way I can't describe.

"I will lead the blind by ways they have not known, along unfamiliar paths I will guide them; I will turn the darkness into light before them and make rough places smooth. These are the things I will do; I will not forsake them." -Isaiah 42:16.

"I will instruct you and teach you in the way you should go; I will counsel you with my loving eye on you." -Psalm 32:8 (Psalm 73:24 and Psalm 143:8-10). God promises to instruct us the way we should go, and counsel us with His loving eye on us. How comforting! How does He instruct? Many cannot confidently say they have audibly heard God's voice tell them which direction to take. I have been as desperate as to put a blank note pad next to my bed with a pen, asking God to write an answer for me to wake up to in the morning. I have learned the Holy Spirit guides us, as the Holy Spirit is how Jesus lives in us and counsels us. But maybe you are still wondering, how? "All of us, then, who are mature should take such a view of things. And if on some point you think differently that too God will make clear to you." -Philippians 3:15.

"But where can wisdom be found? Where does understanding dwell? No mortal comprehends its worth; it cannot be found in the land of the living. The deep says, "It is not in me"; the sea says, 'It is not with me.' It cannot be bought with the finest gold, nor can its price be weighted out in silver." -Job 28:12-15 (Job 28:20).

What is the definition of wisdom? The very nature in person of Jesus. "It is because of him that you are in Christ Jesus, who has become for us wisdom from God—that is, our righteousness, holiness and redemption." -1 Corinthians 1:30. "I am the Lord, your God, who teaches you what is best for you, who directs you in the way you should go. If only you had paid attention to my commands, your peace would have been like a river, your well-being like the waves of the sea." -Isaiah 48:17-18. First, if you are stuck in sin and not listening to His commands, it will be hard to hear His guidance I have come to find. People are rarely in the middle of committing a sin thinking they are getting direction from God. First, I would say we need to make sure our own desires are not clouding our thoughts. Then, if it contradicts His word, we know it is not His will. We should rejoice in His law as one rejoices in riches, meditate on them, and delight in them. They are our counselors. Our soul longs for his law. (See Psalm 119:14-16, Psalm 119:20, Psalm 119:54, Psalm 119:24 and Psalm 119:35-37). Last, if you pray and are seeking His way, He will either send people in your life who you trust as believers to guide you or give you a feeling of peace when you are seeking His ways. "I will praise the Lord, who counsels me; even at night my heart instructs me." -Psalm 16:7. "For God is not a God of disorder but of peace—as in all the congregations of the Lord's people." -1 Corinthians 14:33. God is not a God of confusion but of peace. Satan will usually try to rush you to decide, where God will have you consult Him and pray on it.

"He put a new song in my mouth, a hymn of praise to our God. Many will see and fear the Lord and put their trust in him. Blessed is the one who trusts in the Lord, who does not look to the proud, to those who turn aside to false gods. Many, Lord my God, are the wonders you have done, the things you planned for us. None can compare with you; were I to speak and tell of your deeds, they would be too many to declare." -Psalm 40:3-5.

God will tell you where to go, if you look to Him and not a "false god" in your life. Where we run into the most trouble is when we seek counsel from others and don't seek it from God. God is your creator; He knows you best. Always go to Him first. If I am a volleyball player, I would not go to a football player for direction on how to perform a top spin jump serve. If I am a softball player, I would not go to a soccer player on how to hit a rise ball. God knows the human heart and soul better than anyone, so He needs to be addressed first. Then it is possible He can speak through others in your life as well, to guide you.

God advises us to seek counsel. "Plans fail for lack of counsel, but with many advisers they succeed." -Proverbs 15:22. It is wise to have those in your life to provide you with counsel. "I run in the path of your commands for you have broadened my understanding." -Psalm 119:32 (Psalm 119:74-77, Psalm 119:52, Psalm 119:137-138 and Psalm 119:86 and 119:14). When I first started working for my surgeons, I wasn't always able to read their handwriting, but the more time I spent with them, figuring out their orders, I started to understand. Or with my patients who have a cognitive handicap or stroke, it is hard to understand them at first, but the more time I spend with them, the more it is like talking to anyone else. "and how from infancy you have known the Holy Scriptures, which are able to make you wise for salvation through faith in Christ Jesus." -2 Timothy 3:15. Your counselors should lead you to the word. When we get in the word, our situations become clearer, and even though the pain of this life may stay, we begin to understand why the world is the way it is, and what the redemption plan is moving forward.

"Oh, how I love your law! I meditate on it all day long. Your commands are always with me and make me wiser than my enemies. I have more insight than all my teachers, for I meditate on your statutes. I have more understanding than the elders, for I obey your precepts. I have kept my feet from every evil path so that I might obey your word. I have not departed from your laws, for you yourself have taught me. How sweet are your words to my taste, sweeter than honey to my mouth! I gain understanding from your precepts; therefore, I hate every wrong path. Your word is a lamp for my feet, a light on my path." -Psalm 119:97-105 (Psalm 119:120, Psalm 119:167-168 and Luke 24:32).

It will not seem like a chore if you fall in love with God's law, and the more you meditate on His law the more you fall in love with Jesus. When you love someone, you love what they have to say! When you trust someone, you follow them, knowing they genuinely love and care about you. Until you fall in love with Jesus, you will not see His laws as "good." Only burdensome, and frankly annoying. They won't make sense until you realize these laws are for you, as God created you and knows what is best for you. Then the more you obey the laws, the more you begin to understand. Sweeter than honey! The word of God is our light to keep us from stumbling.

"The commands of the Lord are radiant, giving light to the eyes" Psalms 19:8. God's commands can bring light into your energy and life. "The unfolding of your words gives light; it gives understanding to the simple." -Psalm 119:130. It is one thing to have wisdom and know the Bible, but it is another to gain understanding of what it is saying. It is the same as sports. It is one thing to know about the game of volleyball, but it is another to understand the routes ran between a setter and hitter. You can know basketball, but it is another to know who is setting the screen and who is scoring. You can know football, but it is another to know how the offense works in order to play defense. You can know softball, but it is another to know how to hit a rise ball. Many are intimidated by the Bible simply because they think it is confusing, and yes, it can be. However, the more time you spend in it, the more it makes sense, and you realize a lot of it is straightforward. God will not leave you abandoned. If your heart is desiring to know His Word better, He will provide those in your life to help you grow. Also, looking at different translations can help too.

"Great peace have those who love your law, and nothing can make them stumble." -Psalm 119:165. You want peace? You want to be kept from stumbling? Get in the Word. Every day. Love the law and Word of the Lord. They will guide you; He will guide you. It is the ultimate "how to" instruction book for your life. The best treatment for depression, worthlessness, and anxiousness is to meditate on God's Word every day. Every day?! Yes. Why? Take it from someone who has attempted to get into the word from a young age. It is scary how quickly I either forget what it says or forget to keep it to heart in this fallen world. "All your words are true; all your righteous laws are eternal." -Psalm 119:160 (Psalm 119:89-93). Every single word is true and lasts for eternity. The only things that will last for eternity are the souls of people, God and the celestial beings and His Word. Choose wisely.

Did you know your words can bring someone life? You have the power to take away someone else's anxiety? God says so! With suicide on the rise, it shows this world desperately needs purpose. Suicide happens when the guilt and sin of this world is more than we can take. This world needs Jesus. In my profession as an occupational therapist and certified hand therapist, I have learned suicide is the fourth leading cause of death for adults, and the fifth leading cause for kids. I also see in our clinic stress affects our scapular, GI system, etc., and we must get to the root of that problem. Medication will help, but not cure. We all have stress; it's how you cope. I see in therapy all the time. You need to understand the Old Testament to know the why behind the New; like how in my profession, we must know the why to treat others.

I know I have always taken what others say to heart and taken what they said as truth when it was not. God protects us from the words of others who may not speak truth or be unloving. "You will be protected from the lash of the tongue and need not fear when destruction comes." -Job 5:21. Listen, Heaven will be the best, but God has you here on earth, right now for a purpose. Anything making you think otherwise or wanting to end this journey sooner is from the enemy, do not listen to him. He is using your suffering and depression. He wants to destroy you.

The enemy has people convinced their lives are not worth living. He loves to tell people they are not good enough. Nothing could be further from the truth because what God says is truth. We need to use words of encouragement; it could save a life! Satan loves when we procrastinate or feel discouraged, and wants us to think our attitude, motivation and deeds mean nothing. God promises we will reap a harvest if we have endurance, energy and do not give up!

"Let us not become weary in doing good, for at the proper time we will reap a harvest if we do not give up. Therefore, as we have opportunity, let us do good to all people, especially to those who belong to the family of believers." - Galatians 6:9-10 (1 Peter 4:19).

Occupational therapy started because people who had different injuries and disease were idle, and they wanted to put them in psych wards and institutions. Once they began occupations, they were able to have purpose. Satan wants you idle. Even if you do not benefit immediately, move forward at the proper time. It could be spiritually or physically, but don't stay idle.

"The sins of some are obvious, reaching the place of judgment ahead of them; the sins of others trail behind them. In the same way, good deeds are obvious, and even those that are not obvious cannot remain hidden forever." -1

Timothy 5:24-25.

We can become idle when we make anything the focus of our life rather than God. This can be family, friends, sports, our pets, hobbies, or our job. Is there anything wrong with these? Absolutely not. Only if they become our idol. If we are not constantly renewing our minds and working toward getting closer to Jesus, naturally this broken world is going to pull us back away from Him. Many people do not mean to slip away from their faith, but if we are not consistently putting in the effort, it is easy for our minds to drift. This is not a "works" mentality, in the sense that you can lose your salvation. We are saved by grace alone, through faith for what Jesus did for us at the cross. I fully believe if you abide in Christ, you are fully in Him, however God does command the renewal of our minds consistently.

"He has saved us and called us to a holy life—not because of anything we have done but because of his own purpose and grace. This grace was given us in Christ Jesus before the beginning of time, but it has now been revealed through the appearing of our Savior, Christ Jesus, who has destroyed death and has brought life and immortality to light through the gospel." -2 Timothy 1:9-10.

He calls us to do our best to lead a holy life out of love, but the pressure is off because even *when,* not *if* we mess up, his grace already covers us.

"What good is it, my brothers and sisters, if someone claims to have faith but has no deeds? Can such faith save them? Suppose a brother or a sister is without clothes and daily food. If one of you says to them, "Go in peace; keep warm and well fed," but does nothing about their physical needs, what good is it? In the same way, faith by itself, if it is not accompanied by action, is dead." -James 2:14-17.

Your works do not save you, but James is making a point that when your faith is genuine, your works will come to be out of the love you have for Christ. "You foolish person, do you want evidence that faith without deeds is useless? Was not our father Abraham considered righteous for what he did when he offered his son Isaac on the altar? You see that his faith and his actions were working together, and his faith was made complete by what he did. And the scripture was fulfilled that says, "Abraham believed God, and it was credited to him as righteousness," and he was called God's friend. You see that a person is considered righteous by what they do and not by faith alone." -James 2:20-24.

This is proof it has always been by faith that we are saved and made righteous. This clears up the question people have about how people in the Old Testament got to Heaven. Still by faith in God and His Son to come. "As the body without the spirit is dead, so faith without deeds is dead." -James 2:26. Our faith and actions work together; the works do not accomplish the faith, but the works are produced from our faith.

"Do not say, 'Why were the old days better than these? For it is not wise to ask such questions.'" -Ecclesiastes 7:10. If God is at your side, each stage of your life will be better than you ever imagined. "Even to your old age and gray hairs I am He, I am He who will sustain you. I have made you and I will carry you; I will sustain you and I will rescue you." -Isaiah 46:4. God will not change, even though you will as you age. I am not going to pretend I know what it is like to age being in my 20's. I see patients much older than I every single day telling me not to get old. I see the pain they are in and loss they have experienced, and it breaks my heart. However, I know I will be able to find comfort knowing God will sustain us.

"Children's children are a crown to the aged, and parents are the pride of their children." -Proverbs 17:6. Does the word "age" make you worried like it does to me? Every day is a gift from God. "This is the day that the Lord has made, let us rejoice and be glad in it." -Psalm 118:24. This means every day from when you are born, until the day you die. God has a purpose for it, and surrounding that purpose means the exact age you are that day. "Gray hair is a crown of splendor; it is attained in the way of righteousness." -Proverbs 16:31.

"The righteous will flourish like a palm tree, they will grow like a cedar of Lebanon; planted in the house of the Lord, they will flourish in the courts of our God. They will still bear fruit in old age, they will stay fresh and green, proclaiming, 'The Lord is upright; he is my Rock, and there is no wickedness in him.'" -Psalm 92:12-15.

You will produce fruit your entire life if God is your rock through it all. If you are young, submit to your elders and clothe yourself with humility because God opposes the proud but shows favor to the humble. He will then lift you up with his mighty hand, in his time. (See 1 Peter 5:5-6.) We are to submit and respect our elders, as God has designed an order and desires us to gain from their wisdom. As an elder, you can rejoice in the fact that God has put you in responsibility to guide the next generations. You can either see getting older as a pain, be fearful of it or dread it, or you can ask and see why God designed the order of life He did, and his current purpose for you now, no matter your age. You feel you realized this too late? It is never too late with God. He will use your age and wisdom today.

"Blessed are the poor in spirit, for theirs is the kingdom of Heaven." - Matthew 5:3. I struggled with this verse for a long time wondering what exactly God meant. I have always been so hard on myself thinking I am not spending enough time with God, in His Word, serving His people, using my talents and not taking care of myself with nutrition and exercise like I should. This is when I realized what this verse means. God is saying blessed are those who realize they will never be enough! Crazy backward thinking, but I find peace knowing I will never truly be or do enough, but those who realize that are exactly who God is looking for. God is saying He will bless you when you humble yourself to realize this.

"Many are the woes of the wicked, but the Lord's unfailing love surrounds the one who trusts in him." -Psalm 32:10. You trust God? His unfailing love surrounds you. You have days you do not feel as trusting but have Jesus as your Lord and Savior? His unfailing love continues to surround you, because even though our love fails, His does not.

"This is what the Lord says, he who made the earth, the Lord who formed it and established it- the Lord is his name: 'Call to me and I will answer you and tell you great and unsearchable things you do not know.'" -Jeremiah 33:2-3.

Pray. God will give you answers. Prayer is the catch. God specifically says to call on Him, and *then* He will answer you and tell you unsearchable things you do not know. *We are not meant to know what to do in this life.* Feel like life is a constant change and you do not know what to do? Join the club! Everyone will not admit it, but *every single individual has this struggle.* The good news is, we were designed for a relationship with God and when we do, we are free to call on Him anytime for His guidance that will never disappoint!

"How long must I wrestle with my thoughts and day after day have sorrow in my heart? How long will my enemy triumph over me?" -Psalm 13:2. Does this sound familiar? Every day is a spiritual battlefield, and the decisions we make and what we do with our lives start in the heart and mind. "Why did I ever come out of the womb to see trouble and sorrow and to end my days in shame?" -Jeremiah 20:18. You think everyone in the Bible had it so well and did not have the same struggles we do? Think again.

"But I trust in your unfailing love; my heart rejoices in your salvation. I will sing the Lord's praise, for he has been good to me." -Psalm 13:5-6. The cure to the fight. The cure to our heart ache is simply to *look at Him*. When you look to yourself for control of your mind, control of your sin or control of your peace, you will end up empty, anxious and depressed. When you simply just look to Him and become consumed with Him: "You turned my wailing into dancing; you removed my sackcloth and clothes me with joy, that my heart may sing your praises and not be silent. Lord my God, I will praise you forever." -Psalm 30:11-12. "When I said, 'My foot is slipping,' your unfailing love, Lord, supported me. When anxiety was great within me, your consolation brought me joy." -Psalm 94:18-19. Consolation means His comfort brings us joy to remove our anxiousness.

"In his hand are the depths of the earth, and the mountain peaks belong to him. The sea is his, for he made it, and his hands formed the dry land. Come, let us bow down in worship, let us kneel before the LORD our Maker." -Psalm 95:4-6.

When I get to my lowest and do not understand what the point of life is, what the point of the pain is, I come back to realizing to *whom I belong*. Who am I to question the One who made the earth, everything belongs to Him? "Remember the wonders He has done, His miracles, and judgments He pronounced, you His servants, the descendants of Abraham, His chosen ones, the children of Jacob. He is the Lord our God; his judgements are in all the earth." -Psalm 105:5-7. The only way to fight feeling depressed, when you are at your absolute lowest, is to *remember* His wonders, miracles, justice and the promises He has fulfilled for those who love Him since Abraham thousands of years ago. "The Lord protects the unwary; when I was brought low, He saved me. Return to rest, my soul, for the Lord has been good to you." -Psalm 116:6-7. Remembering what the Lord has done in our past and how He has been good to you will bring rest to your soul.

We try to hide our plans from the Lord, but we can't. We try to hide our short comings, but admitting our short comings to God, who already knows what we did, will create more intimacy with Him. Who are we, the pots, to say to the potter "You did not make me? You know nothing? (See Isaiah 29:15-16).

"Woe to those who quarrel with their Maker, those who are nothing but potsherds among the potsherds on the ground. Does the clay say to the potter, 'What are you making?' Does your work say, 'The potter has no hands?' Woe to the one who says to a father, 'What have you begotten?' or to a mother, 'What have you brought to birth?' 'This is that the Lord says- the Holy One of Israel, and its Maker: Concerning things to come, do you question me about my children, or give me orders about the work of my hands? It is I who made the earth and created mankind on it. My own hands stretched out the Heavens; I marshaled their starry hosts." -Isaiah 45:9-12.

Who are we to say to our Maker why did you make me this way? I am frustrated some days I am not a professional athlete. I love my job as a therapist, but my dream was to be an athlete. Why can't I be taller, stockier, just an overall better athlete? Then I am fully humbled in His truth because who am I to question how I was made? The one who made the Heavens? If this brings you discomfort or anxiousness, you do not have intimacy with God. Change! Draw near to Him! The thought of my creator being in control of what He has made brings me such peace which you can only have if you have a relationship with Him and trust Him.

"Yet you, Lord, are our Father. We are the clay; you are the potter; we are all the work of your hand." -Isaiah 64:8.

"One of you will say to me: "Then why does God still blame us? For who is able to resist his will?" But who are you, a human being, to talk back to God? "Shall what is formed say to the one who formed it, 'Why did you make me like this?'" -Romans 9:19-20.

We talk back because we think we know better, but who we are is all we know. When we realize we are mere human beings, and He is the ultimate creator, it humbles us even when we will never fully understand until we are in Heaven. The beauty is, once you accept you will never understand, but the One who does understand holds you in the palm of His hand, you can let go and find peace within the not knowing, just from knowing His love for *you*.

"Oh, the depth of the riches of the wisdom and knowledge of God! How unsearchable his judgments, and his paths beyond tracing out! "Who has known the mind of the Lord? Or who has been his counselor?" "Who has ever given to God, that God should repay them? "For from him and through him and for him are all things. To him be the glory forever! Amen." -Romans 11:33-36. We underestimate God. I have questioned God so many times in my life, but who am I to question the authority of the universe? Read these verses. He is Lord overall, including us and our life. This should bring us peace during the turmoil.

"Forget the former things; do not dwell on the past. See, I am doing a new thing! Now it springs up; do you not perceive it? I am making a way in the wilderness and streams in the wasteland."-Isaiah 43:18-19. *Do not dwell on the past.* If you are tempted to do so, it is the enemy tempting you to. Notice it says *dwell*. You can look back to better yourself, but do not stay there. God says to look to Him! He is doing something new! Only He can make a way in *your wilderness.* I hope you are realizing my book is not here to justify our shortcomings and purposeful sin against our creator, but it is to show you His power, grace, and love triumphs over them, and bring redemption in our lives in areas that seem impossible.

When we live according to our own desires, that is where our mind is set leading to death but when we live according to God's desires, that is where our mind is set leading to life and peace. The mind in control of our own desires is hostile to God and his law making it impossible to please him since then we do not belong to him. When we having the same spirit living inside that raised Jesus from the dead! Even though our body is will subject to death because of sin, his Spirit will give us life and righteousness to our mortal bodies. (See Romans 8:5-11 and Romans 8:13.) I want to point out God is not hostile toward us, but we are hostile toward Him when we are focused on the flesh, meaning our sinful desires apart from Him.

"For we do not have a high priest who is unable to empathize with our weaknesses, but we have one who has been tempted in every way, just as we are—yet he did not sin. Let us then approach God's throne of grace with confidence, so that we may receive mercy and find grace to help us in our time of need." -Hebrews 4:15-16.

There have been times I have shouted to God that He does not understand what I am going through. I was wrong. Jesus came to be fully human and fully God, to empathize with us. He knows what you need, and He cares. Come to Him with confidence! How amazing is it that we can come completely confident before a holy and righteous God because of what Jesus has done for us!

"Therefore, brothers and sisters, since we have confidence to enter the Most Holy Place by the blood of Jesus, by a new and living way opened for us through the curtain, that is, his body, and since we have a great priest over the house of God, let us draw near to God with a sincere heart and with the full assurance that faith brings, having our hearts sprinkled to cleanse us from a guilty conscience and having our bodies washed with pure water." -Hebrews 10:19-22.

If we can have complete confidence before God, the Creator of every single individual we will ever come across, we can have confidence in front of anyone, for anything, our entire lives.

Many people feel they cannot control a sin because it runs in their family. This is common for alcoholism, anxiety, etc. I am not saying this is not true, but we need to realize sin runs in every family because we are all human beings. We all struggle with different sins, and some may be more physically apparent than others. The beauty in all of this is Jesus has given us a way to overcome sin, even if sometimes that means fleeing a situation in which that sin may be involved. The old is gone and the new is here when we have Him. "Therefore, if anyone is in Christ, the new creation has come: The old is gone, the new is here!" -2 Corinthians 5:17. "Those who belong to Christ Jesus have crucified the flesh with its passions and desires. Since we live by the Spirit, let us keep in step with the Spirit." -Galatians 5:24-25.

"For the grace of God has appeared that offers salvation to all people. It teaches us to say "No" to ungodliness and worldly passions, and to live self-controlled, upright and godly lives in this present age, while we wait for the blessed hope—the appearing of the glory of our great God and Savior, Jesus Christ, who gave himself for us to redeem us from all wickedness and to purify for himself a people that are his very own, eager to do what is good." -Titus 2:11-14.

We will always sin while in this broken world, but when we have Christ in our lives, we should reflect less of it! His grace and forgiveness are so good it's hard for us to fathom.

"Nevertheless, God's solid foundation stands firm, sealed with this inscription: "The Lord knows those who are his," and, "Everyone who confesses the name of the Lord must turn away from wickedness." -2 Timothy 2:19. My grandpa's testimony is about his struggle with alcoholism. He used alcohol to cope. Jesus changed His life. Only He can supply the power needed to overcome afflictions such as alcoholism, addictions, anxiety, you name it! To overcome his addiction, he sadly could not have one sip of alcohol, or he knew he would fall right back where he was; however, this was worth it for his stability. To relieve your anxiety, you need to surrender to God. If you can't, it's a trust issue, but who better to trust with your life than the One who made you?

"The Lord is trustworthy in all he promises and faithful in all he does. The Lord upholds all who fall and lifts up all who are bowed down. The eyes of all look to you, and you give them their food at the proper time. You open your hand and satisfy the desires of every living thing. The Lord is righteous in all his ways and faithful in all he does." -Psalm 145:13-17 (Psalm 111:7-8).

"We are to put to death our natural, sinful human desires such as sexual immorality, lust, greed, anger, rage, slander, filthy language, lying and all evil which is idolatry which God's wrath is coming for. We all have walked in these ways the life you once lived, but now you are renewed in the truth and knowledge of Jesus our Creator where there is no longer Gentile or Jew, circumcised or uncircumcised, barbarian, Scythian, slave or free, but Christ is all, and is in all." -Colossians 3:5-11 (1 Corinthians 10:14).

Do you notice He considers all this idolatry? Many say either tolerance or bigot. Jesus was intolerant of sin to the point of death on the cross. I am a Packers fan. If I go to a Packers game and cheer for both the Packers and Bears, anyone could argue I am not a true fan. There are some things in life you need to be quote "closed minded" about because they are absolute truths. 2+2=4, and Jesus is the only way, truth, and life.

My very wise Pastor Sid Litke once said, "If someone is falling asleep while driving, you would be very intolerant and wake them up to keep you BOTH safe. If I ask for directions, I prefer someone 'closed minded' to tell me where to go, as I think if someone said, 'take any way, it'll get you to the store!' I would get lost. Or even if the answer was 'Just be sincere about where you are going, and you will get there.' You would still get lost. There still is a direction and right answer." Also "I sincerely think that ball was a strike." Then you get a different view of perspective and it's at the person's eyes or below the knees. You can be sincere, and still be completely wrong. There are absolute truths. If one person thinks it is a ball, and another a strike, they cannot both be right. God is who He says He is, and what I "think" about Him or what you "think" about Him does not change the absolute truth of who He tells us He is in His word.

Mental illness and addictions are real. Take it from someone who has experienced it and has studied treatment for it while in graduate school. Occupational therapists help people with addictions return to their occupations which is not necessarily their jobs, but anything in their life they need to return to. Many begin the addiction as a means of coping with something deeper to feel purpose. I remind them the feelings they get from the addiction is not where their sense of purpose lies. One of our professors also conducted research showing sports help prevent addiction as well giving an outlet. The psych portion, which is addressed, is the sense of belonging, as to the team, purpose, and dependability. If an individual knows a team is depending on them, they will be less likely to fall into addiction. Even better, if they know God sees what they are doing, this is the ultimate prevention.

Physical and mental illnesses may be inevitable, but just like preventing physical diagnoses with eating healthy and exercise, we need to do the same for our minds. Brain chemistry has an absolute role, but Satan also has a role, and we have been trained from the Word on how to defend ourselves against him. I have been through it, but I want to emphasize that you cannot let it leave you hopeless. We need to approach it like any other medical condition. Every single individual in this world has experienced anxiety and depression to some extent, but there is a difference when it is the actual diagnosis. As Christians, we need to show these individuals grace as everyone experiences emotions differently. As Christians, we know we are just as susceptible to all diagnoses and illnesses as anyone else. The beauty of being a believer is we can still glorify God through the suffering, through the counseling, through medication if necessary, and still realize Jesus is the Giver and Provider of all treatment and help. No one is less of a believer, though they struggle.

We learned in graduate school that sociopaths have an underdeveloped temporal lobe of their brain. Is it underdeveloped because they have chosen not to use self-control when harming others, which overtime caused the underdevelopment? Even though guilt and shame are not meant to be dwelt in since Jesus covers over them with His death on the cross, I feel they are temporarily needed to appropriately empathize for others and ourselves, and the very essence of what is needed to understand our sin and how much we need a Savior. How we view God and His love will reflect in how we see and treat others. If you never feel guilt or shame, you will think you have done nothing wrong. In your mind you would not see the truth that we all do need a Savior. As occupational therapists and certified hand therapists, we see how pain is affected by anxiety and depression. We can often predict the outcome by the self-confidence and effort put in. I know because I have experienced also treating mental health conditions in my profession. It is not easy, but with God all things are possible. "Jesus looked at them and said, "With man this is impossible, but with God all things are possible." -Matthew 19:26 (Mark 10:27 and Luke 18:27). "Take delight in the Lord, and he will give you the desires of your heart. Commit your way to the Lord; trust in him and he will do this." -Psalm 37:4-5.

Medications are great in helping to manage symptoms, but they will not heal you *if you do not have Jesus*. I have taken the medications; I know how much they help. God has provided those medications, but we need to realize He is the healer. A pill cannot heal sin, only Jesus. I once had a patient who was making significant progress on his shoulder. He went through a tragedy, and we started back at square one. It all begins in the mind. "The Lord sustains them on their sick bed and restores them from their bed of illness." -Psalm 41:3. "At the end of that time, I, Nebuchadnezzar, raised my eyes toward Heaven, and my sanity was restored. Then I praised the Most High; I honored and glorified him who lives forever." -Daniel 4:34

Once you are saved, you have the holy spirit living inside of you, who is also Jesus, and God! "But the fruit of the spirit is love, joy, peace, forbearance, kindness, goodness, faithfulness, gentleness and self-control. Against such things there is no law." (See Galatians 5:22-23 and Philippians 4:5). All this fruit is the evidence of the Holy Spirit living inside of you.

"No good tree bears bad fruit, nor does a bad tree bear good fruit. Each tree is recognized by its own fruit. People do not pick figs from thorn bushes, or grapes from briers. A good man brings good things out of the good stored up in his heart, and an evil man brings evil things out of the evil stored up in his heart. For the mouth speaks what the heart is full of." -Luke 6:43-45 (Matthew 7:17-18, 3 John 1:11 and Hosea 10:12-13).

I have always struggled with this verse. There are many moments in my life in which people I have wronged or hurt would tell you I do not produce good fruit, and some say that I produce bad fruit. I have come to realize though, since I have Christ, He has allowed me to produce good fruit, and has kept my tree from dying through my short comings.

"Whoever seeks good finds favor, but evil comes to one who searches for it." -Proverbs 11:27. Find the good in others. Ask God to help you find the good in others, as every single person has been made in His image. "The mind is governed by the flesh is death, but the mind governed by the Spirit is life and peace." -Romans 8:6. Jehu the 10th king of Israel said it's impossible to have peace with idolatry and witchcraft around (See 2 Kings 9:22). Peace is the presence of Christ calming us during our difficult times. We need to let our mind be governed by the spirit. We cannot escape the evil of the world, but we can control what we listen to, eat, talk about and who we spend time with. Jesus even prayed for us ahead of time for God to not take us out of the world, but to protect us from the evil of the world from the enemy. The only way to be in the world but not of it is getting into the Word of God. As Jesus was sent, He is now sending us, giving us the purpose of our lives and with this mission, He has promised God is faithful to strengthen and protect us from the enemy.

" My prayer is not that you take them out of the world but that you protect them from the evil one. They are not of the world, even as I am not of it. Sanctify them by the truth; your word is truth. As you sent me into the world, I have sent them into the world. For them I sanctify myself, that they too may be truly sanctified." -John 17:15-19.

"God is faithful and will strengthen and protect us from the evil one." -2 Thessalonians 3:2-4.

"Above all else, guard your heart, for everything you do flows from it." - Proverbs 4:23. Guard your mind and heart. We feel and live depending on our thoughts. Your thoughts determine what you do today, to determine your future. Your thoughts not only affect you, but those around you. Think of every tragedy that has ever happened from someone harming others out of hate. It starts with a thought, affecting not only themselves but those around them. Now let's define guarding. I personally know God's character does not feel this means to "hate" or "cut" others out of our lives. I feel people use this verse to do so saying they are "guarding" their heart. I think "guarding" means to protect in a way of how *we* react and respond to others. I need to guard from hating, bitterness and cutting others out of my life. Guarding our heart means guarding our mind. What should we fix our minds on in order to guard?

"Finally, brothers and sisters, whatever is true, whatever is noble, whatever is right, whatever is pure, whatever is lovely, whatever is admirable- if anything is excellent or praiseworthy- think about such things." -Philippians 4:8. You will have peace when you are focused on Jesus.

"The eye is the lamp of the body. If your eyes are healthy, your whole body will be full of light. But if your eyes are unhealthy, your whole body will be full of darkness. If then the light within you is darkness, how great is that darkness." - Matthew 6:22-23 (Luke 11:34-36).

Our mind is more powerful than we think and needs more protection than we realize. Stay away from porn, horror movies, any images that do not reflect this verse. Sin starts in the mind. Anything you say or do reflects your heart. Fear also starts in the mind, which is why if you are consumed with a scary movie, you will be scared every corner. We must read the scriptures to keep our minds focused on such things.

"For in my inner being I delight in God's law; but I see another law at work in me, waging war against the law of my mind and making me a prisoner of the law of sin at work within me." -Romans 7:22-23. "I do not understand what I do. For what I want to do I do not do, but what I hate I do." -Romans 7:15. We are in a battle for our soul, and in spiritual warfare whether you recognize it or not. Just because you close your eyes during a war, does not mean you are not in it.

"I do not understand what I do. For what I want to do I do not do, but what I hate I do. And if I do what I do not want to do, I agree that the law is good. As it is, it is no longer I myself who do it, but it is sin living in me. For I know that good itself does not dwell in me, that is, in my sinful nature. For I have the desire to do what is good, but I cannot carry it out." -Romans 7:15-18 (Romans 7:20).

If we fill our minds with God's truth, we are more equipped to fight the lies from Satan. Your focus changes your mind, which leads to your actions. Even though we cannot always control our minds, we can control the way we think and react. What we stay fixated on in our thoughts we pursue, and then become. "Whoever pursues righteousness and love finds life, prosperity and honor." -Proverbs 21:21. "Therefore, holy brothers and sisters, who share in the Heavenly calling, fix your thoughts on Jesus, whom we acknowledge as our apostle and high priest." - Hebrews 3:1.

"The weapons we fight with are not the weapons of the world. On the contrary, they have divine power to demolish strongholds. We demolish arguments and every pretension that sets itself up against the knowledge of God, and we take captive every thought to make it obedient to Christ." -2 Corinthians 10:4-5.

It is one of the hardest areas of our body to control, and it takes practice. This is called mindfulness. Mindfulness is training your brain to stay in the here and now. Your amygdala is what produces a response in the body called fight or flight. When we are anxious, the amygdala releases this response with adrenaline when there really is nothing to fight or flight from. It is just listening to your thoughts. The best thing that helps with my anxious thoughts is to think that if you cannot stop thinking about it, you can have peace God cares more about it than you do. If it is on your mind, it is already on His heart.

As an athlete, I compare it to practicing like I would for a sport. As an Occupational Therapist who went to graduate school, it takes practice just like studying for an exam. When we have wrong thoughts, God tells us to combat it with truth. "I have told you these things, so that in me you may have peace. In this world you will have trouble. But take heart! I have overcome the world." -John 16:33 "A person is praised according to their prudence, and one with a warped mind is despised." - Proverbs 12:8.

It is not a sin to be praised if the purpose of being praised is that you wanted to please someone else out of service. Where it becomes dangerous and prideful is when we start thinking highly of ourselves from the praise.

"Do not conform to the pattern of this world but be transformed by the renewing of your mind. Then you will be able to test and approve what God's will is—his good, pleasing and perfect will." -Romans 12:2.

Our mind is affected by the world from our own sin and the sin of others daily, and it daily needs to be renewed. If you feel like your emotions are out of control as I have many times, you need to renew your mind. The way you think, affects your emotions. This takes practice, but you will see a change in your emotions when you practice keeping your mind focused on Christ and the control God has in your life.

Jesus gave us the perfect example. After all these years of Satan thinking he has a rule over the earth, there is a man fasting in the wilderness weak from not eating and just think, at this point, there is not one human being who has not sinned. Satan tempts him saying,

"If you are the Son of God, tell these stones to become bread." Jesus answered, "It is written: 'Man shall not live on bread alone, but on every word that comes from the mouth of God.'" Then the devil took him to the holy city and had him stand on the highest point of the temple. "If you are the Son of God," he said, "throw yourself down. For it is written: '"He will command his angels concerning you, and they will lift you up in their hands, so that you will not strike your foot against a stone.'" Jesus answered him, "It is also written: 'Do not put the Lord your God to the test.'" Again, the devil took him to a very high mountain and showed him all the kingdoms of the world and their splendor. "All this I will give you," he said, "if you will bow down and worship me." Jesus said to him, "Away from me, Satan! For it is written: 'Worship the Lord your God and serve him only.'" Then the devil left him, and angels came and attended him." -Matthew 4:3-11 (Luke 4:2-13).

Combat Satan's sinister lies with the truth of scripture just as Jesus did, and he will flee! "Because he himself suffered when he was tempted, he is able to help those who are being tempted. -Hebrews 2:18.

Something none of us can deny is in this world, nothing lasts forever. As much as it hurts me to say, because I love my family, friends and others, our bodies are only temporary, whether you are a believer or not. Obviously, we all know we will die at some point, but can you take a second to really process this. *You are going to die at some point.* I struggle to wrap my mind around this, as it is something we have never yet experienced. This is a fact. As an athlete, this concept has been hard for me as I have gotten older. I felt I could play volleyball, softball, and basketball forever. As an Occupational Therapist, I see it. Our bodies are not made to last forever, and they do age. I know many ways to help slow this process such as exercise, nutrition, activity modification but the truth is it's a process none of us can stop completely. Our jobs are also temporary. Compliments are temporary. When you put your identity in what you do whether it be a job or sports, or in your family, or in relationships, one day it will all come to an end. Am I saying this to be negative? No. Am I saying you should not put your heart into these things? Absolutely not. I am saying this to make sure you are enjoying these things, however, know that Jesus is your solid foundation and ultimately your means to satisfaction. I am saying you cannot let your happiness and joy only rely on something you can lose. God is our strength, our fortress on home we can rely. He will go before me (See Psalm 59:9-10, Isaiah 52:12).

Effective Leadership

"I can do all things through Christ who strengthens me." -Philippians 4:1.

I can *lead with confidence* through Christ who strengthens me.

"...From everyone who has been given much, much will be demanded; and from the one who has been entrusted with much, much more will be asked." -Luke 12:48. I have had to lead in various aspects of my life. As captain of my sport teams, for Bible studies, youth groups, as a mentor, class president and class office, prom queen, Miss Madison and Southern Wisconsin, representative for my Master of Occupational Therapy class and coaching, I have learned many ways to be an effective leader from these experiences.

The ability to lead has never been through one's own power.

"You have delivered me from the attacks of the peoples; you have preserved me as the head of nations. People I did not know now serve me, foreigners cower before me; as soon as they hear of me, they obey me." -2 Samuel

22:44-45.

Jesus has taught us to lead confidently, yet humbly. To lead truthfully yet be encouraging.

"Whoever wants to become great among you must be your servant, and whoever wants to be first must be your slave— just as the Son of Man did not come to be served, but to serve, and to give his life as a ransom for many." -Matthew 20:26-28 (Mark 10:43-45 and Mark 9:33-35).

In Luke 22:24-27 the disciples were fighting about who is the greatest. Jesus replies saying the greatest is the one who serves. I enjoy washing my patients' hands, even when they look and smell less than desirable. It often reminds me of Jesus humbling himself to wash the disciples' feet.

"You call me 'Teacher' and 'Lord,' and rightly so, for that is what I am. Now that I, your Lord and Teacher, have washed your feet, you also should wash one another's feet. I have set you an example that you should do as I have done for you. Very truly I tell you, no servant is greater than his master, nor is a messenger greater than the one who sent him. Now that you know these things, you will be blessed if you do them." -John 13:13-17 (John 13:5).

Is it my first instinct to love doing this? No. Can I train my mind to love doing this? Yes! When you ask Jesus to genuinely give you the desire to serve, not out of pride that you are better and someone is below you, but for Him to create genuine love in your heart for them. Satan will try to tempt us with pride when in leadership. We need to remember to follow Jesus as our example. We are to speak up for those who cannot speak for themselves. "Speak up for those who cannot speak for themselves, for the rights of all who are destitute. Speak up and judge fairly; defend the rights of the poor and needy." -Proverbs 31:8-9.

"Has not my hand made all these things, and so they came into being?" declares the Lord. "These are the ones I look on with favor: those who are humble and contrite in spirit, and who tremble at my word." -Isaiah 66:2. The Bible is the literal word of God, and we should tremble at its holiness, realizing our Holy Father is speaking directly to us through it. When we are in leadership type positions, it is important to remain humble. What exactly is humility and how do we obtain it? After all God does say. "Believers in humble circumstances ought to take pride in their high position." -James 1:9.

"Humility is the fear of the Lord; its wages are riches and honor and life" - Proverbs 22:4. Fearing God helps you realize you are *created*, not the creator. When you are humble, you get peace. "The arrogance of man will be brought low and human pride humbled; the Lord alone will be exalted in that day; and the idols will totally disappear." -Isaiah 2:17 (Isaiah 2:11). God alone should be exalted as He is our creator. If we are being honest, we would say that we want to be exalted. What is ironic is even when you are exalted, you will not be fulfilled because our very nature is we were created to exalt God.

"For the Lord takes pleasure in his people; he crowns the humble with victory." -Psalm 149:4 (James 4:6, Matthew 5:5, Psalm 37:11, Matthew 5:5 and Psalm 37:11). More ironic is when we exalt God, he crowns us with victory. "In the pride of your heart you say, "I am a god; I sit in the throne of a god in the heart of the seas." But you are a mere mortal and not a god, thou you think you are as wise as a god." -Ezekiel 28:2. I have had to help patients bathe at the end of their life. Nothing humbles you more than when you cannot perform your activities of daily living. I have had some raw and real conversations with those in this stage, realizing how dependent we really are on God and one another.

"The pride of your heart has deceived you." -Obadiah 1:3. We need to be careful pride does not deceive us, as pride in its very nature is thinking we are right when we are not. "The greatest among you will be your servant. For those who exalt themselves will be humbled, and those who humble themselves will be exalted." -Matthew 23:11-12 (Luke 14:11 and Proverbs 29:23). God promises "Humble yourself before the Lord, and He will lift you up." -James 4:10. The more we humble ourselves, the more God lifts us up. If you humble yourself strictly for the desire of wanting to be lifted, this is pride. Humility is not self-hatred. It is where you are so focused on Jesus and others, it is hard to remain thinking about yourself, your problems and building yourself up. When I am suffering, I have wanted to sulk in my pain. Then I realize if I continue to sulk, I will not have the energy to share the gospel with others and help them. When you are confident in who you are, you can naturally become humble knowing God has justified you. You will only know who you are, if you are in the word of God. I have always wanted to say what I do, what my accomplishments were until I realized God already knows. When you are confident with yourself, it makes it easier to love others, making them feel like they are the only person who matters.

"The Lord detests all the proud of heart. Be sure of this: They will not go unpunished." -Proverb 16:5. "Do not boast about tomorrow, for you do not know what a day may bring. Let someone else praise you, and not your own mouth; an outsider, and not your own lips." -Proverbs 27:1-2 (1 Corinthians 5:6). Pride brings punishment. Let others praise you, not yourself. Stay confident while staying humble. The world feels a leader should be selfish and use their power to manipulate. They feel it shows their strength. God loves a leader who is courageous through selfless love and justice. Courage does not mean as a leader we have no fear. It means we reply on God with our fears and do not let them stop us from carrying out His purpose.

With my experience, I cannot help but think it is like our muscles. The more we work them out, just like our ability to lead, the better we will get! God is looking for a leader who is willing to trust Him to make himself big and tough the way He is! But He said to me,

"My grace is sufficient for you, for my power is made perfect in weakness. There I will boast all the more gladly about my weaknesses, so that Christ's power may rest on me. That is why, for Christ's sake, I delight in weaknesses, in insults, in hardships, in persecutions, in difficulties. For when I am weak, then I am strong." -2 Corinthians 12:9-10 (2 Corinthians 4:7-9).

Paul asked God to remove a thorn in his side that Satan had put there. God responded saying not that the thorn would be removed, but that His grace is sufficient through the thorn. The same holds true for us. I have begged and pleaded with God to remove the turmoil and hardships in my life, the heart ache and the devastation, only to realize no matter what I go through and no matter who I have in my life, His grace is sufficient. I am not saying this as someone living in a fairy tale world or having empty happiness, pretending everything is ok. God meant what He said. We were created for Him, and He will not fail His responsibility of being enough for us through the worst of this very difficult life and broken world. He will take responsibility for whatever He has called us to. Our shortcomings are not His fault or our sin, but He is that powerful He can still take responsibility for His glory and good to come out of it. His power is made perfect in our weakness. There are many times I have overcome obstacles in my life, knowing very well I was not smart enough or strong enough alone, whether in grad school or in sports, but have still succeeded knowing fully well it was only by the power of Christ. I will boast how I cannot do it on my own, but every accomplishment of my life has been through Christ. "I put no trust in my bow, my sword does not bring me victory; but you give us victory over our enemies, you put our adversaries to shame. In God we make our boast all day long, and we will praise your name forever." -Psalm 44:6-8.

"May I never boast except in the cross of our Lord Jesus Christ, through which the world has been crucified to me, and I to the world. Neither circumcision nor uncircumcision means anything; what counts is the new creation." -Galatians 6:14-15 (Isaiah 45:25).

Did you know we are allowed to boast, but not about ourselves or anything about us, but in Christ? We boast in Christ because nothing else we can accomplish in the world can satisfy like He does. There is nothing wrong with wanting to feel loved and accepted. We were created to be loved and accepted, but we will never find it in this world through fame, by how many people like us, through our success, through the number of friends we have, how many people are in love with us, through even a significant other or your spouse. The second you take your eyes off the cross and look to yourself and to others for this acceptance and purpose you will search your entire life. Human love is incredible, and God did design us, but love is limited so it can never fulfill us. We all know mistakes we have made in relationships, or times we have not loved our spouse, significant others, friend, family member or neighbor unconditionally which is what we were designed for, and it is the type of love God has for us.

"For in Christ Jesus neither circumcision nor uncircumcision has any value. The only thing that counts is faith expressing itself through love." -Galatians 5:6. You can express the faith you have in Christ through love.

"You were taught, with regard to your former way of life, to put off your old self, which is being corrupted by its deceitful desires; to be made new in the attitude of your minds; and to put on the new self, created to be like God in true righteousness and holiness." -Ephesians 4:22-24.

What is the attitude of your mind?

"So, he said to me, "This is the word of the Lord to Zerubbabel: "Not by might nor by power, but by my Spirit," says the Lord Almighty." -Zechariah 4:6. You will not lead efficiently though poser and might but by the spirit of God. No help book or person can give you the supernatural power that only comes from Christ to help you lead and stay confident in your life.

"You have spoken arrogantly against me," says the Lord. "Yet you ask, "What have we said against you?" "You have said, "It is futile to serve God. What do we gain by carrying out his requirements..." -Malachi 3:13-14. We are being arrogant when we have the attitude that God "owes" us when we serve Him. We get to serve Him by being madly in love with Him for giving us His all at the cross. We have the power to say no to sin, and yes to Him. We gain the absolute honor to get to serve the creator of the universe.

Leaders focus on objectives, not the obstacles. Preparation is key to being an effective leader. The Bible tells us to plan.

"Get yourself ready! Stand up and say to them whatever I command you. Do not be terrified of them, or I will terrify you before them. Today I have made you a fortified city, an iron pillar and a bronze wall to stand against the whole land- against the kings of Judah, its officials, its priests and the people of the land. They will fight against you but will not overcome you, for I am with you and will rescue you," declares the Lord." -Jeremiah 1:17-19.

As a leader, God will guide you. As an individual serving and following Christ, He will guide you. "Whether you turn to the right or to the left, your ears will hear a voice behind you, saying "This is the way; walk in it." -Isaiah 30:21.

"This is what the Lord says: "Stand at the crossroads and look; ask for the ancient paths, ask where the good way is, and walk in it, and you will find rest for your souls." -Jeremiah 6:16. To know the way to go, we need to ask God. We may not hear an audible voice, but God desires to guide us through Him, the Holy Spirit. Look for the ancient paths by getting in the word, every day. You will find rest, peace, for your soul.

"Commit to the Lord whatever you do, and he will establish your plans." - Proverbs 16:3. Many people change their beliefs based on the situations they are in. We are called to do the opposite. When you are not sure what God wants you to tell others or show them while leading, ask Him! Fully commit yourself to the Lord, regardless of the outcome and He will establish your plans. "Oh, the depth of the riches of the wisdom and knowledge of God! How unsearchable his judgments, and his paths beyond tracing out." -Romans 11:33. You may not understand or be able to trace out His plan but continue to lean into Him and He will guide you. You do not have to have the answers to follow His will and plan. God desires to make himself known to us. Pray for a clear answer. Accountability and discipline are key. Discipline is what keeps you going when the adrenaline and feelings have worn down. I have tended to blame God for circumstances I have ended up in the past, finding that my own sin was what got me there. Regardless of the circumstances you have in your life, blaming someone else or God is the biggest waste of time and will get you nowhere. All the way back when Adam and Eve took the fall, the first thing they did was blame each other and the devil, and yet everyone still had their consequence. Even if someone else has wronged us, God says we are to take responsibility of how we react.

"Then Daniel returned to his house and explained the matter to his friends Hananiah, Mishael and Azariah. He urged them to plead for mercy from the God of Heaven concerning this mystery, so that he and his friends might not be executed with the rest of the wise men of Babylon. During the night the mystery was revealed to Daniel in a vision. Then Daniel praised the God of Heaven and said: "Praise be to the name of God for ever and ever; wisdom and power are his. He changes times and seasons; he deposes kings and raises up others. He gives wisdom to the wise and knowledge to the discerning. He reveals deep and hidden things; he knows what lies in darkness, and light dwells with him. I thank and praise you, God of my ancestors: You have given me wisdom and power, you have made known to me what we asked of you, you have made known to us the dream of the king." - Daniel 2:17-23.

God reveals deep and hidden things, and even though He himself dwells in the light He exposes the darkness to us.

God does not desire to stay hidden or secretive in His ways. Yes, He is the almighty God and there is no possible way us as humans can comprehend exactly what He is doing and why. However, if we are desiring direction in our own lives, he says he wants to reveal this counsel and His thoughts to mankind. "He who forms the mountains who creates the wind, and who reveals his thoughts to mankind, who turns dawn to darkness, and treads on the heights of the earth- the Lord Almighty is his name." -Amos 4:13 (Amos 5:8).

"...turning your ear to wisdom and applying your heart to understanding— indeed, if you call out for insight and cry aloud for understanding, and if you look for it as for silver and search for it as for hidden treasure, then you will understand the fear of the LORD and find the knowledge of God. For the LORD gives wisdom; from his mouth come knowledge and understanding. He holds success in store for the upright, he is a shield to those whose walk is blameless." -Proverbs 2:2-7 (Psalm 7:10).

"Daniel replied, "No wise man, enchanter, magician or diviner can explain to the king the mystery he has asked about, but there is a God in Heaven who reveals mysteries." -Daniel 2:27-28. I love how Daniel always gave glory back to God, understanding the wisest of His age did not acquire their wisdom on their own.

"The king said to Daniel, 'Surely your God is the God of gods and the Lord of kings and a revealer of mysteries, for you were able to reveal this mystery.' Then the king placed Daniel in a high position and lavished many gifts on him. He made him ruler over the entire province of Babylon and placed him in charge of all its wise men." -Daniel 2:47-48.

Daniel was blessed because of His faith in God, and trust of His provision of wisdom.

"For the kingdom of God is not a matter of talk but of power." -1 Corinthians 4:20. God wants to use you, but we need to not just say He can use us but be completely self-reliant on Him with courage to overcome our fears. He wants us to boast not in ourselves, but in Him. You may feel like you could never lead. You feel you are not good enough, do not talk enough, do not know enough. The list could go on with all the excuses people make. Moses said he could not speak properly. David could have said he was not strong enough. Do we realize who our

God is? You can be an effective leader! Do not give up!

"When David saw the angel who was striking down the people, he said to the Lord, 'I have sinner; I, the shepherd, have done wrong. These are but sheep. What have they done? Let your hand fall on me and my family'." -2 Samuel 24:17 (1 Chronicles 21:17).

"...you, then, who teaches others, do you not teach yourself? You who preach against stealing, do you steal? You who say people should not commit adultery, do you commit adultery? You who abhor idols, do you rob temples? You who boast in the law, do you dishonor God by breaking the law?" -Romans 2:21-23.

As leaders, we have a lot of responsibility. This sounds a lot like practice what you preach, or what you preach is invalid.

"Then Jesus said to the crowds and to his disciples: "The teachers of the law and the Pharisees sit in Moses' seat. So, you must be careful to do everything they tell you. But do not do what they do, for they do not practice what they preach." -Matthew 23:1-3.

Will we ever be perfect? No. Will others look to see what we do when we fail? Absolutely. As leaders we will sin, but how do you respond when you sin? This is what makes an effective leader. We should strive to be as much like Jesus as possible, looking to Him when we fall short. I understand we are not perfect, but we shouldn't look like an unbeliever.

Stay humble and be honest when you have fallen short. God has not called you to fit in.

"But you are a chosen people, a royal priesthood, a holy nation, God's special possession, that you may declare the praises of him who called you out of darkness into his wonderful light. You were not called to fit in! Look at the story of Joseph! He went through trial after trial, and yet God called him to lead in each circumstance he was in. "The Lord was with Joseph so that he prospered, and he lived in the house of his Egyptian master. When's master saw that the Lord was with him and that the Lord gave him success in everything he did, Joseph found favor in his eyes and became his attendant. Potiphar put him in charge of his household, and he entrusted to his care everything he owned." -Genesis 39:2-4.

He was put into leadership, and might I add successful in His leadership due to his devout life to the Lord. Also, was Potiphar a man of God? We do not know but regardless, he was blessed maybe because of Joseph.

God called many in the Bible who are human just like you and me and used them in amazing, mighty ways! There are so many examples in the Bible of those broken exactly like each of us. Abraham who was a liar when he said his wife is his sister to save himself, Noah, who became a drunk, Moses, who was a murderer, Sampson, who was so powerful in physical strength from God had a weakness for women, Abraham, who did not trust God multiple times, David, who had victory from the Lord over giants but had lust, Solomon, who was the wisest man to ever live and wrote proverbs, yet had hundreds of wives and lost his way, Elijah, who ran in fear and depression out of queen Jezebel. In Genesis, Abraham first asks his wife to lie for his life to be spared and she was taken by the Pharaoh of Egypt. He took matters into his own hands when he thought Pharaoh would kill him for his wife. He wants to use every single individual He has made on this earth when they come to Him.

You may think you are not adequate to lead but look at people God uses in the Bible to lead even with their flaws. In Exodus 2:11-12 Moses murders an Egyptian for beating a Hebrew, one of his people.

"Moses said to the Lord, "Pardon your servant, Lord. I have never been eloquent, neither in the past nor since you have spoken to your servant. I am slow of speech and tongue." The Lord said to him, "Who gave human beings their mouths? Who makes them deaf or mute? Who gives them sight or makes them blind? Is it not I, the Lord? Now go; I will help you speak and will teach you what to say." -Exodus 4:10-12 (1 Corinthians 4:5).

Every time I speak at an event, did presentations in Grad school or flat out was nervous to talk to someone, I think of this verse. *Who gave human beings their mouth? Who makes them deaf or mute?* (See Exodus 4:11). If you pray and ask God to guide your words each day, go into that day having full confidence that even if you mess us, stutter, say the wrong thing, He will guide you!

"You must be on your guard. You will be handed over to the local councils and flogged in the synagogues. On account of me you will stand before governors and kings as witnesses to them. And the gospel must first be preached to all nations. Whenever you are arrested and brought to trial, do not worry beforehand about what to say. Just say whatever is given you at the time, for it is not you speaking, but the Holy Spirit. "Brother will betray brother to death, and a father his child. Children will rebel against their parents and have them put to death. Everyone will hate you because of me, but the one who stands firm to the end will be saved." -Mark 13:9-13 (John 17:14).

Even during persecution or in a circumstance you are the most nervous, the Holy Spirit will guide you in what to say. Stand firm until the end.

"This is what we speak, not in words taught us by human wisdom but in words taught by the Spirit, explaining spiritual realities with Spirit-taught words." -1 Corinthians 2:13 The words of wisdom are not from our human understanding but taught by the Holy Spirit.

"I came to you in weakness with great fear and trembling. My message and my preaching were not with wise and persuasive words, but with a demonstration of the Spirit's power, so that your faith might not rest on human wisdom, but on God's power." -1 Corinthians 2:3-5.

The fact that we can speak even through our nervousness and fears for Jesus shows the power of the Spirit.

"But when they arrest you, do not worry about what to say or how to say it. At that time you will be given what to say, for it will not be you speaking, but the Spirit of your Father speaking through you." -Matthew 10:19-20.

Do not be anxious about your words. I have prayed for God to guide my words, remembering God says to ease our anxiousness, we are to bring it to Him in prayer. This includes how we speak and interact with others. The truth says even if it gets to the point of being arrested, not to worry. God will be with us and continue to guide us. It will not be us speaking, but the supernatural power of the Holy Spirit.

"The mouths of the righteous utter wisdom, and their tongues speak what is just. The law of their God is in their hearts; their feet do not slip." -Psalm 37:30-31.

"God desires to speak life through you if you let Him. "The Spirit of the Lord spoke through me; his word was on my tongue. The God of Israel spoke, the Rock of Israel said to me: "When one rules over people in righteousness, when he rules in fear of God, he is like the light of morning at sunrise on a cloudless morning, like the brightness after rain that brings grass from the earth."-2 Samuel 23:2-4.

"I have out my words in your mouth and covered you with the shadow of my hand- I who set the Heavens in place, who laid the foundations of the earth, and who say to Zion, 'You are my people.'" -Isaiah 51:16. Jesus who set the Heavens in place, will give you the words to say. What more reassurance do you need? Who to trust better? "But they could not stand up against the wisdom the Spirit gave him as he spoke." -Acts 6:10. Even when you face the most difficult circumstances, the Spirit is there to guide and speak. God can use even the worst circumstances in our life for His glory His good which is ultimately our good when we trust in Him.

"But Gideon told them, "I will not rule over you, nor will my son rule over you. The Lord will rule over you." -Judges 8:23. When in a leadership position, we stay humble remembering we are only alive and have breath to lead in the first place, because of God. Everything is made for Christ and through Him, including your roles and purpose in life.

"Now then, tell my servant David, "This is what the Lord Almighty says: I took you from the pasture, from tending the flock, and appointed you ruler over my people Israel. I have been with you wherever you have gone, and I have cut off all your enemies before you. Now I will make you name great, like the names of the greatest men on earth." -2 Samuel 7:8-9 (1 Chronicles 17:7-8 and Amos 7:14-16).

God also took Amos from tending sheep to being a prophet for Israel. Whatever position, occupation or role you have in life, we can have confidence God has placed you there for His divine purpose. Do you feel like you are not where you are supposed to be? You could be in a season of preparation, like David was when he was a shepherd before God made him king. I wish I would not have rushed through seasons of my life to get to the next. Even though I was not supposed to remain in those seasons and continue to progress, when I look back, I see the purpose of those seasons was for preparation. Find joy today, understanding and knowing if God can take a small shepherd boy and make him king, there is nothing and no obstacle in your life God will not use or remove to have you where you need to be. I had to work hard in high school to stay an average student. I would have never guessed God would have led me to the career I am in, helped me get through my neuroscience, anatomy, and physiology classes and passing my boards to become a certified hand therapist.

"God said, 'Ask for whatever you want me to give you.' Solomon answered, 'You have shown great kindness to your servant, my father David, because he was faithful to you and righteous and upright in heart. You have continued this great kindness to him and have given him a son to sit on his throne this very day. Now, Lord my God, you have made your servant king in place of my father David. But I am only a little child and do not know how to carry out my duties. Your servant is here among the people you have chosen, a great people, too numerous to count or number. So, give your servant a discerning heart to govern your people and to distinguish between right and wrong. For who is able to govern this great people of yours?' The Lord was pleased that Solomon had asked for this. So, God said to him, "Since you have asked for this and not for long life or wealth for yourself, nor have asked for the death of your enemies but for discernment in administering justice, I will do what you have asked. I will give you a wise and discerning heart, so that there will never have been anyone like you, nor will there ever be. Moreover, I will give you what you have not asked for- both wealth and honor- so that in your lifetime you will have no equal among kings. And if you walk in obedience to me and keep my decrees and commands as David your father did, I will give you a long life. Then Solomon awoke- and he realized it had been a dream." -1 Kings 3:5-15 (2 Chronicles 1:7-12).

Of all the things Solomon could have asked for, he asked for wisdom. It did not matter his age. When he requested wisdom, God granted it to him. Solomon was able to make this wise request because he realized the relationship David and God had. God loves Solomon's request and heart in this situation so much, He blessed him beyond what he asked for. The key is, we cannot ask wisdom with the hopes of gaining more from God. That is not the point. The point is realizing having his wisdom is enough. "…but a ruler with discernment and knowledge maintains order." -Proverbs 28:2 Lead with discernment and knowledge. How do you obtain both? Getting in the word and asking of the Lord. Talking to others who are wise mentors who also have a relationship in the Lord or talking to others in your field of practice who have knowledge from their treatments or experiences.

"Solomon son of David established himself firmly over his kingdom, for the Lord his God was with him and made him exceedingly great." -2 Chronicles 1:1.

"King Solomon was greater in riches and wisdom than all the other kings of the earth. The whole world sought audience with Solomon to hear the wisdom God had put in his heart." -1 Kings 10:23-24 (2 Chronicles 9:22-23, 1 Kings 4:29-34, 1 Kings 4:28, 1 Kings 5:7 and 1 Kings 10:9).

"Even though Solomon was now the wisest man to ever be, his wisdom is still from the Lord, who is willing to give it to you if you ask. King Solomon, however, loved many foreign women besides Pharaoh's daughter—Moabites, Ammonites, Edomites, Sidonians and Hittites. They were from nations about which the Lord had told the Israelites, "You must not intermarry with them, because they will surely turn your hearts after their gods." Nevertheless, Solomon held fast to them in love. He had seven hundred wives of royal birth and three hundred concubines, and his wives led him astray. As Solomon grew old, his wives turned his heart after other gods, and his heart was not fully devoted to the Lord his God, as the heart of David his father had been." -1 Kings 11:1-4.

Even though Solomon asked for wisdom, we can learn from his mistake of straying from the Lord due to many women, political affairs and marrying those who do not have a personal relationship with Jesus. Sex and relationships are a good thing in a marriage covenant, but when we lust and desire multiple people, those who do not have Christ and having relationships for power, you will be led astray to your downfall like Solomon was.

"So, Solomon did evil in the eyes of the Lord; he did not follow the Lord completely, as David his father had done. The Lord became angry with Solomon because his heart had turned away from the Lord, the God of Israel, who had appeared to him twice. Although he had forbidden Solomon to follow other gods, Solomon did not keep the Lord's command. So, the Lord said to Solomon, Since this is your attitude and you have not kept my covenant and my decrees, which I commanded you, I will most certainly tear the kingdom away from you and give it to one of your subordinates. Nevertheless, for the sake of David your father, I will not do it during your lifetime. I will tear it out of the hand of your son. Yet I will not tear the whole kingdom from him but will give him one tribe for the sake of David my servant and for the sake of Jerusalem, which I have chosen." -1 Kings 11:6-12.

There was punishment when Solomon's heart was not serving the Lord. The difference is not that his father, David, had been perfect. He made his mistakes too, but David repented to the Lord. When the Lord appeared to Solomon, he did not repent. He continues to follow other gods due to his wives leading him astray. God cares about our attitude, and our attitude toward Him. We can choose our attitude. I have had the worst attitude toward God, the worst. I have pouted like no one's business, thinking He "owes" me, how can my life be so hard, why am I created the way I am, etc., realizing how terrible my attitude was. Who am I to question an all-powerful God? God kept His promise to David to save His people, us, through Jesus even though those like Solomon were not stepping in line with exactly what He wanted them to do. We have a God more in control and powerful beyond our understanding. My attitude toward Him should be in love and reverence for just that.

"And David became more and more powerful, because the Lord Almighty was with him." -1 Chronicles 11:9. David was able to lead, because God was with him.

"David praised the Lord in the presence of the whole assembly, saying, Praise be to you, Lord, the God of our father Israel, from everlasting to everlasting. Yours, Lord, is the greatness and the power and the glory and the majesty and the splendor, for everything in Heaven and earth is yours. Yours, Lord, is the kingdom; you are exalted as head over all. Wealth and honor come from you; you are the ruler of all things. In your hands are strength and power to exalt and give strength to all. Now, our God, we give you thanks, and praise your glorious name." -1 Chronicles 29:10-13.

Wealth and honor come from the Lord who is ruler of all, David understood this even though he was human and a sinner like you and me.

"The Lord was with Jehoshaphat because he followed the ways of his father David before him. He did not consult Baals but sought the God of his father and followed his commands rather than the practices of Israel. The Lord established the kingdom under his control; and all Judah brought gifts to Jehoshaphat, so that he had great wealth and honor. His heart was devoted to the ways of the Lord; furthermore, he removed the high places and the Asherah poles from Judah." -2 Chronicles 17:3-6.

Devote your heart to the Lord. It is ok to seek advice from others, especially others in your field of practice. For me, I would consult other therapists or surgeons for my job. For life advice I consulted with other fellow believers and mentors, however God should be consulted first before any as He made the human body, has every answer, sees our situation in ways others cannot, sees our heart in ways others cannot and loves us in a perfect love no other is able to. "But Jehoshaphat said to the king of Israel, "First seek the counsel of the Lord." -2 Chronicles 18:4.

"Ezra came up from Babylon. He was a teacher well versed in the Law of Moses, which the Lord, the God of Israel, had given. The king granted him everything he asked, for the hand of the Lord his God was on him." -Ezra 7:6. To be a good teacher, we need to be well verse in the scriptures. We cannot just know the scripture, we must do what it says, but how can we do what it says if we do not know it? How can we guide others, when the scriptures, being very God Himself, is the guidance and purpose of our lives? Because they were considered trustworthy. They were made responsible. (See Nehemiah 13:13). You want to be a good leader, or you have a goal to reach a certain position? Start by being trustworthy. Be a man or woman of your word.

"And David shepherded them with integrity of heart; with skillful hands he led them." -Psalm 78:72. Integrity of heart means your heart does not change depending on who you are around, with others, or alone. We create an integrity of heart knowing God always sees our heart, and we should have the same character and values. This does not mean we cannot ever be different with different people. I am going to act different in a professional environment and sillier with my friends, but your overall character should remain. "Whoever walks in integrity walks securely, but whoever takes crooked paths will be found out." -Proverbs 10:9. "Because of my integrity you uphold me and set me in your presence forever." - Psalm 41:12. God blesses and rewards integrity, it is of high value to Him and should be to us. "Let love and faithfulness never leave you; bind them around your neck, write them on the tablet of your heart. Then you will win favor and a good name in the sight of God and man." -Proverbs 3:3-4. Love and faithfulness shoulder be the anthem of your life, developing for you a good name "A good name is more desirable than great riches; to be esteemed is better than silver and gold." - Proverbs 22:1 (Ecclesiastes 7:1).

"Therefore, this is what the Lord says: "If you repent, I will restore you that you may serve me; if you utter worthy, not worthless, words, you will be my spokesman. Let this people turn to you, but you must not turn to them." -Jeremiah 15:19.

God is looking for those whose words serve a purpose and are not just uttered carelessly.

"The angel of the Lord gave this charge to Joshua: This is what the Lord Almighty says: "If you will walk in obedience to me and keep my requirements, then you will govern my house and have charge of my courts, and I will give you a place among these standing here." -Zechariah 3:6-7.

Walk in obedience to the Lord and keep His requirements, and by doing this you will be able to lead the way He intends you to. "He also told them this parable: "Can the blind lead the blind? Will they not both fall into a pit? The student is not above the teacher, but everyone who is fully trained will be like their teacher." -Luke 6:39-40. Jesus is our teacher, and who we should desire to want to be like every day.

"As Peter entered the house, Cornelius met him and fell at his feet in reverence. But Peter made him get up. "Stand up," he said, "I am only a man myself." -Acts 10:25-26. Even though I am sharing this knowledge and insight with you throughout this book, just like Peter, I am only human, and this is all direction and guidance I need myself. I prayed before writing this book Jesus to guide my hands, words and mouth to share from His word what He wanted with you. He is to be praised.

"When the crowd saw what Paul had done, they shouted in the Lycaonian language, The gods have come down to us in human form!" Barnabas, they called Zeus, and Paul they called Hermes because he was the chief speaker. The priest of Zeus, whose temple was just outside the city, brought bulls and wreaths to the city gates because he and the crowd wanted to offer sacrifices to them. But when the apostles Barnabas and Paul heard of this, they tore their clothes and rushed out into the crowd, shouting: "Friends, why are you doing this? We too are only human, like you. We are bringing you good news, telling you to turn from these worthless things to the living God, who made the Heavens and the earth and the sea and everything in them." -Acts 14:11-15.

Just like Paul and Barnabas, those of us sharing the Word of God are only human as well, with the Holy Spirit guiding us to share with you Jesus' direction, love and purpose for your life and for eternity when we die. Everything in this world, other than people and Christ, is worthless if you make them an idol above Him, Him who made the Heavens, earth, sea and everything in them.

"I myself am convinced, my brothers and sisters, that you yourselves are full of goodness, filled with knowledge and competent to instruct one another." - Romans 15:14. It is good to realize our sin and filth before Christ, but once we have Christ, we can have confidence He alone has made us good, and with this goodness overflows in us the knowledge and competency to help others. I at first hesitated to write this book because I thought "I mess up all the time, who am I to instruct others of their purpose and how to live?!" Then I realized I can have confidence to instruct because of the Word of God which we can be confident in, and the Holy Spirit. God uses us as people for His communication all the time and can use my instruction not to act above anyone, but to encourage one another as the salt and light of the earth. "The hearts of the wise make their mouths prudent, and their lips promote instruction." -Proverbs 16:23. We can teach others when we acquire wisdom ourselves.

"Follow my example, as I follow the example of Christ." -1 Corinthians 11:1 (1 Corinthians 4:16). Paul says to follow his example, imitate him, as he follows the example of Christ. It always goes back to trying to be more like Christ, not like others. I caution you if you have someone you look up to, not to idolize them because they will let you down. There is nothing wrong with looking up to others as a goal for ourselves such as an athlete who may have taken the path we hope to take, a therapist who is a certified hand therapist, which was a goal of mine to obtain, or as a mentor or pastor who can guide us, but if you use this individual to make all your life choices instead of Christ, you will be disappointed every time.

"This is why I write these things when I am absent, that when I come, I may not have to be harsh in my use of authority—the authority the Lord gave me for building you up, not for tearing you down." -2 Corinthians 13:10. We need to use our leadership positions to build others up and encourage them. This comes with tough love at times, but the motive of your heart should always be that out of the tough love in critiquing others. It is that you want to ultimately build them up, letting them know it is because you care.

"So, Christ himself gave the apostles, the prophets, the evangelists, the pastors and teachers, to equip his people for works of service, so that the body of Christ may be built up until we all reach unity in the faith and in the knowledge of the Son of God and become mature, attaining to the whole measure of the fullness of Christ." -Ephesians 4:11-13.

God has equipped each of us for everything we need to provide service for Him and for others, to build one another up.

"Now may the God of peace, who through the blood of the eternal covenant brought back from the dead our Lord Jesus, that great Shepherd of the sheep, equip you with everything good for doing his will, and may he work in us what is pleasing to him, thorough Jesus Christ, to whom be glory forever and ever. Amen." -Hebrews 13:20-21.

God has equipped you through His Son, Jesus, what whatever you need! Self-control, forgiveness, confidence, it is yours through Him! You no longer have an excuse to not pursue whatever it is God has put on your heart. We can always be confident in one, whatever God wants us to do will be accomplished through Him and two, if it is not accomplished, that was not a part of God's will even if you tried your best. Realize God's will is always better. If you do fail a boards exam, have a failed relationship, or did not make the team, it does not mean God does not want you to try again. He can use the failure to equip you, or He may be taking you in a different direction.

"In the presence of God and of Christ Jesus, who will judge the living and the dead, and in view of his appearing and his kingdom, I give you this charge: Preach the word; be prepared in season and out of season; correct, rebuke and encourage—with great patience and careful instruction. For the time will come when people will not put up with sound doctrine. Instead, to suit their own desires, they will gather around them a great number of teachers to say what their itching ears want to hear. They will turn their ears away from the truth and turn aside to myths. But you, keep your head in all situations, endure hardship, do the work of an evangelist, discharge all the duties of your ministry." -2 Timothy 4:1-5.

In 1 Peter 4:2-5, Revelation 11:17-18 and Acts 17:29-32 there are many Scriptures that talk about how people do not live for the will of God but for human desires such as debauchery, lust, drunkenness, orgies, carousing and idolatry and will heap abuse on you, but we all will have to give an account to God who judges the living and the dead. We are told to tell others about the Word of God and to be prepared. Correcting, rebuking and encouraging can all be done well together, if done with patience and love. You can correct while still being encouraging. In today's world, there are many false teachers that people desire to listen to because their teaching matches what our sinful nature wants, even though it leads to our destruction. We are to rebuke such teachings, knowing it is out of love for ourselves and others.

"In fact, though by this time you ought to be teachers, you need someone to teach you the elementary truths of God's word all over again. You need milk, not solid food! Anyone who lives on milk, being still an infant, is not acquainted with the teaching about righteousness. But solid food is for the mature, who by constant use have trained themselves to distinguish good from evil." -Hebrews 5:12-14.

How do we become mature in faith? It is not by how old we are or how much time goes by, but how acquainted we are with the teachings of the word about righteousness, and how we put them into practice. There is a divine wisdom about someone who has done this for a long time. "Therefore, let us move beyond the elementary teachings about Christ and be taken forward to maturity, not laying again the foundation of repentance from acts that lead to death, and of faith in God." -Hebrews 6:1. Spiritual maturity is not automatic. It takes effort, but just like the school you wanted to go to, sport you wanted to play or job you wanted to obtain, the effort is worth it. The difference is this relationship in growth with Jesus is beyond any of these passions. It is one for eternity, and the very essence of why we exist, so what better to put effort into?! The crazy thing is you realize once you are all in for Jesus, the effort becomes more natural because He gives you the strength as you lean in closer to Him, obeying, praying, and sharing with others the hope you have found.

"Therefore, rid yourselves of all malice and all deceit, hypocrisy, envy, and slander of every kind. Like newborn babies, crave pure spiritual milk, so that by it you may grow up in your salvation, now that you have tasted that the Lord is good." -1 Peter 2:1-3. I have always had Jesus, but my relationship has deepened, and I have matured. While living in the world, we will struggle with deceit, hypocrisy, envy and slandering, but the flame and desire to run toward these things should diminish as we mature, letting them have less of a hold on our lives.

"I do not say this to condemn you; I have said before that you have such a place in our hearts that we would live or die with you. I have spoken to you with great frankness; I take great pride in you. I am greatly encouraged; in all our troubles my joy knows no bounds." -2 Corinthians 7:3-4. "I am writing this not to shame you but to warn you as my dear children. -1 Corinthians 4:14. As a leader, make it clear that your rebuking, correction and encouragement are not to condemn, but because of the pride and joy others bring to you. Not to shame, but to warn out of love.

"Remember your leaders, who spoke the word of God to you. Consider the outcome of their way of life and imitate their faith." -Hebrews 13:7. We are to look at the leaders in the Bible, or those in our lives, and see the outcome of their faith. We should use them as our example to follow, if they are pointing us to Christ. Ultimately, Jesus is our leader. If we make Him just that, you will fulfill your purpose of the leader God has designed you to be. What you learn from Him, put into practice. "Whatever you have learned or received or heard from me or seen in me—put it into practice. And the God of peace will be with you." -Philippians 4:9. God will give you peace when you are focused on Him.

Armor Against Evil

"I can do all things through Christ who strengthens me." Philippians 4:13

I can *resist the devil* through Christ who strengthens me.

God rules over the world, over all. He is only allowing Satan to act but has a leash. Satan has been at work since the beginning wanting us to question God. "Now the serpent was craftier than any of the wild animals the LORD God had made. He said to the woman, "Did God really say, "You must not eat from any tree in the garden?" -Genesis 3:1. Satan likes to take what God makes beautiful, you and I, His Word, and twist it. Satan used what God told Adam and Eve plainly, to make them question if God really said what He meant. I see it today. Satan has an act for twisting what God says and making us believe the lies. You may justify certain sins in your life thinking you are just "tweaking" God's rules, but we see just a simple "twist" of God's rules created destruction for humanity for the rest of time. This is how dangerous it is. An example would be that you may think you are not cheating on your spouse because you are not physically performing a sexual act against them but looking at porn or lusting over another girl's pictures online. Another "twist" that can lead to destruction. God promises in His word that when we place our trust in Him, in His son, we are His children and are forgiven of our sins. Satan wants us to question if we are *really* forgiven. I mean, can you really be forgiven of everything you have done wrong? Those are the types of lies he will try and make you believe. God's word is truth.

You know in the end God wins? You know today, God wins? Satan has no hope. He wants you convinced you do not have hope, when he is simply trying to bring you down with him because you do have hope. Your story is not over, but his has been told from beginning to end in scripture. In Isaiah 14:12-15 you will read about the origin of Satan, how he fell from Heaven, was cast down to the earth because he wanted his throne above God. God says because of this he is brought down to the realm of the dead. Satan was perfect before he fell. He was originally supposed to rule the world under God, but that was not enough for him. His very name Lucifer means "light bearer" or "morning star." Therefore, when stars are referenced in the Bible, sometimes we need to realize this could mean angels.

"Now these things occurred as examples to keep us from setting our hearts on evil things as they did. Do not be idolaters, as some of them were as it is written: "The people sat down to eat and drink and got up to indulge in revelry." We should not commit sexual immorality, as some of them did—and in one day twenty-three thousand of them died. We should not test Christ, as some of them did—and were killed by snakes. And do not grumble, as some of them did—and were killed by the destroying angel. These things happened to them as examples and were written down as warnings for us, on whom the culmination of the ages has come. So, if you think you are standing firm, be careful that you don't fall! No temptation has overtaken you except what is common to mankind. And God is faithful; he will not let you be tempted beyond what you can bear. But when you are tempted, he will provide a way out so that you can endure it." -1 Corinthians 10:6-13.

Satan will want you to set your heart on evil things including eating and drinking in access, having sex outside of marriage or with multiple partners, grumbling and complaining. We are told to be careful that we do not fall. God is faithful and will not let us be tempted beyond what we can bear. He provides a way out. You may be wondering how? First, is not to be put into the situations. If some situations are unavoidable, this is where God will provide you with the strength to resist the temptation. An example would be if you struggle with lust or desiring sex with someone other than your spouse. A way to avoid this situation is to not find yourself alone with someone of the opposite sex in a situation where temptation can strike. Now let's say you are a boss, and meeting with the opposite sex alone is unavoidable, then I truly believe God will give you the strength to withstand the temptation if there seems to be no way to avoid the situation.

"Finally, be strong in the Lord and in his mighty power. Put on the full armor of God, so that you can take your stand against the devil's schemes. For our struggle is not against flesh and blood, but against the rulers, against the authorities, against the powers of this dark world and against the spiritual forces of evil in the Heavenly realms. Therefore, put on the full armor of God, so that when the day of evil comes, you may be able to stand your ground, and after you have done everything, to stand. Stand firm then, with the belt of truth buckled around your waist, with the breastplate of righteousness in place, and with your feet fitted with the readiness that comes from the gospel of peace. In addition to all this, take up the shield of faith, with which you can extinguish all the flaming arrows of the evil one. Take the helmet of salvation and the sword of the Spirit, which is the word of God." -Ephesians 6:10-17.

That person that you cannot stand. The one you know personally, the one you know politically, the one in your family, the one who ripped apart your life, the one who ruined your relationship. They are not the enemy. Our enemy is Satan. We are all on the same team as people, and God, Jesus and the Holy Spirit are for us as our Savior and coach to help us. Being bitter and trying to harm another person is like trying to harm someone on your team in a sport or tackle your teammate when you are on offense with them. It does not make sense, because you are fighting for the same purpose. Your enemy is the other team, not each other. The enemy is Satan, disguised within his tactics of temptation toward others who chose to listen to them. The only way to withstand the devil's schemes is God's armor, encouraging others to put on the armor and resting in his armor, which is described as His Word, memorizing it and applying it to our lives. Arrows from the evil one, you may ask. Physical arrows? Could be, or more like envy, discouragement, pride, doubt, fear, laziness, anxiousness, hopelessness, just to name a few. Temptation is not sin, but to fall into the temptations by choice is. However, we can take courage as God promises to always have a way out. We cannot wait until we are tempted. We are to prepare for battle ahead of time!

"But since we belong to the day, let us be sober, putting on faith and love as a breastplate, and the hope of salvation as a helmet. For God did not appoint us to suffer wrath but to receive salvation through our Lord Jesus Christ. He died for us so that, whether we are awake or asleep, we may live together with him." -1 Thessalonians 5:8-10.

Why the emphasis on being sober? Because when you are drunk, you are not ready to act. When we are drunk, you cannot withstand the devil's schemes hence why many will say they have done things they regret or felt they could not control when they are drunk. There is nothing wrong with drinking alcohol, the Bible is clear when it says we can drink and be merry. It is only to the point of drunkenness when it is a sin, or when we rely on it to the point, we become addicted to feel complete, happy or satisfied. God does not want us to suffer. He wants all of us to be saved through Jesus. He died for us so that whether we are alive on this earth now or when we die, we can be with Him.

"...which he revealed his glory; and his disciples believed in him." -John 2:11. You will read in John 2 the first miracle where Jesus turned water into wine, each of the 6 jars help twenty to thirty gallons! The master who tasted the wine didn't know where it came from, but the servants did. The master told the bridegroom most bring out the best wine first, but here the bet was saved for last! In 1st Timothy 5:23 it says a little wine is healing as opposed to only drinking water. There is nothing wrong with alcohol in moderation, but when excessive it effects more than just your liver. There are many Scriptures in Proverbs 23:19-21, Proverbs 20:1, Habakkuk 2:15, and Proverbs 23:31-33 that talk about being careful to be around those who drink too much or eat too much as they become poor and drowsy. "Go, eat your food with gladness, and drink your wine with a joyful heart, for God already approved what you do." -Ecclesiastes 9:7.

"Those who want to get rich fall into temptation and a trap and into many foolish and harmful desires that plunge people into ruin and destruction. For the love of money is the root of all kinds of evil. Some people, eager for money, have wandered from the faith and pierced themselves with many grieves. But you, man of God, flee from all this, and pursue righteousness, godliness, faith, love, endurance and gentleness." -1 Timothy 6:9-11.

Money is not evil. We need money to live and to enjoy much of this world God has given us, whether that is vacations, concerts, sporting games, for our health, school, almost everything.

"This is what I have observed to be good: that it is appropriate for a person to eat, to drink and to find satisfaction in their toilsome labor under the sun during the few days of life God has given them—for this is their lot. [19] Moreover, when God gives someone wealth and possessions, and the ability to enjoy them, to accept their lot and be happy in their toil—this is a gift of God. [20] They seldom reflect on the days of their life, because God keeps them occupied with gladness of heart." -Ecclesiastes 5:18-20.

The *love* of money is evil. Saving your money is a biblical principal as well as sharing with others. "On the first day of every week, each one of you should set aside a sum of money in keeping with your income, saving it up, so that when I come no collections will have to be made." -1 Corinthians 16:2. It is not a sin to save for our family, retirement, go on vacation, play travel sports and have a nice home. "After all, children should not have to save up for their parents, but parents for their children." -2 Corinthians 12:14. We need to make sure our priorities are in check as far as making sure we are also saving to share with others, and remembering whose money it is, God's. We need to make sure we are not letting money change our character or who we spend time with. That is when we know the love for money is evident and will cause evil in our lives.

"...though your riches increase do not set your heart on them." -Psalm 62:10. "People who have wealth but lack understanding are like the beasts that perish." -Psalm 49:20. "Whoever trusts in their riches will fall, but the righteous will thrive like a green lead." -Proverbs 11:28. If God blesses you in the way of financial provision that is great! He did for Hezekiah, David, and others in the Bible. "Hezekiah had very great wealth and honor..." -2 Chronicles 32:27. "...for God had given him very great riches." -2 Chronicles 32:29. He just warns not to set our heart on the money, because money can be fleeting, job changes could be around the corner, a pandemic could take away our business and money in and of itself will not satisfy. To help myself, I chose my priorities and lifestyle I want regardless of my financial income in the sense of my purposes. If my wealth increases, it should not change my mind set or priorities. We need to verbally tell ourselves every day we have enough. If you don't, you will never have enough. "Do not wear yourself out to get rich; do not trust your own cleverness." -Proverbs 23:4. Frankly, when your heart is so set on wealth, it is exhausting. You will wear yourself out, because as humans we are never satisfied, and can always crave and want more. "Whoever loves money never has enough; whoever loves wealth is never satisfied with their income. This too is meaningless."-Ecclesiastes 5:10. The word "meaningless" in Hebrew means "temporary." It is not that money has no worth, but its effects in the here and now of this world are temporary, instead of us craving what is eternal. "Why spend money on what is not bread, and your labor on what does not satisfy?" -Isaiah 55:2.

"Their silver and gold will not be able to deliver them in the day of the Lord's wrath." -Ezekiel 7:19. "Peter answered: "May your money perish with you, because you thought you could buy the gift of God with money!" -Acts 8:20 (Acts 8:21-23). All the money in the world cannot pay for your salvation. Only Jesus can. Only He can provide you with wealth that will never perish or fade and will be here in the life to come.

"Do not store up for yourselves treasures on earth, where moths and vermin destroy, and where thieves break in and steal. But store up for yourselves treasures in Heaven, where moths and vermin do not destroy, and where thieves do not break in and steal. For where your treasure is, there your heart will be also." -Matthew 6:19-21 (Luke 12:33-34, Matthew 19:21, Mark 10:21 and Mark 12:43-44).

When you die, nothing physical will go with you, and this is all going to pass away. What you do today matters for eternity if you are invest in what is eternal. If you accept Jesus, you will experience these treasures in Heaven. "In this way they will lay up treasure for themselves as a firm foundation for the coming age, so that they may take hold of the life that is truly life." -1 Timothy 6:19.

Could you imagine getting to Heaven one day and the individual you helped through your finances God used to save them? Whether it is through your example of generosity, or even buying them a Bible? This leads into tithing. God calls us to put aside our 10%. Remember, God does not need your money. He is after your heart and faithfulness. Who better to trust with your money than God? When you tithe, he promises to bless you. "But you ask, "How are we robbing you?" "In tithes and offerings." -Malachi 3:8. "Test me in this," says the Lord Almighty, "and see if I will not throw open the floodgates of Heaven and pour out so much blessing that there will not be room enough to store it. I will prevent pests from devouring your crops, and the vines in your fields will not drop their fruit before it is ripe," says the Lord Almighty. "Then all nations will call you blessed, for yours will be a delightful land," says the Lord almighty." -Malachi 3:10-12. These blessings may not appear as we would think, but isn't God's will usually better anyway? This requires preparation. "Be sure to set aside a tenth of all that your fields produce each year." -Deuteronomy 14:22 (Nehemiah 10:28 and Deuteronomy 26:12). Make your 10% a priority and budget around it to not run into financial troubles instead of giving God the leftovers. "Honor the Lord with your wealth, with the first fruits of all your crops; then your barns will be filled to overflowing, and your vats will brim over with new wine." -Proverbs 3:9-10. God emphasizes to provide for the foreigner, the fatherless, the widow in the sense of letting them eat with you to be satisfied.

"Woe to you, teachers of the law and Pharisees, you hypocrites! You give a tenth of your spices—mint, dill and cumin. But you have neglected the more important matters of the law—justice, mercy and faithfulness. You should have practiced the latter, without neglecting the former. You blind guides!" -Matthew 23:23-24 (Luke 11:39-42).

Even though giving a tenth is important, Jesus wants us to realize the heart behind all our laws and rules, realizing they are ultimately for justice, mercy and faithfulness, which is the very character and nature of who God is.

"But remember the Lord your God, for it is he who gives you the ability to produce wealth, and so confirms his covenant, which he swore to your ancestors, as it is today." -Deuteronomy 8:18. "The silver is mine and the gold is mine," declares the Lord Almighty." -Haggai 2:8. "Command those who are rich in this present world not to be arrogant nor to put their hope in wealth, which is so uncertain, but to put their hope in God, who richly provides us with everything for our enjoyment." -1 Timothy 6:17. I want to emphasize there is nothing wrong if God blesses you with wealth, but I caution to remember He gives us the ability to do so in the first place, giving glory to Him and remembering He can give or take away. This helps us to remain grateful in these times of fruitfulness and provision financially. All our money is God's in the first place. He wants to guide you with how to spend it, in what ways you are to earn it, in what ways to save and in what ways to give. Our finances are meant to be enjoyed, and we should tell God we know this is His money, what would we like Him to do with it?

"Give generously to them and do so without a grudging heart; then because of this the Lord your God will bless you in all your work and in everything you put your hand to." -Deuteronomy 15:10. More promises of blessing come when we give. Again, these blessings may not be that we get back what we give financially but could be spiritually or in other forms. "One person gives freely, yet gains even more; another withholds unduly, but comes to poverty. A generous person will prosper; whoever refreshes others will be refreshed." -Proverbs 11:24-25 (Proverbs 22:9). You should give to others out of your love for them, not for reward, but ironically when you do give, God says you yourself will be refreshed.

"But who am I, and who are my people, that we should be able to give as generously as this? Everything comes from you, and we have given you only what comes from your hand. We are foreigners and strangers in your sight, as were all our ancestors. Our days on earth are like a shadow, without hope. Lord our God, all this abundance that we have provided for building you a temple for your Holy Name comes from your hand, and all of it belongs to you. I know, my God, that you test the heart and are pleased with integrity. All these things I have given willingly and with honest intent. And now I have seen with joy how willingly your people who are here have given to you. Lord, the God of our fathers Abraham, Isaac and Israel, keep these desires and thoughts in the hearts of your people forever, and keep their hearts loyal to you. And give my son Solomon the wholehearted devotion to keep your commands, statutes and decrees and to do everything to build the palatial structure for which I have provided." -1 Chronicles 29:14-19.

Everything comes from God, from his hand. God tests the heart and is pleased with integrity. "The crucible for silver and the furnace for gold, but the Lord tests the heart." -Proverbs 17:3. We cannot condemn those with wealth, what defines wealth or someone who is rich? As far as other countries are concerned, all of America is rich. Does that mean all of America is evil? I would say no. Again, money is not evil. Money can be a blessing if your heart is not set on it. Your mind should never be so consumed with wealth, that you are not willing to be generous. "Wealth and riches are in his house, And his righteousness endures forever. Light arises in the darkness for the upright; He is gracious and compassionate and righteous. It is well with the man who is gracious and lends; He will maintain his cause in judgement." -Psalm 112:3-5.

"Dishonest money dwindles away, but whoever gathers money little by little makes it grow." -Proverbs 13:11. When your heart is set on money, you will usually do anything to get it, even by dishonest means whether that is in your business, through heart breaking businesses such as sex trafficking, money at the strip club or how addictions to gambling begin. "A man who loves wisdom brings joy to his father, but a companion of prostitutes squanders his wealth." -Proverbs 29:3. "A wicked person earns deceptive wages, but the one who sows righteousness reaps a sure reward." -Proverbs 11:18.

"The wise store up choice food and olive oil, but fools gulp theirs down." -Proverbs 21:20. God is clear we are to save our money as well as be generous. It is a tough balance that if I am being honest, do not know the exact science to. It is something I pray about often, and how God can show you how to spend your money for you and your family, while giving to others, while saving for your retirement, decreasing your debt and saving for your life.

"Do not be one who shakes hands in pledge or puts up security for debts; if you lack the means to pay, your very bed will be snatched from under you." -Proverbs 22:26-27 (Proverbs 22:7). Speaking of debt, it is something you should want to pay off as soon as you can. We are in a society where it is inevitable whether you are paying for college, a house, or a car. Make it your priority to pay back your debt to keep from being snatched under, as the Bible says we are a "slave" to the lender. "He does not oppress anyone but returns what he took in pledge for a loan. He does not commit robbery but gives his food to the hungry but gives clothing for the naked." -Ezekiel 18:7. "Let no debt remain outstanding, except the continuing debt to love one another, for whoever loves others has fulfilled the law." -Romans 13:8. The only debt we should continue to have is the obligation, or to be a slave to loving others as Christ has loved us to fulfill the law! "The wicked borrow and do not repay, but the righteous give generously." -Psalm 37:2.

"I tell you, use worldly wealth to gain friends for yourselves, so that when it is gone, you will be welcomed into eternal dwellings. Whoever can be trusted with very little can also be trusted with much, and whoever is dishonest with very little will also be dishonest with much. So, if you have not been trustworthy in handling worldly wealth, who will trust you with true riches? And if you have not been trustworthy with someone else's property, who will give you property of your own?"No one can serve two masters. Either you will hate the one and love the other, or you will be devoted to the one and despise the other. You cannot serve both God and money." -Luke 16:9-13 (Matthew 6:24).

I was very convicted when the truth talks about if you cannot be trusted with worldly wealth, who will trust you with true riches? This was when I knew I had to reevaluate my finances and what I was spending and ultimately going into too much debt. Also, using worldly wealth to gain friends for yourself may sound almost selfish, but I take that as what better way to spend money than on people who are eternal? These are more reasons how God can use money, and why we cannot just view it as evil. Money is not evil if the matter you are serving is God. You cannot serve both Him and money. Serve Him, and you will learn how to handle your finances, and where He wants them to come from.

"Tell us then, what is your opinion? Is it right to pay the imperial tax to Caesar or not?" - Matthew 22:17. "Caesar's," they replied. Then he said to them, 'So give back to Caesar what is Caesar's, and to God what is God's'." - Matthew 22:21 (Mark 12:14-17 and Luke 20:20-25). You would probably think I am crazy to say this, but what if we were joyful to pay our taxes? "A proclamation was then issued in Judah and Jerusalem that they should bring to the Lord the tax that

Moses the servant of God had required of Israel in the wilderness. All the officials and all the people brought their contributions gladly." -2 Chronicles 24:9-10. I am not naïve to the fact that there is corruption in our world, and unfortunately our tax system is not exactly how it should be, but overall God has set up government to give back to our leaders but giving God also what is His. We should pay our taxes gladly, knowing regardless of the corruption, this is what God intends and will use for His and our good!

"Don't collect any more than you are required to," he told them. Then some soldiers asked him, "And what should we do?" He replied, "Don't extort money and don't accuse people falsely—be content with your pay." -Luke 3:13-14 (Luke 3:11-12). I have been frustrated at times in my life, feeling like I was not getting paid what I should. I have learned to pray and ask God what it is He feels I should get paid and have learned to be content. There is nothing wrong with asking questions to those who pay you as to how you can work your way to more, but after that, it is out of your control, and in the hands of God.

You can read in, Matthew 25:16-30 and Luke 19:12-27, a man received 5 bags of gold and another 2 bags of gold. They put the money to work and gained double of what they had. Another man received one bag of gold and hid his master's money in the ground. When their master returned, he was pleased with the two servants who put their money to work saying "Well done, good and faithful servant!" to each of them, saying since they have been faithful with a few things they will oversee many things. He invited them to share in his happiness. The man with one bag of gold tried to protect himself from his strict master out of fear, but showed he was only being selfish and hid the gold for himself, but then gave back to his master when asked for it. "His master said, "You wicked, lazy servant!" The master said how the men knew he could harvest where he has not sown and gather where he has not scattered seed. "Well then, you should have put my money on deposit with the bankers, so that when I returned, I would have received it back with interest. 'So, take the bag of gold from him and give it to the one who has ten bags." - Matthew 25:27-28. Even though this is a parable referencing investing our time and talent for Jesus, I also think it is very beneficial to apply to money. When we put our money away to collect interest within our savings, this is a biblical principle.

"Then he said to them, "Watch out! Be on your guard against all kinds of greed; life does not consist in an abundance of possessions." -Luke 12:15. Greed is the value you put on your possessions, not how much you have. No matter how much you have you can still be greedy. If you want people to get taxed so much so you can acquire whatever you want in a sense of stealing their money against their will, that is also greed. We are stewards of everything. You will be less anxious if you remember everything you own is God's, including your life. I feel like it is possible to own so much, you forget what you own. I was at the airport once and envied someone's suitcase, wishing I had one and not the large athletic bag causing me shoulder pain. Then later, I was cleaning my room and found the exact same suitcase under my bed. Think I may have owned too much I couldn't even keep track of my own things, and envied something I already owned? I was completely humbled. Life is so much more than things. Again, possessions are not bad or evil, only when our life is centered around collecting an abundance of these possessions does it become dangerous.

"All the believers were one in heart and mind. No one claimed that any of their possessions was their own, but they shared everything they had. With great power the apostles continued to testify to the resurrection of the Lord Jesus. And God's grace was so powerfully at work in them all that there were no needy persons among them. For from time to time those who owned land or houses sold them, brought the money from the sales and put it at the apostles' feet, and it was distributed to anyone who had need." -Acts 4:32-35.

This is the definition of a church family. Anytime someone asks to borrow something of mine that I innately want to keep for myself, I remember this truth. God's grace can be shown in how we share.

"Remember this: Whoever sows sparingly will also reap sparingly, and whoever sows generously will also reap generously. Each of you should give what you have decided in your heart to give, not reluctantly or under compulsion, for God loves a cheerful giver. And God is able to bless you abundantly, so that in all things at all times, having all that you need, you will abound in every good work. As it is written: "They have freely scattered their gifts to the poor; their righteousness endures forever." -2 Corinthians 9:6-9 (Acts 10:31).

I have used this verse to justify either not giving or barely giving, thinking "well I am not cheerful and do not want to give which means I should not" instead of changing my heart to choose to be cheerful to give my 10%.

"You will be enriched in every way so that you can be generous on every occasion, and through us your generosity will result in thanksgiving to God. This service that you perform is not only supplying the needs of the Lord's people but is also overflowing in many expressions of thanks to God. Because of the service by which you have proved yourselves, others will praise God for the obedience that accompanies your confession of the gospel of Christ, and for your generosity in sharing with them and with everyone else. And in their prayers for you their hearts will go out to you, because of the surpassing grace God has given you. Thanks be to God for his indescribable gift!" -2 Corinthians 9:11-15.

God provides for you and your family so you can be generous. Your generosity leads others to look toward the provider, Jesus, creating the perfect opportunity to share the gospel!

I can't stand the outlook that Christians or those who have God "don't like to have fun" and we're just so "good" all the time. God is fun! Living in freedom is insanely fun, and I have so much fun every day. I live in this freedom I am not good, but Christ is who makes us good! Satan makes sin look fun, full of pleasure but hides the consequences. Many say whatever feels good must be good but look here "Do not be deceived: God cannot be mocked. A man reaps what he sows. Whoever sows to please their flesh, for the flesh will reap destruction; whoever sows to please the Spirit, from the Spirit will reap eternal life." -Galatians 6:7-8 (Proverbs 21:17).

Flesh means selfishness. God does not give us the law because he wants our lives to be miserable. It is the opposite. He wants to protect us! When we sin, we are not breaking the law but destroying ourselves, falling into your own trap you might not even realize is set up. "Evildoers are snared by their own sin." -Proverbs 29:6.

"Your wrongdoings have kept these away; your sins have deprived you of good." -Jeremiah 5:25 (Hosea 14:1-2). "Have you not brought this on yourselves by forsaking the Lord your God when he led you in the way?" -Jeremiah 2:17. Every sin is forgiven when in Christ, but there are consequences. "Joy is gone from our hearts; our dancing has turned to mourning. The crown has fallen from our head. Woe to us, for we have sinned! Because of this our hearts are faint, because of these things our eyes grow dim." -Lamentations 5:15-17. "Hear, you earth: I am bringing disaster on this people the fruit of their schemes, because they have not listened to my words and have rejected my law." -Jeremiah 6:19.

Today, many people say it is ok to break the law or go our own way if we are following our hearts. The only problem with this is our hearts are very deceitful. "The heart is deceitful above all things and beyond cure. Who can understand it? I the Lord search the heart and examine the mind, to reward each person according to their conduct, according to what their deeds deserve." -Jeremiah 17:9-10 "...great are your purposes and mighty are your deeds. Your eyes are open to the ways of all mankind; you reward each person according to their conduct and as their deeds deserve." -Jeremiah 32:19 (Matthew 16:27).

The problem is not things, guns, drugs; the problem is our sin. Who is the cure for our sin? Jesus. Even though Satan will continue to tempt us, he cannot see in our hearts. Only God can.

"...then hear from Heaven, your dwelling place. Forgive and act; deal with everyone according to all they do, since you know their hearts (for you alone know every human heart), so that they will fear you all the time they live in the land you gave our ancestors." -1 Kings 8:39-40 (2 Chronicles 6:30 and Acts 1:24).

"And you, my son Solomon, acknowledge the God of your father, and serve him with wholehearted devotion and with a willing mind, for the Lord searches every heart and understand every desire and every thought. If you seek him, he will be found by you; but if you forsake him, he will reject you forever. Consider now, for the Lord has chosen you to build a house as the sanctuary. Be strong and do the work." -1 Chronicles 28:9-10 (Proverbs 5:21).

"He said to them, "You are the ones who justify yourselves in the eyes of others, but God knows your hearts." -Luke 16:15 (Psalm 44:21). "From Heaven the Lord looks down and sees all mankind; from his dwelling place he watches all who live on earth- he who forms the heart of all, who considers everything they do." -Psalm 33:13-15.

Since Satan cannot see in your heart, sometimes it helps to tell him to flee out loud! "Submit yourself, then, to God. Resist the devil, and he will flee from you." -James 4:7. "Resist him (Satan), standing firm in the faith, because you know that the family of believers throughout the world is undergoing the same kind of sufferings." -1 Peter 5:9. It takes a team of us to resist Him. God has provided us as the body of believers as a team to resist his schemes. Just like watching film before a game to know your opponent, we must do the same, and to do so we need to read the play book (the Bible) and get other perspectives of those we trust on our team. Of course, the best help is going to be from the coach himself, Jesus, who literally crushed Him under his feet when he died and rose again on the cross. "Be alert and of sober mind. Your enemy the devil prowls around like a roaring lion looking for someone to devour." -1 Peter 5:8. The devil prowls like a roaring lion, looking for any way to devour you.

Have you seen The. Lion King? Who doesn't love that movie? When Mufasa takes Simba for "pouncing" lessons, he tells him to stay low to the ground, tells him not to make a sound and comes out of nowhere to take him out. The devil may do this by acting like he wants what is best for you, when really, he is waiting for the moment to devour you. This is why the truth tells us to be alert and sober minded, to be prepared and aware of his attacks.

You know that little voice in your head, telling you that you are not good enough, strong enough, pretty enough, worthy enough to live. Those are all lies from the liar himself!

"Why is my language not clear to you? Because you are unable to hear what I say. You belong to your father, the devil, and you want to carry out your father's desires. He was a murderer from the beginning, not holding to the truth, for there is no truth in him. When he lies, he speaks his native language, for he is a liar and the father of lies. Yet because I tell the truth, you do not believe me! Can any of you prove me guilty of sin? If I am telling the truth, why don't you believe me? Whoever belongs to God hears what God says. The reason you do not hear is that you do not belong to God." -John 8:43-47.

He wants you to be envious when you see others. He wants you to be prideful. Satan became the fallen angel he is, due to pride. He wanted the glory instead of

God. It destroyed why God created him, and it will destroy us. Pride is one of the sins I struggle with the most. Pride destroys marriages and relationships because it is what keeps us from showing grace to others. Jesus is the truth, and we need to read and speak the truth to ourselves and each other.

He never wants you to be satisfied when Jesus has paid it all for us. This is truth. Stick to truth. Once you see yourself the way God sees you, you will be able to stand firm no matter what others say. I have always received mixed compliments as far as if I was pretty or not, whether my teeth were straight or not, whether I was skinny or not, whether I was the most athletic or not, smart or not, and I would base my view off these comments. Satan had me believe my value was based off others. Once I knew who I was in Christ, it isn't that other people's opinions did not affect me, but I was able to pick myself up much quicker. I care about what others say in the sense that I truly care about them, and value what they say. I pray about what others say about me, asking God if I should take it as truth to make me better. However, I ultimately know what He says is truth, and when you are confident in who you are, it is tough for others to bring you down.

"Then the Lord your God will make you most prosperous in all the work of your hands and in the fruit of your womb, the young of your livestock and the crops of your land. The Lord will again delight in your ancestors, if you obey the Lord your God and keep his commands and decrees that are written in this Book of the Law and turn to the Lord your God with all your heart and with all your soul." - Deuteronomy 30:9-10 (Proverbs 12:14).

Satan is not only trying to get you to do evil deeds with your life, but he wants you to waste your life. He wants you to become idle. "Our people must learn to devote themselves to doing what is good, in order to provide for urgent needs and not live unproductive lives." -Titus 3:14.

Don't eat anyone's food without paying for it, work night and day to not be a burden not because you don't deserve the help. Paul was being a model for us to imitate. He says the one who is unwilling to work shall not eat. Do not be idle and disruptive. It's ok to be busy, but don't be a busybody, instead be productive. They command in Jesus to earn the food you eat. Never tire of doing good. Pay attention if someone does not follow this instruction and warn them as a fellow believer. 2

Thessalonians 3:7-15 and 1 Thessalonians 5:14 says the same, to encourage the disheartened, help the weak and to be patient with everyone. We are to work and find joy in our work. Part of the fall was how our work unfortunately is toilsome, but when we realize this is what God made us for and is part of our spiritual gift, it can still bring us joy and make us excited within the turmoil. It is only with His help. There are many times in my life I have been a busybody instead of being productive. Paul is clear when we are busy, to make sure it is productive instead of looking like we are being productive.

"God is not unjust; he will not forget your work and the love you have shown him as you have helped his people and continue to help them. We want each of you to show this same diligence to the very end, so that what you hope for may be fully realized. We do not want you to become lazy, but to imitate those who through faith and patience inherit what has been promised." -Hebrews 6:10-12. God sees when you are working and when you love him by loving on his people. This is the opposite of being lazy.

"The lazy do not roast any game, but the diligent feed on the riches of the hunt." -Proverbs 12:27 (Proverbs 21:25 and Proverbs 12:24). "…but the desires of the diligent are fully satisfied" -Proverbs 13:4. "All hard work brings a profit, but mere talk leads only to poverty." -Proverbs 14:23. "Do not love sleep or you will grow poor; stay awake and you will have food to spare." -Proverbs 20:13 (Proverbs 19:15). "The plans of the diligent lead to profit as surely as haste leads to poverty." -Proverbs 21:5. "There I call her Rahab the Do-Nothing." -Isaiah 30:7. "You women who are so complacent, rise up and listen to me." -Isaiah 32:9. "Tremble, you complacent women." -Isaiah 32:11. Amos 6:1 says, "woe to all who are complacent in Zion." "…and punish those who are complacent, who are like wine left on its dregs, who think, "" The Lord will do nothing, either good or bad." -Zephaniah 1:12. "Lazy hands make for poverty, but diligent hands bring wealth." -Proverbs 10:4 (Proverbs 10:5, Proverbs 12:11 and Proverbs 28:19). The proverbs are not promises and I know there are exceptions to this, but the overall wisdom of proverbs tells us that lazy hands, if we sleep too much and if we only talk without work, will make for poverty, and diligent hands will help provide financially. Do not be complacent. God is clear to come to Him in prayer with assistance for our finances, however part of God's design is our work, for us to enjoy our work the best we can and if we aren't to pray to Him about it whether we should get a job or career change, or overall, just change our attitude. It makes me sad when people say like "I can't just pray, I have to do something!" Prayer is the first best thing you can do and is part of the good work. Pray about what physical steps God wants you to take, and then act once you have taken it to Him in prayer. "...Be strong, all you people of the land,' declares the Lord, and work. For I am with you,' declares the Lord Almighty." -Haggai 2:4.

God also wants you to rest. However, God always wants us to work hard and balance with rest. Satan wants you to use your entire life to rest and procrastinate, so you miss out on the awesome opportunities God has for you. Do not let him! "A curse on anyone who is lax in doing the Lord' work! A curse on anyone who keeps their sword from bloodshed!" -Jeremiah 48:10.

Listen, we have all failed at some point in our lives and sometimes this makes you give up. Giving up is Satan's way of convincing you God does not have another plan in mind for your next step. Have you read the promises God has for you?! "This is what the Lord says: I anoint you king over Israel." Then open the door and run; don't delay!" -2 Kings 9:3. "The men in charge of the work were diligent, and repairs progressed under them." -2 Chronicles 24:13. The repairs of your life will progress if you remain diligent and rely on the Lord.

"David also said to Solomon his son, "Be strong and courageous, and do the work. Do not be afraid or discouraged, for the Lord God, my God, is with you. He will not fail you or forsake you..." -1 Chronicles 28:20. Do the work without fear for God is always with us. A door for effective work was opened, and people oppose Paul in 1 Corinthians 16:9. Paul says when he went to Troas to preach the gospel, he saw the Lord open a door. (See 2 Corinthians 2:12). He sees your work. Solomon stood before the altar of the Lord spread out his hands toward Heaven and said, "There is no one like you God in Heaven or on earth who keeps their covenant of love with his servants who continue in you wholeheartedly who kept his promise with David by mouth and his hands have fulfilled it." -1 Kings 8:22-24 (2 Chronicles 6:4 and 1 Kings 8:54).

"Then David said to God, "I have sinned greatly by doing this. Now, I beg you, take away the guilt of your servant. I have done a very foolish thing." -1

Chronicles 21:8. What a wretched man I am! Who will rescue me from this body that is subject to death? Thanks be to God, who delivers me through Jesus Christ our Lord!" -Romans 7:24-25 (Psalm 37:40). God has rescued us from ourselves. We are no longer a slave to Satan, to sin. When we ask God to take away our guilt, to save us from death, He delivers.

"Then, after desire has conceived, it gives birth to sin; and sin, when it is full-grown, gives birth to death." -James 1:15. Sin starts in our minds, our hearts as our desires. It grows, becomes actions, and eventually the consequence for our sin is spiritual death, Hell, where Satan will be and where he wants us to join him. "The plans of the righteous are just, but the advice of the wicked is deceitful." -Proverbs 12:5. The devil's advice is deceitful, and even if others don't realize it, if they do not have the Holy Spirit, their advice can be deceitful too.

"Jesus was disappointed the disciples could not stay up to keep watch while he prayed, and he said to watch and pray so we do not fall into temptation because the spirit is willing, but the flesh is weak." -Matthew 26:40-41 (Mark 14:37-38). Prayer is so important because having a personal relationship with Jesus is the only way we can overcome our fallen flesh with its desires and wickedness. Even if we are willing to do what is right, we do not have the power without prayer, without Jesus. Therefore, the best self-help book cannot help you, because it cannot give you the power you need to overcome the dark spiritual forces and the desires of the flesh.

Peter says how Ananias's heart must have been filled with Satan because he lied to the Holy Spirit for money. What made him do such a thing? Ananias did not just lie to human beings but to God. (See Acts 5:3-4). There are false apostles, deceitful workers, and even Satan and his servants come off like angels of light. (See 2 Corinthians 11:13-15). I think people think of finding the schemes of Satan in the darkest places, and this is true. However, as we can see, he also appears as light. This can be in the church, or anyone who appears to have the light but is not living by the truth or other religions. "The coming of the lawless one will be in accordance with how Satan works. He will use all sorts of displays of power through signs and wonders that serve the lie." -2 Thessalonians 2:9. "This is how you can recognize the Spirit of God: Every spirit that acknowledges that Jesus Christ has come in the flesh is from God." -1 John 4:2 (1 John 4:5-6).

"We know that anyone born of God does not continue to sin; the One who was born of God keeps them safe, and the evil one cannot harm them. We know that we are children of God, and that the whole world is under the control of the evil one. We know also that the Son of God has come and has given us understanding, so that we may know him who is true. And we are in him who is true by being in his Son Jesus Christ. He is the true God and eternal life. Dear children, keep yourselves from idols." -1 John 5:18-21.

I am amazed that God chooses us to be a part of his family. He already saw our whole lives before we were born, all the wrong choices we were going to make, and still decided to adopt us into his family! I think people struggle at the word adoption, as they think their parents didn't want them, when if you think about it, the parents who adopted you chose you!

"Therefore rejoice, you Heavens and you who dwell in them! But woe to the earth and the sea, because the devil has gone down to you! He is filled with fury, because he knows that his time is short." -Revelation 12:12. Satan knows his time is short and is trying to destroy all he can here on earth, including me, you, us. "Then the dragon was enraged at the woman and went off to wage war against the rest of her offspring—those who keep God's commands and hold fast their testimony about Jesus." -Revelation 12:17. We must be always ready.

The devil who deceived them, the beast and the false prophet will all be in the lake of fire in torment forever. (See Revelation 20:10 and Matthew 25:41). You can read in Revelation 20:15 that it says all who are not in the lamb's book of life will as well. The good news is, if you come to Christ, you will be in the book of life, saved for eternity with Christ, giving you hope in the darkest times we will face while in this world! "There will be a time of distress such as has not happened from the beginning of nations until then. But at that time your people- everyone whose name is found written in the book- will be delivered." -Daniel 12:1. If you do not have Jesus as your Lord to save you from Satan, you will have his same destiny. The amazing news is you do not have to if you choose Him as your Savior!

The second you do not think Satan is real, he has that much more of an advantage because you won't be prepared against his tactics. He is the one putting all the negative self-talk in your head. Tell Satan to back off! God speaks the truth, that you are forgiven. "The thief comes only to steal and kill and destroy; I have come that they may have life and have it to the full." -John 10:10. "When I am lifted up from the earth, I will draw people to myself." -John 12:32. When Jesus is talking about having life to the fullest, it is not a life in which you get everything you desire. It is a life where with Jesus, He is always enough no matter what you have or what you are going through. God's will is not easy for us to understand, and by not easy I mean impossible, but we know the ending. Naturally being an athlete, I am going to compare it to a softball game. Many different strategies and skills go into a win, but the end is home base. Stay focused on home, and all the steps leading up to it God, our coach, will make sense to defeat Satan, the enemy!

A Broken Heart

"I can do all things through Christ who strengthens me." Philippians 4:13

I can have *hope and overcome death physically and emotionally* through Christ who strengthens me.

It's not supposed to be this way. All the problems, stress and heart break were not how God created this world to work in His original design. There are situations and circumstances in our lives where we just cannot find the words to express to others how we feel. Even the ones we love most cannot seem to bring us comfort during these times. You know the times I am talking about where it feels like you can't breathe. Sometimes to the point where you wonder if life is worth it. Situations where you question God. Question how a good God can let something like this happen. Death. Life altering diagnosis. Break-Up. Divorce. Affairs. Losing your job. Infertility. Imprisonment. Rejection of your life dreams, goals, and schools. Times where you are convinced there is not even the smallest speck of hope. I am here to tell you, there is. You have been knocked down, but after you read this, God will help you get back up. "The Lord makes firm the steps of the one who delights in him; though he may stumble, he will not fall, for the Lord upholds him with his hand." -Psalm 37:23-24 (1 Chronicles 12:18). "I consider that our present sufferings are not worth comparing with the glory that will be revealed in us." -Romans 8:18. The worst of what you are going through now cannot compare with the glory that will be reveled in us, when we have Jesus.

Life is hard, really hard. However, God has equipped us to be able to cope with it. One of my best friends, Lauren, once boldly and confidently stated that if God has allowed a painful situation to happen, whether it was in her life through a relationship or problems with miscarriages and infertility, God would put it on her heart to be ok and to have peace. What amazed me was her trust in God even though she had tears and was hurting. She trusted God as the giver and taker of life, the child is His to give and take, and on His timing. Our life is not our own, it is God's, and this can either frustrate us (I have been there) or completely comfort us. He cares more about our lives, pain and situations than we do, and He wants His story written out perfectly for us.

Flashbacks and nightmares are part of healing that result from trauma, helping us process what we are going through. We do relaxation techniques and social support. It is proven in therapy if you have people with the same diagnosis treated at the same time it improves their outcome. Cognitive-behavioral therapy (CBT) where the therapist acts as an educator teaching patients to become more aware of what and how they are thinking and feeling, and how to change their thinking and behavior based on the knowledge.

"Blessed are those who mourn, for they will be comforted." -Matthew 5:4. There is a big difference how the Bible tells us to mourn and the world. When I experienced pain, I was shocked at how many people say to move on immediately. It was almost as if the world felt the source of healing is simply distraction, instead of going to the healer himself. "Those who sow with tears will reap with song of joy. Those who go out weeping, carrying see to sow, will return with songs of joy, carrying sheaves with them." -Psalm 126:5-6. Pain is real. God can turn your pain to peace, but the only way is to go through pain and get in the Word. Search after Him many times before you feel the peace. Grief is a way of God letting us know something is not right, that something is happening that He did not design for us to originally go through before sin entered the world. This world is beyond broken. When we experience these situations where we find it hard to breathe and go on, God says to mourn. I think as Christians, we have the false impression God always expects us to have a smile on our face. Yes, he does call us to have an eternal joy, but this is so much different than a temporary earthly happiness. God wants us to be genuine.

Never force yourself or anyone out of their grief, but simply be there alongside them as they grieve, checking in on them. I am one that desires to fix everyone's problems, but I am not God. However, Jesus can and reminding someone of our Savior's love by being with them in the hard time is everything. As much as I want to help, especially when someone has lost a loved, all you can do is let the individual know how sorry you are and that you are praying for them, continuing to check-in. It is a tough balance in the sense you never want to be forceful by asking someone if you can bring them a meal, but often they appreciate it, and even if they are not ready to see you or have interaction with others, you can always drop it off. Sometimes when we ask others to let us know when they need help, they do not feel comfortable doing so.

Jesus knows the pain. He experienced every hurt we could possibly imagine all at one time. Abandonment from his disciples and family, even abandonment from Himself (aka God) for a split second when God had to pour the wrath of all our sins on Him. Even though we mourn, we mourn with hope. Hope that this world is not all there is, and hope being with Christ in Heaven is better than here. The thought of going to Heaven should make us excited, not because we have this vision of getting everything we could ever want, but because Jesus is there. We are so in love with Him that that is the only place we want to be. "The righteous cry out, and the Lord hears them; he delivers them from all their troubles. The Lord is close to the brokenhearted and saves those who are crushed in spirit." -Psalm 34:17-18 (Psalm 54:7). Jesus is here to heal your broken heart. Many times, we feel a sense of guilt when moving forward with our lives after losing someone who could not be closer to us. We need to remind ourselves it is not that we are moving on, only moving forward. If we do not mourn, we can fall into depression. Kubler-Ross stages of grief are denial, anger, depression and integration. Also, depression can come off as denial and poor attention to substance abuse. I feel we rotate between all of these when grieving and there does not always seem to be the clear-cut order. I want to encourage you that if you try to avoid grieving and mourning, it does not get rid of the feelings. Even if in the moment you do not feel the weight and depth of the cut, it will linger. Just like my patients who may think that not looking at their arm or not doing their therapy will make their diagnosis "get better," but they will soon realize the pain continues to linger. Be patient with yourself during this hard time, and understand even when your emotions change, God has not. God is deeper than your feelings, wants you to talk to Him about how you feel and know He cares.

People will say they have tried to find God, not have had no luck but this can't be true. "Come near to God and he will come near to you." -James 4:8 (Lamentations 3:57). Tired of waiting on God? Maybe he is waiting on you! Just like other relationships, you will also come to find if you do not actively pursue or put that time into practice, you may feel the intimacy fading. This is never because God has moved, but we do. God is ever present no matter how we feel. Our feelings are not truth. We do not feel his presence because in our darkest times we tend to withdraw. I know I have. God is saying to stay near to him by continuing to pray, talking to him, even if you're talking is tears and yelling. This also means talking to people God has given you. Do not leave yourself in isolation. Satan loves when we are isolated, because he can better get into our head and thoughts, using our weaknesses to destroy us. Lay your pride down and get help. "Love the Lord, all his faithful people! The Lord preserves those who are true to him, but the proud he pays back in full. Be strong and take heart, all you who hope in the Lord." -Psalm 31:23-24.

Ask others to pray for you. You do not even have to talk about the situation if you do not want. Just surround yourself with your family and friends. Even though our circumstances are not always good, God still is. Only he can have the power to turn our dark situations into hopeful circumstances. When I have gone through dark times, sometimes it helps remembering Jesus gave his all for me, and that is enough. Sometimes I feel as if God owes me. As if he needs to turn this situation around for me. Even though He wants to, and ultimately will, I know in the end He has already given more than I could ever need. We deserve condemnation, and anything good we ever get is a blessing. I think we forget that. "We are hard pressed on every side, but not crushed; perplexed but not in despair; persecuted, but not abandoned; struck down, but not destroyed." -2 Corinthians 4:8-9. Through the worst hurts, God will heal what is impossible to do on our own. "No one will be able to stand against you all the days of your life. As I was with Moses, so I will be with you; I will never leave nor forsake you." -Joshua 1:5.

When we are diagnosed with a life-threatening or life-changing disease, it can be hard to see the purpose. "When he heard this, Jesus said, "This sickness will not end in death. No, it is for God's glory so that God's son may be glorified through it." -John 11:4. Nothing can happen to you without God's permission. Does this mean God creates evil or if you sin and there are consequences, that its God's fault? No. He does not cause evil but with our free will He allows it and uses them because He is more powerful. You see, if He did not give us the ability to have free will, there would be no ability for us to freely choose to love him either. God knew the wrong choices we would make but having a genuine love and relationship with us must mean He thought it was worth it.

When I am in pain, I want to argue that God should have never created us in the first place. Why make us or put us in situations that are only going to hurt? We have all experienced this type of pain. What I realize though when I argue that God should not have created me, is that I am arguing with the very being that gave me the ability to argue at all. When you let your kids choose their gender, or if you yourself have chosen to have a different gender, you are going against the very being which gave you the ability to choose in the first place. If you love God, He will work this out for your good. He will work this out for you. I may not know you, but I am confident in this because I am confident in Him. "I prayed to the Lord my God and confessed: "Lord, the great and awesome God, who keeps his covenant of love with those who love him and keep his commandments." -Daniel 9:4 (Nehemiah 4:14). This is hard for us to wrap our minds around because God is clear "For my thoughts are not your thoughts, neither are your ways my ways," declares the Lord. "As the Heavens are higher than the earth, so are my ways higher than your ways and my thoughts higher than your thoughts." -Isaiah 55:8-10. "Yes, from ancient days I am he. No one can deliver out of my hand. When I act, who can reverse it?" -Isaiah 43:13. "As you do not know the path of the wind, or how the body is formed in a mother's womb, so you cannot understand the work of God, the Maker of all things." -Ecclesiastes 11:5 (Isaiah 44:24-25 and Jeremiah 50:19).

"So is my word that goes out from my mouth: It will not return to me empty but will accomplish what I desire and achieve the purpose for which I sent it. You will go out in joy and be led forth in peace; the mountains and hills will burst into song before you, and all the trees of the field will clap their hands. Instead of the thornbush will grow the juniper, and instead of briers the myrtle will grow. This will be for the Lord's renown, for an everlasting sign, that will endure forever." -Isaiah 55:11-13 (Ecclesiastes 3:14).

"For the foolishness of God is wiser than human wisdom, and the weakness of God is stronger than human strength." -1 Corinthians 1:25.

Listen, this does not mean God approves sin such as murder, divorce, rape or any other tragedy that happens in our life. All this means is God is more powerful than it. His thoughts, ways and plan can make good out of it when we turn to Him. God creating good in our lives is not saying He approved of the sin, but it is His grace overcoming our sin and others that are affecting us. "The anger of the Lord will not turn back until he fully accomplishes the purpose of his heart. In days to come you will understand it clearly." -Jeremiah 23:20 (Jeremiah 30:24).

Death. It is hard to wrap our minds around and for many is even scary to think about.

"For if we have been united with Him in a death like His, we will certainly also be united with Him in a resurrection like His. For we know that our old self was crucified so that the body rules by sin might be done away with, that we should no longer be slaves to sin- because anyone who has died has been set free from sin. Now if we died with Christ, we believe that we will also live with Him. For we know that since Christ was raised from the dead, he cannot die again; death no longer has mastery over Him." -Romans 6:5-9.

There you have it. We who has died with Christ have overcome death. Defeated it.

This is the only way we can see the true power of Christ in full circle. Even though we will die on this earth, it will end up being our biggest blessing. "For we know that if the earthly tent we live in is destroyed, we have a building from God, an eternal house in Heaven, not built by human hands. Meanwhile we groan, longing to be clothed instead with our Heavenly dwelling." -2 Corinthians 5:1-2.

" Now the one who has fashioned us for this very purpose is God, who has given us the Spirit as a deposit, guaranteeing what is to come. Therefore, we are always confident and know that as long as we are at home in the body we are away from the Lord. For we live by faith, not by sight. We are confident, I say, and would prefer to be away from the body and at home with the Lord. So, we make it our goal to please him, whether we are at home in the body or away from it. For we must all appear before the judgment seat of Christ, so that each of us may receive what is due us for the things done while in the body, whether good or bad." -2 Corinthians 5:5-10.

When you die and are before God, it will not matter what your friend, family member, patients or neighbors think of you. The truth of your thoughts, deeds and actions will be fully exposed in truth in front of God. What will we do when the "curtain" is pulled away and this world that we think is all there is, is gone? What will you say when you are in the presence of complete power and holiness? Death is scary to think about, but it no longer has the power to physically destroy us. "I am the resurrection and the life; he that believes in me, though he were dead, yet shall live and whosoever lives and believe in me shall never die." -John 11:25-26. The pain when you lose someone you love is more than we can handle on our own. I know. This is not to tell you the pain is not real. This is to give you hope through the pain and through my love for you. I am telling you this because I need to hear it it too. We all do. I think what makes death so hard for us to understand is that it seems permanent because this world is all we know. Once we remember this world is only temporary, it helps us cope a little bit more. Heaven will be the most perfect place, beyond anything we can long for. "Better is one day in your courts than a thousand elsewhere." -Psalm 84:10.

At a funeral, a common question for both the giving and receiving end is "What should I say?" We have all been in these situations. You are hurting for the individual and cannot find the words you think will bring comfort. Advice is not all we need in dark times. When I have a loved one going through a dark time, sometimes the best thing you can do is just be there for them, even if you do not know what to say. Sit with them, hug them and cry with them. We do not know what to say because we were never made for death until sin entered the world. Death is where humanity is confronted with God because it is out of our control, and we know it cannot be the end. When people are asked after a funeral what they remember, many times they honestly do not remember words, but who was there. When my Grandpa passed away, my Grandma asked, "Why would God take my Dad and now my husband?" Do you think this is a moment when God wants us to say this is His plan? People need your presence more than your advice, so do not be anxious or worry about what to say. God is bigger than your words and bigger than the worst trauma. Keep their hope alive, even if they do not believe there is hope, you can believe it for them. Do not force anyone to feel anything they cannot when they are struggling. Just be there for them, through every stage. Just continue to be the quiet whisper letting them know there is hope. Also, remembering anniversaries of the dates people have lost their loved ones, including miscarriages, and sending them texts, cards, or reminders that you are thinking of them, can make all the difference.

"Brothers and sisters, we do not want you to be uninformed about those who sleep in death, so that you do not grieve like the rest of mankind, who have no hope. For we believe that Jesus died and rose again, and so we believe that God will bring them with Jesus those who have fallen asleep with him." -1 Thessalonians 4:13-14 (Isaiah 26:19).

Funerals are a gift from God telling us there is more than this. If you do not have Jesus, you have no hope of resurrected life, but the great news is you can come to Him today and have hope, even through death.

"Taste and see that the Lord is good; blessed if the one who takes refuge in him." -Psalm 34:8. Here comes the famous question. "If God is good, why do bad things happen?" "'This is the verdict: Light has come into the world, but people loved darkness instead of light because their deeds were evil." -John 3:19. Free will. We have the choice every day to choose God or our own way. As people, all of us, every single one of us want our own way. When we choose anything apart from God, this is what is known as sin. Psychologists say there is something wrong with people, we call it sin. It has affected every part of us to our minds. "I say to the Lord, "You are my Lord; apart from you I have no good thing." -Psalm 16:2. You may be thinking, "Why can't God just get rid of all of the evil?" Then He would have to get rid of us. He created us knowing He would have to sacrifice His son for us. It tells us we have more purpose, even through the pain and suffering more than we can imagine.

Sin has consequences. The Bible makes that quite clear. Therefore, God gives us instruction in the Bible. Not to restrain us but quite the opposite. To free us from sin and its chains because he loves us. "...to say to the captives, "Come out," and to those in darkness, "Be free!" -Isaiah 49:9 (Psalm 107:14-15, Psalm 107:21 and Psalm 107:31).

"Here is my servant, whom I uphold, my chosen one in whom I delight; I will put my Spirit on him, and he will bring justice to the nations. He will not shout or cry out or raise his voice in the streets. A bruised reed he will not break, and a smoldering wick he will not snuff out. In faithfulness he will bring forth justice; he will not falter or be discouraged till he establishes justice on earth. In his teaching the islands will put their hope." This is what God the Lord says—the Creator of the Heavens, who stretches them out, who spreads out the earth with all that springs from it, who gives breath to its people, and life to those who walk on it: "I, the Lord, have called you in righteousness; I will take hold of your hand. I will keep you and will make you to be a covenant for the people and a light for the Gentiles, to open eyes that are blind, to free captives from prison and to release from the dungeon those who sit in darkness." -Isaiah 42:1-7.

It is not freedom to make choices that will lead to death or destroy our lives. Therefore, the mentality that we are free to sin, since Christ has set us free, is all wrong. Sinning is not freedom, it is destruction.

Alright, next question you may be wondering. "Why the heck would God give us free will when He knew how broken this world would become!?" The word is love. What? Yes, love. Even though we can choose our own way, He also knows we can choose Him. God doesn't want robotic people He forces to love him. He is not an evil dictator. God does not need us. He decided to create you because when He pictured His family, He saw you in it. When you love someone, no matter how hard it is, you do not force them to love you back. You know this would not be genuine love. To answer the ultimate question of "Why is there so much bad if God is good?" Free will.

However, good happens because of grace. God does not create bad or pain but uses our suffering for a greater purpose. God knew we would all fail. Therefore, since the beginning of time He has had the salvation plan already made. This plan is Jesus and His death on the cross for you and for me. "Here is a trustworthy saying: If we died with him, we would also live with him; if we endure, we will also reign with him. If we disown him, he will also disown us; If we are faithless, he remains faithful, for he cannot disown himself." -2 Timothy 2:11-13. "What if some were unfaithful? Will their unfaithfulness nullify God's faithfulness? Not at all! Let God be true, and every human being a liar." -Romans 3:3-4. "All the ways of the Lord are loving and faithful..." -Psalm 25:10. "...nor will he see the good things I will do for my people." -Jeremiah 29:32.

"And if not, He is still good." -Daniel 3:18. God loves you; do you know that? We live in a broken world where it seems like the pain will never end. To be honest, it will never end while we are here. "In this world you will have trouble but take heart! I have overcome the world." -John 16:33. "For everyone born of God overcomes the world. This is the victory that has overcome the world, even our faith. Who is it that overcomes the world? Only the one who believes that Jesus is the Son of God." -1 John 5:4-5. It is clear we will have trouble and should not be surprised by it. However, it is also clear we are to take heart. "The righteous person may have many troubles, but the Lord delivers him from them all." -Psalm 34:19 (2 Samuel 4:9 and Psalm 32:7).

Life is short. Ask someone in their old age. Many will say it seems like everything happened in the blink of an eye. Thinking of this perspective does not make it any easier to face our pain, however it gives us hope the suffering will end. In the end, Jesus wins. In the end it will all be alright. Until then, we are to take heart while we are here in the world to help us sleep a little better at night knowing God has everything under control even when we do not. We will never be able to understand our pain because our minds are so finite here on earth. We need to put our trust in our God who is infinite. God is the one who gave us a mind to be able to comprehend pain and situations in our lives in the first place.

Who better to trust with it? God will do more than you can imagine even when his answer is no. A no from God means He may have something better in mind. Trust Him. His plan is better than ours. Every. Time. Whenever I question God why I was made, why I have the body I do, why do I have to experience pain. I realize who am I to question. "Trust in him at all times, you people; pour out your hearts to him, for God is our refuge." -Psalm 62:8. David is telling us to pour out our hearts. If we do not pour out our hearts to God, we will pour them out in ways that will hurt us whether in anger, rage or depression. "Ah, Sovereign Lord, you have made the Heavens and the earth by your great power and outstretched arm. Nothing is too hard for you." -Jeremiah 32:17.

You may be suffering worse than you can handle on your own but take hope nothing is too hard for God. Pray. Do not give up. Trust not in your situations, but God's character. "Since ancient times no one has heard, no ear has perceived, no eye has seen any God besides you, who acts on behalf of those who wait for him." -Isaiah 64:4.

"For when you did awesome things that we did not expect, you came down, and the mountains trembled before you. Since ancient times no one has heard, no ear has perceived, no eye has seen any God besides you, who acts on behalf of those who wait for him. You come to the help of those who gladly do right, who remember your ways." -Isaiah 64:3-5.

That glorious day when we see Jesus, it will all make sense. "He will wipe every tear from their eyes. There will be no more death or mourning or crying or pain, for the old order of things has passed away." -Revelation 21:4.

We need to be excited, Jesus is coming back! God will make everything right. For now, even though it seems impossible, know we can have a peace from God that will not make sense to the world. "And the peace of God, which transcends all understanding, will guard your heart and your minds in Christ Jesus." -Philippians 4:7. "All this comes from the Lord Almighty, whose plan is wonderful, and whose wisdom is magnificent." -Isaiah 28:29. The only thing that keeps me going when my world is falling apart is starting from the book of Genesis to the end of the Bible. God's purpose is unstoppable if you read from beginning to end, even though the horrible brokenness. You see us, people, messing up our lives or others, and God making it for good. I think of Joseph, the son of Jacob and Rachel "You intended to harm me, but God intended it for good to accomplish what is now being done, the saving of many lives." -Genesis 50:20. Joseph was sold into slavery by his brothers out of envy, accused of adultery when he was clean, forgotten in prison when he helped someone else escape, but God ultimately led him to rule with Pharaoh during the famine through his interpretation of dreams. At the end, he tests his brothers' character by placing silver on the table, accusing the brother Benjamin of taking it, but then his brother Judah offers to take his brothers place when he says he must stay. He knows God used this situation for good. Then, Jacob and Joseph are reunited. In the end, we will see how he used our fall of humanity for his divine plan. He will use the wrong that happens to us and the mistakes we make for good. It will all make sense once we are in Heaven.

Have you ever heard the phrase; time heals all wounds? I have never bought it. You never stop missing someone once they die, you just train your mind to focus on eternity. I think if you talk to people who have lost their parents, a child, a spouse, or have experienced rape, an affair, abuse, a broken heart or whatever the situation, they will tell you the same thing. The only one who heals wounds is God. Only God has the power. Even if time temporarily cover up a wound, it cannot heal something so deep. God knows the pain of losing a child, only He can understand. "Have you not heard? Long ago I ordained it. In days of old I planned it; now I have brought it to pass..." -2 Kings 20:22. This is the very essence of the Bible. It is one big redemptive plan from the beginning of Abraham, all the way to his descendant Jesus, our Savior. "This man will not be your heir, but a son who is your own flesh and blood will be your heir." He took him outside and said, "Look up at the sky and count the stars-if indeed you can count them." Then he said to him, "So shall your offspring be." -Genesis 15:4-5. Seems simple enough, but Abraham and Sarah became inpatient in God's perfect timing. "Now Sarai, Abram's wife, had borne him no children. But she had an Egyptian slave named Hagar, so she said to Abram," The Lord has kept me from having children. Go, sleep with my slave; perhaps I can build a family through her." Abram agreed to what Sarai said. So, after Abram had been living in Canaan ten years, Sarai, his wife, took her Egyptian slave Hagar and gave her to her husband to be his wife. He slept with Hagar, and she conceived." - Genesis 16:1-4. This was Ishmael. "...and Abram (that is, Abraham).

"The sons of Abraham: Isaac an Ishmael." -1 Chronicles 1:27-28. "Abraham was the father of Isaac. The sons of Isaac: Esau and Israel." -1 Chronicles 1:34.

"I will bless her so that she will be the mother of nations; kings of peoples will come from her." Abraham fell facedown; he laughed and said to himself," Will a son be born to a man a hundred years old? Will Sarah bear a child at the age of ninety?" -Genesis 17:16-17.

"Then God said, "Yes, but your wife Sarah will bear you a son, and you will call him Isaac. I will establish my covenant with him as an everlasting covenant for his descendants after him." -Genesis 17:19 (Leviticus 26:9). "But the Lord was gracious to them and had compassion and showed concern for them because of his covenant with Abraham, Isaac and Jacob. To this day he has been unwilling to destroy them or banish them from his presence." -2 Kings 13:23 (Leviticus 26:42 and Leviticus 26:45).

Then the Lord said to Abraham, "Why did Sarah laugh and say, 'Will I really have a child, now that I am old?' Is there anything too hard for the Lord?" -Genesis 18:13-14. "Now the Lord was gracious to Sarah as he had said, and the Lord did for Sarah what he had promised. Sarah became pregnant and bore a son to Abraham in his old age, at the very time God had promised him. Abraham gave the name Isaac to the son Sarah bore him." -Genesis 21:1-3. Then, after finally having his son, God tested Abraham's faith asking him to sacrifice Isaac. God did not do this to tempt Abraham, God is not interested in child sacrifice and was not sinning, however we are all to put God even before our own family, and this was also a look into the future of how God would have to sacrifice Jesus for our sins. "Then God said, 'Take your son, you only son, whom you love-Isaac-and go to the region of Moriah. Sacrifice him there as a burnt offering on the mountain I will show you.'" - Genesis 22:2.

"Do not lay a hand on the boy," he said, "Do not do anything to him. Now I know that you fear God, because you have not withheld from me your son, your only son." -Genesis 22:12. "The angel of the Lord called to Abraham from Heaven a second time and said, "I swear by myself, declares the Lord, that because you have done this and have not withheld your son, your only son, I will surely bless you and make your descendants as numerous as the stars in the sky and as the sand on the seashore. Your descendants will take possession of the cities of their enemies and through your offspring all nations on earth will be blessed, because you have obeyed me." -Genesis 22:15-18.

Isaac married Rebekah and had twins, Jacob and Esau. "When Isaac was old and his eyes were so weak that he could no longer see, he called for Esau his older son and said to him, "My son." "Here I am," he answered. Isaac said, "I am now an old man and don't know the day of my death. Now then, get your equipment-your quiver and bow- and go out to the open country to hunt some wild game for me. Prepare me the kind of tasty food I like and bring it to me to eat, so that I may give you my blessing before I die." -Genesis 27:1-4. Genesis 27:6-14 says Rebekah told Jacob to steal the blessing and to pretend he is his brother. Even through adultery, lying, distrusting God and more sin, God still chose to work through and ultimately Jesus came from Abraham's line just as He will work through each of us. God chose to bless Jacob even when he sinned against Him, because of Jacob's heart desiring God. God does not depend on our sins and our free will and will use you even if you have deceived or sinned in other ways like Jacob.

When I die, I want my loved ones to rejoice knowing God's timing is perfect, even when it does not make sense on our timing. He is the best friend; Savior and Father I could ever hope for. I hope He changes your heart the same way He has changed mine. You want proof God exists? You want proof Jesus died and rose again? Look at my heart. He has changed it. Our hearts and our lives will never have full and complete satisfaction until we are in Heaven, our true home. Think of who you love more than anyone. If I asked you if they were real, you would say of course! I feel the same about God. Of course, He is real because I love Him, have a relationship with Him and He has changed my life. I can't just tell you the person you love doesn't exist because you love them. I would be crazy if I claimed that, wouldn't I? I once had to break up with an individual because they did not have faith. Their response was, "This is stupid, you are breaking up with me over someone/something you can't see or know exists." They couldn't see the love that was more real to me than anything in my life, and you may not realize it, but in your life too. "I love you Lord, my strength." -Psalm 18:1.

"David sang to the Lord the words of this song when the Lord delivered him from the hand of all his enemies and from the hand of Saul. He said: "The Lord is my rock, my fortress and my deliverer; my God is my rock, in whom I take refuge, my shield and the horn of my salvation. He is my stronghold, my refuge, and my savior-from violent people you save me. "I called to the Lord, who is worthy of praise, and have been saved from my enemies. The waves of death swirled about me; the torrents of destruction overwhelmed me. The cords of the grave coiled around me; the snares of death confronted me. "In my distress I called to the Lord; I called out to my God. From his temple he heard my voice; my cry came to his ears." -2 Samuel 22:1-7 (Psalm 18:2-6).

I think most would argue the worst experience we can have in this life is death. Even if it coils around you, or those you love, God hears you and is right there to sustain you as your rock, refuge and shield, your Savior through the worst of this life.

"He reached down from on high and took hold of me; he drew me out of deep waters. He rescued me from my powerful enemy, from my foes, who were too strong for me. They confronted me in the day of my disaster, but the Lord was my support. He brought me out into a spacious place; he rescued me because he delighted in me. The Lord has dealt with me according to my righteousness; according to the cleanness of my hands he has rewarded me. For I have kept the ways of the Lord; I am not guilty of turning from my God. All his laws are before me I have not turned away from his decrees. I have been blameless before him and have kept myself from sin. The Lord has rewarded me according to my righteousness, according to my cleanness in his sight. To the faithful you show yourself faithful to the blameless you show yourself blameless, to the pure you show yourself pure, but to the devious you show yourself shrewd. You save the humble, but your eyes are on the haughty to bring them low. You, Lord, are my lamp; the Lord turns my darkness into light. With your help I can advance against a troop; with my God I can scale a wall. As for God, his way is perfect: The Lord's word is flawless; he shields all who take refuge in him. For who is God besides the Lord? And who is the Rock except our God? It is God who arms me with strength and keeps my way secure. He makes my feet like the feet of a deer; he causes me to stand on the heights. He trains my hands for battle; my arms can bend a bow of bronze. You make your saving help my shield; your help has made me great. You provide a broad path for my feet, so that my ankles do not give way." -2 Samuel 22:17-37 (Psalm 18:16-36).

God rescues those who confide in Him. How do you confide in Him? Getting in his word, which is flawless. It will be your shield. I have been so completely disappointed in myself when I have been so upset at God to the point, at my lowest, I have thrown my Bible against the wall. The thing was, after I did it, I eventually picked it up and continued to pursue Him at my weakest, when I felt hopeless at my lowest, I can attest His word will be your shield when you cannot be lower, at your lowest. As I was faithless, He remained faithful when I picked it back up. He picked me up, emotionally, mentally, and physically as I wept.

"Let the beloved of the Lord rest secure in him, for he shields him all day long, and the one the Lord loves rests between his shoulders." -Deuteronomy 33:12. "I trained them and strengthened their arms, but they plot evil against me." -Hosea 7:15. "Why has the Lord done such a thing to this land and to this temple?" People will answer, "Because they have forsaken the Lord their God, who brought their ancestors out of Egypt, and have embraced other gods, worshiping and serving them- that is why the Lord brought all this disaster on them." -1 Kings 9:8-9, (2 Chronicles 7:22 and Jeremiah 22:8-9). "Though his disease severe, even in his illness he did not seek help from the Lord, but only from the physicians. Then in the forty-first year of his reign Asa died and rested with his ancestors." -2 Chronicles 16:12-13. I work for upper extremity surgeons and with upper extremity therapists and let me tell you, they are phenomenal. I have learned so much working for and with them, however I understand God has given them the ability to heal and has rewarded all their incredibly hard work through our practice. Without His healing power over His people we treat, I know it would not be possible to have the success we do, considering the reason we even take our next breath is because of Him. When we are struggling with trauma or coping, this is humbling and relieving to remember.

Then the Lord said to Satan, "Have you considered my servant Job? There is no one on earth like him; he is blameless and upright, a man who fears God and shuns evil." Does Job fear God for nothing? Satan replied. "You have blessed the work of his hands." -Job 1:8-10 (Job 1:1). The Lord said to Satan, "Very well, then, everything he has is in your power, but on the man, himself do not lay a finger." -Job 1:12. Now, Job 1:14 says his animals were taken. Job 1:19 says his sons and daughters were taken when a wind struck the house. Satan argued Job worshiped and served God because He blessed Him for his life. God knew Job's heart. He did not serve God because of the blessings, He served God because He loves Him.

"At this, Job got up and tore his robe and shaved his head. Then he fell to the ground in worship and said: "Naked I came from my mother's womb, and naked I will depart. The Lord gave and the Lord has taken away; may the name of the Lord be praised." In all this, Job did not sin by charging God with wrongdoing." -Job 1:20-22.

"Then the Lord said to Satan, "Have you considered my servant Job? There is no one on earth like him; he is blameless and upright, a man who fears God and shuns evil. And he still maintains his integrity, though you incited me against him to ruin him without any reason." -Job 2:3. Job still mourned. Job was not told to be happy when his life fell apart, simply trust God that He would make it right. Job realized we do not deserve anything. We came into the world with nothing and will leave with nothing.

"…strike his flesh and bones, and he will surely curse you to your face." The Lord said to Satan, "Very well, then, he is in your hands; but you must spare his life." So, Satan went out from the presence of the Lord and afflicted Job with painful sores from the soles of his feet to the crown of his head." -Job 2:5-7. "His wife said to him, "Are you still maintaining your integrity? Curse God and die!" He replied, "You are talking like a foolish woman. Shall we accept good from God, and not trouble?" In all this, Job did not sin in what he said." -Job 2:9-10. Even though

Satan had free reign, God was still in control as he had to spare his life. When Job's wife told Job to curse God for what He was going through, it proved Job's heart was not to gain from God. He served God because He has a genuine relationship with Him and loves Him.

In Job 2:11 Job's friends heard his trouble and went to sympathize and comfort him. Job 2:13 says his friends sat with him for 7 days and nights and didn't say a word because they saw how much he was suffering. "He performs wonders that cannot be fathomed, miracles that cannot be counted. He provides rain for the earth; he sends water on the countryside. The lowly he sets on high, and those who mourn are lifted to safety." -Job 5:9-11. I love how Job's friends comfort him. They sat with him, stayed with him and knew no words could heal the pain he was going through; however, he needed their presence. I believe God designed something powerful in our presence that words cannot do justice when we are suffering at our worst. Let this give you peace when you want to comfort others and do not know what to say. Those who mourn will be lifted to safety through the God whose miracles cannot be counter, the ultimate provider of all things.

"...but whoever listens to me will live in safety and be at ease, without fear of harm" Proverbs 1:33. "Indeed, this will turn out for my deliverance." -Job 13:16. "I know that my redeemer lives, and that in the end he will stand on the earth. And after my skin has been destroyed, yet in my flesh I will see God; I will see him with my eyes- I, and not another. How my heart yearns within me!" -Job 19:25-27. I think everyone wants to live at ease, and God offers just that. We will always be yearning to see Jesus' face to face our entire lives, and we can always live with hope that no matter what we go through when we have a personal relationship with Him, that is our future.

"After the Lord had said these things to Job, he said to Eliphaz the Temanite, "I am angry with you and your two friends, because you have not spoken the truth about me, as my servant Job has." -Job 42:7. "After Job had prayed for his friends, the Lord restored his fortunes and gave him twice as much as he had before. All his brothers and sisters and everyone who had known him before came and ate with him in his house. The Lord blessed the latter part of Job's life more than the former part." -Job 42:10-12. Two of Job's friends told Job the reason He had all these terrible events was due to something he had done wrong, which angered God as this was not true. What I love is Job's response. He was accused of wronging God, which was not true, however he prays God does not punish his friends. When we have such a confident relationship with God and truly see how much we have done wrong, it helps soften our hearts to others even when they hurt us so deeply. God ends up restoring Job's fortunes, twice as much. God is just. He will make a purpose when He sees none.

"Brothers and sisters, as an example of patience in the face of suffering, take the prophets who spoke in the name of the Lord. As you know, we count as blessed those who have persevered. You have heard of Job's perseverance and have seen what the Lord finally brought about. The Lord is full of compassion and mercy." -James 5:10-11.

In this world we will have suffering, but when we persevere God sees, knows, cares and will bless you from his compassion and mercy. I know what it feels like to suffer, and it is a pain beyond comprehension or being able to explain, but so is His peace when we realize He is in ultimate control, the pain will not last forever as this life will not last forever, and He knows what He is doing. "Who can say to him, "What are you doing?" -Job 9:12.

"...His dominion is an eternal dominion; his kingdom endures from generation to generation. All the peoples of the earth are regarded as nothing. He does as he pleases with the powers of Heaven and the peoples of the earth. No one can hold back his hand or say to him: "What have you done?" While my sanity was restored, my honor and splendor were returned to me for the glory of my kingdom. My advisers and nobles sought me out, and I was restored to my throne and became even greater than before. Now I, Nebuchadnezzar, praise and exalt and glorify the King of Heaven, because everything he does is right, and all his ways are just. And those who walk in pride he is able to humble." -Daniel 4:34-37 (Psalm 135:6-7).

"Why, my soul, are you downcast? Why so disturbed within me? Put your hope in God, for I will yet praise him, my Savior and my God." -Psalm 42:5. "Our God comes and will not be silent." -Psalm 50:3. God is active in your life right now, regardless of how you are feeling. He is never silent. When our soul is at its lowest, we can still praise Him. Why? Not that the pain is not more than you can bear, but because God is more than this life or anything you can face in it. "But I am like an olive tree flourishing in the house of God; I trust in God's unfailing love for ever and ever. For what you have done I will always praise you in the presence of your faithful people. And I will hope in your name, for your name is good." -Psalm 52:8-9.

"The Lord is a refuge for the oppressed, a stronghold in times of trouble. Those who know your name trust in you, for you, Lord, have never forsaken those who seek you." -Psalm 9:9-10. Continue to seek His face. When I am at my lowest and suffering, I tend to isolate and turn away from God and others. Seek Him, He is right there.

"As for me, I call to God, and the Lord saves me. Evening, morning and noon I cry out in distress, and he hears my voice. He rescues me unharmed from the battle raged against me, even though many oppose me. God, who is enthroned from of old, who does not change." -Psalm 55:16-19 (Psalm 50:15).

God hears you, and He has not changed since the beginning of time. The one who knew exactly when to make you, every wrong turn you would face, every challenge you would encounter, hears you and loves you. We are all looking for someone to be there for us with consistency, who is not going to change like we do and those around us. God will not change, and knows exactly how to love you, what you need and when you need it the most.

"I call as my heart grows faint; lead me to the rock that is higher than I. For you have been my refuge, a strong tower against the foe. I long to dwell in your tent forever and take refuge in the shelter of your wings. For you, God, have heard my vows; you have given me the heritage of those who fear your name." -Psalm 61:2-5.

As we face suffering, our hearts grow faint. We were not meant to endure suffering, it entered as soon as sin infected the world. We must be led to a source higher than us, Jesus. We will always long for Heaven, for eternal peace and freedom from the suffering.

"Your righteousness, God, reaches to the Heavens, you who have done great things. Who is like you, God? Though you have made me see troubles, many and bitter, you will restore my life again; from the depths of the earth, you will again bring me up. You will increase my honor and comfort me once more. I will praise you with the harp for your faithfulness, my God; I will sing praise to you with the lyre, Holy One of Israel. My lips will shout for joy when I sing praise to you—I whom you have delivered. My tongue will tell of your righteous acts all day long." -Psalm 71:19-24.

God will restore your life again, on this earth and ultimately in the end in Heaven. He alone brings comfort. I always search for comfort in all of those around me, which God provides such as friends, family, spouse, things, experiences and even yourself. However, ultimately for healing, it must come from Him. Only with the love of God can praise come from someone in their worst pain.

"Record my misery; list your tears on your scroll- are they not in your record?" -Psalm 56:8 (Psalm 31:7). God knows every tear you have cried, your entire life. Even the ones you do not want to talk about to others. He knows. "And earth has nothing I desire besides you. My flesh and my heart may fail, but God is the strength of my heart and my portion forever." -Psalm 73:26. As we hang onto this world and our physical being, scared of death, we must face that fact our flesh and heart will someday fail. We are not guaranteed today, nor are we guaranteed tomorrow. If your focus is to keep from dying, you will only become anxious and lose your peace as you try to keep the inevitable from happening. The only way to fully have peace is for God to be our portion and strength.

"All night long I flood my bed with weeping and drench my couch with tears. My eyes grow weak with sorrow; they fail because of all my foes. Away from me, all you who do evil, for the Lord has heard my weeping. The Lord has heard my cry for mercy; the Lord accepts my prayer." -Psalm 6:6-9. We have all had these nights, more than we admit. "For his anger lasts a moment, but his favor lasts a lifetime; weeping may stay for the night, but rejoicing comes in the morning." -Psalm 30:5. I have thought many times that God is testing me, He wants to see my faith in this heart shattering circumstance, in my suffering. His favor outweighs His anger.

"I cried out to God for help; I cried out to God to hear me. When I was in distress, I sought the Lord; at night I stretched out untiring hands, and I would not be comforted. I remembered you, God, and I groaned; I meditated, and my spirit grew faint. You kept my eyes from closing; I was too troubled to speak. I thought about the former days, the years of long ago; I remembered my songs in the night. My heart meditated and my spirit asked: "Will the Lord reject forever? Will he never show his favor again? Has his unfailing love vanished forever? Has his promise failed for all time? Has God forgotten to be merciful? Has he in anger withheld his compassion?" Then I thought, "To this I will appeal: the years when the Most High stretched out his right hand. I will remember the deeds of the Lord; yes, I will remember your miracles of long ago. I will consider all your works and meditate on all your mighty deeds." Your ways, God, are holy. What god is as great as our God? You are the God who performs miracles; you display your power among the peoples. With your mighty arm you redeemed your people, the descendants of Jacob and Joseph." -Psalm 77:1-15 (Psalm 143:4-6, Psalm 119:27, Deuteronomy 7:18 and Psalm 107:43).

We have all had nights of tears, where our spirit feels faint, where we cannot find the words. What is the cure when the pain is too real? To focus on the former days. Do not dwell on your past, dwell on *His* past. His faithfulness since the beginning of time. The fulfillment of every promise. Remember His deeds and miracles. Meditate on His holy ways since Jacob and Joseph.

Put one step in front of the other and choose to remember what you have done and who you are. This is what Kathy Burros chose to do when she lost her daughter. I can't think of a worst pain, the pain of losing a child.

"How lovely is your dwelling place, Lord Almighty! My soul yearns, even faints, for the courts of the Lord, my heart and my flesh cry out for the living God. Even the sparrow has found a home, and the swallow a nest for herself, where she may have her young— a place near your altar, Lord Almighty, my King and my God. Blessed are those who dwell in your house; they are ever praising you. Blessed are those whose strength is in you, whose hearts are set on pilgrimage." -Psalm 84:1-5 (Psalm 146:5).

"I am a stranger on earth." -Psalm 119:19. "If they had been thinking of the country they had left, they would have had opportunity to return. Instead, they were longing for a better country—a Heavenly one." -Hebrews 11:15-16. This is not our home. Until we're in Heaven, we are always going to be searching for more fulfillment. Keep your mind and heart set on where it is. He will give you peace and the strength to endure the here and now, making the most of the incredible blessings in friends, family, spouse, talents, experiences, work and physical blessings He has provided for today.

"The Lord bestows favor and honor; no good thing does he withhold from those whose walk is blameless. Lord Almighty, blessed is the one who trusts in you." -Psalm 84:11-12. Who is blameless? Are we? Only when we have Christ does God consider us blameless. Job was considered blameless before Christ came physically on the earth, but his faith in God made him blameless. He will bestow his favor and honor, wanting good things for His children when we trust in Him.

"...and the dust returns to the ground it came from, and the spirit returns to God who gave it." -Ecclesiastes 12:7 (Ecclesiastes 3:20). God created the very Spirit inside of you. When we die, even though our physical bodies remain, our spirit returns to God, since you belong to Him in the first place.

"They eagerly turned to him again. They remembered that God was their Rock, that God Most High was their Redeemer. But then they would flatter him with their mouths, lying to him with their tongues; their hearts were not loyal to him, they were not faithful to his covenant. Yet he was merciful; he forgave their iniquities and did not destroy them. Time after time he restrained his anger and did not stir up his full wrath. He remembered that they were but flesh, a passing breeze that does not return." -Psalm 78:34-39.

God takes care of what He creates. Even when we are not loyal, he remains merciful and faithful. He sees us how we really are. Humbly, we are flesh and a breeze that does not return. Even though our souls will last forever, our time here is quick and fleeting. If you remember this, it changes how you live your life, and changes how you view God our Father.

"...the span of my years is as nothing before you. Everyone is but a breath, even those who seem secure." -Psalm 39:5. "But do not forget this one thing, dear friends: With the Lord a day is like a thousand years, and a thousand years are like a day." -2 Peter 3:8 (Psalm 90:3-4). Jesus has seen your life from the second you were born, until the day you die, and as it is happening now. A thousand years is like a day to our God.

"Whoever dwells in the shelter of the Most High will rest in the shadow of the Almighty. I will say of the Lord, "He is my refuge and my fortress, my God, in whom I trust. Surely, he will save you from the fowler's snare and from the deadly pestilence. He will cover you with his feathers, and under his wings you will find refuge; his faithfulness will be your shield and rampart. You will not fear the terror of night, nor the arrow that flies by day, nor the pestilence that stalks in the darkness, nor the plague that destroys at midday. A thousand may fall at your side, ten thousand at your right hand, but it will not come near you. You will only observe with your eyes and see the punishment of the wicked. If you say, "The LORD is my refuge," and you make the Most High your dwelling, no harm will overtake you, no disaster will come near your tent. For he will command his angels concerning you to guard you in all your ways; they will lift you up in their hands, so that you will not strike your foot against a stone. You will tread on the lion and the cobra; you will trample the great lion and the serpent. "Because he loves me," says the LORD, "I will rescue him; I will protect him, for he acknowledges my name. He will call on me, and I will answer him; I will be with him in trouble, I will deliver him and honor him. With long life I will satisfy him and show him my salvation." -Psalm 91:1-16 (Zechariah 13:9).

When we love God, He says He will protect us. When we acknowledge his name, He says He will rescue. He says He will answer us in times of trouble, deliver us and honor us. God desires to save and satisfy us, however in His love He never wants to force it. He wants us to desire and come to Him.

"Then they cried to the Lord in their trouble, and he saved them from their distress. He sent out his word and healed them; he rescued them from the grave." -Psalm 107:19-20 (Psalm 107:6-7, 107:13). "For you, Lord, have delivered me from death, my eyes from tears, my feet from stumbling, that I may walk before the Lord in the land of the living." -Psalm 116:8-9 (Psalm 86:13). "Precious in the sight of the Lord is the death of his faithful servants. Truly I am your servant, Lord." -Psalm 116:15-16. "...for you have given me hope. My comfort in my suffering is this: Your promise preserves my life." -Psalm 119:49-50. God has overcome death. The worst loss we can experience in this life, something we cannot process or wrap our mind around, was trampled at the cross where Jesus died in our place. My comfort in my suffering is that the promises of our Savior who died in our place, preserves our short lives here on earth to be a co-heir with Him for eternity. Our help comes from Him who created the earth and our lives in the first place. "I lift my eyes to the mountain- where does my help come from? My help comes from the Lord, the maker of Heaven and earth. He will not let your foot slip- he who watches over you will not slumber." -Psalm 121:1-3.

"He heals the brokenhearted and binds up their wounds. He determines the number of the stars and calls them each by name. Great is our Lord and mighty in power; his understanding has no limit. The LORD sustains the humble but casts the wicked to the ground. Sing to the LORD with grateful praise; make music to our God on the harp. He covers the sky with clouds; he supplies the earth with rain and makes grass grow on the hills. He provides food for the cattle and for the young ravens when they call. His pleasure is not in the strength of the horse, nor his delight in the legs of the warrior; the LORD delights in those who fear him, who put their hope in his unfailing love. Extol the LORD, Jerusalem; praise your God, Zion. He strengthens the bars of your gates and blesses your people within you. He grants peace to your borders and satisfies you with the finest of wheat. He sends his command to the earth; his word runs swiftly. He spreads the snow like wool and scatters the frost like ashes. He hurls down his hail like pebbles." -Psalm 147:3-17.

If I were to tell you He feels our broken heart and binds up our wounds, you may ask how? He determines the stars in the sky and knows them by name. That is how. His understanding has no limit. He sustains the humble. I cannot explain to you exactly how, but I can confidently tell you He does in a way even though I cannot explain, you can experience when you bring Him your broken heart and praise Him. He will delight in you if you fear Him and put your hope in His unfailing love. His word runs swiftly, and He is not slow in keeping His promises.

"...but even in death the righteous seek refuge in God." -Proverbs 14:32. "...in their misery they will earnestly seek me." -Hosea 5:15. God is our refuge at the worst of times. "In the same way I will not cause pain without allowing something new to be born," says the Lord. "If I cause you the pain, I will not stop you from giving birth to your new nation," says your God." -Isaiah 66:9. God will use your pain for something greater than you can imagine, but only He can do it because pain is not a "good" thing. I truly believe He has designed life in such a way that because He knew we would fail; His power is more than enough to create our exact purpose way we cannot mess up when we surrender to Him. Sin created the pain, but God's power is shown by how he takes the disaster we create as people and turns it into something beautiful. "The human spirit can endure in sickness but a crushed spirit who can bear?" -Proverbs 18:14. I have many times said I would rather deal with physical ailments than a crushed spirit. Nothing brings us down more than when our heart is shattered. "...the day of death better than the day of birth." -Ecclesiastes 7:1. When our heart is crushed, we long for death and to be freed from this life. "Consider what God has done: Who can straighten what he has made crooked? When times are good, be happy but when times are bad, consider this: God has made the one as well as the other". -Ecclesiastes 7:13. However, we find hope in the here and now, knowing God can fix the suffering sin and Satan have created, affecting us and our daily lives. We can have peace knowing even though God does not purposely inflict pain on us, sometimes the bad times are needed for reasons we cannot explain, however we trust knowing this. He loves you, wants what is best for you *and* those around you that may be affected in the same suffering you are, and this pain *will not* last forever. He would not allow the bad times to happen unless there is an eternal purpose behind it.

"For there is a proper time and procedure for every matter, though a person may be weighed down by misery. Since no one knows the future, who can tell someone else what is to come? As no one has the power over the wind to contain it, so no one has power over the time of their death." -Ecclesiastes 8:6-8. Knowing God has already determined your death date can either bring you peace or anxiety. The answer lies in your relationship with Him. If you understand He created you and has set out an exact purpose for your life, and you understand there is so much more to this life after, you will have peace.

"So, he sent two of his disciples, telling them, "Go into the city, and a man carrying a jar of water will meet you. Follow him. Say to the owner of the house he enters, 'The Teacher asks: Where is my guest room, where I may eat the Passover with my disciples?' He will show you a large room upstairs, furnished and ready. Make preparations for us there. The disciples left, went into the city and found things just as Jesus had told them. So, they prepared the Passover." -Mark 14:13-16.

Jesus told the disciples exactly what would happen, and the same is true for us. He leads us gently in the direction to go, keeping us close to his arms and heart.

"He tends his flock like a shepherd: He gathers the lambs in his arms and carries them close to his heart; he gently leads those that have young. Who has measured the waters in the hollow of his hand, or with the breadth of his hand marked off the Heavens? Who has held the dust of the earth in a basket, or weighed the mountains on the scales and the hills in a balance? Who can fathom the Spirit of the Lord, or instruct the Lord as his counselor? Whom did the Lord consult to enlighten him, and who taught him the right way? Who was it that taught him knowledge, or showed him the path of understanding?" -Isaiah 40:11-14 (Ezekiel 34:2-10).

There have been many times (I am ashamed to tell you) when I was suffering, I talked back to God. I am so grateful He is so loving, patient and merciful with me, as I am yelling at the very one who wants to help me. The one who gives me the ability to even type the next word right now. The one who provides our next breath. He knows all and is all.

"But now, this is what the Lord says—he who created you, Jacob, he who formed you, Israel: "Do not fear, for I have redeemed you; I have summoned you by name; you are mine. When you pass through the waters, I will be with you; and when you pass through the rivers, they will not sweep over you. When you walk through the fire, you will not be burned; the flames will not set you ablaze. For I am the Lord your God, the Holy One of Israel, your Savior; I give Egypt for your ransom, Cush and Seba in your stead. Since you are precious and honored in my sight, and because I love you." -Isaiah 43:1-4 (2 Kings 14:27).

"The God of Israel, who summons you by name." -Isaiah 45:3. God says when we pass through the waters and fire, He will be with us. It does not say "if." He is in the fire with us. We are precious and honored in His sight, He loves us! He summons you by your name with such a personal love!

"Shout for joy, you Heavens; rejoice, you earth; burst into song, you mountains! For the Lord comforts his people and will have compassion on his afflicted ones. But Zion said, "The Lord has forsaken me, the Lord has forgotten me." "Can a mother forget the baby at her breast and have no compassion on the child she has borne? Though she may forget, I will not forget you! See, I have engraved you on the palms of my hands; your walls are ever before me." -Isaiah 49:13-16.

"As a mother comforts her child, so I will comfort you." -Isaiah 66:13. God will comfort you with His compassion, and we are to show this same compassion for others. God uses the example of a mother. How could she forget the baby she bore? Unfortunately, being in a broken world, we know sometimes parents do not stay in the picture as God designed. However, God is saying He will not leave you as some parents do. He will be a Father to us better than even the best earthly Dad.

"Was my arm too short to deliver you? Do I lack strength to rescue you? By a mere rebuke I dry up the sea, I turn rivers into a desert." -Isaiah 50:2. God in the Old Testament and Jesus in the New Testament love to answer with a question. By a mere rebuke, God can change your circumstance. I can see where this very statement can either cause you peace, or complete anger. I have been angered thinking God is witnessing me experiencing something He can change. This is where the love and trust come back into play. "Those who walk uprightly enter into peace; they find rest as they lie in death." -Isaiah 57:2. When my Great Grandpa Joe found out he was dying of cancer, I was distraught and asked him how he was feeling. His response? "Isn't it a joy?" I had to take a minute to process what he said as I was heartbroken. I am not for a split second saying to "rejoice" when we face the worst because of the worst that is happening to us, but the joy comes from keeping our eyes fixated on the Cross no matter what news we face in this life. "...the Lord will be your everlasting light, and your days of sorrow will end." -Isaiah 60:20 (Revelation 22:3-5). Your days of sorrow *will* have an end *if* you have received Jesus as your Lord and Savior. This is how we can have joy today. Not because of the sorrow, but in the midst of it! "It is I, proclaiming victory, mighty to save." -Isaiah 63:1.

What will the end look like for those who are in Christ? "See, I will create new Heavens and a new earth. The former things will not be remembered, nor will they come to mind. But be glad and rejoice forever in what I will create, for I will create Jerusalem to be a delight and its people a joy. I will rejoice over Jerusalem and take delight in my people; the sound of weeping and of crying will be heard in it no more. "Never again will there be in it an infant who lives but a few days, or an old man who does not live out his years; the one who dies at a hundred will be thought a mere child." -Isaiah 65:17-20.

No more weeping, only rejoicing! A new Heaven and a new earth. "I will turn their mourning into gladness; I will give them comfort and joy instead of sorrow." - Jeremiah 31:13.

"The Lord is good to those whose hope is in him, to the one who seeks him." -Lamentations 3:25. "But you did not honor the God who holds in his hand your life and all your ways." -Daniel 5:23. Why would we not honor God who holds our very life in His hands? "The Lord is good, a refuge in times of trouble. He cares for those who trust in him." -Nahum 1:7 (Psalm 37:18, Mark 6:18, Mark 6:27, Matthew 14:10, and Luke 3:19-20). I know some may argue what His refuge looks like and His care when those who love Him very much have been martyred. An example people have brought up to me is John the Baptist. He was beheaded in prison strictly for telling Herod it is wrong for him to have his brother's wife. He was a true servant of God, a cousin of Jesus who prepared the way for Him as was prophesied, beheaded. My word of hope in this, is God is bigger than what we can see and comprehend. It is hard for me to stomach the thought of how this happened, and the injustice of it. However, God's word stands true, and God promises to take care of those He loves. In the end, it must be worth it even if circumstances such as this come in our lives.

"Then you will be handed over to be persecuted and put to death, and you will be hated by all nations because of me. At that time many will turn away from the faith and will betray and hate each other, and many false prophets will appear and deceive many people. Because of the increase of wickedness, the love of most will grow cold, but the one who stands firm to the end will be saved. And this gospel of the kingdom will be preached in the whole world as a testimony to all nations, and then the end will come. "So when you see standing in the holy place 'the abomination that causes desolation,' spoken of through the prophet Daniel—let the reader understand." -Matthew 24:9-15 (Matthew 24:3).

We are not to be surprised by the fiery trials of this world or the persecution we will face as believers. Many will turn from faith and hate one another. Many leaders will lead people astray, telling them information and laws that are not in the Word of God. Love will grow cold, but we must stand firm, loving each other and proclaiming the gospel. Then the end will come as prophesied in Daniel, however, the Bible is clear we will not know exactly when the end will be.

"When Jesus looked up and saw a great crowd coming toward him, he said to Philip, "Where shall we buy bread for these people to eat?" He asked this only to test him, for he already had in mind what he was going to do." -John 6:5-6. Jesus and God love to ask questions to provide an answer for us.

"Jesus called his disciples to him and said, 'I have compassion for these people; they have already been with me three days and have nothing to eat. I do not want to send them away hungry, or they may collapse on the way.' His disciples answered, 'Where could we get enough bread in this remote place to feed such a crowd?' 'How many loaves do you have?' Jesus asked. 'Seven,' they replied, "and a few small fish." He told the crowd to sit down on the ground. Then he took the seven loaves and the fish, and when he had given thanks, he broke them and gave them to the disciples, and they in turn to the people. They all ate and were satisfied. Afterward the disciples picked up seven basketfuls of broken pieces that were left over. The number of those who ate was four thousand men, besides women and children." -Matthew 15:32-38 (Mark 8:1-9, Mark 6:37-38, Mark 6:41-44, Matthew 14:15-21, Luke 9:13-17, John 6:11-13 and Acts 27:35-36).

The miracle of Jesus' provision for the many should bring you confidence He will provide for you from what seems like a little in our life. You may be thinking "What can he do with the small amount of education I have? The small town I am from? The few people I have in my life? The little bit of money and possessions I own? The little bit of talent I have?" He can multiply it beyond what you can comprehend when you answer His question in your own life of "Who shall I use to feed my people?" It would be physically feeding, spiritually feeding, socially feeding or emotionally feeding others through His Holy Spirit living inside of you. It is amazing what God can do and use. You may even think you are running out of time depending on your age, but God saved the entire world in one day. "...says the Lord Almighty, "and I will remove the sin of this land in a single day. In that day each of you will invite your neighbor to sit under your vine and fig tree," declares the Lord Almighty."-Zechariah 3:9-10.

"For then there will be great distress, unequaled from the beginning of the world until now—and never to be equaled again." -Matthew 24:21 (Mark 13:19, 2 Timothy 3:1-6. Matthew 24:26-27 says as obvious as we see lightning, we will know when he returns. Until then, the Word says no one knows the time Jesus will return. All we know is the world will continue to get worse as people get further away from Jesus, God and His teaching in the scripture.

"Blessed is the one who reads aloud the words of this prophecy, and blessed are those who hear it and take to heart what is written in it, because the time is near." -Revelation 1:3. You will be happier if you read the Bible. You can read many scriptures in Matthew 24:36-50, Matthew 24:51, Mark 13:32-33, Mark 13:36-37, 1 Thessalonians 5:1-2, Revelation 3:3, Luke 12:41-48, Luke 12:36-40, and 2 Peter 3:10 that says how no one knows the day or hour, not the angels or even Jesus. Only God. It will be like the flood with Noah, when no one believed it was coming. People were just living their life like normal and eating, drinking, marrying, etc. Two will be working, and one of each taken. We must be ready as a faithful servant who has been put in charge of His people, His possessions and His work when He comes back. If we can be trusted with this, He will put us in charge of it all. But if you take advantage and do what you want as a wicked servant thinking either He won't come back or it will be a long time until He does and you continue hurting others and getting drunk, the master will come when He does not expect. "But you, brothers and sisters, are not in darkness so that this day should surprise you like a thief." -1 Thessalonians 5:4 (Revelation 16:15 and Acts 1:6-11).

We do not know the exact date, so what now? What about today?

"Since everything will be destroyed in this way, what kind of people ought you to be? You ought to live holy and godly lives as you look forward to the day of God and speed its coming. That day will bring about the destruction of the Heavens by fire, and the elements will melt in the heat. But in keeping with his promise we are looking forward to a new Heaven and a new earth, where righteousness dwells. So then, dear friends, since you are looking forward to this, make every effort to be found spotless, blameless and at peace with him. Bear in mind that our Lord's patience means salvation, just as our dear brother Paul also wrote you with the wisdom that God gave him. He writes the same way in all his letters, speaking in them of these matters. His letters contain some things that are hard to understand, which ignorant and unstable people distort, as they do the other Scriptures, to their own destruction. Therefore, dear friends, since you have been forewarned, be on your guard so that you may not be carried away by the error of the lawless and fall from your secure position. But grow in the grace and knowledge of our Lord and Savior Jesus Christ. To him be glory both now and forever! Amen." -2 Peter 3:11-18 (Isaiah 51:6 and 2 Peter 3:10).

Do not be swayed by opinions, stay firm in the truth of His word. We will never be blameless in ourselves but lead into Jesus' desiring to be like Him who is blameless while resting in his grace when we constantly fall. He sees your heart. Continue to look forward to the hope of the new Heaven and the new earth, realizing Jesus has not returned yet, God is patient, wanting more people to come to salvation and have a relationship with Him. Be on guard.

"My soul is overwhelmed with sorrow to the point of death," he said to them. "Stay here and keep watch." Going a little farther, he fell to the ground and prayed that if possible, the hour might pass from him. "Abba, Father," he said, "everything is possible for you. Take this cup from me. Yet not what I will, but what you will." -Mark 14:34-36 (Matthew 26:36-39 and Matthew 26:42). My soul has been overwhelmed to the point I felt it would be better to die than bear the pain. I have cried out with all I have that God take the cup of pain from me in order to fulfill His will. "My Father will honor the one who serves me. "Now my soul is troubled, and what shall I say? 'Father, save me from this hour'? No, it was for this very reason I came to this hour." -John 12:26-27 (John 12:23-24).

Even though there have been times I did not understand why my soul experienced the immense pain, but then I think about how Jesus endured the cross knowing this was the Father's will.

"As he went along, he saw a man blind from birth. His disciples asked him, "Rabbi, who sinned, this man or his parents, that he was born blind?" "Neither this man nor his parents sinned," said Jesus, "but this happened so that the works of God might be displayed in him." -John 9:1-3 (John 9:4-7). Sometimes we go through the pain and worst of times, not because we are being punished, but for God's glory to be on display. "So, the sisters sent word to Jesus, "Lord, the one you love is sick." When he heard this, Jesus said, "This sickness will not end in death. No, it is for God's glory so that God's Son may be glorified through it." -John 11:3-4. We live in a broken world, and I know we all have stories where the sickness we have experienced with others resulted in death. However, the miracle and hope can come through our loved ones dying, when they are in Christ, they live in Heaven where God is glorified! "So, then he told them plainly, "Lazarus is dead, and for your sake I am glad I was not there, so that you may believe. But let us go to him." -John 11:14-15.

" Lord," Martha said to Jesus, "if you had been here, my brother would not have died. But I know that even now God will give you whatever you ask." Jesus said to her, "Your brother will rise again." Martha answered, "I know he will rise again in the resurrection at the last day." Jesus said to her, "I am the resurrection and the life. The one who believes in me will live, even though they die; and whoever lives by believing in me will never die. Do you believe this?" -John 11:21-26.

Martha and Mary were hurt Jesus was not there sooner. They felt if He was, this would have kept Lazarus from dying. He said it was for their sake He was not there, so that they may believe. If you believe in Christ, you never truly die.

"When Mary reached the place where Jesus was and saw him, she fell at his feet and said, "Lord, if you had been here, my brother would not have died." When Jesus saw her weeping, and the Jews who had come along with her also weeping, he was deeply moved in spirit and troubled. "Where have you laid him?" he asked. 'Come and see, Lord,' they replied. Jesus wept. Then the Jews said, "See how he loved him!" -John 32-36.

When we are in pain, we tend to run from God, thinking He is causing the pain. Jesus is so sad when you experience pain or are hurting. He wept.

"Then Jesus said, "Did I not tell you that if you believe, you will see the glory of God?" So, they took away the stone. Then Jesus looked up and said, "Father, I thank you that you have heard me. I knew that you always hear me, but I said this for the benefit of the people standing here, that they may believe that you sent me." When he had said this, Jesus called in a loud voice, "Lazarus, come out!" The dead man came out." -John 11:40-44.

There are scriptures in Luke 8:50-55, Mark 5:23-30, Mark 5:34-36, Mark 5:41-43, Mark 5:39, Matthew 9:18-29, Mark 10:50-52 and Luke 18:35-43 that give other examples of Jesus saying if we are not afraid, believe the child will be healed. He was laughed at, but when He told the child to get up, she did. Jesus is never in a rush, have you noticed? Yet He always acts. He even told Mary, His mother, when she informed Him there was no wine, that his hour had not yet come. In our lives He always acts as well, but on His time which if you noticed is always perfect. Why would God be rushed? When indeed life and the world in and of itself is His story. He has the pen. Would it make sense that He would ever be in a rush?

"Jesus replied, "You do not realize now what I am doing, but later you will understand." -John 13:7.

"Do not let your hearts be troubled. You believe in God; believe also in me. My Father's house has many rooms; if that were not so, would I have told you that I am going there to prepare a place for you? And if I go and prepare a place for you, I will come back and take you to be with me that you also may be where I am. You know the way to the place where I am going." -John 14:1-4.

"But I, by your great love, can come into your house." -Psalm 5:7. There is an eternal plan for your life now that we cannot see.

"Who shall separate us from the love of Christ? Shall trouble or hardship or persecution or famine or nakedness or danger or sword? As it is written: "For your sake we face death all day long; we are considered as sheep to be slaughtered." No, in all these things we are more than conquerors through him who loved us. For I am convinced that neither death nor life, neither angels nor demons, neither the present nor the future, nor any powers, neither height nor depth, nor anything else in all creation, will be able to separate us from the love of God that is in Christ Jesus our Lord." -Romans 8:35-39.

No matter how hard life gets, the mistakes we make, the suffering we go through, the death we face, nothing, absolutely nothing, will separate us from Christ's love and pursuit after our heart.

We tend to think that if we have all the answers and explanations from God, we will then be happy. Look at the Israelites or others throughout the Bible when He would tell them what was going to happen such as the promised land. They still complained. We just need to rest in Him and trust Him.

"For now we see only a reflection as in a mirror; then we shall see face to face. Now I know in part; then I shall know fully, even as I am fully known." -1 Corinthians 13:12.   It is by faith that we walk, even when we cannot see. We cannot fully see as sin has made the way foggy, but through the fog there is still a clear light, Jesus, and even though we cannot directly see His face we know His light is home, and we eagerly, confidently and continually follow the light until our race is over, when He will be reveled and then fully known.

"I face death every day—yes, just as surely as I boast about you in Christ Jesus our Lord. If I fought wild beasts in Ephesus with no more than human hopes, what have I gained?" -1 Corinthians 15:31-32. Paul feels it was worth it to face death for the sake of Christ, comparing if he only had merely human hopes, what would he gain?

"For you have been born again, not of perishable seed, but of imperishable, through the living and enduring word of God. For, "All people are like grass, and all their glory is like the flowers of the field; the grass withers and the flowers fall, but the word of the Lord endures forever." -1 Peter 1:23-25 (Isaiah 40:8 and Matthew 24:35, Mark 13:31, Luke 21:33, and 1 Corinthians 15:53-54).

The only things that will last for eternity is the Word of God, Jesus, celestial beings and our souls.

"I will deliver this people from the power of the grave; I will redeem them from death. Where, O death, are your plagues? Where, O grave, is your destruction?" -Hosea 13:14. "Death has been swallowed up in victory." "Where, O death, is your victory? Where, O death, is your sting?" The sting of death is sin, and the power of sin is the law. But thanks be to God! He gives us the victory through our Lord Jesus Christ." -1 Corinthians 15:54-57 (1 Corinthians 15:25-26, 1 Corinthians 15:42-45, Proverbs 12:28). Death no longer has its sting! The pain remains, but Jesus has overcome.

"Praise be to the God and Father of our Lord Jesus Christ, the Father of compassion and the God of all comfort, who comforts us in all our troubles, so that we can comfort those in any trouble with the comfort we ourselves receive from God. For just as we share abundantly in the sufferings of Christ, so also our comfort abounds through Christ. If we are distressed, it is for your comfort and salvation; if we are comforted, it is for your comfort, which produces in yo patient endurance of the same sufferings we suffer. And our hope for you is firm, because we know that just as you share in our sufferings, so also you share in our comfort. We do not want you to be uninformed, brothers and sisters, about the troubles we experienced in the province of Asia. We were under great pressure, far beyond our ability to endure, so that we despaired of life itself. Indeed, we felt we had received the sentence of death. But this happened that we might not rely on ourselves but on God, who raises the dead. He has delivered us from such a deadly peril, and he will deliver us again. On him we have set our hope that he will continue to deliver us, as you help us by your prayers. Then many will give thanks on our behalf for the gracious favor granted us in answer to the prayers of many." -2 Corinthians 1:3-11 (Romans 15:13).

I am so grateful our Father is a God of comfort and compassion for us, His children and creation. The saying God does not give you more than you can handle is not true. Life is way more than we can bear! Ask anyone if they are truthful about the pain they have felt. The truth is there is nothing in this life that is more than *God* can handle. *He* will help you through. Paul said they faced death to the point they despaired life itself. This happened so that they would not rely on themselves but on our God who raises the dead. He is our hope.

In 2 Corinthians 7:5-6, God comforts the downcast by the coming of Titus showing God can comfort through those he has put in your life.

"Rather, as servants of God we commend ourselves in every way: in great endurance; in troubles, hardships and distresses; in beatings, imprisonments and riots; in hard work, sleepless nights and hunger; in purity, understanding, patience and kindness; in the Holy Spirit and in sincere love; in truthful speech and in the power of God; with weapons of righteousness in the right hand and in the left; through glory and dishonor, bad report and good report; genuine, yet regarded as impostors; known, yet regarded as unknown; dying, and yet we live on; beaten, and yet not killed; sorrowful, yet always rejoicing; poor, yet making many rich; having nothing, and yet possessing everything." -2 Corinthians 6:4-10.

"I served the Lord with great humility and with tears and in the midst of severe testing by the plots of my Jewish opponents. You know that I have not hesitated to preach anything that would be helpful to you but have taught you publicly and from house to house. I have declared to both Jews and Greeks that they must turn to God in repentance and have faith in our Lord Jesus. "And now, compelled by the Spirit, I am going to Jerusalem, not knowing what will happen to me there. I only know that in every city the Holy Spirit warns me that prison and hardships are facing me. However, I consider my life worth nothing to me; my only aim is to finish the race and complete the task the Lord Jesus has given me—the task of testifying to the good news of God's grace." -Acts 20:19-24.

Paul was not saying his life is worthless but saying any gain he could achieve in this world is nothing now that He has found his purpose in Christ. With a true athlete mentality, he saw the end goal, the finish line, and was determined to complete the race set before him at any cost. Just like a dedicated athlete during a basketball game, it does not matter how many times I was fouled, how many charges I took, how many times I had the wind knocked out of me being elbowed in the side, hand checked, bleeding or tired from the game. Any competitive athlete knows you keep your eyes focused on that basket until you win, and when your adrenaline is going and you are down, you do not feel the pain when your eyes are fixed on the basket. There is something powerful about what happens to our soul depending what the brain is fixated on. How much more confident and determined will we be if we fix our eyes on Jesus? He tells us He is fully content, realizing His purposes are to have a relationship with Jesus and to help others find it. "When we heard this, we and the people there pleaded with Paul not to go up to Jerusalem. Then Paul answered, "Why are you weeping and breaking my heart? I am ready not only to be bound, but also to die in Jerusalem for the name of the Lord Jesus." -Acts 21:12-13.

"I eagerly expect and hope that I will in no way be ashamed but will have sufficient courage so that now as always Christ will be exalted in my body, whether by life or by death. For to me, to live is Christ and to die is gain." -Philippians 1:20-21. If someone were to threaten your life today and you are a believer in Christ, you can be confident that to die is to gain. We are to love life! It is a beautiful gift from God, but we hang onto the unwavering hope that one day when this life is over, we will receive Christ's reward and the perfection our hearts so badly long for. When you have Christ, you love this life knowing God has created you for a purpose, but you are only able to do that because you are not afraid to die, knowing it will ultimately be your gain. "I am torn between the two: I desire to depart and be with Christ, which is better by far; but it is more necessary for you that I remain in the body." -Philippians 1:23-24. Paul is torn, telling us that we have a purpose in our life today, and by all means need to do all we can to live a healthy life to stay alive, but ultimately trusting and realizing our bodies will eventually fail. We all have a death date, but we do not need to be anxious for it but be excited knowing the best thing in the world is going to be being with the one who loves us more than anyone.

"But whatever were gains to me I now consider loss for the sake of Christ. What is more, I consider everything a loss because of the surpassing worth of knowing Christ Jesus my Lord, for whose sake I have lost all things. I consider them garbage, that I may gain Christ and be found in him, not having a righteousness of my own that comes from the law, but that which is through faith in[a] Christ—the righteousness that comes from God on the basis of faith. I want to know Christ—yes, to know the power of his resurrection and participation in his sufferings, becoming like him in his death, and so, somehow, attaining to the resurrection from the dead. Not that I have already obtained all this, or have already arrived at my goal, but I press on to take hold of that for which Christ Jesus took hold of me. Brothers and sisters, I do not consider myself yet to have taken hold of it. But one thing I do: Forgetting what is behind and straining toward what is ahead, I press on toward the goal to win the prize for which God has called me Heavenward in Christ Jesus." -Philippians 3:7-14.

When you know Christ, you realize He is all you need. As athletes, we continue to press on to train toward our goal in knowing Him. It takes practice, time, energy and work like any sport or relationship. Getting in the Word, talking to Him regularly and obeying Him are how you practice and develop this relationship.

"Join together in following my example, brothers and sisters, and just as you have us as a model, keep your eyes on those who live as we do. For, as I have often told you before and now tell you again even with tears, many live as enemies of the cross of Christ. Their destiny is destruction, their god is their stomach, and their glory is in their shame. Their mind is set on earthly things. But our citizenship is in Heaven. And we eagerly await a Savior from there, the Lord Jesus Christ, who, by the power that enables him to bring everything under his control, will transform our lowly bodies so that they will be like his glorious body." -Philippians 3:17-21.

Jesus is our model and where we are to fix our lives on how to live. Keep your mind away from earthly desires or pleasures that can never satisfy. Our citizenship is in Heaven where we will have a new glorious body.

"Fight the good fight of the faith. Take hold of the eternal life to which you were called when you made your good confession in the presence of many witnesses. In the sight of God, who gives life to everything, and of Christ Jesus, who while testifying before Pontius Pilate made the good confession, I charge you to keep this command without spot or blame until the appearing of our Lord Jesus Christ, which God will bring about in his own time—God, the blessed and only Ruler, the King of kings and Lord of lords, who alone is immortal and who lives in unapproachable light, whom no one has seen or can see. To him be honor and might forever. Amen." -1 Timothy 6:12-16.

Life is going to be a constant fight, but our fight is with joy and faith, keeping our eyes fixed on eternity; the source of our hope from God, who literally created life itself. We cannot see God right now and our hearts long to, but we can still lean into our personal relationship with Him today. When we love one another, He is seen through us since He himself is love.

"When God made his promise to Abraham, since there was no one greater for him to swear by, he swore by himself, saying, "I will surely bless you and give you many descendants." And so after waiting patiently, Abraham received what was promised. People swear by someone greater than themselves, and the oath confirms what is said and puts an end to all argument. Because God wanted to make the unchanging nature of his purpose very clear to the heirs of what was promised, he confirmed it with an oath. God did this so that, by two unchangeable things in which it is impossible for God to lie, we who have fled to take hold of the hope set before us may be greatly encouraged. We have this hope as an anchor for the soul, firm and secure. It enters the inner sanctuary behind the curtain, where our forerunner, Jesus, has entered on our behalf. He has become a high priest forever, in the order of Melchizedek." -Hebrews 6:13-20.

Even when my life is in shambles and I cannot make sense of the pain and tragedies, the anchor for my soul is that since God's promise to Abraham, since the beginning, God has been Sovereign in His design and plan, orchestrating everything to fulfill his purposes and his goodness. The promise of our Savior who has come, Jesus, has become our high priest to justify for us before the Father.

"Since you call on a Father who judges each person's work impartially, live out your time as foreigners here in reverent fear." -1 Peter 1:17. We are foreigners in this world, it is not our home. "Do not be afraid. I am the First and the Last. I am the Living One; I was dead, and now look, I am alive for ever and ever! And I hold the keys of death and Hades." -Revelation 1:17-18. Since we know this is not our home and we have an eternal home in Heaven, it helps ease our fears! Jesus, God, is the first and last who holds the keys of death and Hades, and our very lives and He loves you. "Whoever has ears, let them hear what the Spirit says to the churches. To the one who is victorious, I will give the right to eat from the tree of life, which is in the paradise of God." -Revelation 2:7. When we have Christ, we are crowned victorious and will get to eat from the tree of life, the one we were supposed to eat from in the beginning before we chose sin.

"Then one of the elders said to me, "Do not weep! See, the Lion of the tribe of Judah, the Root of David, has triumphed." -Revelation 5:5. Even though we will mourn here, we do not need to stay weeping as the Lion of the tribe of Judah, the Root of David, Jesus, has triumphed and we are already victorious! The worst pain you can feel *will pass away some day.* I am here as a friend to you to say, I understand this does not bring comfort in this moment as the pain is too real, but what I do hope it brings you, as it brings me; is *hope*. Hope that this pain will end, even though my feelings do not align, the truth is I know one day all will be made new and right. There will be no more tears or heartache. Jesus, the worthy lamb of God who was slain in our place, has confirmed this through his Word, forever and ever!

"Worthy is the Lamb, who was slain, to receive power and wealth and wisdom and strength and honor and glory and praise!" Then I heard every creature in Heaven and on earth and under the earth and on the sea, and all that is in them, saying: "To him who sits on the throne and to the Lamb be praise and honor and glory and power, for ever and ever!" -Revelation 5:12-13.

"Never again will they hunger; never again will they thirst. The sun will not beat down on them,' nor any scorching heat. For the Lamb at the center of the throne will be their shepherd; 'he will lead them to springs of living water.' 'And God will wipe away every tear from their eyes." -Revelation 7:16-17. The tragedies of this life, people going hungry, natural disasters, death and broken relationships, all gone. No more tears.

"...he will swallow up death forever. The Sovereign Lord will wipe away the tears from all faces; he will remove his people's disgrace from all the earth. The Lord has spoken. In that day they will say: "Surely this is our God; we trust in him, and he saved us. This is the Lord, we trusted in him; let us rejoice and be glad in his salvation." -Isaiah 25:8-9.

We can rejoice and be glad today knowing the evil will end and good will prevail. How relieving to know we know that the end of the story!

"Then I saw "a new Heaven and a new earth," for the first Heaven and the first earth had passed away, and there was no longer any sea. I saw the Holy City, the new Jerusalem, coming down out of Heaven from God, prepared as a bride beautifully dressed for her husband. And I heard a loud voice from the throne saying, "Look! God's dwelling place is now among the people, and he will dwell with them. They will be his people, and God himself will be with them and be their God. 'He will wipe every tear from their eyes. There will be no more death' or mourning or crying or pain, for the old order of things has passed away." He who was seated on the throne said, "I am making everything new!" Then he said, "Write this down, for these words are trustworthy and true." He said to me: "It is done. I am the Alpha and the Omega, the Beginning and the End. To the thirsty I will give water without cost from the spring of the water of life. Those who are victorious will inherit all this, and I will be their God and they will be my children." -Revelation 21:1-7 (Revelation 34:4 and Jeremiah 33:6-9).

The old order will pass away. The days and nights in which I have questioned God as to why I am alive, why do I need to experience the pain that this life brings that is all too real, will soon make sense when there is a new Heaven and a new earth. It will all be done. The ultimate wedding ceremony is us, God's church to himself. We are His children, and will live on a new earth and Heaven, with no more sin. We will be dancing on streets of gold! "The twelve gates were twelve pearls, each gate made of a single pearl. The great street of the city was of gold, as pure as transparent glass." -Revelation 21:21.

"Look, I am coming soon! Blessed is the one who keeps the words of the prophecy written in this scroll." -Revelation 22:7 (Revelation 22:10). We do not know when Jesus is returning, but we know it is soon!

"And do this, understanding the present time: The hour has already come for you to wake up from your slumber, because our salvation is nearer now than when we first believed. The night is nearly over; the day is almost here. So let us put aside the deeds of darkness and put on the armor of light. Let us behave decently, as in the daytime, not in carousing and drunkenness, not in sexual immorality and debauchery, not in dissension and jealousy. Rather, clothe yourselves with the Lord Jesus Christ, and do not think about how to gratify the desires of the flesh." -Romans 13:11-14.

The enemy wants us to live "nonchalantly" thinking we have all this time, when we do not! Even if Jesus does not come back in your lifetime, your life will fly by. Has it not already? Salvation is closer than when you first believed. Put on the armor of light today. This requires we put off the ways of the world, and focus on what Jesus would have us do, to bring true fulfillment, productivity and joy producing fun!

The pain and heartache you are experiencing leaves you with two options. You can curse God or give up fighting Him. The only thing is He always wins. I have wrongly chucked my Bible against the wall, I have screamed and cried to take away the pain, I have blamed others, I have done everything I should not, but please understand He will still have His will, and regardless of the pain I promise *His will is good*. The other thing is, He is on your side. Even when I do not understand that why bad things happen, I trust God is good. I don't have a secret deal with God that if I serve Him, I am going to receive the best in life or all these blessings. I serve God because I am in love with Him, regardless of the circumstances. However, the good news is when we have this relationship, God uses every situation for our good.

Love Your Neighbors

"I can do all things through Christ who strengthens me." Philippians 4:13.

I can *love unconditionally and genuinely* through Christ who strengthens me.

"My command is this: Love each other as I have loved you. Greater love has no one than this: to lay down one's life for one's friends. You are my friends if you do what I command. I no longer call you servants, because a servant does not know his master's business. Instead, I have called you friends, for everything that I learned from my Father I have made known to you. You did not choose me, but I chose you and appointed you so that you might go and bear fruit—fruit that will last—and so that whatever you ask in my name the Father will give you. This is my command: Love each other." -John 15:12-17.

This is when you know your love is true. Jesus died for me, the least I could do is lay down my life for Him. When you understand and experience Jesus' love, it literally pours out of you. You cannot help but love those around you! We are commanded to love one another, just as Christ loves us, to the point of laying down our lives for others as He did for us. It is incredible that Jesus, the King of the universe, calls us *friend*. How are we friends? He has shared with us in His sufferings, His victory and in His commands, His thoughts and His desires. He chose us to bear His fruit, His love regardless of all our flaws and imperfections. I think the question is how? How can you really, genuinely love someone that much, even if you barely know them, to the point of being able to do this? Think of your best friends. You know they have flaws and imperfections, but you accept them regardless because you love them so much.

"One of the teachers of the law came and heard them debating. Noticing that Jesus had given them a good answer, he asked him, 'Of all the commandments, which is the most important?' 'The most important one,' answered Jesus, 'is this: 'Hear, O Israel: The Lord our God, the Lord is one. Love the Lord your God with all your heart and with all your soul and with all your mind and with all your strength. 'The second is this: 'Love your neighbor as yourself.' There is no commandment greater than these.' 'Well said, teacher,' the man replied. 'You are right in saying that God is one and there is no other but him. To love him with all your heart, with all your understanding and with all your strength, and to love your neighbor as yourself is more important than all burnt offerings and sacrifices' When Jesus saw that he had answered wisely, he said to him, 'You are not far from the kingdom of God.' And from then on no one dared ask him any more questions." - Mark 12:28-34 (Luke 10:27, 1 Samuel 12:20, 2 Kings 23:24-25, and Hebrews 13:1).

God is love in and of itself, so He gave us the ability to love and is the definition of what love truly is. We must love God with all we have first, and the second is to love our neighbors as ourselves. When we love God first, only then will we have the true direction and capacity of how to love our neighbors the way they need. It says to love our neighbor as ourselves, and the Bible is clear we are to put others before ourselves. When asked of God, He provides us with a balance of loving ourselves without becoming prideful or self-centered in a healthy, humble manner, allowing us to love others in the same way.

"The commandments, "You shall not commit adultery," "You shall not murder," "You shall not steal," "You shall not covet," and whatever other command there may be, are summed up in this one command: "Love your neighbor as yourself." Love does no harm to a neighbor. Therefore, love is the fulfillment of the law." -Romans 13:9-10.

When we love others, genuinely, it makes it easier to follow God's commands as our motivation is from the heart as opposed to feeling an obligation to follow the law. When you genuinely love someone, you will understand and empathize with their pain. We are human, imperfect and will still be tempted in these ways even when we genuinely love someone, but God can provide us with a way to overcome our temptations.

"For the entire law is fulfilled in keeping this one command: "Love your neighbor as yourself." -Galatians 5:14. God saw love as so important; He says all other commands can be fulfilled from this one. He understands when you love someone, the other commands follow more "naturally" when they are motivated by love. When you love your neighbor, you desire to tell them about Jesus as you realize He has changed everything. As we know, our world is falling apart, and many are heading for destruction. If people sense you genuinely love and care for them, they usually won't be quite as defensive if you ask if they know Christ.

"We remember before our God and Father your work produced by faith, your labor prompted by love, and your endurance inspired by hope in our Lord Jesus Christ. For we know, brothers and sisters loved by God, that he has chosen you, because our gospel came to you not simply with words but also with power, with the Holy Spirit and deep conviction." -1 Thessalonians 1:3-5.

Work is produced by faith; labor is prompted by love and endurance is inspired by hope in Jesus. Jesus chooses each one of us. Our words can produce power with the Holy Spirit to others. This is where genuine love, genuine faith, genuine labor and genuine endurance that cannot be shaken comes from. "You became imitators of us and of the Lord, for you welcomed the message in the midst of severe suffering with the joy given by the Holy Spirit." -1 Thessalonians 1:6.

"But for those who are self-seeking and who reject the truth and follow evil, there will be wrath and anger." -Romans 2:8. Without Jesus, love is either not genuine or self-seeking. Jesus allows us to love people for who they are, flaws and all. When we love without Him, we generally only love for our own gain from what we can get from others or for our own protection. When you see others through God's eyes, you cannot help but love them! "Teacher, which is the greatest commandment in the law?" Jesus replied, "Love the Lord your God with all your heart and with all your soul and with all your mind. This is the first and greatest commandment. And the second is like it: "Love your neighbor as yourself" All the law and the prophets hang on these two commandments." -Matthew 22:36-40.

The greatest commandment. Love God and your neighbor with all your heart. You are to be God's living expression of His love! Put others before yourself. Some may argue we need self-care first before taking care of others. I do not disagree in the sense, it is hard to properly care for others when you are sleep deprived, haven't eaten, etc., however, if your motivation to take care of yourself is so you can better take care of others, I believe your heart is still in the right place. I get into the habit of saying "I am spending time with God serving His people" and while that is true, we need alone time with him as well. There will always be more people to help while in this broken world. "He told them, "The harvest is plentiful, but the workers are few. Ask the Lord of the harvest, therefore, to send out workers into his harvest field." -Luke 10:2 (Matthew 9:37-38).

To be genuine, real, we need to care about God's approval over man. When we care about man's approval, we will be swayed left and right because it is impossible to keep people happy. Even worse, not everyone has God and has the heart He desires for us which could lead you down the wrong path. You will be consistent with your ways, answers and life when your focus is on God. God is always genuine. Follow His example and keep it real. I try my best to genuinely love everyone in my life, but I fall short. The important thing is I point others to God who genuinely love them and who will never fail. "Love must be sincere. Hate what is evil; cling to what is good." -Romans 12:9. "Whoever leads the upright along an evil path will fall into their own trap, but the blameless will receive a good inheritance." -Proverbs 28:10.

"You have heard that it was said, 'Love your neighbor and hate your enemy.' But I tell you, love your enemies and pray for those who persecute you," -

Matthew 5:43-44. Love your enemy. This is foreign in our culture today, as we are told to live for ourselves, do what is best for ourselves and if anyone gets in the way of us, get them out of your life ASAP. Now I am asking you to love your enemy and pray for those who persecute you. How? Why? Because this is exactly what God does for us!

"But to you who are listening I say: Love your enemies, do good to those who curse you, pray for those who mistreat you. If someone slaps you on one cheek, turn to them the other also. If someone takes your coat, do not withhold your shirt from them. Give to everyone who asks you, and if anyone takes what belongs to you, do not demand it back. Do to others as you would have them do to you. If you love those who love you, what credit is that to you? Even sinners love those who love them. And if you do good to those who are good to you, what credit is that to you? Even sinners do that. And if you lend to those from whom you expect repayment, what credit is that to you? Even sinners lend to sinners, expecting to be repaid in full. But love your enemies, do good to them, and lend to them without expecting to get anything back. Then your reward will be great, and you will be children of the Most High, because he is kind to the ungrateful and wicked. Be merciful, just as your Father is merciful." -Luke 6:27-36.

Again why? Why would we do this for those who do not treat us right? Because we realize at some point in our lives, we were the enemy in someone else's life.

I once had a co-worker yell at me for things they were venting about. I wanted to yell back, but we are taught to have a gentle approach, possibly even asking what else I can work on or ask how they are feeling. I even received a message later from this individual thanking me for my heart. Trust me when I say I never would have thought I would receive this kind of message. "So, in everything, do to others what you would have them do to you, for this sums up the Law of the Prophets." -Matthew 7:12.

Is there someone in your life no matter how hard you try to get along with, you feel like you can't? Pray for them. Prayer will take away your bitterness. Instead of thinking "jerk," try to think lost or misunderstood just as Jesus did. "Jesus said, "Father, forgive them, for they do not know what they are doing." -Luke 23:34. In Acts 7:55-60 and Acts 6:15 you can read how Stephen was another great example, while being stoned, he prayed the same message for Jesus to receive his spirit and not to hold their sins against them as he died.

True love is a man who wipes your tears away, even when you are the reason He died on the cross. If Jesus can forgive those crucifying Him (aka all of us), there is no one we cannot forgive. I am grateful to have parents who when I tell them I am upset with someone, the first thing they tell me to do is pray for them. It is not always my first instinct even though it should be and would save me a lot of trouble. I can't begin to tell you how much better I feel once I pray for them. It is as if God removes all the bitterness and gives me a new heart for them right there and then.

"As iron sharpens iron, so one person sharpens another." -Proverbs 27:17. "Perfume and incense bring joy to the heart, and the pleasantness of a friend springs from their heartfelt advice. Do not forsake your friend or a friend of your family." -Proverbs 27:9-10. "A true friend is always loyal, and a brother is born to help in time of need." -Proverbs 17:17. We need to make people in our lives a priority. The best way to do this is to make time for others. Even though our own loved ones will hurt us, could gossip about us, and could be cruel to us, we need to forgive and love.

A lot of people wonder why they can't see God. "But "he said, 'you cannot see my face, for no one may see me and live'."-Exodus 33:20. Here in this broken world, His holiness and glory would overwhelm us, however there is a way to see and know Him while here. "No one has ever seen God, but the one and only Son, who is himself God and is in closest relationship with the Father, has made him known." -John 1:18. Want to know who God is? Jesus has made Him known through His word and our personal relationship with Him.

"Dear friends, since God so loved us, we also ought to love one another. No one has ever seen God; but if we love one another, God lives in us, and his love is made complete in us. This is how we know that we live in him and he in us: He has given us of his Spirit. And we have seen and testify that the Father has sent his Son to be the Savior of the world. If anyone acknowledges that Jesus is the Son of God, God lives in them and they in God. And so, we know and rely on the love God has for us. God is love. Whoever lives in love lives in God, and God in them." -1 John 4:11-17 (1 John 3:23-24).

238

"Blessed are the pure in heart, for they will see God." -Matthew 5:8. When we love one another, since the very nature of love is God Himself, we can know Him.

"Dear friends, let us love one another, for love comes from God. Everyone who loves has been born of God and knows God. Whoever does not love does not know God, because God is love." -1 John 4:7-8. "And now, dear lady, I am not writing you a new command but one we have had from the beginning. I ask that we love one another. And this is love: that we walk in obedience to his commands. As you have heard from the beginning, his command is that you walk in love." -2 John 1:5-6. Since we have defined that love is God Himself, He says we show our love for Him when we walk in obedience with Him. "Now that you have purified yourselves by obeying the truth so that you have sincere love for each other, love one another deeply, from the heart." -1 Peter 1:22. When we are obedient, it flows into love for others!

"A new command I give you: Love one another. As I have loved you, so you must love one another. By this everyone will know that you are my disciples, if you love one another." -John 13:34-35 (Romans 15:7 and John 15:8). What makes a Christian stand out? Our love! When we show others love and acceptance, we are showing the very characteristic and love of God. This acceptance does not mean approval of sinful actions. Does God accept our sinful nature? Of course not! Does He accept us due to His love and grace? Absolutely! He expects us to do the same for others.

Even though we may struggle to show genuine love when others wrong us, this is where God steps in. He gives us the ability; you do not have to do it alone. "The righteous choose their friends carefully, but the way of the wicked leads them astray." -Proverbs 12:26. We are to love on and spend time with believers and unbelievers, however, we are to be careful who we spend most of our time with. "Walk with the wise and become wise, for a companion of fools suffers harm. -Proverbs 13:20. We want to love others and stay wise.

"Anyone who runs ahead and does not continue in the teaching of Christ does not have God; whoever continues in the teaching has both the Father and the Son. If anyone comes to you and does not bring this teaching, do not take

239

them into your house or welcome them. Anyone who welcomes them shares in their wicked work." -2 John 1:9-11.

"Do not be misled: "Bad company corrupts good character." Come back to your senses as you ought and stop sinning; for there are some who are ignorant of God—I say this to your shame." -1 Corinthians 15:33-34.

"But avoid foolish controversies and genealogies and arguments and quarrels about the law because these are unprofitable and useless. Warn a divisive person once, and then warn them a second time. After that, have nothing to do with them." -Titus 3:9-10. To summarize, do not get involved in drama and try to cause quarreling.

"But among you there must not be even a hint of sexual immorality, or of any kind of impurity, or of greed, because these are improper for God's holy people. Nor should there be obscenity, foolish talk or coarse joking, which are out of place, but rather thanksgiving. For of this you can be sure: No immoral, impure or greedy person—such a person is an idolater—has any inheritance in the kingdom of Christ and of God. Let no one deceive you with empty words, for because of such things God's wrath comes on those who are disobedient. Therefore, do not be partners with them. For you were once darkness, but now you are light in the Lord. Live as children of light (for the fruit of the light consists in all goodness, righteousness and truth) and find out what pleases the Lord. Have nothing to do with the fruitless deeds of darkness, but rather expose them. It is shameful even to mention what the disobedient do in secret. But everything exposed by the light becomes visible—and everything that is illuminated becomes a light." -Ephesians 5:3-13.

Do not join into evil deeds of others but try to lovingly expose them by showing others why they are hurting themselves and more importantly why you care for them. Be the light in their life. Sometimes what they are doing can be exposed without words when they sense the genuine love you have for them.

"Do not be yoked together with unbelievers. For what do righteousness and wickedness have in common? Or what fellowship can light have with darkness?" -2 Corinthians 6:14.

"I urge you, brothers and sisters, to watch out for those who cause divisions and put obstacles in your way that are contrary to the teaching you have learned. Keep away from them. For such people are not serving our Lord Christ, but their own appetites. By smooth talk and flattery, they deceive the minds of naive people. Everyone has heard about your obedience, so I rejoice because of you; but I want you to be wise about what is good, and innocent about what is evil." -Romans 16:17-19.

We can love others and spend time with them without becoming "yoked" with them if we feel they are trying to cause divisions in our relationships. Flattery is when people are kind for their own gain. When you notice the difference between someone just showing flattery around you as opposed to genuine love, pray for them. Even if their intentions are evil, we should have compassion on them and realize they are trying to fill a void that cannot be filled by whatever they feel they are trying to gain. We are all on the same team. Those against you are wearing the same jersey but haven't had a chance to look down at it because they are blinded by the actual enemy, Satan.

Loving our neighbors means letting go of the right to judge. This term "judge" means letting go of the right to condemnation. However, many people will use this as an excuse in order to not be held accountable. We can assess and evaluate, but do not judge. We are to judge the ones we love by holding them accountable for their own good, as they should do for us. It is quite unfortunate many feel we need to be permissive to show love. If I have something on my face, someone who loves me would tell me no matter how awkward. Let's get even more serious. Let's say you have a life-threatening illness. Would I be loving you if I had the cure, and did not give it to you? Sin is worse than a life-threatening illness and destroys you from the inside out. If I had the answer and did not tell you, you would argue that I am your enemy. If hell is real (and it is) and you don't want those you love to go there, it can help as motivation to share even when it might feel uncomfortable. Love causes us to do some crazy things!

If someone knows I am sinning and destroying my life, true love is someone telling me to get back on track. "Brothers and sisters, if someone is caught in a sin, you who live by the Spirit should restore that person gently. But watch yourselves, or you also may be tempted. Carry each other's burdens, and in this way, you will fulfill the law of Christ."-Galatians 6:1-2. Restore *gently* and carry each other's burdens within the process.

"Even if I caused you sorrow by my letter, I do not regret it. Though I did regret it—I see that my letter hurt you, but only for a little while— yet now I am happy, not because you were made sorry, but because your sorrow led you to repentance. For you became sorrowful as God intended and so were not harmed in any way by us. Godly sorrow brings repentance that leads to salvation and leaves no regret, but worldly sorrow brings death. See what this godly sorrow has produced in you: what earnestness, what eagerness to clear yourselves, what indignation, what alarm, what longing, what concern, what readiness to see justice done. At every point you have proved yourselves to be innocent in this matter." -2 Corinthians 7:8-11.

"If you really keep the royal law found in Scripture, "Love your neighbor as yourself," you are doing right. But if you show favoritism, you sin and are convicted by the law as lawbreakers." -James 2:8-9 (James 2:1). "Anyone who does wrong will be repaid for their wrongs, and there is no favoritism." -Colossians 3:25. "Then Peter began to speak: "I now realize how true it is that God does not show favoritism but accepts from every nation the one who fears him and does what is right." -Acts 10:34-35 (Galatians 2:6, Romans 2:11, Colossians 4:1, and Ephesians 6:9).

There is nothing wrong with making your spouse, family and friends' priority, however, we are called to show love to all and not play favorites. Jesus had His close group of disciples, but was sure to show love, attention and take care of all who were around him. I remind myself of this when I have patients of many kinds such as famous athletes, judges, politicians, professors or those from prisons. I try to treat them all with the love God has for each of them. He even showed love to those who treated Him poorly, asking God to forgive them. "Therefore, as God's chosen people, holy and dearly loved, clothe yourselves with compassion, kindness and humility, gentleness and patience." -Colossians 3:12.

"Then the King will say to those on his right, 'Come, you who are blessed by my Father; take your inheritance, the kingdom prepared for you since the creation of the world. For I was hungry, and you gave me something to eat, I was thirsty, and you gave me something to drink, I was a stranger and you invited me in, I needed clothes, and you clothed me, I was sick and you looked after me, I was in prison and you came to visit me.' "Then the righteous will answer him, 'Lord, when did we see you hungry and feed you, or thirsty and give you something to drink? When did we see you a stranger and invite you in, or needing clothes and clothe you? When did we see you sick or in prison and go to visit you?' "The King will reply, 'Truly I tell you, whatever you did for one of the least of these brothers and sisters of mine, you did for me.'" -Matthew 25:34-41 (Colossians 1:9-14, Proverbs 19:17, Proverbs 28:27, and Proverbs 19:17).

What if we pictured every single individual we met as Jesus himself? This is exactly what He is saying we do when we serve others. As parents, nothing makes you feel better than knowing someone is taking good care of your children. We are taking care of God's children when we serve others.

"Do not forget to show hospitality to strangers, for by so doing some people have shown hospitality to angels without knowing it."-Hebrews 13:2. "Offer hospitality to one another without grumbling." -1 Peter 4:9 (Romans 12:13 and 3 John 8).

"Anyone who welcomes you welcomes me, and anyone who welcomes me welcomes the one who sent me. Whoever welcomes a prophet as a prophet will receive a prophet's reward, and whoever welcomes a righteous person as a righteous person will receive a righteous person's reward. And if anyone gives even a cup of cold water to one of these little ones who is my disciple, truly I tell you, that person will certainly not lose their reward." -Matthew 10:40-42.

"When you enter a house, first say, 'Peace to this house.' If someone who promotes peace is there, your peace will rest on them; if not, it will return to you." -Luke 10:5-6. "Greet Rufus, chosen in the Lord, and his mother, who has been a mother to me, too." -Romans 16:13. Jesus is so clear when we help others and show them hospitality, because He loves each person so much, it is as if we are welcoming Him into our homes. Now it is one thing to show hospitality, and it is one thing to do it without grumbling. It can be very inconvenient and depending on who stays, not fun to be hospitable, however, if God tells us to not grumble, there is a way to do it with joy. Ask Him to show you! Trust me, my parents were very hospitable to the point of allowing strangers access to our home. One time I came down for a snack late in the evening, and one of our family friends was in the dining room. I was a little startled once in a while, but I loved their example of their hospitality, and it was so cool to see how God used it to share His love. I also think what is hard is many people feel they don't have the finances to be hospitable to all. I had roller skating parties when I was younger, and it was the same price to rent the roller rink no matter how many people came. With some prayer and creativity, anything is possible. David even when as far as to restore the land and invite Jonathan to always eat at his table. Jonathan is the grandchild of his enemy Saul who tried to kill him. Usually when a new king took the throne, you did not associate with the old king's family, and David was trying to be killed by the old king! Since he was a man after God's own heart, he chose to go against the grain, and we should too. "Don't be afraid," David said to him.... I will restore to you all the land that belonged to your grandfather Saul, and you will always eat at my table." -2 Samuel 9:7.

"But when you give a banquet, invite the poor, the crippled, the lame, the blind, and you will be blessed. Although they cannot repay you, you will be repaid at the resurrection of the righteous." -Luke 14:13-14. The "least of these" is not just the poor, it is everyone. "After that, he poured water into a basin, and began to wash his disciples'' feet, drying them with the towel that was wrapped around him." -John 13:5. The night before Jesus knew he would be crucified; he chose to wash his disciples' feet. He knew they were going to abandon Him, and He would be alone on the cross. He chose to do it anyway. We say loving others is risky and it is. Others can hurt us, talk negative about us and even leave us. We are called to love anyway, as we have the best example to follow.

Sometimes to love our neighbor means inconveniencing ourselves. This would be a time we all have busy schedules and obligations. Satan will always try to give you an excuse to put yourself before someone else. When you give time, attention, and love to others, you are telling them they matter. We all know how precious time is, and when you give it to others you are telling them how valuable they are. Also, be genuine. "As water reflects the face, so one's life reflects the heart." -Proverbs 27:19. Don't fake it. Do not be on your phone while talking to others. People notice. Are you the friend people come to when they are down? Do people feel they can come to you and be real without judgment as in condemnation? Are you the friend people know will tell the truth and hold them accountable if they are sinning or in other words, only harming themselves? Are you a true friend during the best times and the worst? Are you trustworthy, even behind peoples backs? Pray for friends. There is nothing better you can do for them to display these attributes. "...not looking to your own interests but each of you to the interests of the others." - Philippians 2. We need to make time for others. Giving time is one of the best ways to show love because everyone knows how precious and short it is. This means put down the phone when you are with others. This means writing a letter. This means reaching out to others. This means choosing to make those in your life a priority and meeting their needs before your own. It will not only benefit others, but God says it will benefit you.

"An honest answer is like a kiss on the lips." -Proverbs 24:26. "A gossip betrays a confidence, but a trustworthy person keeps a secret." -Proverbs 11:13. "A perverse person stirs up conflict, and a gossip separates close friends." -Proverbs 16:28. We all struggle with it. We forget it is a sin. Also, the worst is once your loved ones know you are gossiping, your trust is broken. I find it hardest not to gossip when others come to you to gossip. You feel awkward asking them to stop or awkward if you do not add to the conversation. Let the individual know you are there to listen and help them; however, try to help them find something positive about the individual they are talking about. If this person coming to you is truly distressed by an individual, offer to pray with them and talk in such a way that if the person you are talking about were listening, they could tell you are talking out of sincere concern and not to tear them down. If you are talking about someone's appearance, you are talking down on the very beautiful creation God hand crafted himself, in His image. "But the Lord said to Samuel, "Do not consider his appearance or his height, for I have rejected him. The Lord does not look at the things people look at. People look at the outward appearance, but the Lord looks at the heart." -1 Samuel 16:7. God looks at the heart, and we should too. "Like a snow-cooled drink at harvest time is a trustworthy messenger to the one who send him; he refreshes the spirit of his master." -Proverbs 25:13.

"Timothy, guard what has been entrusted to your care. Turn away from godless chatter and the opposing ideas of what is falsely called knowledge, which some have professed and in so doing have departed from the faith. Grace be with you all." -1 Timothy 6:20-21.

"There are six things the Lord hates, seven that are detestable to him: haughty eyes, a lying tongue, hands that shed innocent blood, a heart that devises wicked schemes, feet that are quick to rush into evil, a false witness who pours out lies and a person who stirs up conflict in the community." -Proverbs 6:16-19.

"A false witness will not go unpunished, and whoever pours out lies will not go free." -Proverbs 19:5.

What do we do if others are gossiping about us and we are hurt, our trust broken? "For I hear many whisperings, "Terror on every side!" They conspire against me and plot to take my life. But I trust in you, Lord; I say, "You are my God." My times are in your hands." -Psalm 31:13-15 (2 Chronicles 20:12). First, trust God and understand He is the one who defines you, not what others say. "…you keep them safe in your dwelling from accusing tongues." -Psalm 31:20. "Many have become my enemies without cause; those who hate me without reason are numerous. Those who repay my good with evil lodge accusations against me, though I seek only to do what is good." -Psalm 38:19-20. Sometimes people gossip out of their own insecurities, and it is good to realize this. This does not make you a "push over" but truly compassionate as to understand why others would talk negative behind your back. I have had best friends talk behind my back that are still my close friends today. I forgave them, realizing even though in the moment what they said hurt, they were struggling with their own hurt. Now if gossip becomes a consistent thing within a friendship, this may be a time to have a talk with that person. "One who has unreliable friends soon comes to ruin, but there is a friend who sticks closer than a brother." -Proverbs 18:24. You can remain loving toward them, but it might be healthy to not have them as one of your closest friends. Pray to God, talk to your friends reminding them that gossip is a sin, and even when they talk about others, they are hurting themselves. You cannot sin against God and not have some form of hurt. "Even my close friend, someone I trusted, one who shared my bread, has turned against me." -Psalm 41:9. Talk to Jesus if you are hurt by a friend gossiping about you. He had the ultimate betrayal when one of His closest friends sold Him to be crucified, for the sum of money they would sell a slave.

"You shall have no other gods before me." -Exodus 20:3. We like to remember the golden calf. However, this could mean our phones. For me it can be sports or even other people in our lives. God calls us to love our family, friend and strangers, but they are not supposed to take God's number one priority in our lives. We love others better when we put God first. Also, we don't realize how much we idolize celebrities. When we are looking to them as examples instead of Jesus, we are asking for trouble. When we are more worried about what is happening in their lives as compared to our own, we are idolizing.

"And I tell you that you are Peter, and on this rock, I will build my church, and the gates of Hades will not overcome it." In Matthew 16:18, God is saying his church is going to last forever. Many churches may be failing, but the church of believers who follow the Word of God will never be abolished completely. Who is the church? We are. We are called to be a family in Christ, and to go to the ends of the earth to make disciples. Jesus loved the church so much He died for it, His bride. We are to do the same. However, how do we gather with other believers as God calls us to do? Many times, in a building on Sunday! I understand people like to emphasize that the church is not a building, and even though that is true, there is something beautiful about gathering all together in one area to worship our Jesus together!

We need to make sure as the body of Christ we are keeping the church as God intended.

"Jesus entered the temple courts and drove out all who were buying and selling there. He overturned the tables of the money changers and the benches of those selling doves. "It is written," he said to them, "'My house will be called a house of prayer,' but you are making it 'a den of robbers.'" The blind and the lame came to him at the temple, and he healed them. But when the chief priests and the teachers of the law saw the wonderful things, he did and the children shouting in the temple courts, "Hosanna to the Son of David," they were indignant. "Do you hear what these children are saying?" they asked him. "Yes," replied Jesus, "have you never read, "'From the lips of children and infants you, Lord, have called forth your praise'?"" -Matthew 21:12-16 (Mark 11:15-18).

I want to show you how powerful prayer is for reconciling relationships. There was

247

one point I felt some of my friendships were drifting apart. I truly cared about these friendships. I prayed for them to be rekindled. God answered, and I ended up standing up as bridesmaids in their weddings. There was a time I really took seriously those I thought I may have not given the best impression of myself to, and I prayed I could make up for it. I ended up moving out on my roommate after only a week. Not because of my roommate, but because I was frustrated that they did not put me where I originally wanted to live. She ended up being a student at the clinic I am at, and I was able to talk to her more! I was so frustrated when I could not be roommates with the friends, I met initially my freshmen year of college. However, it worked out, because it led me to room with one of my best friends whom I still have today. God desires reconciliation, and prayer is powerful. Of course, we cannot force people to reconcile but I encourage you to pray for those you feel you need to pray for the situation, reach out to them and see God work, even if it is not immediate because He is faithful, and oh so good! "I will praise your name, Lord, for it is good." -Psalms 54:6.

"Then God said, "Let us make mankind in our image, in our likeness, so that they may rule over the fish in the sea and the birds in the sky, over the livestock and all the wild animals, and over all the creatures that move along the ground." -Genesis 1:26. We are made in God's image, which is why nothing else will ever satisfy. No money, fame, substance or person. Then He said we will rule over the earth when Satan was ruling the earth. We are also called to take care and love the environment. God has given us power and authority over the earth and other livings creatures. I am not saying you must take care of the environment to the point of not being able to live your daily life and go bankrupt, but at least appreciate His creation and take care of the earth when opportunities arise. If you do have pets or livestock, take care of their needs. I understand some people have had a bad experience and are afraid of animals, but just like with people who hurt us, it is good to remember they are God's creation too and we are asked by God to take care of them, even if that care may be more at a distance for you. "The righteous care for the needs of their animals." -Proverbs 12:10.

"Consider therefore the kindness and sternness of God." -Romans 11:22 (1 Samuel 20:14). God has the perfect way of handling us with kindness but being stern when He needs to be like a Father shoulder. "Anyone who withholds kindness from friend forsakes the fear of the Almighty." -Job 6:14. God asks us to be kind to our friends. "A kindhearted woman gains honor." -Proverbs 11:16. God asks us to be kind to all around us. "Those who are kind benefit themselves." -Proverbs 11:17. Even though when we are kind it *can* benefit us as Proverbs says, be careful that the motivation of your heart is not for personal gain, or it could turn to flattery. We are human and this can easily happen, and constant heart checks are important. "It is a sin to despise one's neighbor, but blessed is the one who is kind to the needy." -Proverbs 14:21. Do not despise *anyone but* be kind to those in need. Who is in need? Everyone. Just ask, we all are in need whether it is a physical, spiritual, emotional, or a social need. "Blessed are those who have regard for the weak; the Lord delivers them in times of trouble." -Psalm 41:1.

"Absalom said to Hushai, "So this is the love you show your friend? If he's your friend, why didn't you go with him?" -2 Samuel 16:17. Friends join one another in this adventure called life. "Then Job replied: "I have heard many things like these; you are miserable comforters, all of you!" -Job 16:1-2. "I could make fine speeches against you and shake my head at you. But my mouth would encourage you; comfort from my lips would bring you relief." -Job 16:4-5. Job's "friends" blamed him for the pain he was going through, thinking God must be punishing him instead of comforting him. In this broken world, we will experience heartache whether it is our fault or not. Regardless of what you feel about someone's situation and whether it was self-inflicted, or not, we are called to comfort and show grace. You may have friends in which tough love is needed to help them move forward if they are causing their own pain. But there is a time and place, and during the initial hurt, the time to simply be there and comfort them, even if words are exchanged. Job said we should instead be encouraging, as our comforting words can sometimes bring others relief.

'My son, if sinful men entice you, do not give in to them" Proverbs 1:10. "Hatred stirs up conflict, but love covers all wrongs." -Proverbs 10:12. If people are trying to encourage you to hate someone, do not give in. Hatred only brings about heartache, turmoil and frankly, God simply commands we do not hate. "Above all, love each other deeply, because love covers over a multitude of sins." -1 Peter 4:8. Even if you have been hurt beyond belief by someone, love covers over a multitude of sins. Genuine love. "Through love and faithfulness sin is atoned for; through the fear of the Lord evil is avoided." -Proverbs 16:6.

"Be careful not to practice your righteousness in front of others to be seen by them. If you do, you will have no reward from your Father in Heaven. "So, when you give to the needy, do not announce it with trumpets, as the hypocrites do in the synagogues and on the streets, to be honored by others. Truly I tell you, they have received their reward in full. But when you give to the needy, do not let your left hand know what your right hand is doing, 4 so that your giving may be in secret. Then your Father, who sees what is done in secret, will reward you." -Matthew 6:1-4.

Part of being genuine is your integrity. You do not change because of who is watching. Even if no one realized the good you were doing, you should do it anyways. I do not know about you, but I struggle with this. It took some serious heart checking and asking God to make sure my heart was genuine, helping others because of a genuine love for them and a gain from others watching.

"The Lord says: "These people come near to me with their mouth and honor me with their lips, but their hearts are far from me. Their worship of me is based on merely human rules they have been taught. Therefore, once more I will astound these people with wonder upon wonder; the wisdom of the wise will perish, the intelligence of the intelligent will vanish." -Isaiah 29:13-14.

To be genuine, our hearts must match our words. To become genuine, we need to be held accountable to God and in His word which does not change, unlike humans who do change. Nothing can separate His love for you. His *personal* love for you.

"On one occasion an expert in the law stood up to test Jesus. "Teacher," he asked, "what must I do to inherit eternal life?" "What is written in the Law?" he replied. "How do you read it?" He answered, "'Love the Lord your God with all your heart and with all your soul and with all your strength and with all your mind'; and 'Love your neighbor as yourself.'" "You have answered correctly," Jesus replied. "Do this and you will live." But he wanted to justify himself, so he asked Jesus, "And who is my neighbor?" In reply Jesus said: "A man was going down from Jerusalem to Jericho, when he was attacked by robbers. They stripped him of his clothes, beat him and went away, leaving him half dead. A priest happened to be going down the same road, and when he saw the man, he passed by on the other side. So too, a Levite, when he came to the place and saw him, passed by on the other side. But a Samaritan, as he traveled, came where the man was; and when he saw him, he took pity on him. He went to him and bandaged his wounds, pouring on oil and wine. Then he put the man on his own donkey, brought him to an inn and took care of him. The next day he took out two denarii and gave them to the innkeeper. 'Look after him,' he said, 'and when I return, I will reimburse you for any extra expense you may have.' "Which of these three do you think was a neighbor to the man who fell into the hands of robbers?" The expert in the law replied, "The one who had mercy on him." Jesus told him, "Go and do likewise." -Luke 10:25-37.

Who is our neighbor? Anyone in need. Who is in need? Everyone. It does not matter your job, title, circumstance, where you live, God has provided the opportunity for you to be a neighbor to those around you. You might not find someone lying on the side of the road, there are many lying on the sides of our lives that need your help and encouragement to get back up. Be their neighbor with your genuine love!

You cannot love God without loving others, as he is saying when we love others, we are loving him and ultimately ourselves. Jesus said to Peter "if you love me, you will feed my sheep." -John 21:17 (John 21:15-16). "The Jews were amazed how Jesus had so much knowledge without being taught. Jesus said his teaching is not his own, it is from God who sent him. Anyone who speaks on their own does for personal glory, but he who seeks the glory God is one of truth, there is nothing false about him." -John 7:15-18.

"Devote to breaking bread and praying, gather with other believers, give to anyone in need and every day continue to meet. Break bread in your homes with a glad and sincere heart, praising God and enjoying the favor of all the people. The Lord added to their number daily to those being saved," -Acts 2:42-47 (1 Corinthians 11:26, 1 Corinthians 29-30, 1 Corinthians 11:26 and 1 Corinthians 10:16-17, and Acts 9:28). How are we to strengthen and grow as a church? What are some ideas in ways to help our neighbors? An example God gives is having others over for meals in our homes, praying, gathering and seeing what their needs are. Only God himself can meet every individual's needs, so this is not to put pressure on you, but to see how God can use you when you are willing to meet the needs of others. Many times, He will provide for you to help someone else. He wants your heart sincere when you help, and sometimes helping others may not be physical but just your encouragement or time spent.

"In everything I did, I showed you that by this kind of hard work we must help the weak, remembering the words the Lord Jesus himself said: 'It is more blessed to give than to receive." -Acts 20:35. Giving to others will always benefit you more than receiving.

"For by the grace given me I say to every one of you: Do not think of yourself more highly than you ought, but rather think of yourself with sober judgment, in accordance with the faith God has distributed to each of you. For just as each of us has one body with many members, and these members do not all have the same function, so in Christ we, though many, form one body, and each member belongs to all the others. We have different gifts, according to the grace given to each of us. If your gift is prophesying, then prophesy in accordance with your faith; if it is serving, then serve; if it is teaching, then teach; if it is to encourage, then give encouragement; if it is giving, then give generously; if it is to lead, do it diligently; if it is to show mercy, do it cheerfully. Love must be sincere. Hate what is evil; cling to what is good. Be devoted to one another in love. Honor one another above yourselves." -Romans 12:3-10.

We all have gifts from God, and He wants us to use them cheerfully. Love must be sincere. His definition of sincerity is to love someone above yourself. We are to love ourselves, knowing we are valuable and loved in Christ, and when you do, God can help you love others that much more. We live in a culture that is all about doing what is best for ourselves and not necessarily what is best for others. The ironic thing is I am so much more fulfilled in joy and love when loving others above myself.

"Rejoice with those who rejoice; mourn with those who mourn. [16] Live in harmony with one another. Do not be proud but be willing to associate with people of low position. Do not be conceited." -Romans 12:15-16. Rejoice with those who rejoice and mourn with those who mourn. There is true supernatural power in increasing someone's joy when you rejoice with them and lighten the burden of someone who is mourning when you are there in the painful process with them. As much as it depends on you, live in harmony with one another and be humble. God wants you to comfort others because you are comforting those He loves. Now you can care for someone going through a hard time or depression by carrying the burden while not becoming obsessed or overwhelmed with grief, which can affect your own family and life. Let your heart break with those you are comforting, but then realize since they are weak, you can also be their strength in prayer by giving their situation to God. My own example would be my work at the clinic. With my patients, I mourn their loss, physically, psychologically, spiritually and emotionally; however, at the end of the day I must give it to God in prayer because if I brought it home every night, it could affect my other relationships by causing burnout. We can ask God for the balance of grieving with others, but also staying joyful as their light of hope. "Comfort, comfort my people, says your God." -Isaiah 40:1.

"For if someone with a weak conscience sees you, with all your knowledge, eating in an idol's temple, won't that person be emboldened to eat what is sacrificed to idols? So, this weak brother or sister, for whom Christ died, is destroyed by your knowledge. When you sin against them in this way and wound their weak conscience, you sin against Christ. Therefore, if what I eat causes my brother or sister to fall into sin, I will never eat meat again, so that I will not cause them to fall." -1 Corinthians 8:10-13 (Romans 14:21).

For example, if I want to have a drink, it is not wrong. However, if I am with my alcoholic friend, having a drink may tempt them into getting drunk, which is a sin. Although there is nothing wrong with me having a drink, I would not be loving them if I choose to drink in their presence.

"Just as a body, though one, has many parts, but all its many parts forms one body, so it is with Christ." -1 Corinthians 12:12.

"Now if the foot should say, "Because I am not a hand, I do not belong to the body," it would not for that reason stop being part of the body. And if the ear should say, "Because I am not an eye, I do not belong to the body," it would not for that reason stop being part of the body. If the whole body were an eye, where would the sense of hearing be? If the whole body were an ear, where would the sense of smell be? But in fact, God has placed the parts in the body, every one of them, just as he wanted them to be. If they were all one part, where would the body be? As it is, there are many parts, but one body. The eye cannot say to the hand, "I don't need you!" And the head cannot say to the feet, "I don't need you!" On the contrary, those parts of the body that seem to be weaker are indispensable, and the parts that we think are less honorable we treat with special honor. And the parts that are unpresentable are treated with special modesty." -1 Corinthians 12:15-23 (1 Corinthians 12:13-14).

Even though we each have different roles in God's design, story and plan, each are equally as important. I think if you were to ask someone if they would rather lose their hearing, eyesight, mobility, or smell, they may be funny and tell you which they feel is most important, but we know how hard it would be to lose one of these functions.

"If one part suffers, every part suffers with it; if one part is honored, every part rejoices with it. Now you are the body of Christ, and each one of you is a part of it. And God has placed in the church first of all apostles, second prophets, third teachers, then miracles, then gifts of healing, of helping, of guidance, and of different kinds of tongues." -1 Corinthians 12:26-28.

God is redeeming the Earth through Christ, who is the Church, from the enemy through each one of us. If one part of the body suffers, we all suffer which is why we must look out for one another. As a therapist, if our trunk or neck has a nerve impingement, it can affect the entire arm down to the fingertips, whether from pain or loss of motion. When we hurt one another, we are only hurting ourselves.

"Such people should realize that what we are in our letters when we are absent, we will be in our actions when we are present." -2 Corinthians 10:11. We need to do what we say we will do. "Am I now trying to win the approval of human beings, or of God? Or am I trying to please people? If I were still trying to please people, I would not be a servant of Christ." -Galatians 1:10.

"Isaiah said this because he saw Jesus' glory and spoke about him. Yet at the same time many even among the leaders believed in him. But because of the Pharisees they would not openly acknowledge their faith for fear they would be put out of the synagogue;]' for they loved human praise more than praise from God." -

John 41-43.

When you try to please people, you will lose your genuineness about you, because many people will ask of different tasks from you which may affect your morals of how you want to live. When you are a God pleaser, you will do all you can to love people. God loves people more than anyone, and of course it is ok to want to please them *if* it is out of love for them and approving to the Lord. However, if anyone ever asks you to do anything apart from God's word or will, we need to uphold our relationship and wanting to please God more. Receiving praise from others is not bad, and is encouraging, however do not live your life in a way as to seek it out or you will continue to be disappointed your whole life, as no matter what you do someone will disapprove and people cannot see the big picture like God can. Seek praise from God, as He is truthful, encouraging and sees your potential better than anyone. "On the contrary, we speak as those approved by God to be entrusted with the gospel. We are not trying to please people but God, who tests our hearts." -1 Thessalonians 2:4.

"Instead, speaking the truth in love, we will grow to become in every respect the mature body of him who is the head, that is, Christ. From him the whole body, joined and held together by every supporting ligament, grows and builds itself up in love, as each part does its work." -Ephesians 4:15-16. Speaking the truth in love is a tough skill that God will help you with if you ask. Tone and demeanor is everything. Most of the time, people can tell when you are being truthful because you care, as opposed to trying to bring them down. As each of us gets stronger in our faith, we can build up and support others. When working with patients for example, if one ligament of the joint is weak, the entire joint is, however, sometimes you can strengthen the muscles around the joint to create stability.

"Follow God's example therefore, as dearly loved children." -Ephesians 5:1. We are God's children, and He wants us to grow up and mimic Him as a child mimics their Father. Who is God's example? Jesus! How did Jesus act?

"Do nothing out of selfish ambition or vain conceit. Rather, in humility value others above yourselves, not looking to your own interests but each of you to the interests of the others. In your relationships with one another, have the same mindset as Christ Jesus: Who, being in very nature God, did not consider equality with God something to be used to his own advantage; rather, he made himself nothing by taking the very nature of a servant, being made in human likeness. And being found in appearance as a man, he humbled himself by becoming obedient to death— even death on a cross!" -Philippians 2:3-8.

"Do nothing out of selfishness and think of others as higher than yourself but looking into the interests of others over your own. Jesus who was equal to God, being God Himself did not even take advantage of this but became a servant. He served all the way to the cross for us, sacrificing all He had for us, those He loves. We are to do the same, and the only way you can comprehend serving to this point is to realize what Jesus has done for you. Until we stay fixated on Him, us putting others above ourselves or serving to this point will seem like foolishness, but once you experience this intense and life changing love, it completely pours out of you to others. No one should seek their own good, but the good of others." -1 Corinthians 10:24.

"I have no one else like him, who will show genuine concern for your welfare. For everyone looks out for their own interests, not those of Jesus Christ." -Philippians 2:20-21. When we are humble, we are not degrading ourselves or thinking we have less value. When I meet humble people, they are usually overall cheerful, smart, and care about you as a person. He doesn't think about Himself, only others.

"Continue to remember those in prison as if you were together with them in prison, and those who are mistreated as if you yourselves were suffering." -Hebrews 13:3. "Religion that God our Father accepts as pure and faultless is this: to look after orphans and widows in their distress and to keep oneself from being polluted by the world." -James 1:27. Other than loving the very ones God has placed in your life genuinely, He also points out to show genuine love to those in prison, orphans and widows.

"Anyone who claims to be in the light but hates a brother or sister is still in the darkness. Anyone who loves their brother and sister lives in the light, and there is nothing in them to make them stumble. But anyone who hates a brother or sister is in the darkness and walks around in the darkness. They do not know where they are going, because the darkness has blinded them." -1 John 2:9-11.

You cannot hate your brother and sister when you have Christ, because God is love in His nature, who is living in you. Even though we are sinners and stumble in this area, it makes me sick to my stomach when I feel the feelings of hate even begin to seep into me and who it turns me into. The truth of recognizing we cannot be in Christ and hate convicts me more than anything in a beautiful way, to soften my heart toward my neighbor who has wronged me. When we have Christ, we recognize how evil we are. When people do not have Christ, they are blind to the bad and think they are good. "Whoever claims to love God yet hates a brother or sister is a liar. For whoever does not love their brother and sister, whom they have seen, cannot love God, whom they have not seen. And he has given us this command: Anyone who loves God must also love their brother and sister." -1 John 4:20-21.

"For this is the message you heard from the beginning: We should love one another. Do not be like Cain, who belonged to the evil one and murdered his brother. And why did he murder him? Because his own actions were evil, and his brothers were righteous. Do not be surprised, my brothers and sisters, if the world hates you. We know that we have passed from death to life, because we love each other. Anyone who does not love remains in death. Anyone who hates a brother or sister is a murderer, and you know that no murderer has eternal life residing in him. This is how we know what love is: Jesus Christ laid down his life for us. And we ought to lay down our lives for our brothers and sisters. If anyone has material possessions and sees a brother or sister in need but has no pity on them, how can the love of God be in that person? Dear children, let us not love with words or speech but with actions and in truth." -1 John 3:11-18.

Cain murdered his brother because of jealousy. God gave him multiple times to repent, but his pride would not let him. We have all been jealous. It is a strong and terrible feeling in which you may feel a lack of control and hate for someone else. Do not let it get to that point. When the enemy throws these feelings at you, comparing yourself to someone else, pray immediately for God to remove those feelings and express how you do not want to feel this way. If you linger and keep your thoughts fixated on the individual, hate will begin to creep in. If you hate, in God's eyes of justice, you have murdered that individual in your heart. This shows how serious it is to hate others, and why we need to strive toward love. What is love? How can we love? As Christ died for us, we ought to do the same for others. Love is action. Words of affirmation are beautiful, do not get me wrong, but if we tell someone we love them without action, the truth is not being expressed through us.

"This is how God showed his love among us: He sent his one and only Son into the world that we might live through him. This is love: not that we loved God, but that he loved us and sent his Son as an atoning sacrifice for our sins." -1 John 4:9-10 (Ephesians 5:2). His love is better than life. Never say you are unloved, or that someone else is unloved. He loves you so much that our sin did not stop Him from dying for us, no matter the cost. When we understand and have this love, it overflows out of us to others.

"Everyone who believes that Jesus is the Christ is born of God, and everyone who loves the father loves his child as well. This is how we know that we love the children of God: by loving God and carrying out his commands." -1 John 5:1-2. When we are in love with Christ, He leads us to genuinely love His children. His children are all of those around us, that we come across every single day. "Greet the friends there by name." -3 John 1:14. Call them by name. I have noticed a difference in how others respond to me, and even how I respond to others when I feel they have a personal love and interest in me, generally calling me by name. Let His love shine through you in such a way people do not see you, but Him.

Faith Over Fear

"I can do all things through Christ who strengthens me. -" Philippians 4:13

I can *be courageous* through Christ who strengthens me.

"Have I not commanded you? Be strong and courageous. Do not be afraid; do not be discouraged, for the Lord your God will be with you wherever you go." - Joshua 1:9 (1 Chronicles 22:13, Joshua 1:6, Deuteronomy 31:6-8 and Deuteronomy 31:23). God tells us not to be afraid for a reason. If we do not have Him, this world is something we should be fearful of. The only way to push past your fear is to realize He is with us wherever we go. "The Lord himself goes before you and will be with you; He will never leave nor forsake you. Do not be afraid; do not be discouraged." -Deuteronomy 31:8. "The Lord said to Joshua, "Do not be afraid of them; I have given them into your hand. Not one of them will be able to withstand you." -Joshua 10:8.

Courage is what is used to overcome fear, but it does not mean you are not afraid. "There is no fear in love, perfect love drives out fear." -1 John 4:18. The opposite of fear is not courage, it is love, and God is love. God does not make mistakes. We never have to fear for our life, because He uses ours for His perfect will. "So do not fear, for I am with you; do not be dismayed, for I am your God. I will strengthen you and help you; I will uphold you with my righteous right hand... For am the Lord your God who takes hold of your right hand and says to you, do not fear; I will help you." -Isaiah 41:10 (Isaiah 41:13, Isaiah 43:5 and Haggai 2:4-5).

One of my biggest fears in life is that I will not use every ounce of my potential God has given me to glorify Him. Do not be afraid to use your gifts! Pray and ask God what your gifts are and how He wants you to use them. We are His body, and our hands need to start reaching out and not letting fear stop us. "Do not be afraid, Abram. I am your shield, your very great reward." -Genesis 15:1.

"Are not two sparrows sold for a penny? Yet not one of them will fall to the ground apart from the will of your Father. And even the very hairs on your head are numbered. So don't be afraid; you are worth more than many sparrows." -Matthew 10:29-31 (Luke 12:6-7). You are valued. Not one bird in this world falls without our God knowing it. How much more are you worth?! Beyond measure! God knows every single hair on your head. What do we have to be afraid of? Only God Himself!

There was a furious storm on the water with waves coming over the boat as Jesus was sleeping. The disciples yelled to him for help, saying they were going to drown. Jesus said, "You of little faith, why are you so afraid?" He got up and rebuked the storm. Complete calmness. "What kind of man is this? Even the winds and the waves obey him!" -Matthew 8:24-27 (Mark 4:37-41 and Luke 8:24-25). When we focus on the storms in the world and in our lives, you will become fearful which will lead to discouragement. When you focus on Jesus, while it doesn't make your storm less scary, but it does remind you who oversees the storm, this world and this life. "The people were all so amazed that they asked each other, "What is this? A new teaching—and with authority! He even gives orders to impure spirits, and they obey him." -Mark 1:27. "He taught as one who had authority." -Matthew 7:28-29 (Mark 1:22). Jesus has the authority over all the earth and mankind. Who are we to be afraid of?

What happens around us and to us have small effects compared to the God who lies within us. "He will have no fear of bad news; his heart is steadfast, trusting in the Lord." -Psalm 112:7. I know we have all received news that leaves us so afraid and hurt that we find ourselves numb, shaken and experiencing pain so deep we cannot put it into words. When we are steadfast in a relationship with the Lord and His word, and we hear bad news, it does not take away the sting and pain we feel deep down, but we can have trust in the One who created us and Who allows us to take our next breath.

"So, this is what the Sovereign Lord says: 'See, I lay a stone in Zion, a tested stone, a precious cornerstone for a sure foundation; the one who relies on it will never be stricken with panic.'"-Isaiah 28:16. With Jesus, there is no panic. "When you go to war seeing an army greater than yours, do not be afraid, fainthearted or panic because the Lord your God will be with you. For the Lord your God is the one who goes with you to fight for you to give you victory." - Deuteronomy 20:1-4. We can trust God is never surprised by the news we hear. He already knows. He knows the heart and we never have to be afraid because He already has plans to work out these situations for our good when we rely on Him. "But the plans of the Lord stand firm forever, the purposes of his heart through all generations." -Psalm 33:11 (Jeremiah 50:12 and Revelation 17:17).

"The disciples caught nothing all night, and in the morning, Jesus was on the shore, but they did not recognize him. He said to them "Friends, haven't you any fish?" "No," they answered. He said, "Throw your net on the right side of the boat and you will find some." When they did, they were unable to haul the net in because of the large number of fish. Then John said, "It is the Lord!" Peter jumped into the water. The other disciples followed in the boat. Jesus said to them, "Bring some of the fish you have just caught." It was full of large fish, 153, but even with so many the net was not torn. Jesus said, "Come and have breakfast." -John 21:3-12 (John 21:13-14).

Sometimes I think of what I have already went through, and the pain I know will come being in a world of sin, and I cannot help but feel fearful, anxious and sometimes angry with God to allow me to experience the pain. Then I remember, Jesus knows our exact purpose, where He needs us and wants to pour His goodness on us. Even though we may not see what side of the boat His goodness is waiting for us on, we can have courage that He already knows, and is already there.

"The Lord is my Shepard, I lack nothing. He makes me lie down in green pastures, he leads me beside quiet waters, he refreshes my soul. He guides me along the right paths for his name's sake. Even though I walk through the valley of death, I will fear no evil, for you are with me; your rod and your staff, they comfort me. You prepare a table before me in the presence of my enemies. You anoint my head with oil, my cup overflows. Surely your goodness and love will follow me all the days of my life, and I will dwell in the house of the Lord forever." -Psalm 23:1-6.

Even though here on earth we are walking through the valley of the shadow of death, Christ is granting us His goodness and mercy in this life, while at the same time leading us home to Heaven in perfection forever! We have no need to fear. We can enjoy life *today* knowing the ultimate goodness is promised in its perfect form once we are in Heaven, but He also promises His goodness here on earth while we are in the valley.

"Be on guard; stand firm in the faith; be courageous; be strong. Do everything in love." -1 Corinthians 16:13-14. Be on guard. What about when "fear" is healthy? Is it not unhealthy to "fear" a venomous snake if you come across one and run the other direction to protect yourself? Instead of fear, I like to call this "being on guard" or being aware which is necessary to live a life God desires. The same with redirection. If you desire to go to a certain school, accept a job, move across the country or play a certain sport, you may have an unsettled feeling or lack of peace. It can be tough to differentiate, but God will guide you if it is fear holding you back from your dreams, or redirection from Him.

"God is our refuge and strength, a very present help in trouble. Therefore, we will not fear; though the earth should change, though the mountains shake in the heart of the sea; though its waters roar and foam, though the mountains quake with their surging. There is a river whose streams make glad the city of God, the holy place where the Most High dwells. God is within her; she will not fall; God will help her at break of day. The Lord Almighty is with us; the God of Jacob is our fortress." -Psalm 46:1-5.

Picture the mountains shaking into the heart of the sea. Picture being in the middle of a hurricane with no barrier. God commands us to not be afraid, knowing He surrounds us during the storm. God is within you, the same power that rose Jesus from the dead. He is our fortress, and He keeps these promises.

"I am leaving you with a gift-peace of mind and heart. And the peace I give is a gift the world cannot give. So don't be troubled of afraid." -John 14:27. Without God, it is impossible to not be troubled or afraid. It is impossible to have true genuine peace. Even though we will always have moments of trouble and fear being human, our foundation on Him will be a peace that only comes from Him. If you look for peace from the world, you will realize it is only temporary. What you may have put your peace in continues to either change or fade, and you realize you never really had peace when you thought you did. Keeping your minds steadfast by getting in His word and talking to Him will give you peace. This peace is eternal and cannot be taken from you. "You will keep in perfect peace those whose minds are steadfast because they trust in you. Trust in the Lord forever, for the Lord, the Lord himself, is the Rock eternal." -Isaiah 26:3-4.

"As mother comforts her child, God will comfort us." -Isaiah 66:13. You are never alone. You may feel alone; I know I have. Our feelings are not the truth. Do you think Jesus was afraid the night before the crucifixion? He sweat blood. Jesus tells us to pray we do not fall into temptation. He prayed "Father, if you are willing, please take this cup from me; yet not my will but yours be done. An angel then strengthened him. In anguish, he prayed more earnestly, and he sweat blood." -Luke 22:40-44 (Luke 22:46 and Mark 14:36). Jesus was fully committed to God and His will, but His expression of His genuine concern for what He was about to endure shows how personal and real our God is, and how we can do the same. We can be honest with God about our concerns and fears, while still obeying and keeping faith. Jesus had courage and fear did not stop him. Why? Love. Perfect love drives out fear. He loves us so much; fear could not stop Him from dying for you and for me. He also went to God in prayer to handle His fear. Jesus experienced the worst, most unfair punishment, yet He trusted God's will. We are to do the same even when we are in situations that seem unfair or do not make sense.

When we take courage and have faith, we will see God's work. Not because we are strong enough, but He is. Therefore, we need to be courageous when sharing our gifts. Each of you should use whatever gift you have received to serve others, as faithful stewards of God's grace in its various forms." -1 Peter 4:10. When we know our gifts come from God, we don't need to be scared.

Did you know that a risk factor for falling is... fear of falling! We all have fear but you can't let it take over your life. Fear is telling God you do not trust Him to take care of you. Sometimes, patients hold back from coming to therapy or performing their therapy correctly because of fear. Even though there are challenges we fear we can't handle on our own, there is nothing we are facing that God cannot help us overcome. "God is our salvation, defense and strength. We are to trust and not be afraid." -Isaiah 12:2. Instead of saying "God how will this ever work out?" Try saying, "God, I can't wait to see how you will help me stand courageous through this!"

"The Lord is my light and my salvation-whom shall I fear? The Lord is the stronghold of my life-of whom shall I be afraid." -Psalm 27:1. When we know nothing can take away our salvation, there is nothing else to fear. Everything else is temporary. When afraid, I ask, "Will this affect my eternal salvation?"

"And if the spirit of him who raised Jesus from the dead is living in you, he who raised Christ from the dead will also give life to your mortal bodies because of his Spirit who lives in you." -Romans 8:11. The same power that rose Jesus from the dead is living inside of you. I ask again, of who should we be afraid?

"I pray that the eyes of your heart may be enlightened in order that you may know the hope to which he has called you, the riches of his glorious inheritance in his holy people, and his incomparably great power for us who believe. That power is the same as the mighty strength he exerted when he raised Christ from the dead and seated him at his right hand in the Heavenly realms, far above all rule and authority, power and dominion, and every name that is invoked, not only in the present age but also in the one to come. And God placed all things under his feet and appointed him to be head over everything for the church, which is his body, the fullness of him who fills everything in every way." -Ephesians 1:18-23.

This scripture right here is what helps me stand in front of hundreds of people to compete for Miss Wisconsin, while talking about Jesus. This right here is what even helps me talk to a stranger about Jesus, knowing I will get rejected. This is what can help you every day to play in that game, go to that school, take that test, start that conversation or just the strength you need to face the everyday tasks that can so easily create so much fear in us we do not even want to walk outside into the world.

"When you boast, boast in the Lord for you are not approved if you commend yourself, but if the Lord commends you." -2 Corinthians 10:17-18 (1 Corinthians 1:31). "If I must boast, I will boast at what shows my weakness." -2 Corinthians 11:30-31. You say you can't because you're weak. We all are. David was weak when facing Goliath. Even if you are not physically weak, there has been a point in your life that this broken world has made you weak spiritually, emotionally, or psychologically. If you tell me no, you are lying. God is saying when you trust in Him with your weakness, He won't only make you strong, but He is saying his power is made perfect in your weakness. If you are telling God, you are strong enough without Him, you are telling the very source who gave you life and who made your body and spirit in the first place.

"Yes, my soul, find rest in God; my hope comes from him. Truly he is my rock and my salvation; he is my fortress; I will not be shaken. My salvation and my honor depend on God, he is my mighty rock, my refuge. Trust I him at all times, you people; pour out your hearts to him, for God is our refuge." -Psalm 62:5-8 (Psalm 62:1-2, Psalm 92:12-15 and Psalm 18:2-3). To find your trust in God to understand the refuge and this courage He provides; you have to pour your heart out to Him. Caleb said "...with confidence they could take possession of the land, but the other men were afraid the people were stronger than them." -Numbers 13:30-31. "The Lord said to Joshua, I have delivered Jericho into your hands. March around the city and on the seventh day march around the city seven times blowing the trumpets. When you hear the sound, give a loud shout and the walls of the city will collapse." -Joshua 6:2-5. "When he trumpets sounded, the army shouted, and the walls collapsed." -Joshua 6:20. Only Caleb and Joshua were able to make it to the promise land because of their courage and trust in God. Even though the Philistines were scary and could have easily killed them, they chose to focus on God instead.

"See, the Lord your God has given you the land. Go up and take possession of it as the Lord, the God of your ancestors, told you. Do not be afraid; do not be discouraged." -Deuteronomy 1:21. "Then I said to you, 'Do not be terrified; do not be afraid of them. The Lord your God, who is going before you, will fight for you, as he did for you in Egypt, before your very eyes, and in the wilderness. There you saw how the Lord your God carried you, as a father carries his son, all the way you went until you reached this place.'" -Deuteronomy 1:29-31. Remember the stories in the Bible when God carried those, He loved with the continual reminder He gives us today to not be afraid.

"And now, Israel, what does the Lord your God ask of you but to fear the Lord your God, to walk in obedience to him, to love him, to serve the Lord your God with all your heart and with all your soul, and to observe the Lord's commands and decrees that I am giving you today for your own good? To the Lord your God belong the Heavens, even the highest Heavens, the earth and everything in it. Yet the Lord set his affection on your ancestors and loved them, and he chose you, their descendants, above all the nations—as it is today. Circumcise your hearts, therefore, and do not be stiff-necked any longer. For the Lord your God is God of gods and Lord of lords, the great God, mighty and awesome, who shows no partiality and accepts no bribes. He defends the cause of the fatherless and the widow, and loves the foreigner residing among you, giving them food and clothing. And you are to love those who are foreigners, for you yourselves were foreigners in Egypt. Fear the Lord your God and serve him. Hold fast to him and take your oaths in his name. He is the one you praise; he is your God, who performed for you those great and awesome wonders you saw with your own eyes. Your ancestors who went down into Egypt were seventy in all, and now the Lord your God has made you as numerous as the stars in the sky." - Deuteronomy 10:12-22 (Joshua 22:5).

It is a command to fear God, walk in obedience with Him, submit to Him and to serve Him with all your heart for your own good. When we fear others and not the Lord, we are in a sense idolizing, thinking that they have greater power than He does.

"Everything on earth belongs to God, he founded it all." -Psalm 241-2 (1 Corinthians 10:26).

"For the Lord God dried up the Jordan before you until you had crossed over. The Lord your God did to the Jordan what he had done to the Red Sea when he dried it up before us until we had crossed over. He did this so that all the peoples of the earth might know that the hand of the Lord is powerful and so that you might always fear the Lord your God.' The Lord." -Joshua 4:23-24.

God performed the miracles He did with many purposes, and one of them being that we may understand the power and might of our God, and that even in your life when it seems there is no way, He can create a way by parting the sea.

"The Lord gives victory to his anointed." -Psalm 20:6. Joshua says to "give him the hill country the Lord promised this day. The Anakites were large and fortified, but with the Lord helping me, I will drive them out just as he said." -Joshua 14:12. Even if your hardships seem larger than what you can handle on your own and grip you frozen with fear, God promises to give victory to His anointed, His children. Victory may look different in the eyes of the Lord than us. Many people saw Jesus' death at the cross as defeat initially, but the victory came when He was raised from the dead. Even if you seem defeated, thinking this cannot be true because of your circumstances, God can use the hardships and death in your life to bring you and your circumstance from the dead to bring you life. Let His power defeat your fear. We do not even have to fear death itself! All we ever have to fear is God himself, and when we fear Him, He looks on us as His child, giving us literally nothing to fear. "Do not be afraid of those who can kill the body but be afraid of the One who can destroy both soul and body." -Matthew 10:28 (Luke 12:4-5).

"When the angel of the Lord appeared to Gideon, he said, "The Lord is with you, mighty warrior." "Pardon me, my lord," Gideon replied, "but if the Lord is with us, why has all this happened to us? Where are all his wonders that our ancestors told us about when they said, 'Did not the Lord bring us up out of Egypt?' But now the Lord has abandoned us and given us into the hand of Midian." The Lord turned to him and said, "Go in the strength you have and save Israel out of Midian's hand. Am I not sending you?" -Judges 6:12-14.

Gideon asked a question we all wonder. We all doubt. We read these stories and think "Yes, I know these are true and incredible, but where are the results and miracles in my own life?" The Lord responded, "Am I not sending you?" God would not have created you to live on this Earth if you did not have the capacity to obtain the courage from His Holy Spirit that lives inside you when you are a believer in Jesus. He has in a sense "sent you" to live this life, knowing very well you were going to have the temptation to be paralyzed and gripped with fear. Therefore, He provides us with His word to free you from the bondage of fear and chains and into His freedom to obtain courage!

The Spirit of the Lord is so powerful, it gave Samson the power to tear apart a lion with his bare hands. -Judges 14:6. "It was not by their sword that they won the land, nor did their arm bring them victory; it was your right hand, your arm, and the light of your face, for you loved them." -Psalm 44:3. God provides physical strength in victory as well as triumph through love and light. We may not understand or know how God will provide during our hardships but when we have courage, we can trust He will, and His way is *best*. All Israel's surrounding nations lot their self-confidence because they realized this was from the help of our God. (See Nehemiah 6:16).

Esther 2:7 describes how Mordecai had a cousin who did not have a mother or father and so he brought her up, her name was Esther. Esther 2:17 says the king was attracted to Esther and won over all the other women so he set a royal crown on her head and made her Queen instead of Vashti. Esther 2:21-22 says Mordecai

267

caught Bigthana and Teresh who were two of the king's officers who wanted to assassinate King Xerxes. Mordecai told Queen Esther who told the king who gave credit to Mordecai. Esther 3:2 says everyone paid honor to Haman the King's right-hand man, but Mordecai refused to kneel or worship him. Esther 3:6 says Haman conspired how to destroy all the Jews, Mordecai's people and Mordecai himself. Esther 4:8 says Mordecai told Ester to tell the king to save the Jews. Esther 4:10-11 says Esther was scared because everyone knows if anyone approaches the king without being summoned, they will be put to death unless he extends the gold scepter and spares their life. Mordecai sent back this answer: "…For if you remain silent at this time, relief and deliverance for the Jews will arise from another place, but you and your father's family will perish. And who knows but that you have come to your royal position for such a time as this?" -Esther 4:14. "…a time to be silent and a time to speak." -Ecclesiastes 3:7

Esther could have been killed for simply approaching the king without being summoned, let alone to approach him to request he save her people, the Jews, from Haman's evil scheme. The courage she had was with the help of her cousin who reassured her that God brought her to power for such a time as this. God puts people in our lives to encourage us to have the confidence to be courageous. Sometimes we may feel alone and ultimately our courage comes from the Lord, but God loves when we are surrounded by community with the same mind set. We should also be an encouragement to others, helping them feel more confident in order to be courageous in areas of their life in which God calls them to be. The enemy attacks us best when we are isolated. It is so important to encourage one another with these words.

Esther 5:14 says Haman planned to have Mordecai impaled on a pole. Esther 6:1-12 says the king could not sleep one night, so he ordered the book of chronicles, the record of his reign, to be read to him. The readings reminded him of Mordecai, who saved him from his assassins. The king asked, "what honor did he get for this!" Nothing, his servant said. As this was happening, Haman happened to walk in with his request to impale Mordecai on a pole. The king asked Haman "What should be done for the man the king delights to honor?" Now Haman thought to himself, "Who is there that the king would rather honor than me?" So, he answered the king, "For the man the king delights to honor, have them bring a royal robe the king has worn and a horse the king has ridden, one with a royal crest placed on its head. Then let the robe and horse be entrusted to one of the king's most noble princes. Let them robe the man the king delights to honor and lead him on the horse through the city streets, proclaiming before him, 'This is what is done for the man the king delights to honor!' The king said "Go! Get the robe and the horse and do just as you have suggested for Mordecai the Jew. So, Haman robed Mordecai, and led him through the city streets. After Haman was overwhelmed with grief.

Esther 7:2-7 says the King asked Queen Esther whatever she wants, it will be given even half the kingdom. Queen Esther says to grant her life and to spare her people for they have been sold to be killed. The King asked who he is?! Esther said, Hamen! The king in a rage. Hamen begged Queen Esther for his life. Esther 8:1-6 says King Xerxes found out now Mordacai was related to Queen Ester and gave him his signet ring he was going to give to Haman and Esther appointed him in Haman's position. The king extended the gold scepter to Esther, and she said let an order be written overruling Haman who wrote to destroy the Jews. For how can I bear to see disaster fall on my people and family. Esther 8:11 says the king overruled and saved the Jews. Esther 9:4 says Mordecai was prominent in the palace and his reputation spread throughout the provinces. Ester has no idea when God made her the King's wife that part of her purpose was going to be to save His people. Even if your life seems uncertain, I can promise God is at work.

"Who is like me and who can challenge me?" -Jeremiah 50:19 (Job 9:19). No one compares to God that we can say we should fear more. "I lie down and sleep; I wake again, because the Lord sustains me. I will not fear though tens of thousands assail me on every side." -Psalm 3:5-6 (Psalm 27:3). The only way we can lie down and sleep knowing trouble and evil lurk at every corner is His peace. "So, we say with confidence, "The Lord is my helper; I will not be afraid. What can mere mortals do to me?" -Hebrews 13:6 (Psalm 56:3-4 and Psalm 56:10-11). "Hear me, you who know what is right, you people who have taken my instruction to heart: Do not fear the reproach of mere mortals or be terrified by their insults." -Isaiah 51:7. It is easy to be scared or very hurt by others. We all have been. We need to remember God's power as opposed to human power. God is vast and infinite, and we are finite. What others see and think of you is their own judgment and much of the time not true. We need to remember only God's judgment is perfect. When others insult you strictly to bring you down or even threaten your life, only God has the power after this life over your soul.

David says when hard pressed, "I cried to the Lord who brought me to a spacious place. Do not be afraid for God is with you as your helper. What can mortals do to me? We will have triumph over your enemies. It is better to take refuge in the Lord than trust in humans or princes." -Psalm 118:5-9. Paul said, "no more boasting in human leaders including himself, all things are God's including the world, life, death the present and the future." -1 Corinthians 3:21-23. "Do not trust in people who can be taken at any time." -Isaiah 2:22 (Proverbs 11:7). "You will be deceived if you depend on your own strength or the strength of others." -Hosea 10:13. When we fear others, we are fearing those who are only temporary on this earth even though their souls live on forever in Heaven or Hell. If you rely simply on the strength of others, or even your own, it will fail as the years press on. "Fear of man is a trap, but whoever trusts in the Lord is kept safe." -Proverbs 29:25.

"Do not be afraid of disgrace, you will not be humiliated. You will forget the shame of your youth." -Isaiah 54:4. We may not think of fear in the sense of being scared of embarrassment, however this fear paralyzes people just as much as fear of being harmed. When you have committed shameful acts throughout your life, God wipes your sin clean in Christ and His perfect love continues to drive out fear of all forms. It is healthy to temporarily feel shame and guilt towards others in how we may have hurt them, ourselves or God with our sin, but God never intended for us to live there. If you never felt shame or guilt, your heart would become hardened toward others. "For God has not given us a spirit of fear, but of power, love and self-discipline." -2 Timothy 1:7.

"Jesus went to a mountain side by himself to pray. After dawn, Jesus went out to the disciples on the lake. When they saw him, they were terrified saying "it's a ghost!" Jesus said "Take courage! It is I. Don't be afraid." Peter said Lord, if it's you have me come out on the water by you." Jesus said to come. Peter got out of the boat and walked on the water toward Jesus but when he saw the wind, he was afraid and began to sink shouting "Lord, save me!" Jesus reached out his hand and said, "You of little faith, why did you doubt?" The storm stopped and the disciples worshiped Jesus saying, "Truly you are the Son of God." -Matthew 14:23-33 (Mark 6:48-51 and John 6:18-21).

When you look at the world and see the storms, every single human being in this world will be afraid. If you look to Jesus, you might still see the storm in your peripheral, but you will feel His hand supporting you through it.

But now I urge you to keep up your courage, because not one of you will be lost; only the ship will be destroyed. Last night an angel of the God to whom I belong and whom I serve stood beside me and said, 'Do not be afraid, Paul. You must stand trial before Caesar; and God has graciously given you the lives of all who sail with you.' So, keep up your courage, men, for I have faith in God that it will happen just as he told me." -Acts 27:22-25.

"The Spirit you received does not make you slaves, so that you live in fear again; rather, the Spirit you received brought about your adoption to sonship. And by him we cry, *"Abba,* Father." -Romans 8:15.

"Therefore, since we have such a hope, we are very bold." -2 Corinthians 3:12.

Joy & Thanksgiving

"I can do all things through Christ who strengthens me." -Philippians 4:13

I can *have joy and be content* through Christ who strengthens me.

"Rejoice in the Lord always, I will say it again: Rejoice!" -Philippians 4:4 (1 Thessalonians 5:16). Guess where Paul was when he said to rejoice? Prison. In prison for simply for standing up for Jesus and what he believes in, not because of anything he did wrong. One of the beautiful things is that Paul had no clue at the time that God was going to use the letters he would write at this low time in his life to influence others for thousands of years. We can rejoice today knowing our current suffering or hardship is not in vain. "I am not saying this because I am in need, for I have learned to be content whatever the circumstances. I know what it is to be in need, and I know what it is to have plenty. I have learned the secret of being content in any and every situation, whether fed or hungry, whether living in plenty or in want." -Philippians 4:11-12. He found joy not because his situation or being in prison was good, but because God is.

We have joy because we are going to Heaven, always, always giving us hope. It does not mean we shouldn't enjoy the here and now. As God's goodness is evident today and every day, but we can have joy even during the struggles. "Do not fret because of evildoers or be envious of the wicked, for the evildoer has no future hope." -Proverbs 24:19-20. Even though our circumstances, our needs and our feelings change, God does not. As much as we feel our circumstances, wants, needs and feelings are what dictate our happiness, there is no substitute for Jesus. To be content and have joy, we need to consciously say we do not need to worry, for God has everything under control. We need to pray with thanksgiving, knowing this is what God says the antidote to relieve us of anxiety. God is more concerned about your life than you are.

Take control of your mind. This takes practice, but sin (aka worry and discontentment) starts in the mind. You will think about what you focus on and where you direct yourself each day. In volleyball, I would be confused why my pass would not go to the setter, where it was supposed to. My coach would tell me my arms and body were pointed in the opposite direction. I was shocked how obvious it was once it was pointed out. Then when I directed my form to the setter, there the ball went. The same goes with our focus. What we consume ourselves with is where our minds will be, which ultimately determines our life course. "And the peace of God, which transcends all understanding, will guard your hearts and your minds in Christ Jesus." -Philippians 4:7. Peace of mind. Isn't this what we all want? "How great are you, Sovereign Lord! There is no one like you, and there is no God but you, as we have heard with our own ears." -2 Samuel 7:22 (1 Chronicles 17:20). It is impossible to be near God and not have life and joy, and it is impossible to be away from God and have it. When separated from God, you are separated from the true source of joy and life.

"Sing to the Lord, all the Earth; proclaim his salvation day after day. Declare his glory among the nations, his marvelous deeds among all peoples. For great is the Lord and most worthy of praise; he is to be feared above all gods. For all the gods of the nations are idols, but the Lord made the Heavens. Splendor and majesty are before him; strength and joy are in his dwelling place. Ascribe to the Lord, all you families of nations, ascribe to the Lord glory and strength. Ascribe to the Lord the glory due his name; bring an offering and come before him. Worship the Lord in the splendor of his holiness. Tremble before him, all the earth! The world is firmly established; it cannot be moved. Let the Heavens rejoice, let the earth be glad; let them say among the nations, 'The Lord reigns!' Let the sea resound, and all that is in it; let the fields be jubilant, and everything in them! Let the trees of the forest sing, let them sing for joy before the Lord, for he comes to judge the earth. Give thanks to the Lord, for he is good; his love endures forever. Cry out, "Save us, God our Savior; gather us and deliver us from the nations, that we may give thanks to your holy name, and glory in your praise." Praise be to the Lord, the God of

Israel, from everlasting to everlasting. Then all the people said 'Amen' and 'Praise the Lord.'" -1 Chronicles 16:23-36 (Psalm 96:1-3 and Psalm 108:3).

It is not an option to sing. We don't sing because we have a great voice or we want to, but He deserves it! When we don't feel like it, we need it!

"A cheerful heart is good medicine, but a crushed spirit dries up the bone." -Proverbs 17:22 (Proverbs 15:15). Keep your sense of humor! Listen, actual medicine works. Counseling helps. However, our hearts and lives can't be changed without Christ. We can't be saved without Christ. "Stand up and praise him." - Nehemiah 9:5. "Let them praise His name with dancing and make music to Him with timbrel and harp. For the Lord takes delight in his people; he crowns the humble the victory." -Psalm 149:3-4 (1 Chronicles 23:5, 2 Chronicles 7:6, 2 Chronicles 5:13 and Psalm 119:67-68). Dance! Make music! Sing! Raise your hands! Praising God is to be embraced and make us feel set free! Sometimes singing and dancing makes many of us feel uncomfortable, but isn't feeling uncomfortable worth it to heal your soul and bond with God?

"Sing to him a new song; play skillfully, and shout for joy." -Psalm 33:3. "...the music of the strings makes you glad." -Psalm 45:8. Now I know we have all been in church, next to that "free spirited woman" who has her hands in the air like she's just trying to swat a bird or even become a bird. "Let us lift up our hearts and our hands to God in Heaven." -Lamentations 3:40-41. "Lift up your hands in the sanctuary and praise the Lord." -Psalm 134:2 (Psalm 63:4). I was afraid to stand and lift my hands because one, I did not grow up in a hand raising church. Two, I did not want my praise to be on display or distracting. Three, I flat out was uncomfortable, especially if others around me were not doing it as well. Once I saw in the Word God commands us to stand and lift our hands in worship, I felt more courage to do so that it even still felt awkward at times. I realized who I was worshipping and surrendered my own insecurities and focused on the glory my worship produced as opposed to my own pride. This is what it means to lift your hands and your heart. As an athlete, it is very natural for me to raise my hands at sporting events and games, so why not get even more excited for the one who saved my soul?! "Enter his gates with thanksgiving and his courts with praise; give thanks to him and praise his name. For the Lord is good and his love endures forever; his faithfulness continues through all generations." -Psalm 100:4-5 (Revelation 19:11).

"Come, let us sing for joy to the Lord; let us shout aloud to the Rock of our salvation. Let us come before him with thanksgiving and extol him with music and song." -Psalm 95:1-2 (Psalm 68:32-35, Psalm 59:16-17 and 1 Chronicles 13:8). "Praise the Lord, now and forever more from morning to night. He is exalted over all the nations and his glory above the Heavens. Who is like the Lord our God, who sits enthroned on high and looks down on Heaven and earth?" -Psalm 113:1-6 (Psalm 89:7-8). "Give thanks to the Lord, his love endures forever. As they began to praise and sing, the Lord set ambushes against the men invading Judah and they were defeated." -2 Chronicles 20:21-22 (Psalm 106:1, 107:1, 118:1, 118:29, Jeremiah 33:11, Psalm 136:1-26 and Luke 1:74). Having joy requires gratefulness, even when life gives us a lot of situations and circumstances that leave us feeling less than. As you sing, God is preparing an army of joy around you, just like He set an ambush of defense around the men in Judah while they were praising Him! Our weapon is our praise and joy as believers, and it is the strongest weapon we can have. Frankly it's the only one that works as it seems the struggles never end.

"...tell of his works with songs of joy." -Psalm 107:22 (Psalm 100:1-2). Complaining is the opposite of worship. Telling of His works with songs of joy heals your heart in ways you may not feel or understand in the moment.

"Praise the Lord. Praise God in his sanctuary; praise him in his mighty Heavens. Praise him for his acts of power; praise him for his surpassing greatness. Praise him with the sounding of the trumpet, praise him with the harp and lyre, praise him with timbrel and dancing, praise him with the strings and pipe, praise him with the clash of cymbals, praise him with resounding cymbals. Let everything that has breath praise the Lord. Praise the Lord." -Psalm 240:1-6 (Psalm 47:6-7, Psalm 147:1 and Hebrews 13:15).

"Great is the Lord and most worthy of praise; his greatness no one can fathom." -Psalm 145:3. "Let them shout from the mountaintops. Let them give glory to the Lord and proclaim his praise in the islands. The Lord will march out like a champion, like a warrior he will stir up his zeal; with a shout he will raise the battle cry and will triumph over his enemies." -Isaiah 42:11-13 (Jeremiah 13:16).

To have joy every day, it must be based on something that will never go away, something that is eternal. Our feelings, circumstances and joy that comes from others are inconsistent. Many say, "follow your heart." I think "lead" your heart and feelings, for God is the only one you should follow. C.S Lewis says, "look inside yourself and you will only find hate, rage, loneliness, and decay but look for Christ and you will find Him, and with Him everything else." Jesus gives us a joy that is eternal. Joy is what helps us release our anxiety. I want you to love everyone in your life with your whole heart, put all your enthusiasm into your career, use all your talents for sports and instruments, and get the most out of your life as God calls us to do. My gosh, this is my life motto. We routinely see carpal tunnel releases at my clinic, and one time I had a patient ask me "Do you always get this excited about carpal tunnel?" A little over the top, I know. I just always want you to know He is the only one that is eternal. Our loved one's souls are eternal and will be in Heaven, but on this earth nothing is. You are way too valuable for only this life! You were made to last forever; you were made for more than this.

God is the one constant, and the good news is He is all you need. He will provide! "Ask the Lord for rain in the springtime it is the Lord who sends the thunderstorms. He gives showers of rain to all people, and plants of the field to everyone." -Zechariah 10:1. "How abundant are the good things that you have store up for those who fear you." -Psalm 31:19. God promises good in abundance, but that good is Christ!

"Who is like the wise? Who knows the explanation of things? A person's wisdom brightens their face and changes its hard appearance." -Ecclesiastes 8:1. This wisdom means more knowledge of the Lord which increases your joy, brightening your face. "Those who are wise will shine like the brightness of the Heavens, and those who lead many to righteousness, like the stars forever and ever." -Daniel 12:3. God does not play favorites, but those in Him shine because we allow him to work in us.

"But godliness with contentment is great gain. For we brought nothing into the world, and we can take nothing out of it. But if we have food and clothing, we will be content with that." -1 Timothy 6:6-8 (Psalm 49:17 and Ecclesiastes 5:15). When we are best friends with God and content, we understand we brought nothing into this world, and we will take no physical thing out. Things are not evil, but they can consume us. God wants us to know we will take nothing out of the world to decrease the stress and load we feel from acquiring more and more. Being content does not mean we are to be lazy. You can be happy and enjoy, striving to better yourself. This is not a form of being passive because we can care but not have to carry the load.

No material item you have is going to last forever. I am not saying owning things is wrong and God is not saying that. However, He does not want us to base our contentment on something that will eventually not be there anymore. This is the same with experience. I have had many people tell me once they get to a particular part of the world, then they will be happy. I was sad but not surprised when they returned, still feeling unfulfilled and unsatisfied. Is traveling and going on adventures exciting and something God would want us to do? Absolutely! Is it something on which we should base our contentment and joy? Not at all. Experiences, just like our material items, are temporary. God wants us to have a joy that is eternal, and the only thing that is eternal is Him and each other. "Death and destruction are never satisfied, and neither are human eyes." -Proverbs 27:20.

The fall of mankind happened because Satan tempted us saying we could "be like God." Ever since, we, as people, have tried everything outside of God to make us happy bringing all destruction of humanity. Nothing will make you happy outside of God. God created us, knows exactly what makes you tic, and you cannot function without him. It's like a car trying to function without gas. It's like trying to use a hair dryer when it's not plugged in. It's like trying to hit a ball without a bat. You cannot know your purpose in life until you know the very one who created you for a purpose and for *the* purpose in the first place.

We do not find joy in trails because of the pain we go through, but we find joy knowing how God will use the result. Even though we have not physically seen Jesus, we find joy in Him as our best friend. Just as the verse says, it is hard for me to put into words or express this joy. It comes solely from having a relationship with Him. It is a joy no one else can take away, a joy I have had since I accepted Him as a little girl. I have encountered every emotion since then including anxiety, depression, fear, guilt, anger, you name it. These emotions and my circumstances never took away my joy. To the world this does not make sense. How can I have joy when I am depressed? Angry? Anxious? Hurt? Joy is different than happiness. Even in my sorrows, I have joy deep down knowing in the end, Jesus will make it all ok. Joy also helps us release those worries and anxiety.

Jesus wants us to have joy, to choose joy. Joy comes from the Lord, the truth of the Word. If you let joy come from your circumstances, you will never have it. Never let joy depend on something you may lose. "...This day is holy to our Lord. Do not grieve, for the joy of the Lord is your strength." -Nehemiah 8:10. Joy gives us strength. Satan wants you to be weak. When we are weak, it is easier to bring us down from the purposes God has for us. "This is the day the Lord has made, let us rejoice and be glad in it." -Psalm 118:24. Today isn't your day? No, it's not. It is God's day. This God happens to love you and cherish you, more than you love yourself. Trust Him and find your joy. I was in Walgreens in the middle of the Coronavirus pandemic, and a guy said to me, "Well you sure seem happy!" People notice!

"Let us not become conceited, provoking and envying each other." - Galatians 5:26 (Proverbs 23:17-18). "Each one should test their own actions. Then they can take pride in themselves alone, without comparing themselves to someone else." -Galatians 6:4. Comparison is the thief of joy. "Resentment kills a fool, and envy slays the simple." -Job 5:2. "A heart at peace gives life to the body, but envy rots the bones." -Proverbs 14:30. Envy literally destroys you. "Anger is cruel and fury overwhelming, but who can stand before jealousy?" -Proverbs 27:4.

I can tell you not to envious but a valid question you could ask me is "Why not?" Someone may have something you want. Why can't you want that? Someone might have something you think you deserved. Why not you? The thing is, God promises: "Keep your lives free from the love of money and be content with what you have, because God has said, "Never will I leave you; never will I forsake you." -Hebrews 13:5. God has given you all you need, and if you have desired something that is not yours, the answer is either He knows that will not fulfill you the way you think it will, or maybe His answer is simply just "not yet."

"Since you trust in your deeds and riches, you too will be taken captive." -

Jeremiah 48:7. Money is not evil; the love of money is. Do you ever notice how content we are until we see what someone else has? Remember, do not compare, and let it steal your joy. When we envy, we are telling God we do not trust Him to meet our needs. The only time you can compare, is if instead of comparison, you are looking to someone else as *encouragement* or as a *role model* to someone you want to achieve similar goals you may have or work in the same way they did to help you achieve your goals. However, this comparison should never lead you to want to be someone else, as God literally hand designed you since the beginning of time with a purpose and task only you can fulfill. "And my God will meet all your needs according to the riches of his glory in Christ Jesus." -Philippians 4:19.

"Who is wise and understanding among you? Let them show it by their good life, by deeds done in the humility that comes from wisdom. But if you harbor bitter envy and selfish ambition in your hearts, do not boast about it or deny the truth. Such "wisdom" does not come down from Heaven but is earthly, unspiritual, demonic. For where you have envy and selfish ambition, there you find disorder and every evil practice." -James 3:13-16.

I was convicted when I realized envy is demonic in nature.

"You are still worldly. For since there is jealousy and quarreling among you, are you not worldly? Are you not acting like mere humans? For when one says, "I follow Paul," and another, "I follow Apollos," are you not mere human beings? What, after all, is Apollos? And what is Paul? Only servants, through whom you came to believe—as the Lord has assigned to each his task. I planted the seed, Apollos watered it, but God has been making it grow. So, neither the one who plants nor the one who waters is anything, but only God, who makes things grow." -1 Corinthians 3:3-7.

"I sent you to reap what you have not worked for. Others have done the hard work, and you have reaped the benefits of their labor." -John 4:38 (John 4:36-37).

We all do it, and when you start to pray, thank God for what you have. Think, someone is probably envious of you, and here you are envious of someone else! It is a vicious cycle. I think we need to be careful too, because often we envy others and do not realize what it takes to be in their spot of position in life or on the team. In the wise words from Spiderman, "with great power comes great responsibility." Appreciate others while embracing yourself. This took me a while to practice. I have always been competitive in school with grades, class president and various officers, prom queen and sports. Even when I would be in different positions, I caught myself envying and many times still wanting more. When I appreciated others, it helped me further appreciate myself for us to work as a team. Even if I did not "feel" appreciative, I would pray God would give me these genuine feelings. Guess what? It happened. It is ok to want that spot on the team, to want those grades, to want that relationship, but do not simply want it because others have it or because you want to be them. Work hard for that spot on the team. Study for those grades

"The Lord has blessed you in all the work of your hands. He has watched over your journey through this vast wilderness. These forty years the Lord your God has been with you, and you have not lacked anything." -Deuteronomy 2:7. Pray God changes your heart to help you find the relationships you are looking for. You can search the whole world for satisfaction, but I promise you, you will not find it until you have Jesus. You will covet others until you have Jesus. You will still struggle with it when you have Him, but He will help you through. Have you ever thought you would be happy if you just had a little more money? Little more clothes? A few more friends? If you were a little better at a sport? A little more famous? Married? Then it happens, and you realize you are still not content and are still coveting. No matter where you are in life, do not compare. Just like He provided for the Israelites, He will provide for us, His children.

"I know what it is to be in need, and I know what it is to have plenty. I have learned the secret of being content in any and every situation, whether well fed or hungry, whether living in plenty or in want." -Philippians 4:12. Practice contentment, it will happen. His grace is sufficient for you. Have full confidence every day that God knows your needs. Live in such a way that you have so much joy, people wonder what God is all about? "Dear friends, I urge you, as foreigners and exiles, to abstain from sinful desires, which wage war against your soul. Live such good lives among the pagans that, though they accuse you of doing wrong, they may see your good deeds and glorify God on the day he visits us." -1 Peter 2:11-12.

"Give thanks in all circumstances; for this is the will of God in Christ Jesus for you." -1 Thessalonians 5:18. It says to give joy in all circumstances, not that we must be grateful for all circumstances. People tend to feel Christians have to live in a fake, fairy tale land and be happy all these horrible things happen. As Christians, we are not called to fake it until we make it. We are called to give thanks within the suffering, genuinely. Suffering is caused by sin, which does not make God happy either. However, because of Him and His son, we can have peace and give thanks, genuinely, in all circumstances.

"You are the light of the world. A town built on a hill cannot be hidden. Neither do people light a lamp and put it under a bowl. Instead, they put it on its stand, and it gives light to everyone in the house. In the same way, let your light shine before others, that they may see your good deeds and glorify your Father in Heaven." -Matthew 5:14-16 (Luke 11:33, Luke 8:16 and Mark 4:21).

When you have joy, you have a light that is not meant to be hidden, and there is no need to boast or become prideful from it is natural. We perform our good deeds for God's glory and not our own. "The light of the righteous shines brightly." -Proverbs 13:9. "For God, who said, "Let light shine out of darkness," made his light shine in our hearts to give us the light of the knowledge of God's glory displayed in the face of Christ." -2 Corinthians 4:6. God's light can literally brighten up our faces when we are with others. People will notice something different, not perfection, but that light in their life. Even though this light is within, there is something powerful it does in our expressions that we may never understand. When we converse with others, we cannot see our own face, but we trust His word is true.

"For once you were darkness, but now in the Lord you are light. Live as children of light- for the fruit of the light is found in all that is good and right and true. Try to find out what is pleasing to the Lord." -Ephesians 5:8-10 (Psalm 118:29). There is no light in us alone; it is reflected from Jesus living inside of us. Even if someone seems sincere, they can be sincerely wrong if they do not have Christ. The average person may perform good works to receive the approval of God or man, but a Christian believes any good in them is because of Jesus himself working in us. I am not being good to make God love me, but because God loves me, I am able to produce good. "I sought the Lord, and he answered me; he delivered me from all my fears. Those who look to him are radiant; their faces are never covered with shame." -Psalm 34:4-5. Shame is ok to feel for a moment as it is good to have emotions or feel bad when we hurt others or God, but we are not to live there as Christ has redeemed it. Part of understanding this redemption brings us joy. When we have Jesus, the Holy Spirit, living in us, His light shines through. Ask if you can pray for them. You are a light, and your joy is a light! God does not want you to hide your light. He is telling you that is the surest thing you can do. Do not throw away your light. Joy is a choice and a weapon; choose well and fight well.

"Though the fig tree does not bud and there are no grapes on the vines, though the olive cup fails, and the fields produce no food, though there are no sheep in the pen and no cattle in the stalls, yet I will rejoice in the LORD, I will be joyful in God my Savior. The Sovereign Lord is my strength; he makes my feet like the feet of a deer; he enables me to tread on the heights. For the director of music. On my stringed instruments." -Habakkuk 3:17-19.

You know Jesus? Yeah... I want to hear a "Yeah!" Get excited people! Others will know Jesus through your joy. In my life, I have noticed those who have Christ through their love first, but second has been through their joy and grace. Though there is no food or possessions, we can still rejoice and be joyful in Jesus our strength. You can eat clean, exercise, lose all the weight, travel, be the best athlete, continue to buy what you think will make you happy, have the best holiday celebrations, take care of yourself and have the best job in the world. But if you do not have Jesus or read your Bible, you will never find your true purpose of fulfillment. Until Jesus is enough, nothing will ever be.

Exercising and losing weight to be happy, being an athlete, this is a passion of mine, but I always have something to criticize about my body. We all do. Then I realized, who am I to critique the body God designed? Now do not get me wrong, I am totally for a healthy lifestyle by eating healthy foods, participating in sports, training, and exercising. But let's say I am motivated and disciplined enough to be consistent in these categories, if we are not happy with Christ, we will continue to dislike like how your body looks, I can promise you because that is our human nature.

I desired to be Prom Queen just like my mom. I won and found that title did not bring contentment. I was Miss Southern Wisconsin United States, Miss Madison

Wisconsin United States, captain of my volleyball, basketball and softball teams, class president, and earned my master's degree. I am an occupational therapist, supposedly one of the top jobs in the country, and world, combining both satisfaction and payment perspectives. It does not bring fulfillment. It's not enough, and it never will be. Not only does it not bring fulfillment, but it also made me want more. First Homecoming Attendant, then Prom Queen, then Homecoming Queen of my college. When I was nominated for Miss Southern Wisconsin, I wanted Miss Wisconsin, then I desired Miss Wisconsin to be Miss America; then I would've wanted to be Miss World. You see where I am going? I also used to think I was getting excited for Jesus when I would sing in the car around Christmas time, realizing I was only excited with the thought of having someone to love around Christmas time. I realized no matter what I had or accomplished in my life, only Jesus brought contentment. I used to say this, but now I mean it. All these other desires are not bad or wrong, but they are not your Creator. They are not what you were purposely and skillfully made from and for. Something will always be missing no matter what you have in life. You need to realize He is what you are missing, and alone He is enough.

"...for riches do not endure forever, and a crown is not secure for all generations." -Proverbs 27:24. It is all a lie. I would fall into the trap, and this is when I would become depressed and anxious. I am not saying there is anything wrong with having dreams and wanting to be or do these things, but until you have Jesus you will never find satisfaction for your soul. He is your purpose. I continued to wonder why I was never truly content and felt empty, like many of you may feel. These are all great things but put your fulfillment and purpose in Jesus to find true contentment that cannot be shaken. Our purpose being here is to share Him with others. My one purpose is to help others find a personal relationship with God, Jesus. You can have the best marriage, the best sex, the best travel, the best house, the best friend, the best body, the most money, the best job and it never seems to be able to satisfy you, right? Then you think you married the wrong person or traveled to the wrong place when they aren't the issue at all. It is just that you are missing Jesus. Some may say to never get your hopes up which is not a good way to live either, because we do have an eternal hope! Nothing will satisfy you unless you have Jesus.

"Because you did not serve the Lord your God joyfully and gladly in the time of prosperity, therefore in hunger and thirst, in nakedness and fire poverty, you will serve the enemies the Lord sends against you." -Deuteronomy 28:47-48. When we serve God, He wants us to do it joyfully, not out of obligation. The great thing is with the awesome and persona God we serve, that is easy to do when you have the right perspective about Him! The ironic thing is we may feel sometimes it is hard to find joy, but He provides it. "He will yet fill your mouth with laughter and your lips with shouts of joy." -Job 8:21.

"Surely you know how it has been from of old, ever since mankind was placed on the earth, that the mirth of the wicked is brief, the joy of the godless lasts but a moment." -Job 20:4-5. It is easy to find joy if you have Jesus, but impossible if you do not. If you do not have Jesus, the feelings you have in good times is times of happiness which is a great feeling too! The only thing is joy is eternal and cannot be taken from you, regardless of your circumstances. God created us and the world to be enjoyed, and what has kept us from feeling joy always is sin. The beautiful thing is, God has still made it possible to enjoy life and still make it fun, but we can make sure life is fun no matter how hard it gets by realizing Jesus always provides the joy. "The Lord is my strength and my shield; my heart trusts in him, and he helps me. My heart leaps for joy, and with my song I praise him." -Psalm 28:7. Part of joy comes from understanding God is our strength, and our strength is our joy in Him. When we have full trust in Him and His sovereignty in our life regardless of our circumstances or choices when we make mistakes, you cannot help but have joy knowing He helps you.

"Clap your hands, all you nations, shout to God with cries of joy. For the Lord Most High is awesome, the great King over all the earth." -Psalm 47:1-2. Why have joy? Because God is awesome!

"Shout for joy to God, all the earth! Sing the glory of his name; make his praise glorious. Say to God, "How awesome are your deeds! So great is your power that your enemies cringe before you. All the earth bows down to you; they sing praise to you; they sing the praises of your name." Come and see what God has done, his awesome deeds for mankind! He turned the sea into dry land, they passed through the waters on foot— come, let us rejoice in him. He rules forever by his power, his eyes watch the nations." -Psalm 66:1-7.

Our God is so great, He turns seas into dry land for rescue, and He will rule forever. He is everywhere all at once, with His eyes on all nations. When our joy leads to praise, we discover the wonders of God. "You, Lord, reign forever; your throne endures from generation to generation." -Lamentations 5:19.

"But may the righteous be glad and rejoice before God; may they be happy and joyful. Sing to God, sing in praise of his name, extol him who rides on the clouds; rejoice before him, his name is the Lord. A father to the fatherless, a defender of widows, is God in his holy dwelling." -Psalm 68:3-5. "...he leads the prisoners with singing." -Psalm 68:6. The joy of the Lord is so powerful; it even leads prisoners to sing. I have seen those from the prison as patients, and even when they come in cuffs with guards on either side of them, I have been shocked at some of their joy, knowing some found God in prison, making them grateful for their punishment leading them to repentance. Paul and Silas were stripped and beaten with rods and flogged and put in prison. (See Acts 16:22-24). At midnight Paul and Silas were praying and singing hymns to God in prison and the other prisoners listened to them. There was a violent earthquake, and the prison doors flew open. The jailer woke up and was about to kill himself when he saw the prisoners had escaped, but Paul told him not to. (See Acts 16:25-28). Joy defines a Christian as well as love. People should know we are Christians by our love, and joy no matter our circumstance, even being beat and put in prison!

"Blessed are those who have learned to acclaim you, who walk in the light of your presence, Lord. They rejoice in your name all day long; they celebrate your righteousness. For you are their glory and strength, and by your favor you exalt our horn. Indeed, our shield belongs to the Lord, our king to the Holy One of Israel." -Psalm 89:15-18.

Praise is a discipline. It is tough to make praise a habit, but the more you practice the more natural it becomes. The more you walk with Him, the more you notice how his presence brings light. When you are in the light, you rejoice and celebrate life and who has given it to you. "For you make me glad by your deeds, Lord; I sing for joy at what your hands have done. How great are your works, Lord, how profound your thoughts!" -Psalm 92:4-5 (Isaiah 42:11). It is very anti culture to get excited about the unknown. It does not come naturally, but when you think of how profound

God's thoughts are, what He has done to provide for you in your past, what He has done for those in the scriptures and who He is through his works, you will find joy in the unknown.

"Let the Heavens rejoice, let the earth be glad; let the sea resound, and all that is in it. Let the fields be jubilant, and everything in them; let all the trees of the forest sing for joy. Let all creation rejoice before the Lord, for he comes, he comes to judge the earth. He will judge the world in righteousness and the peoples in his faithfulness." -Psalm 96:11-13.

Does it not also seem anti-cultural to have joy in judgment? Joy in judgment comes from knowing the judge is just, fair and ultimately *gracious*. It brings joy to know not one sin or wrongdoing committed in this world will go unpunished, but it can also immediately bring thinking of everything *you* have done that will not go unpunished. The joy comes in knowing if you believe in Jesus as your Savior, know that he took the place of your judgment at the cross. What joy serving a God who is Holy, just and graceful brings! "Shouts of joy and victory resound in the tends of the righteous: "The Lord's right hand has done mighty things! The Lord's right hand is lifted high; the Lord's right hand has done mighty things!" I will not die but live and will proclaim what the Lord has done." -Psalm 118:15-17.

"Sing, Daughter Zion; shout aloud, Israel! Be glad and rejoice with all your heart, Daughter Jerusalem! The Lord has taken away your punishment, he has turned back your enemy. The Lord, the King of Israel, is with you; never again will you fear any harm. On that day they will say to Jerusalem, "Do not fear, Zion; do not let your hands hang limp. The Lord your God is with you, the Mighty Warrior who saves. He will take great delight in you; in his love he will no longer rebuke you but will rejoice over you with singing." -Zephaniah 3:14-17.

"Therefore, since we are receiving a kingdom that cannot be shaken, let us be thankful, and so worship God acceptably with reverence and awe, for our 'God is a consuming fire.'" -Hebrews 12:28-29 (Deuteronomy 4:24). Joy is possible because of eternity. The kingdom we are now a part of and will be when we die cannot be shaken. God is a consuming fire, and this fire is now inside of you. "The earth is filled with your love, Lord..." -Psalm 119:64. Even though we live in a hard world, it is ultimately still God's world and full of His love if you look for it. Life is meant to be enjoyed, and for us to produce joy for one another. "Your statutes are my heritage forever; they are the joy of my heart. My heart is set on keeping your decrees to the very end." -Psalm 119:111-112. The joy comes from following His statutes, which in the moment may seem like a responsibility but then we realize the joy they produce. "I rejoice in your promise." -Psalm 119:162. We can have joy knowing God keeps every single one of His promises. "Seven times a day I praise you for your righteous laws." -Psalm 119:164.

"The prospect of the righteous is joy, but the hopes of the wicked come to nothing." -Proverbs 10:28. The only way to be righteous is to have Christ, and once you have the Holy Spirit living in you it produces joy naturally, one of the natural fruits of the spirit. "Deceit is in the hearts of those who plot evil, but those who promote peace have joy." -Proverbs 12:20.

Promoting peace brings joy, while trying to plan harm to others does just the opposite. "This too, I see, is from the hand of God, for without him, who can eat or find enjoyment? To the person who pleases him, God gives wisdom, knowledge and happiness." -Ecclesiastes 2:24-26. Without God, it is impossible to find joy.

"In that day you will say: 'I will praise you, Lord. Although you were angry with me, your anger has turned away and you have comforted me. Surely God is my salvation; I will trust and not be afraid. The Lord, the Lord himself, is my strength and my defense; he has become my salvation.' With joy you will draw water from the wells of salvation. In that day you will say: 'Give praise to the Lord, proclaim his name; make known among the nations what he has done, and proclaim that his name is exalted. Sing to the Lord, for he has done glorious things; let this be known to all the world. Shout aloud and sing for joy, people of Zion, for great is the Holy One of Israel among you.'" -Isaiah 12:1-6.

Even though the work has just begun once you are saved, instead of seeing it as a tiring journey of laws and regulations to follow as a Christian maybe you find as you "draw water" it is, might I say fun? Maybe fulfilling is a better word? Again, allow the joy to come naturally. As Christians, we do not live in a fantasy world that all this work is fun, but it is genuine when you see the purpose behind your work, and when you have Jesus there is always purpose behind your work, whether for your job, work within your family, friends, training for sports or hobbies.

"But only the redeemed will walk there, and those the Lord has rescued will return. They will enter Zion with singing; everlasting joy will crown their heads. Gladness and joy will overtake them, and sorrow and sighing will flee away." -Isaiah 35:9-10. Joy literally overtakes you. Even if times of sorrow that every single human being comes across, joy will always fill you in the end as a believer in Christ no matter the pain. "I delight greatly in the Lord; my soul rejoices in my God. For he has clothed me with garments of salvation and arrayed me in a robe of his righteousness, as a bridegroom adorns his head like a priest, and as a bride adorns herself with her jewels." -Isaiah 61:10. Joy comes from the thought of God being as excited to see you just as a groom sees his bride.

"Surely, he has done great things! Do not be afraid, land of Judah; be glad and rejoice. Surely the Lord has done great things! Do not be afraid, you wild animals, for the pastures in the wilderness are becoming green. The trees are bearing their fruit; the fig tree and the vine yield their riches. Be glad, people of Zion, rejoice in the Lord your God, for he has given you the autumn rains because he is faithful. He sends you abundant showers, both autumn and spring rains, as before. The threshing floors will be filled with grain; the vats will overflow with new wine and oil." -Joel 2:20-24.

Joel is saying that instead of being fearful, to have joy. Joy may seem to be an odd alterative to fear, but have you ever had a super exciting time in your life and felt unstoppable? If you think about it, joy did make you brave erasing your fears. We have joy because God is faithful and He always provides, even if the provision is not what you are expecting. In those instances, the joy comes from understanding you are the created being, the creator knows best and loves your more than you can understand.

"And Mary said: "My soul glorifies the Lord, and my spirit rejoices in God my Savior." -Luke 1:46-47. We find joy when we are glorifying God in all we do, when He becomes our motivator and purpose for life. "At that time Jesus, full of joy through the Holy Spirit." -Luke 10:21. He must become greater; I must become less." -John 3:30. The more our purpose revolves around ourselves, the more we rob ourselves of joy because we were not made for ourselves alone. This is not cliché, but a fact. When He becomes greater as the One, we aim to please, instead of ourselves and others, you will have joy. For instance, think of someone you have tried so hard to please and it's never enough. It is absolutely exhausting. Now, think of trying to please God who already loves you the same now as He did even when you accomplished a task He has assigned for you. How freeing and again, what joy it brings to serve someone who accepts you without a doubt.

"Very truly I tell you, you will weep and mourn while the world rejoices. You will grieve, but your grief will turn to joy. A woman giving birth to a child has pain because her time has come; but when her baby is born, she forgets the anguish because of her joy that a child is born into the world. So, with you: Now is your time of grief, but I will see you again and you will rejoice, and no one will take away your joy." -John 16:20-22.

Having joy does not mean everything will be good, or that there is not a time to mourn. For example, when a woman is giving birth, she is in anguish, but she forgets the anguish when she holds her child which results in her joy. Jesus promises no matter what anguish we feel in life, no one can take away our joy. Even when we mourn, joy can still be present and just as something as the indescribable joy of having a newborn baby in your arms, Jesus is our indescribable joy even when experiencing the worst pains in life.

"The jailer brought them into his house and set a meal before them; he was filled with joy because he had come to believe in God—he and his whole household." -Acts 16:34. When you are married for a long time, sometimes it is easy to forget the joy you had when you first started dating. The same holds true with our relationship with God. Sometimes we get into the mundane of life and forget how much joy we had when we first came to believe. Just like in your marriage when you chose to focus on what makes you excited about being with your spouse, when we focus on how insanely awesome God is, we can have the same joy as when we first came to believe. The story of the gospel and the cross has such immense power; it never gets "old."

"But what does it matter? The important thing is that in every way, whether from false motives or true, Christ is preached. And because of this I rejoice. Yes, and I will continue to rejoice, for I know that through your prayers and God's provision of the Spirit of Jesus Christ what has happened to me will turn out for my deliverance." -Philippians 1:18-19.

It is hard to have joy when you feel someone has false motives, particularly when sharing the gospel or maybe it seems like they are using Jesus to their own advantage. First, we can never, ever judge someone's heart. Second, who cares! Regardless of what we may feel someone's motive is, Christ is being preached to others! The thought of someone hearing about Christ should bring us joy, regardless of what the motives are.

"Let the peace of Christ rule in your hearts, since as members of one body you were called to peace. And be thankful. Let the message of Christ dwell among you richly as you teach and admonish one another with all wisdom through psalms, hymns, and songs from the Spirit, singing to God with gratitude in your hearts. And whatever you do, whether in word or deed, do it all in the name of the Lord Jesus, giving thanks to God the Father through him." -Colossians 3:15-17.

Peace and joy come from thankfulness, and thankfulness comes with trust and reflection on the word. We are to really consider what we say and do, making sure our motivator is God and being thankful we have the capacity to complete what He asks of us. "So then, just as you received Christ Jesus as Lord, continue to live your lives in him, rooted and built up in him, strengthened in the faith as you were taught, and overflowing with thankfulness. -Colossians 2:6-7.

"Don't be deceived, my dear brothers and sisters. Every good and perfect gift is from above, coming down from the Father of the Heavenly lights, who does not change like shifting shadows. He chose to give us birth through the word of truth, that we might be a kind of first fruits of all he created." -James 1:16-18.

I know how easy it is to take credit for our work. Maybe we bought something because we worked hard for it. It is important to remember everything and anything we own is God's, and it is Him who has granted us the talent and abilities to acquire what we own or have. We are the first fruits of His creation, the best of what He has created. He takes joy when we choose to use the talents, He has given us. God loves to see when we chose to work hard with the ability, He has given us. We just need to remember the very reason we can even take another breath is because God says we can, and through His sovereignty is the only way we can acquire any good or perfect gift.

"I have much to write to you, but I do not want to use paper and ink. Instead, I hope to visit you and talk with you face to face, so that our joy may be complete." -2 John 1:12. Letters are phenomenal. I love how social media connects us with family and friends. I know life gets busy and I am grateful technology can keep us connected through the craziness, but never underestimate the joy that could come into your life when we make face to face time with others. Sometimes it is scary and intimidating, depending on the relationship with the individual or what you are discussing, but with some prayer and God's guidance, face to face is always better. It can also sometimes be hard to really know what another is saying online as tone and facial expressions are a huge part of communication. Do not give up meeting together, to make your joy complete!

Confidence & Self-Esteem

"I can do all things through Christ who strengthens me." -Philippians 4:13

I can *have confidence and discipline* through Christ who strengthens me.

"But blessed is the one who trusts in the Lord, whose confidence is in him. They will be like a tree planted by the water that send out its roots by the stream. It does not fear when heat comes; its leaves are always green. It has no worries in a year of drought and never fails to bear fruit." -Jeremiah 17:7-8.

I am confident. "Blessed is the one who comes in the name of the Lord." -Psalm 118:26. I am not confident in myself, but I am confident in God who lives in me. I do not wish, and I do not believe in luck. I believe in God, prayer and God given ability to work hard. When our confidence is in things of this world, that is why confidence wavers because people, circumstances, jobs, athletic abilities and health all waver. God does not, which is why you will be like a tree who always has water, able to withstand the immense droughts of life and still produce fruit.

"Be strong and courageous. Be careful to obey all the law my servant Moses gave you; do not turn from it to the right or to the left, that you may be successful wherever you go. Keep this Book of the law always on your lips, meditate on it day and night, so that you may be careful to do everything written in it. Then you will be prosperous and successful." -Joshua 1:7-8.

When you are confident in the Word of God, it helps you not to waiver to the right or left, but on the straight and narrow path. If you could even get a glimpse of the potential God made you with, you would stop doubting yourself. It would change everything right here, right now. Your confidence is not in yourself, but in God and for His glory. "Blessed is she who has believed that the Lord would fulfill his promises to her!" -Luke 1:45.

"There is something powerful about the confidence of God fulfilling his promises. There was a champion named Goliath from Gath who came from the Philistine camp. He was 9 feet and 9 inches including a coat of bronze that weighed 125 pounds, with a helmet and a spear shaft with the point weighing 15 pounds." -1 Samuel 17:4-7.

"Just at the look of him, the Israelites fled in fear." -1 Samuel 17:24. However, David said "Who is this Philistine to defy the armies of the living God?!" -1 Samuel 17:26. I am sure when David saw Goliath, he was fearful as any of us would be, but what gave Him courage was the thought of someone, no matter how big that individual was, to defy the God, His God, the creator of all that He loved. Love for God gives you confidence and courage, regardless of how bad and real the trial is in front of you.

"When a lion or a bear came and carried off a sheep from the flock" David said to Saul, 'Let no one lose heart on account of this Philistine; your servant will go and fight him.' Saul said there was no way David could do it, he is young, and Goliath has been training since youth. David said he has been defending his sheep from predators." -1 Samuel 17:32-34. David said with confidence "this Philistine will be killed just like the lions and bears that attacked his sheep, because he has defied the armies of the living God. David said the Lord will rescue him from the

Philistine just like the predators of his sheep." -1 Samuel 17:36-37. David was confident because of the training he had. He did not go into battle without preparation. He was not prepared how most would have thought one would be for battle. God made him a shepherd and used his role as a shepherd to become all he needed to be to defeat Goliath. You may feel you are in a smaller role than you want in your life, whether it is through your job, a clinical or an internship. But remember, where we are is not always our end goal. Sometimes where we are does not make sense to accomplish our main goal that God has put on our hearts, as we don't know how He could be using it. In school and college, there are many general classes you need to take. In the moment, you may be frustrated as you feel those classes may not be helping you with your specific major or career choice. However, God will not leave them without purpose and preparation in ways you may not understand at the time.

"He took stones with a sling to the Philistine. The Philistine saw David was a little more than a boy. He said to David, "Am I a dog that you come at me with sticks?" Then the Philistine cursed David by his own gods. David said "You come against me with sword, but I come against you in the name of the Lord Almighty, the God of the armies of Israel. This day the Lord will deliver you into my hands. The whole world will know there is a God in Israel. All gathered will know it is not by sword the Lord saves, for the battle is the Lord's and he will give all of you into our hands." The Philistine moved closer to attack him, and David ran to the battle line to meet him. He took out a stone, slung it and struck the Philistine in the forehead. He fell face down to the ground David triumphed with sling and stone, without a sword and killed him." -1 Samuel 17:40-50 (1 Samuel 17:471 and 1 Chronicles 5:22).

When we are confident in God, it does not matter our age, what others feel about us or what we have. God will use what we have, even if it is a sling and some rocks, to defeat our greatest fears. We are human and there will be times we do not feel confident, but the beauty is God still has our backs when we are weak and will pick us right back up. Our confidence comes directly from Him.

"If you fight against God, you will not succeed." -2 Chronicles 13:12. "No wisdom, insight or plan can succeed against God." -Proverbs 21:30. You can have confidence knowing if someone does defy you because of God, it is impossible for them to succeed. David, the small shepherd boy came to the giant goliath with confidence. He knew he could not defeat him, but he knew God would. This is how we should live each day. My giants have been heart break, losing a loved one, getting my master's degree in occupational therapy, becoming a certified hand and upper extremity therapist, becoming a collegiate athlete, playing guitar or even everyday goals of being the best family member, friend, being God's light, you name it. Pray about your goals. Go confidently toward them knowing God is on your side if whatever you are doing is to glorify Him. No longer do we say, "I hope I can." Your new slogan is "I know I can do all things through Christ who strengthens me." - Philippians 4:13. The theme of the book. "Then Job replied to the Lord: "I know that you can do all things; no purpose of yours can be thwarted." -Job 42:1-2.

"Who can speak and have it happen if the Lord has not decreed it? Is it not from the mouth of the Most High that both calamities and good things come? Why should the living complain when punished for their sins?" -Lamentations 3:37-39. We can have confidence knowing God is an absolute. God is either completely in control, or He is not. The answer is He is. "Do not tremble, do not be afraid. Did I not proclaim this and foretell it long ago?" -Isaiah 44:8. Everything He has predicted in his word has come to be. "Surely, as I have planned, so it will be, and as I have purposed, so it will happen."-Isaiah 14:24. Confidence comes from understanding regardless of our downfalls, mistakes and short comings, He will use you and your imperfections for His perfect purpose. "This is the plan determined for the whole world; this is the hand stretched out over the nations. For the Lord Almighty has purposed, and who can thwart him? His hand is stretched out, and who can turn it back?" -Isaiah 14:26-27. No one can get in the way of His plans, not your imperfections and not those who purposefully try to stop His goodness. Think of Jesus. Satan, Judas, the Pharisees, chief priests and the entire Sanhedrin thought they could get rid of Jesus by crucifying Him, and God used what the enemy meant for evil, and it turned out to be our salvation.

"Lord, you are my God; I will exalt you and praise your name, for in perfect faithfulness you have done wonderful things, things planned long ago." - Isaiah 25:1. He has perfect faithfulness, and we can be confident knowing He is faithful to us and for us. "Remember the former things, those of long ago; I am God, and there is no other; I am God, and there is none like me. I make known the end from the beginning, from ancient times, what is still to come. I say, 'My purpose will stand, and I will do all that I please.' From the east I summon a bird of prey; from a far-off land, a man to fulfill my purpose. What I have said that I will bring about; what I have planned, that I will do." -Isaiah 46:9-11. He makes known the end from the beginning and has seen the entire story of mankind and the world before He created it in His sovereignty, and He created the world in love by His perfect wisdom. We acquire confidence from remembering who God is from long ago, and how He is the same God today.

Alright, now you may thinking, "Lexi, I have tried to have confidence and failed to accomplish my goal, dream and deepest desire." Maybe you did not get into the school you wanted, the degree you wanted, the relationship you wanted, or maybe you didn't make the team. You failed. Get back up, today! As you are reading this. God will use every failure and make you and even your situation better *if* you let him. It is a command from God that we get back up. Always get back up. "...for though the righteous fall seven times, they rise again." -Proverbs 24:16. Have you ever snowboarded? Talk about needing to get back up when every ounce of your body hurts. I picked it up and love it but let me tell you how sore my body was when I first started. I fell almost as much as I got up. If I did not continue to get back up and pray, I would have never enjoyed the beauty of the mountains, snow and the wonder of what our bodies can do.

It is easy to let others take away your confidence. I have always been confident in myself, however the second a teacher, coach, adult, co-worker or other person in general would question me, I would start to question myself. Then I would remember, what others think about me is not the truth. When Satan tries to bring self-doubt into my head, that is not the truth. The truth is God is my confidence, and all we need. Satan is powerful, but God is more. Even David felt doubt when King Saul questioned his abilities. David had to refocus his confidence in the Lord, the truth. If you have God, you are always on the winning team no matter what the current score is.

"I will walk among you and be your God, and you will be my people. I am the Lord your God, and you will be my people. I am the Lord your God, who brought you out of Egypt so that you would be no longer slaves to the Egyptians; I broke the bars of your yoke and enabled you to walk with heads held high." -Leviticus 26:12-13.

Confidence means keeping your head held high with good posture. I teach others daily in postural education but am very hypocritical with my constant poor posture. I am working at improving it and taking for truth that God tells us to keep our heads held high knowing we are his children. "Many are saying of me, 'God will not deliver him." But you, Lord, are a shield around me, my glory, the One who lifts my head high.'" -Psalm 3:2-3.

I do not necessarily agree with the phrase "Do not care what others think about you." Here is why. Ultimately yes, God's view of you is the only thing that matters and is completely accurate. However, I do think God wants us to care, to an extent, what others think to show love toward them. If you say you ultimately never care what others think, you are in a sense saying they do not matter which I do not think God wants us to portray. If someone says I hurt them, even if I did not have an intention to, they are still hurt, and I should care.

Confidence comes with practice. Of course, you are not going to feel confident at something you don't practice or something you are not good at. In college, I never took out the trash one year and I swear it was not out of laziness, I just didn't know where the trash went. I wanted to quit at volleyball when I first started in 5th grade because I was not good, but the more I practiced, the better I got and the more I was excited to play. When I first took neuroscience, I wanted to quit because I did not understand the anatomy and physiology. The more I studied, the more confident I felt. When I first became an occupational hand and upper extremity therapist, some days I would feel sick to my stomach to go to work in fear I would hurt someone and felt there was so much I did not know. The more I practiced, the better I was and the more I was excited to go to work. I was always fearful when we had a pitcher over 60 mph, until I practiced, setting that speed with the pitching machine. I would be fearful to pray in front of others or even meet with others when they wanted to talk about deep, heartfelt topics thinking maybe I would not be able to help them or know what to say. The more I did, the more confident I became. Practice also needs prayer. Before the game, before work, or before meeting with others, I would pray for God's confidence, guidance and to be my hands and mouth.

Think of your best version of God. Now understand He is bigger, more powerful and more than what you just imagined. Not only is He more, but more beyond anything we can comprehend. "...then I saw all that God has done. No one can comprehend what goes on under the sun. Despite all their efforts to search it out, no one can discover its meaning. Even if the wise claim they know, they cannot really comprehend it." -Ecclesiastes 8:17. Are you confident yet in God's power, and not only his power but his willingness to help you? Believe in yourself because the very one who created you believes in you. By faith Enoch was taken from this life, so that he did not experience death: "He could not be found, because God had taken him away." For before he was taken, he was commended as one who pleased God. And without faith it is impossible to please God, because anyone who comes to him must believe that he exists and that he rewards those who earnestly seek him." -Hebrews 11:5-6 (1 Samuel 26:23 and Proverbs 28:20).

"By faith Noah, when warned about things not yet seen, in holy fear built an ark to save his family. By his faith he condemned the world and became heir of the righteousness that is in keeping with faith. By faith Abraham, when called to go to a place he would later receive as his inheritance, obeyed and went, even though he did not know where he was going. By faith he made his home in the promised land like a stranger in a foreign country; he lived in tents, as did Isaac and Jacob, who were heirs with him of the same promise. For he was looking forward to the city with foundations, whose architect and builder is God. And by faith even Sarah, who was past childbearing age, was enabled to bear children because she considered him faithful who had made the promise. And so from this one man, and he as good as dead, came descendants as numerous as the stars in the sky and as countless as the sand on the seashore." -Hebrews 11:7-12.

It is easy to lose our confidence when we cannot see the future, but our confidence comes from the faith we have that God will act and do the impossible. Abraham and his wife Sarah were past childbearing age, and it seemed impossible, but God promised Abraham he would have as many descendants as stars in the sky. The confidence and faith came not from their situation, but God's faithfulness.

"By faith Abraham, when God tested him, offered Isaac as a sacrifice. He who had embraced the promises was about to sacrifice his one and only son, even though God had said to him, "It is through Isaac that your offspring will be reckoned." Abraham reasoned that God could even raise the dead, and so in a manner of speaking he did receive Isaac back from death. By faith Isaac blessed

Jacob and Esau regarding their future. By faith Jacob, when he was dying, blessed each of Joseph's sons, and worshiped as he leaned on the top of his staff. By faith Joseph, when his end was near, spoke about the exodus of the Israelites from Egypt and gave instructions concerning the burial of his bones. By faith Moses' parents hid him for three months after he was born, because they saw he was no ordinary child, and they were not afraid of the king's edict. By faith Moses, when he had grown up, refused to be known as the son of Pharaoh's daughter. He chose to be mistreated along with the people of God rather than to enjoy the fleeting pleasures of sin. He regarded disgrace for the sake of Christ as of greater value than the treasures of Egypt, because he was looking ahead to his reward. By faith he left Egypt, not fearing the king's anger; he persevered because he saw him who is invisible. By faith he kept the Passover and the application of blood, so that the destroyer of the firstborn would not touch the firstborn of Israel. By faith the people passed through the Red Sea as on dry land; but when the Egyptians tried to do so, they were drowned. By faith the walls of Jericho fell, after the army had marched around them for seven days. By faith the prostitute Rahab, because she welcomed the spies, was not killed with those who were disobedient. And what more shall I say? I do not have time to tell about Gideon, Barak, Samson and Jephthah, about David and Samuel and the prophets, who through faith conquered kingdoms, administered justice, and gained what was promised; who shut the mouths of lions, quenched the fury of the flames, and escaped the edge of the sword; whose weakness was turned to strength; and who became powerful in battle and routed foreign armies. Women received back their dead, raised to life again. There were others who were tortured, refusing to be released so that they might gain an even better resurrection. Some faced jeers and flogging, and even chains and imprisonment. They were put to death by stoning; they were sawed in two; they were killed by the sword. They went about in sheepskins and goatskins, destitute, persecuted, and mistreated— the world was not worthy of them. They wandered in deserts and mountains, living in caves and in holes in the ground. These were all commended for their faith, yet none of them received what had been promised, since God had planned something better for us so that only together with us would they be made perfect." -Hebrews 11:17-40.

Faith is being confident God will come through. Confidence comes from our faith. The Word says how God promised Abraham the Messiah would come from Isaac.

Then God tests his faith by asking him to offer Isaac. Talk about being confused as a human being and not knowing the plan. However, instead of rationalizing in his human thoughts, cursing God for taking away the son he had been longing for, and doubting God's promise, He reckoned that even God could raise the dead, and if He is asking Him to sacrifice His only Son, that must be the option. I want us to live in the same way. Even when God asks us to have a dream so big it does not seem possible, instead of listing all the reasons it does not make sense, we reason that God must have something up His sleeve to pull us through. I have seen God work to get me through graduate school for occupational therapy, sports and flourish my relationships when I put my faith in him.

"Your beauty should not come from outward adornment, such as elaborate hairstyles and the wearing of gold jewelry or fine clothes. Rather, it should be that of your inner self, the unfading beauty of a gentle and quiet spirit, which is of great worth in God's sight. For this is the way the holy women of the past who put their hope in God used to adorn themselves." -1 Peter 3:3-5.

You will be confident when you are content. This is not saying as girls we cannot get ready with clothes and make up. It is saying do not put your value and true beauty based on these details. "Charm is deceptive, and beauty if fleeting; but a woman who fears the Lord is to be praised." -Proverbs 31:30. It is simply recognizing that clothing styles and our collagen supply are fleeting as our time on goes quickly, and making sure our beauty comes from our fear of the Lord, our inner self, a gentle and quiet spirit and as a wife submitting to our husbands, like Sarah did. "And your fame spread among the nations on account of your beauty, because the splendor I had given you made your beauty perfect, declares the Sovereign Lord." -Ezekiel 16:14. God is talking about Jerusalem, but He uses Jerusalem as an example of His bride. God has made you beautiful! You can be confident in your beauty because you were hand designed to the very last detail. If you ever question anything about your looks, and this goes for everyone, men and women, God the Creator of the universe, whom we can't even wrap our minds around, hand designed you.

"Alas, Sovereign Lord," I said, "I do not know how to speak; I am too young." But the Lord said to me, "Do not say, "I am too young." You must go to everyone I send you to and say whatever I command you. Do not be afraid of them, for I am with you and will rescue you.," declares the Lord. Then the Lord reached out his hand and touched my mouth and said to me, "I have put my words in your mouth. See, today I appoint you over nations and kingdoms to uproot and tear down, to destroy and overthrow, to build and to plant." -Jeremiah 1:6-10.

"Do not let anyone look down on you because you are young, but set an example for the believers in speech, conduct, love, faith and purity." -1 Timothy 4:12. "How can a young person stay on the path or purity? By living according to your word. I seek you with all my heart." -Psalm 119:9-10 (Proverbs 1:1-6). Proverbs 1:1-6 says it provides knowledge and discretion for the young. Even if we are young, with a relationship with God, He will put the words we need in our mouths if we let Him. Many ask how we can stay on the right path, even when we are young. The answer is the word of God.

In grade school, high school, college and even today, I am teased for aspects of being a believer, but guess who people come to when they are in trouble? When you have Christ and have stability in your life, people see that difference in you and know they can come to you when they are at their lowest. Therefore, it is so important to love on people whether they are a believer or not. This does not mean to go and join the unbeliever at the strip club, but rather join them at the gym, sporting event, invite them for dinner or find other ways to love on them.

"For you have been my hope, Sovereign Lord, my confidence since my youth. From birth I have relied on you; you brought me forth from my mother's womb. I will ever praise you. I have become a sign to many; you are my strong refuge. My mouth is filled with your praise, declaring your splendor all day long." -Psalm 71:5-8.

God can be your hope and confidence from the beginning, no matter your age. "Once you spoke in a vision, to your faithful people you said: "I have bestowed strength on a warrior; I have raised up a young man from among the people." -Psalm 89:19. God loves using all ages. Jesus was 12 when He was in the temple courts, listening and asking the teachers questions. They were amazed at His understanding and answers. His parents were looking for Him, and He replied

You Can, Through Christ

saying they should know He would be in His Father's house. However, He did go to Nazareth with them when they asked him to. Jesus grew in wisdom and stature, and in favor with God and man." -Luke 2:46-52. Feel like you are too young?

2 Chronicles 24:1 says Joisha was seven when he became king. There are scriptures in 2 Chronicles 24:2 and 2 Chronicles 34:1-2 that says Josiah was eight when he became king, and he reigned in Jerusalem thirty-one years. He did what was right in the eyes of the Lord and followed the ways of his father David. Unbeknownst to contrary belief, just because you are young does not mean you know things. Yes, there is something to say about experience for advice, absolutely. I will always emphasize to have complete respect for anyone older than you, and we should be respecting any other human being in general.

I think of experience with driving. When I first received my license, I had to be at my high school early for an open gym for softball. I was one of the captains, so I had to be there extra early before the sun was up and the parking lot was plowed to set up. You can probably tell I am making excuses for myself for what I am about to say. Open gym ended, and I went to my math class. Over the speaker I hear, "Lexi Car, can you please move your vehicle so our students can get into the parking lot." What?! My car was parked in such a way it was blocking my entire D1 high school from coming in one of our entrances by the stoplight. Everyone knew this was my car because of my license plate! After more driving experience, you can say I am more to be confident in my parking. I want you confident; however, if you are trying to follow what God says and an adult is not, you are the one setting the example. Spiritual maturity many times comes from obedience as opposed to simply age.

I was in many leadership positions and was told I was too young to be in them. If I did not stand confident, showing an example in speech, conduct, love, faith and purity, I would have failed. God is right next to you, no matter your age. When I first started graduate school, I was with other physical and occupational therapists much older than me. I was also a lot of times one of the youngest players on my sport teams. It did not stop me from trying to be the American Occupational Therapy Association representative for my class or a captain of my team. When I first started my job as an Occupational Therapist, I felt discouraged at times being the youngest. Even though I did not have confidence in myself, I know Jesus put me in this position because He has equipped me and has confidence in me. He has a reason for having us where He needs us, at whatever age we are at that time.

Some people feel they do not want to show their confidence because they feel they are being prideful. When we are prideful, we are thinking more about ourselves. This can take place either thinking higher about our own selves or this could also mean thinking less of ourselves. Even when we think less, we are being prideful because the focus is on ourselves. We have confidence in who is with us, not who we are. We are His handiwork!

"As for you, you were dead in your transgressions and sins, in which you used to live when you followed the ways of this world and of the ruler of the kingdom of the air, the spirit who is now at work in those who are disobedient. All of us also lived among them at one time, gratifying the cravings of our flesh and following its desires and thoughts. Like the rest, we were by nature deserving of wrath. But because of his great love for us, God, who is rich in mercy, made us alive with Christ even when we were dead in transgressions—it is by grace you have been saved. And God raised us up with Christ and seated us with him in the Heavenly realms in Christ Jesus, in order that in the coming ages he might show the incomparable riches of his grace, expressed in his kindness to us in Christ Jesus. For it is by grace you have been saved, through faith—and this is not from yourselves, it is the gift of God— not by works, so that no one can boast. For we are God's handiwork, created in Christ Jesus to do good works, which God prepared in advance for us to do." -Ephesians 2:1-10 (Romans 9:30-32, Acts 15:11, Galatians 3:10-12, and Romans 5:2).

We are to *work out* our salvation, not work *for* our salvation. And if by grace, then it cannot be based on works; if it were, grace would no longer be grace." -Romans 11:6. There will be a big difference in your character and life when you work out your salvation, knowing you are serving out of love for God, our creator, as opposed to working for salvation (not possible by the way) out of fear of trying to get to Heaven and not go to hell. Everything about you was so intentionally designed, and He delights in you. He planned exactly how you were to look, where you were to be born, where you were to grow up, who your parents are and the time in history when you were to be and who is supposed to be in your life during that same time. Do not let His work go to waste! "Those who cleanse themselves from the latter will be instruments for special purposes, made holy, useful to the Master and prepared to do any good work." -2 Timothy 2:21.

Social media can really affect our self-esteem; and I am so ashamed but need to tell you this story, so you do not make the same mistake. Satan prowls online, just as he does in our day-to-day lives. One time I shared a post for a couple from our church who was looking for a house. I was the first to share their post. No one liked it, not even them, so I deleted it. The following Sunday in church, they came up to me thanking me sharing that I was the first to share. They told me that sharing demonstrated God's faithfulness in their struggle and search knowing they can rely on their church family and on me. Wow. Complete and total conviction. The kind of conviction that shatters your heart. When I realized my own selfishness drove me to delete a post when others could not thank me enough for, I was deeply convicted. Please share what you want and more importantly what God wants you to post, regardless of likes or comments. You have no idea who you are impacting, and the conviction you will feel. Be confident, not in how others respond to your posts, but in your motivation behind the posts. We cannot control others. If we feel what we are sharing is pleasing to God and going to motivate others, I am asking you to please share and with *confidence*!

"Then Deborah said to Barak, "Go! This is the day the Lord has given Sisera into your hands. Has not the Lord gone ahead of you?" -Judges 4:14. We can have confidence knowing God is present past, present, and future all at the same time...today. Nathan replied to the king, "Whatever you have in mind, go ahead and do it, for the Lord is with you." -2 Samuel 7:3 (1 Chronicles 17:2). We can have confidence every day knowing where we are is where God has called us to be. "So, David's fame spread throughout every land, and the Lord made all the nations fear him," -1 Chronicles 14:17 (2 Samuel 5:10). "He has declared that he will set you in praise, fame and honor high above all the nations he has made and that you will be a people holy to the Lord your God, as he promised." -Deuteronomy 26:19. "Be strong and courageous. Do not be afraid or discouraged because of the king of Assyria and the vast army with him. With him is only the arm of flesh, but with us is the Lord our God to help us and to fight our battles." And the people gained confidence from what Hezekiah king of Judah said." -2 Chronicles 32:7-8. God wants us to be strong and courageous because He has won, and we are on

His team. No one can overcome Him. He wants us to be as bold as a lion! "The righteous are as bold as a lion." -Proverbs 28:1.

"Blessed is the one whom God corrects; so do not despise the discipline of the Almighty." -Job 5:17. Ah, discipline. Something as human beings we naturally try to avoid, as it does not make us feel adequate or like we are "the best." The key to learning to accept and maybe even dare I say "like" discipline is to realize who is correcting you. If God is correcting you, you know it will end for your good as He is developing your character. As an athlete, discipline from practice is what grows your skills and mind set.

"Does he who fashioned the ear not hear? Does he who formed the eye not see? Does he who disciplines nations not punish? Does he who teaches mankind lack knowledge? The Lord knows all human plans; he knows they are futile. Blessed is the one you discipline, Lord, the one you teach from your law; you grant them relief from days if trouble." -Psalm 94:9-13 (Proverbs 20:12).

Discipline will end up bringing you relief from trouble, even though you initially feel *in* trouble while it is happening. "Whoever heeds discipline shows the way to life, but whoever ignores correction leads others astray." -Proverbs 10:17. If we pay attention to discipline and accept correction, it will only make you better. If someone is disciplining you with what you may feel are "Wrong" motives, even if their heart is in it to bring you down, the amazing thing is God can still use their critique to help you. The key is praying and asking God if what the individual says about you is true. For example, if someone says you are selfish. Don't take what they say to heart in the sense that you are "defined" by their words. Pray that God may show it to you out of love that maybe you have been caring more about yourselves than others lately.

"Whoever loves discipline love knowledge, but whoever hates correction is stupid." -Proverbs 12:1. It is a lie the enemy gives that you are "inadequate" if someone corrects you. We will be corrected our entire lives, as there is always more to learn and always someone who is able to teach and help you grow whether it is for your career, sports, hobbies or life. The key is learning to love discipline, understanding this love comes from the desire to want to grow and be better to help further God's kingdom. I have found this is the only way to love discipline, otherwise. To be honest I just get annoyed and angry with who is correcting me, whether it has been a coach, someone I love, teacher, colleague or coworker. When you understand it is something God desires for you, to use to help you, you accept the command. "The wise in heart accepts commands." -Proverbs 10:8. "The fear of the Lord is the beginning of knowledge, but fools despise wisdom and instruction." -Proverbs 1:7 (Psalm 111:10). The fear of the Lord is the beginning of wisdom, and knowledge of the Holy One is understanding." -Proverbs 9:10. "Whoever scorns instruction will pay for it, but whoever respects a command is rewarded." -Proverbs 13:13 (Proverbs 29:1).

"Whoever disregards discipline comes to poverty and shame, but whoever heeds correction is honored." -Proverbs 13:18. If you continue your entire life thinking you know everything and do not desire to be corrected and learn, you may stay where you are now and it could possibly keep you from getting that job, spot on the team or relationship you desire. "Whoever gives heed to instruction prospers and blessed is the one who trusts in the Lord." -Proverbs 16:20. Desiring instruction and trusting the Lord go hand in hand, because many times when we are instructed, we are trying something new we are not comfortable with. This goes back to needing to have confidence God wants us to desire.

"...though war break out against me, even then I will be confident." -Psalm 27:3. "I remain confident of this: I will see the goodness of the Lord in the land of the living. Wait for the Lord; be strong and take heart and wait for the Lord." -Psalm 27:13-14 (Matthew 22:31-33, Mark 12:26-27 and Luke 20:37-39). Confidence does not come naturally, but it is possible even during wars. The key is waiting on the Lord, knowing His goodness. "The fruit of righteousness will be peace; its effect will be quietness and confidence forever. My people will live in peaceful dwelling places, in secure homes, in undisturbed places of rest. Though hail flattens the forest, and the city is leveled completely, how blessed you will be." -Isaiah 32:17-20 (Psalm 85:10). God promises His people can live in confidence and peace. It does not mean our lives will be rid of the hail, but through the storms of life this is one thing we can be sure of.

"This is what the great king, the king of Assyria, says: On what are you basing this confidence of yours? You say you have counsel and might for war- but you speak only empty words. On whom are you depending, that you rebel against

305

me?" -Isaiah 36:4-5. When people ask you where you get your confidence from, you reply. "the Lord." When Jesus taught, people couldn't believe He was the carpenter's son because He was so wise. Others couldn't believe the courage of Peter and John when they realized they were unschooled "ordinary" men, but they realized they had been with Jesus. (See Matthew 13:54-55 and Acts 4:13). "And he did not do many miracles there because of their lack of faith." -Matthew 13:58. Even as I was writing this book, I was hesitant what others would think, knowing I am not a theologian. However, my confident comes that I am a daughter of the King, and though I waver and do it imperfectly, my life goal is to try and fulfill the duty and purpose He has on my life. I can be confidence, because I am His, and you are too! "Kings will see you and stand up, princes will see and bow down, because of the Lord who is faithful, the Holy One of Israel, who has chosen you." -Isaiah 49:7. "At that time I will gather you; at that time, I will bring you home. I will give you honor and praise among all the peoples of the earth when I restore your fortunes before your very eyes," says the Lord." -Zephaniah 3:20.

"With flattery he will corrupt those who have violated the covenant, but the people who know their God will firmly resist him." -Daniel 11:32. When we are not confident and firm in our beliefs in the word, it is easy to be persuaded with others flattery, simply meaning they act like they genuinely care about you when all they want is self-gain. When we are firm and confident, it does not matter how others try to persuade us because we fully know what our purpose is and who it is from.

"Then the disciples came to Jesus in private and asked, 'Why couldn't we drive it out?' He replied, 'Because you have so little faith. Truly I tell you, if you have faith as small as a mustard seed, you can say to this mountain, Move from here to there, and it will move. Nothing will be impossible for you.'" -Matthew 17:19-21 (Matthew 17:14-18 Mark 9:15-29).

"If you can?" said Jesus. "Everything is possible for one who believe." Immediately the boy's father exclaimed, "I do believe; help me overcome my unbelief!" -Mark 9:23-34. Jesus then healed the man's son form the demon that was possessing him. I love how Jesus answered his request, as the father humbled himself, realizing he did not have the belief he should but asking for help with his unbelief. That's what God is looking for! Doubts will always creep into our heads, but through them continue to pray to God to help us see past the unbelief, keeping our eyes on Him and asking Him to strengthen our faith. We are never going to be perfect as Jesus was with a complete and full trust in God without a doubt, but even with our doubt when you continue in the direction. He has called you, you are saying you have faith He will pull through even if it's as small as a mustard seed.

Jesus has a parable for those who are confident in their own righteousness and looked down on everyone else. Two men went to the temple to pray, one a Pharisee and the other a tax collector. The Pharisee thanked God that he is not like other evil people who rob and are adulterers, or like the tax collector next to him. He talked to God about how he fasts and gives a tenth of his money. The tax collector could not even look up at Heaven, and simply said Lord, have mercy on me, I am a sinner. Jesus said the tax collector was... "justified before God, for those who exalt themselves will be humbled, and those who humble themselves will be exalted." - Luke 18:9-14. Emphasis on confidence is not pride. Confidence is sure of the perfection of our maker who has called us to His purposes in this life that we are able to fulfill through Him. We can admit we are sinners and as we humble ourselves, He will lift us up. If we are self-righteous and if what we think is "confidence" may be pride, we can be sure He will humble us.

The Pharisees said they know Jesus is a sinner, but the blind man said whether He is or not, all I know is I was blind and now, I see! I love this because it reminds me of how people may try to take away your confidence in Christ today by saying things such as you cannot see Him or how can you really know he exists? How can you put your confidence in Him? My response would be I was blind but now I see! My heart was desiring evil, but now it wants what is best for those around me! I was not sure of my purpose or what life was about, wondering in sin and confusion but now I know exactly why I am here, and what is to come after this life. The Pharisees kept questioning, and the man who was blind said "do you want to be his disciples too?" They hurled insults at Him and said they are disciples of Moses. The man said "You don't know where he came from, yet he opened my eyes. We know God does not listen to sinners but to the one who does his will. If this man were not from God, he could do nothing!" -John 9:24-33. We know Jesus is God, because only God can change our hearts, help us genuinely love others and have confidence in a world that consistently tries to break us down and tells us we are less than.

Jesus says He is the vine, His Father in the gardener. He cuts off any branches that does not bear fruit but prunes those that are producing fruit to multiply. He says remain in me, and I will remain in you because you cannot bear fruit on your own. Apart from Him, you can do nothing. If you do not remain in him, you will begin to wither and tossed into the fire, (See John 15:1-6) Jesus doesn't want you in misery but wants to kill your current self to give you new life, a better life. We cannot do this on our own. We do not bear fruit by trying harder or giving more of our self, but by abiding in Him. Try to please people and you will be running around in circles and stressed out your whole life. Try to please God, and you will find rest for your soul. Christ just wants you. Christ has no more to gain and simply wants you out of pure love for you.

Instead of recommendation letters, you yourself can be a recommendation letter known and read by everyone in how you live. Show you are a letter from Christ like those in Corinth did because of Paul's ministry, written not with ink but with the Holy Spirit which gives life and, on your heart, giving us a confidence through Christ before God. Not that we are competent ourselves, but because our competence comes from God (See 2 Corinthians 3:5 & 2 Corinthians 3:1-6).

Paul says we get to serve the gospel by God's gift of grace through His power. He says although he is the least of all the Lord's people, (and I feel the same way) he gets to preach the boundless riches of Christ, making plain the mystery. God's intent is through the church; his wisdom will be made known in Heaven and on earth according to his eternal purpose he accomplished in Jesus. We get to approach God with freedom and confidence because of this! Paul says to "not be discouraged from his sufferings, which are for our glory." -Ephesians 7-13 (Revelation 4:10-11). The fact that Jesus spoke in parables was even the fulfillment of a prophesy saying he will "reveal things hidden since the creation of the world." -Matthew 13:34-35.

Paul says we are to thank God for our brothers and sisters because God chose them to be saved through the gospel so we can share in glory with Jesus. Paul says to "stand firm and hold fast to the teachings whether by word of mouth of writings." -2 Thessalonians 2:13-15 (1 Corinthians 1:4). "Christ is faithful as the Son of God's house, and we are in this house with Him if we hold firmly to our confidence and hope in glory!" -Hebrews 3:6 (Hebrews 10:23 and Thessalonians 3:2-4). Sometimes you will be publicly insulted with persecution and other times you will stand by those treated this way. "Joyfully accept this confiscation of your property, because you know that you have a better and lasting possession. Never throw away your confidence, it will be richly rewarded." -Hebrews 10:32-35.

"This is how we know that we belong to the truth and how we set our hearts at rest in his presence: If our hearts condemn us, we know that God is greater than our hearts, and he knows everything. Dear friends, if our hearts do not condemn us, we have confidence before God and receive from him anything we ask, because we keep his commands and do what pleases him." -1 John 3:19-22.

When we confess our sins to God, we can be confident He is righteous and just to forgive us. We can be confident we are loved. We can be confident we are enough in Christ. We can be confident He has blessed us with gifts and talents He desires to use for us and others. We can be confident He will always use us to fulfill His purpose no matter our mistakes and downfalls. We can be confident no matter how impossible the task looks before us. We can be confident in Jesus, today and always. Confident because of His unconditional love, His unconditional guidance, unconditional strength, and unconditional grace.

Marriage & Relationships

"I can do all things through Christ who strengthens me." -Philippians 4:13

I can *have thriving marriage* through Christ who strengthens me.

When looking for a spouse, Caleb once said run as fast as you can toward God and if someone is able to keep up, introduce yourself.

"So, God created mankind in his own image, in the image of God he created them; male and female he created them. God blessed them and said to them, "be fruitful and increase in number; fill the earth and subdue it. Rule over the fish in the sea and the birds in the sky and over every living creature that moves on the ground." -Genesis 1:27-28.

Marriages seem to be falling apart left and right. I bet if every couple was completely honest, the thought of divorce has at least crossed their mind. So, what is the difference? Why do some stay together and others divorce? No one can deny relationships are very challenging, but what produces the joy and bliss in the relationships as well?

Not just in a marriage, but in general it seems people are depending on their spouses, their jobs, their athletic careers, or other achievements in their life for fulfillment, instead of the fulfillment only God can provide. As a little girl, everything I watched whether movies, TV shows or general cultural influence made you feel that you needed a soul mate to complete you. Marriage is the most beautiful gift God has given us in a relationship, other than a relationship with Him, and the most important relationship next to His. However, marriage was never meant to fulfill you but to be a part of the fulfilling plan and purpose God has for your life. The problem with looking for your spouse to fulfill you is that they are not perfect. They can never fully meet all your expectations. Only God can. So, when you have a clear mind of this concept in your marriage, it helps to show your spouse more grace resulting in more enjoyment of your relationship.

To love your spouse better, you need to put God first. "Rebecca, Isaac's wife, not only offered water to her husband when he asked but also his camels." (See Genesis 24). This means loving them, as well as those who are important to them or their hobbies that mean a lot to them. It does not mean you need to pretend to like something that they love as a hobby, but at least show that you love their interest and are happy it makes them happy.

"If I speak in the tongues of men or of angels, but do not have love, I am only a resounding gong or a clanging cymbal. If I have the gift of prophecy and can fathom all mysteries and all knowledge, and if I have a faith that can move mountains, but do not have love, I am nothing. If I give all I possess to the poor and give over my body to hardship that I may boast, but do not have love, I gain nothing. Love is patient, love is kind. It does not envy, it does not boast, it is not proud. It does not dishonor others, it is not self-seeking, it is not easily angered, it keeps no record of wrongs. Love does not delight in evil but rejoices with the truth. It always hopes, always perseveres. Love never fails. But where there are prophecies, they will cease; where there are tongues, they will be stilled; where there is knowledge, it will pass away." -1 Corinthians 13:1-8. "And now these three remain: faith, hope and love. But the greatest of these is love." -1 Corinthians 13:13.

When you move mountains, you will be satisfied for the moment, then it repeatedly leaves us empty. Unless you are in love and have love from the one who made the mountain and gives you the ability to move it in the first place, you will not find the purpose of life, love. Love is the most important aspect of life, and who is love? God. Who loves your spouse more than you do? God. Who loves you more than your spouse does? God. Who can help you love your spouse the best? God!

One of the qualities of love is patience. How do we acquire patience and keep from being easily angered? Understanding that your spouse is not perfect and showing them grace, seeing their side and perspective through empathy. Love is kind. How do we be kind? Understanding how kind God is to us and how much God values your spouse as another one of his children. Love does not envy. It is easy to get jealous of your spouse in many ways, but realizing you are on the same team together helps as well as praying for a genuine love and seeing yourself as God sees you. When you see yourself as God sees you, with your exact design and purpose, it helps to not get as envious toward others. Love does not boast or become prideful. It does not try to demean or rise above your spouse, realizing your gifts are from God. Love does not dishonor others. It's showing respect for others as well as your spouse, looking out for their best interest. Love keeps no record of wrongs. Oh, this is tough. Where is the line between forgetting and forgiving? I believe we should never keep a record of wrongs in the sense of condemning our spouse from their mistakes. However, you can, out of love, communicate and ask them to work on certain aspects of your relationship to help each other in the downfalls of your relationship. Love rejoices in being truthful and vulnerable with one another. When it is in Christ, it never fails. It always hopes, and always perseveres. Faith and hope are important, but the greatest commandment is love. Love fulfills every single commandment in the Bible, because only by love and through love, the person of Jesus, can we fulfill the purpose in the relationships

God has placed on our lives.

"The Lord God said, "It is not good for the man to be alone. I will make a helper suitable for him." -Genesis 2:18.

"But for Adam no suitable helper was found. So, the Lord God caused the man to fall into a deep sleep; and while he was sleeping, he took one of the man's ribs and then closed up the place with flesh. Then the Lord God made a woman from the rib he had taken out of the man, and he brought her to the man". The man said, "This is bone of my bone and flesh of my flesh; she shall be call 'woman,' fir she was taken out of man." That is why a man leaves his father and mother and is united to his wife, and they become one flesh." -Genesis 2:20-23.

This gift has instructions from its Maker to bring us the most joy. When your marriage glorifies God, it will reach its full potential. When you get married, you literally become one.

Marriage was created to glorify God, to make you each more like Christ. Your marriage will not reach its full potential unless there are three people in it. What Three? Marriage is a team of three!

"Two are better than one, because they have a good return for their labor: If either of them falls down, one can help the other up. But pity anyone who falls and has no one to help them up. Also, if two lie down together, they will keep warm. But how can one keep warm alone? Though one may be overpowered, two can defend themselves. A cord of three strands is not quickly broken." -Ecclesiastes 4:9-12.

Being an athlete, I naturally can't help but think of it this way. You chose to pick up your teammates and chose to love them. Think of Christ as the coach. When you are out on the field playing, the coach sees the big picture, what the defense or enemy has in store and maybe can see your teammates in a way you cannot by their work ethic, gifts and talents. When you pray for your spouse, you are going to the direct source that knows them better than anyone and can counsel you in the play to make next.

When Jesus is at the center, it will not fall apart. Not because we do not fall apart, but because He does not. We are called not only to love each other in a marriage, but to cherish. God wants us not only to love everything about the person, but to appreciate. This will take a lot of forgiveness, as marriage is two sinners living together, however God is enough to give you the power to cherish something about your spouse each day. You will never agree on everything. That would not be an actual relationship but a robotic partnership. The key is being patient to understand one another when you do not agree and using each other's disagreements or thoughts to either strengthen your relationship or figure out together how to compromise.

You cannot go by how you feel each day. Even the days you do not "feel" love, you must choose it. "Therefore, confess your sins to each other and pray for each other so that you may be healed. The prayer of a righteous person is always effective." - James 5:16. When your spouse has hurt you or you have hurt your spouse, apologize. Confess your sin and pray together. When I get really upset if someone has hurt me, the first thing that calms me down is the individual coming to me genuinely apologizing and admitting they were wrong. Remember this when you have wronged someone else too!

"We love because he first loved us." -1 John 4:19 (Colossians 3:14). There is no falling out of love. Love comes from God, who is love Himself. He is always constant. Love is a choice. It represents commitment to someone, even when the feelings come and go. Don't get me wrong, there are many amazing feelings which come with loving your spouse which God has granted us. However, talk to any married couple and they will tell you these feelings are not around all the time. I do not want your relationship to come and go like your feelings do. Always pray for each other, and for your own heart toward your spouse. Think about it. God knows your spouse better than you do and He always will. He knows their deepest desires and struggles. Who better to talk about them with? Many say we're incompatible. We're all incompatible. You need to go into your marriage saying we will do anything and everything and will make this work. God will bless you. You cannot go into thinking if this does not work, I will always have a way out. Write what you love about your spouse. Do what they love. Wash each other's feet.

Looking for happiness in your marriage? Here it is!

"Submit to one another out of reverence for Christ. Wives, submit

313

yourselves to your own husbands as you do to the Lord. For the husband is the head of the wife as Christ is the head of the church, his body, of which he is the Savior. Now as the church submits to Christ, so also wives should submit to their husbands in everything. Husbands, love your wives just as Christ loved the church and gave himself up for her to make her holy, cleansing her by the washing with water through the word, and to present her to himself as a radiant church, without stain or wrinkle or any other blemish, but holy and blameless. In this same way, husband's ought to love their wives as their own body. He who loves his wife loves himself. After all, no one ever hated their own body, but they feed and care for their body, just as Christ does the church— for we are members of his body. For this reason, a man will leave his father and mother and be united to his wife, and the two will become one flesh. This is a profound mystery, but I am talking about Christ and the church. However, each one of you also must love his wife as he loves himself, and the wife must respect her husband." -Ephesians 5:21-33.

Women, when you submit to your husband, you are submitting to God, even if you do not always agree with Him. Remember in your submission, even though your husband is flawed, and not perfect, God is, and He gives this command for a reason that we may not fully understand. Even scripture says this is a mystery, but our heart trusts in the Lord. Husbands, you have a huge responsibly in return. You are to love your wife as Christ loves the church, so much that you are willing to put down your life for her. Husbands, you need to understand that when you are married you are one flesh now, meaning when you love your wife, you are benefitting and loving yourself. The ironic thing is if the main motivation to love your wife is out of selfishness for yourself, you will not love her in the same sense. When your motivation is out of love for God and her, only then will it benefit you. Since marriage does not last into eternity according to His word, we find the point of it here and now. It is supposed to be a beautiful love picture and romantic story of how much God, Jesus, loves the church.

"Now then, at the resurrection, whose wife will she be of the seven, since all of them were married to her?" Jesus replied, "You are in error because you do not know the Scriptures or the power of God. At the resurrection people will neither marry nor be given in marriage; they will be like the angels in Heaven." -Matthew 22:28-30 (Mark 12:23-25 and Luke 20:32-36).

It can be hard to become one when in-laws can make it difficult. In laws can be challenging, but God can use them to be a blessing. I love the story of Ruth, and how she stayed faithful to her mother-in-law Naomi, even though she even became an ex-mother-in-law. "But Ruth replied, "Don't urge me to leave you or turn back from you. Where you go, I will go, and where you stay, I will stay. Your people will be my people and your God my God." -Ruth 1:16. They had a beautiful relationship, and even though there are many challenges with in-laws, this story can be great to pray over your relationship with them. Try to meet with them and develop a relationship to form the truth, love and respect you desire from them.

As a woman, it is easy to say we do not want to submit or respect as our husbands may not display this quality God calls of them consistently. You're right. They do not deserve respect, and you do not deserve love. This is the whole point of Jesus. Even though we do not deserve love, grace, or forgiveness, Jesus gave it to us anyway out of love. If I only was showed love when I deserved it, I would not be shown love very often. We are to love, submit and respect because God commands us to regardless of the circumstance, just as Jesus gave it all for each of us.

When our spouse is going through a difficult time, the best thing we can do is pray for him or her and forgive, which may take prayer in order to do. There will be difficult times and there will be sins you each commit. Can you imagine having a spouse or someone else in general who is continually praying for you? There is no greater power. God has given us free will because without it, we would be robots. He wanted us to choose to love him, and in the same way we need to choose to love our spouse even in their shortcomings. You have the choice to walk away from your spouse, and you always have the choice to stay. I hope you always choose to stay.

You may be thinking, "What if I really messed up? Or my spouse really messed up? God is more powerful than our free will. We have free will, but it is still limited in the power of a Sovereign God ultimately. When we come to him in repentance and want to make things right, you bet he will help us. The God of second chances is our Father! "Judah has been unfaithful. A detestable thing has been committed in Israel and in Jerusalem: Judah has desecrated the sanctuary the Lord loves by marrying women who worship a foreign god." -Malachi 2:11. "Saul died because he was unfaithful to the Lord; he did not keep the word of the Lord and even consulted a medium for guidance and did not inquire of the Lord. So, the Lord put him to death and turned the kingdom over to David son of Jesse." -1 Chronicles 10:13-14. "...she is free to marry anyone she wishes, but he must belong to the Lord." -1 Corinthians 7:39 (Nehemiah 13:26-27). It gives the example of how Solomon was led astray by marrying women who did not have God. When looking for a spouse, God wants us to find someone who has the same faith as we do, because He wants our marriage to thrive and become everything, He designed it. As women, we are to submit to our husbands. You will find it easier if you find someone you know is after God's own heart. Next you may be saying, "What is my spouse does not believe and I am married?" "Thy, without a word, may be won by the conduct of their wives." -1 Peter 3:1-2. Your conduct and prayers for your spouse are not wasted. God loves your spouse more than you do and loves you more than you know. He hears, he knows, keep praying.

You will read in 2 Samuel 11:4 the dreaded story where David sleeps with Bathsheba the wife of Uriah the Hittite and then in 2 Samuel 11:15, 2 Samuel 11:62 Samuel 11:17 David realizes that Uriah will not sleep with his wife upon his return because of the guilt he felt while his fellow soldiers were still out at war, David then puts Uriah in the front line to die. 2 Samuel 11:26-27 tells us how Bathsheba mourned for her husband and then married David. However, what David did displease the Lord. In 2 Samuel 12:11-18, Nathan comes to tell David that God is bringing calamity on him, and David admits he has sinned against the Lord. Nathan says the Lord is taking away his sin, but the consequence of the contempt he has shown for God by his sin is the death of his son born from Bathsheba. "Then David got up from the ground. After he had washed, put on lotions and changed his clothes, he went into the house of the Lord and worshipped." -2 Samuel 12:20. I truly believe David's repentance after he had the affair is what makes David truly a man after God's own heart. The repentance is the difference as he is human, just like all of us.

"You have heard that it was said, 'You shall not commit adultery.' But I tell you that anyone who looks at a woman lustfully has already committed adultery with her in his heart. If your right eye causes you to stumble, gouge it out and throw it away. It is better for you to lose one part of your body than for your whole body to be thrown into Hell. And if your right hand causes you to stumble, cut it off and throw it away. It is better for you to lose one part of your body than for your whole body to go into hell." -Matthew 5:27-30.

We all have wandering minds and disagreements in our marriage. These will be inevitable. We need to be careful to take control of our minds, especially when upset with our spouse. The second Satan tempts you with interests in others outside of your marriage, stop right there. Temptation is inevitable, but your response to temptation is in your control. The Holy Spirit gives us the power to overcome. Sin, adultery, and unfaithfulness start in the mind. This means self-talk to focus on your spouse, prayer, and date night. Marriage takes this kind of work, but it is good work which God offers a reward for. Never believe the lies that you married the wrong person or that there is someone better out there. Once you are married, God is saying you have made the vow not only to them, but to Him. You need to keep it. God loves you and your spouse so much; He treasures your marriage and is on your side to make it flourish. Come to Him.

"Wisdom will save you from the adulterous woman, from the wayward woman with her seductive words, who has left the partner of her youth and ignored the covenant she made before God." -Proverbs 2:16-17. "Keep to a path far from her, do not go near the door of her house." -Proverbs 5:8. Adultery usually starts because you think it is a casual or meaningless flirtation, like, text or gesture. God is clear. Do not go near the door or even let the thoughts in because it is so easy to get entrapped and snared. "May your fountain be blessed, and may you rejoice in the wife of your youth. A loving doe, a graceful deer, may her breasts satisfy you always, may you ever be intoxicated with her love." -Proverbs 5:18-19. "For lack of discipline they will die, led astray by their own great folly." -Proverbs 5:23.

"My son, keep your father's command and do not forsake your mother's teaching. Bind them always on your heart; fasten them around your neck. When you walk, they will guide you; when you sleep, they will watch over you; when you awake, they will speak to you. For this command is a lamp, this teaching is a light, and correction and instruction are the way to life, keeping you from your neighbor's wife, from the smooth talk of a wayward woman. Do not lust in your heart after her beauty or let her captivate you with her eyes. For a prostitute can be had for a loaf of bread, but another man's wife preys on your very life. Can a man scoop fire into his lap without his clothes being burned? Can a man walk on hot coals without his feet being scorched? So is he who sleeps with another man's wife; no one who touches her will go unpunished." -Proverbs 6:20-29 (Proverbs 5:3-4, Proverbs 7:5 and Proverbs 7:22-25).

It is impossible to have an affair and not have side effects spiritually for yourself. I tell you this out of love, not judgment, as I want to keep you from getting burned.

"No one is greater in this house than I am. My master has withheld nothing from me except you because you are his wife. How then could I do such a wicked thing and sin against God?" And though she spoke to Joseph day after day, he refused to go to bed with her or even be with her." -Genesis 39:9-10.

Joseph literally fled when Potiphar's wife was tempting him. Temptation is inevitable in life, but if you flee or not is up to you.

"But since sexual immorality is occurring, each man should have sexual relations with his own wife, and each woman with her own husband. The husband should fulfill his marital duty to his wife, and likewise the wife to her husband. The wife does not have authority over her own body but yields it to her husband. In the same way, the husband does not have authority over his own body but yields it to his wife. Do not deprive each other except perhaps by mutual consent and for a time, so that you may devote yourselves to prayer. Then come together again so that Satan will not tempt you because of your lack of self-control." -1 Corinthians 7:2-5 (Song of Songs 3:1).

God encourages all married couples to not deprive one another and to stay active in your sex life. He specifically says if you are not, you are giving the enemy the opportunity to tempt one of you. The only time is when you are both in mutual agreement to refrain for a temporary amount of time to pray. I cannot emphasize enough how God create sex, and it is a very good thing in a marriage.

"The Lord said to me, 'Go, show your love to your wife again, though she is loved by another man and is an adulteress. Love her as the Lord loves the Israelites, though they turn to other gods and love the sacred raisin cakes.' So, I bought her for fifteen shekels of silver and about a homer and a lethek of barley. Then I told her, "You are to live with me many days; you must not be a prostitute or be intimate with any man, and I will behave the same way toward you."

-Hosea 3:1-3.

"Then she will say, "I will go back to my husband as at first, for then I was better off than now." -Hosea 2:7. (Hosea to his wife Gomer as well as God to Israel). God continued to fight and show His love toward Israel even when they were having an "affair" with other gods or countries. Even though the Bible does state you are allowed to leave your marriage if your partner has had an affair, with God there is always an option for reconciliation and forgiveness. The process will be hard and painful, but it is possible. Divorce is also hard and painful too, regardless the reason.

"It is God's will that you should be sanctified: that you should avoid sexual immorality; that each of you should learn to control your own body in a way that is holy and honorable, not in passionate lust like the pagans, who do not know God; and that in this matter no one should wrong or take advantage of a brother or sister. The Lord will punish all those who commit such sins, as we told you and warned you before. For God did not call us to be impure, but to live a holy life. Therefore, anyone who rejects this instruction does not reject a human being but God, the very God who gives you his Holy Spirit." -1 Thessalonians 4:3-8.

"Marriage should be honored by all, and the marriage bed kept pure, for God will judge the adulterer and all the sexually immoral."-Hebrews 13:4. What gets dangerous when we think about love being a feeling is this is what often leads to adultery. Who is to say adultery is wrong if it is justified by the "love" feeling with the one they are cheating with? Adultery is wrong as specifically spoken by God. God knows you better than you know yourself and wants your marriage to thrive! "Does not he who guards your life know it?" -Proverbs 24:12. He designed the marriage you are in just for you, and He wants you to make the most of it. He is there to help. I truly believe the person you marry God hand-picked just for you, but once you are married God has given you the responsibility to take care of His child, your spouse. God does not talk about soul mates in the Bible, but even better than that, He talks about how to have a great marriage. Jesus is our soul mate, and Heaven is our perfect place. He tells husbands to love their wives as Christ loves the church. A love where Jesus died for the church! He commands wives to respect their husbands. Both require selflessness. Trust me, I always want to be the leader and submitting is something I constantly must try to do. When God talks about submission, this is not to be frowned upon as women giving up their rights or their best as many view it. God designed the woman to submit to the husband who is a servant leader, guiding her and loving her as much as He would die for her. He is not placing more value on one more than the other, simply different roles.

"They submitted themselves to their own husbands, like Sarah, who obeyed Abraham and called him her lord. You are her daughters if you do what is right and do not give way to fear. Husbands, in the same way be considerate as you live with your wives and treat them with respect as the weaker partner and as heirs with you of the gracious gift of life, so that nothing will hinder your prayers." -1 Peter 3:6-7.

God created sex between one man and one woman from the time they are married for the rest of their lives. God is not keeping us from the pleasures of sex because of this rule, He is saving us as He wants to protect your heart because He knows how intimate sex is and that it is more than just physical, but a spiritual experience, as well. He knows the impact such intimacy has on our hearts. He knows we will be happiest being only with one individual, and even better, studies show how much better the sex is. He knows the spiritual, physical, emotional, and mental rewards it will have on us. Think about it again, He created it for us. Who else would know better? You might think you know you are eventually going to marry this person, thus making premarital sex ok. You do not know who God has planned for you, and even if you do end up marrying this person, God considers sex a sin, outside of a covenant with Him. He wants to protect you. He does not want the individual leaving you and wants you to be in this covenant because you are so precious. It is the hardest, let me repeat, the hardest struggle waiting until you are married. I cannot stress this enough. However, God promises great reward when we do. Now if you already have had sex before marriage, God does not want you to live in shame. You are so loved, and God loves to redeem. From here going forward, I encourage you to wait until marriage for your own heart's sake.

I know people argue that sex is our instinct. Well, so is eating. What if we indulged in food every single time, we have a craving? There is a purpose behind the self-control that is for our own benefit. God created sex and Christians celebrate it for what it was created. I can see as a parent it might be hard to address with your kids, but as far as I've witnessed, if people are quiet about it, it can be perverted and if people blatantly just show kids, it can be perverted. I think there is a way to truthfully talk about it. C.S Lewis addresses how in psychology, they talk about "repression" and that to "repress" our sexual desires is "dangerous." He points out "repress" does not mean suppressed or complete denial. He states that when an individual is actively regressing this desire and waits for something greater, committing to one person, we are actual that much more aware of how strong this desire is. (Lewis, "Mere Christianity, 1952). Sex is a beautiful act designed by God, but in it of itself will not fulfill you.

The marriage I look up to the most is my parents of 35 years. Their advice is to find a spouse who loves God more than you, they also say to put yourself before your spouse, and to find a spouse who supports your passions They also always remind me to be grateful for each other every day, even if some days are harder. They stress the importance of always talking positively about your spouse to your kids and pray for each other and forgiveness. Only in loving God more than your spouse, can you love your spouse more than you can ever imagine or do on your own. I admired how my mom would thank my dad for being a leader in our home. She thanked him for making Jesus a priority and living by example. Dad would thank Mom for accepting him as he is and would say how he is looking forward to growing closer to God the rest of their lives together. Falling in love is easy, but staying in love takes God, persistence, and prayer. Being in love is an incredible feeling, but it is still a feeling.

Ask most married couples and the ones who are honest with you will not say they feel that exact same feeling every day for 20 or more years, heck I'd even argue those married a couple years. Do not base off what you see of your friends' marriages, and this includes strangers you see on social media True love is a choice, not a feeling. What happens is people get married, and once that "in love" feeling goes away, they assume they married the "wrong" person. Same with the thrills people seek in life. All temporary. It does not mean where they travel to and who they marry is not a beautiful thing, just that you cannot base all your decisions off feelings. This is where the word of God is so important because when it is your foundation, you will stay married even if the feeling is not there.

"A wife of noble character is her husband's crown, but a disgraceful wife is like decay in his bones." -Proverbs 12:4. "He who finds a wife finds what is good and receives favor from the Lord." -Proverbs 18:22. "A quarrelsome and nagging wife is compared to the constant dripping of a roof and God says it is better to live in a desert or in the corner of a roof than to share a house with one." -Proverbs 19:13 (Proverbs 27:15, Proverbs 21:9, Proverbs 25:24 and Proverbs 21:19). God has such a sense of humor, I love it. In relationships, I cannot stand my nagging voice! It drives me nuts; I cannot even imagine how it has affected others. I understand how tempting it is to nag, I mean come on, can they not get it right?! How do they not see what they are doing wrong?! God has included this in His Word because nagging will not change the situation, them, or their heart. Pray God changes you and your spouse instead of nagging, and try to have a conversation, watch your tone, and speak out of love.

"Houses and wealth are inherited from parents, but a prudent wife is from the Lord." -Proverbs 19:14.

"A wife of noble character who can find. She is worth far more than rubies. Her husband has full confidence in her and lacks nothing of value. She brings him good, not harm, all the days of her life. She selects wool and flax and works with eager hands. She is like the merchant ships, bringing her food from afar. She gets up while it is still night; she provides food for her family and portions for her female servants. She considers a field and buys it; out of her earnings she plants a vineyard. She sets about her work vigorously; her arms are strong for her tasks. She sees that her trading is profitable, and her lamp does not go out at night. In her hand she holds the distaff and grasps the spindle with her fingers. She opens her arms to the poor and extends her hands to the needy. When it snows, she has no fear for her household; for all of them are clothed in scarlet. She makes coverings for her bed; she is clothed in fine linen and purple. Her husband is respected at the city gate, where he takes his seat among the elders of the land. She makes linen garments and sells them and supplies the merchants with sashes. She is clothed with strength and dignity; she can laugh at the days to come. She speaks with wisdom, and faithful instruction is on her tongue. She watches over the affairs of her household and does not eat the bread of idleness. Her children arise and call her blessed; her husband also, and he praises her: "Many women do noble things, but you surpass them all." Charm is deceptive, and beauty is fleeting; but a woman who fears the Lord is to be praised. Honor her for all that her hands have done, and let her works bring her praise at the city gate." -Proverbs 31:10-31 (Ruth 3:11).

You are capable. The Proverbs 31 woman should be our goals, knowing even though we will fail, with the help of God we can be trustworthy so others can have confidence in us, self-control, have genuine love and provide for our spouses, families, and others to bring them good, supply food, work hard whether at home or at jobs, stay strong to complete our physical tasks, full of wisdom from the word and remain faithful. All these qualities can be acquired when we fear the Lord. "Build houses and settle down; plant gardens and eat what they produce." -Jeremiah 29:5 (Jeremiah 29:28).

For those who may think being romantic is worldly or not in the Bible, you have not read the book Song of Songs! God loves romanticism and has designed it between a man and woman. Marriage is the example of how much Jesus loves the church, to give His life for her. I do not think it gets more romantic than that. "Let him kiss me with the kisses of his mouth- for your love is more delightful than wine." -Song of Songs 1:2 (Ezekiel 24:16). God loves the physical touch of being romantic. "...when I found the one my heart loves. I held him and would not let him go." -Song of Songs 3:4 "Place me like a seal over your heart." -Song of Songs 8:6. God loves the commitment in being romantic. "You are altogether beautiful...there is no flaw in you." -Song of Songs 4:7. God loves the admiration of the outer and inner beauty.

"You have stolen my heart, my sister, my bride; you have stolen my heart with one glance of your eyes, with one jewel of your necklace. How delightful is your love, my sister, my bride! How much more pleasing is your love than wine, and the fragrance of your perfume more than any spice! Your lips drop sweetness as the honeycomb, my bride; milk and honey are under your tongue." -Song of Songs 4:9-11 (Song of Songs 7:6).

God loves when people are so in love, they are focused on each other and not the temporary going on around them. "...my heart began to pound for him." -Song of Songs 5:4 (Song of Songs 5:16). God loves the butterflies. Song of Songs 7:10-12 talks about going on a date to the countryside, to the village in the vineyards to see the flowers! God loves date nights and date days!

"Another thing you should do: Flood the Lord's altar with tears. You weep and wail because he no longer looks with favor on your offerings or accepts them with pleasure from your hands. You ask, "Why?" It is because the Lord is the witness between you and the wife of your youth. You have been unfaithful to her, though she is your partner, the wife of your marriage covenant. Has not the one God made you? You belong to him in body and spirit. And what does the one God seek? Godly offspring. So be on your guard, and do not be unfaithful to the wife of your youth. "The man who hates and divorces his wife," says the Lord, the God of Israel, "does violence to the one he should protect," says the Lord Almighty. So be on your guard, and do not be unfaithful." -Malachi 2:13-16.

God loves you if you are divorced, just like He loves any of us and does not want you to live in guilt. He warns against divorce because He knows it causes "violence" where He wants there to be love. It is for your protection that God commands not to get divorced. I want to be real here. I bet if you asked anyone who is married if they have thought about divorce and they say "no", they probably aren't being honest. There are no way two sinners can live together and divorce not at least cross their mind. This is where spiritual warfare is significant, in the mind. I think it is unrealistic for me to ask you not to be tempted by divorce as all are; however, when the thought enters your mind, I encourage you to do something about it and the way you think about your spouse. A tactic I use with my patients when they complain about their spouse is to acknowledge that the complaint may be real and valid, but instead of complaining turn it around with something positive about their spouse and why they married them in the first place. The mind is powerful and can help recreate those "feelings" of love people long for when they first fell in love or got married. Reminder, God loves romanticism! Pray. He can bring it back into your marriage. If your marriage is struggling, pray for your spouse. You cannot change their thoughts, but God can. God wants your marriage to work more than anyone, and cares about you, your spouse, and your marriage more than anyone. God cares about you more than you know. He cares about your intimacy, hurts with you and wants to help. Give it all to Him.

"To the married I give this command (not I, but the Lord): A wife must not separate from her husband. But if she does, she must remain unmarried or else be reconciled to her husband. And a husband must not divorce his wife. To the rest I say this (I, not the Lord): If any brother has a wife who is not a believer and she is willing to live with him, he must not divorce her. And if a woman has a husband who is not a believer and he is willing to live with her, she must not divorce him." -1 Corinthians 7:10-13.

"It has been said, 'Anyone who divorces his wife must give her a certificate of divorce.' But I tell you that anyone who divorces his wife, except for sexual immorality, makes her the victim of adultery, and anyone who marries a divorced woman commits adultery." -Matthew 5:31-32 (Luke 16:18). When Jesus was asked if it is lawful to get a divorce, Jesus responded saying in the beginning the Creator made them male and female, to leave their father and mother and the two will be united flesh. Therefore, what God has joined together, let no man separate. The Pharisees then asked why Moses allowed it. Jesus replied, "because our hearts are so hardened even though it is not supposed to be this way." Jesus says, "if anyone divorces his wife except for sexual immorality and marries another woman, he commits adultery." -Matthew 19:2-9 (Mark 10:2-12). When you divorce, you are physically pulling apart one flesh. The reason God does not want you to get divorced is because He knows the serious emotional, physical, psychological, and spiritual effects on you. Marriage is the only time in the Bible we are making a specific vow to God and the vow to God should be our motivator, especially when you have struggles with your spouse because, ask anyone, struggles will happen. "When you make a vow to God, do not delay to fulfill it." -Ecclesiastes 5:4.

If you are reading this and already divorced or have had sex before marriage, this is not to make you feel guilty. This can mean remarrying your ex-wife or husband if they are not already remarried. If this is not an option, look to your next marriage to love in this way. This is only to guide you from here on out, showing you God's purpose for marriage and sex. God is all about grace and second chances if you haven't been able to tell so far! You are just as loved by God as anyone else. This is not to condone sin, but despite all our sin, every single human being, His grace is a gift!

"Or do you not know wrongdoers will not inherit the kingdom of God? Do not be deceived: Neither the sexually immoral nor idolaters nor men who have sex with men nor thieves nor the green nor drunkards nor slanderers nor swindlers will inherit the kingdom of God. And that is what some of you were. But you were washed, you were sanctified, you were justified in the name of the Lord Jesus Christ and by the Spirit of our God." -1 Corinthians 6:9-11 (Deuteronomy 22:5).

If you struggle with any of these desires, here God is saying he is giving you the ability to change.

"The body, however, is not meant for sexual immorality but for the Lord, and the Lord for the body. By his power God raised the Lord from the dead, and he will raise us also. Do you not know that your bodies are members of Christ himself? Shall I then take the members of Christ and unite them with a prostitute? Never! Do you not know that he who unites himself with a prostitute is one with her in body? For it is said, "The two will become one flesh." But whoever is united with the Lord is one with him in spirit. Flee from sexual immorality. All other sins a person commits are outside the body, but whoever sins sexually, sins against their own body. Do you not know that your bodies are temples of the Holy Spirit, who is in you, whom you have received from God? You are not your own; you were bought at a price. Therefore, honor God with your bodies." -1 Corinthians 6:13-20.

Our life is not our own. We deserve the worst, and God still blesses us. When we have this mentality, which is truth, it helps you have a different perspective of how good God is to us and more peace of His control. If we are not our own, someone needs to take responsibly for us, and God is ready to do just that. The only catch is He does not force us, and is not responsible for our bad decisions, as we make those out of our sinful nature. However, when you trust in Him and have a personal relationship with Him, He does promise to use your hurt and wrong decisions for His good and glory. Are you ready to give your life to Him?

"But I want you to realize that the head of every man is Christ, and the head of the woman is man, and the head of Christ is God." -1 Corinthians 11:3. "A man ought not to cover his head, since he is the image and glory of God; but woman is the glory of man. For man did not come from woman, but woman from man; neither was man created for woman, but woman for man." -1 Corinthians 11:7-9.

"Wives, submit yourselves to your husbands, as is fitting in the Lord. Husbands, love your wives and do not be harsh with them. Children, obey your parents in everything, for this pleases the Lord. Fathers do not embitter your children, or they will become discouraged. Slaves, obey your earthly masters in everything; and do it, not only when their eye is on you and to curry their favor, but with sincerity of heart and reverence for the Lord." -Colossians 3:18-22.

"I also want the women to dress modestly, with decency and propriety, adorning themselves, not with elaborate hairstyles or gold or pearls or expensive clothes, but with good deeds, appropriate for women who profess to worship God. A woman should learn in quietness and full submission. I do not permit a woman to teach or to assume authority over a man; she must be quiet. For Adam was formed first, then Eve. And Adam was not the one deceived; it was the woman who was deceived and became a sinner. But women will be saved through childbearing—if they continue in faith, love and holiness with propriety." -1 Timothy 2:9-15.

Part of the curse from the fall is women will now desire to rule over their husbands, but he will rule over her according to Genesis 3:16. Before the fall, Eve loved to let Adam rule over her. Submission can be a scary word when we do not understand what it means. I love how my friend Anya Meeks, with 20 years of experience, puts it. She says, "Jesus is my Savior and I believe ALL of God's Word to be true. I have learned that what He has said about marriage is perfect and true. Submission to my husband is HIS best for me since the moment I said, "I Do". I believe submission to my husband is humbly accepting the headship, leadership, & protection he has over me. A dying of myself because I am now one with another. Yet, still living with and using the strengths and gifts God has given uniquely to me. When I use them best, they benefit my husband and children and those around me, but if I can't use them dependently and only try to "run" with my gifts independently, it can be a disaster and never how God intended it! When I THINK I know better, I usually ask the Lord to show me through the wisdom of my husband, if I am thinking properly. God made this world with an order and when we function in that order, it runs smoothly! This is why it is important for me to constantly lift my husband up in prayer for His relationship with God to be at its best. If he has a beautiful union with our Savior, he will lead me well. In moments or relationships where God is not part of the husband's life, we, as women should pray and ask God for strength to follow even when things aren't done perfectly. We then must trust God and His sovereignty with our loved one. Even in submission, your opinion does matter! You can talk with your husband about how you feel and discuss important decisions within the family. God wants you apart of the process. Trust that your husband has your best interest in mind, and if you feel they do not, trust that God has your best interest in mind, even if you do not necessarily agree with the decision. It is just understanding that if he is not asking you to sin or go against God, he has the final decision. Even if you may disagree, this is where we need to trust God and His sovereignty that He has the order He does for a reason. I can tell you that our instinct since the fall is to rebel and want to be the leader, to take control of our husbands, but you will be shocked how much happier you, and your marriage will be when you submit. It makes it easier for men to love you and appreciate you when you serve with joy, you will not regret it. Ultimately, we are all children of God, and He is our Father. He designed the order, and He loves us more than we can imagine. We can trust Him! "Nevertheless, in the Lord woman is not independent of man, nor is man independent of woman. [12] For as woman came from man, so also man is born of woman. But everything comes from God." -1 Corinthians 11:11-12.

Many will say they need to feel appreciated. That is not a biblical concept other than finding fulfillment and reward in what you are doing for the Lord. Do not get me wrong, one of the best feelings in the world is feeling appreciated, but even if you do not, sometimes it does not mean your spouse doesn't appreciate you but could mean your feelings are not aligned with truth, which happens often in all our lives. I would hate to see you end a marriage because you do not feel appreciated, when it maybe you are putting your contentment in the wrong area. "As a prisoner for the Lord, then, I urge you to live a life worthy of the calling you have received. Be completely humble and gentle, be patient, bearing one another in love." -Ephesians 4:1-2.

Passion & Perseverance

"I can do all things through Christ who strengthens me." -Philippians 4:13

I can *be passionate, enthusiastic, encouraging, motivated and dedicated* through Christ who strengthens me.

"Never be lacking in zeal, but keep your spiritual fervor, serving the Lord. Be joyful in hope, patient in affliction, faithful in prayer." -Romans 12:11-12. Never be lacking in zeal or in other words, passion, and enthusiasm. What does this look like? Joy, patience and staying faithful in prayer. "When they heard this, they praised God. Then they said to Paul: "You see, brother, how many thousands of Jews have believed, and all of them are zealous for the law." -Acts 21:20. How can we be passionate about the law? By falling in love with it. Zeal is ultimately powered by love. I grew up being taught passion, it makes me laugh to this day. My Dad once said to me, "You know our rule, God wants you to put your heart into everything you do" "But dad, we're cutting cheese?!" Literally......everything. However, the older I get, the more I appreciate my parents' passion. When we make goals, it is common to be super enthusiastic when you first start, and then eventually tapering off. We need to stay enthusiastic. There arc so many motivational books out there but if they do not discuss Jesus, they do not provide the *power* needed to keep your zeal and passion. Our enthusiasm and encouragement must come from God. Be in God and take heart to continue to chase your dreams and passions. "A dream comes when there are many cares, and many words mark the speech of a fool." -Ecclesiastes 5:3.

"Do not let any unwholesome talk come out of your mouths, but only what is helpful for building others up according to their needs, that it may benefit those who listen. And do not grieve the Holy Spirit of God, with whom you were sealed for the day of redemption." -Ephesians 4:29-30. What we say to others should be to build them up. "If anyone speaks, they should do so as one who speaks the very words of God. If anyone serves, they should do so with the strength God provides, so that in all things God may be praised through Jesus Christ. To him be the glory and the power for ever and ever. Amen." -1 Peter 4:11. Building others up does not mean flattery in the sense of being nice to others for hidden motives. Something we can ask of God is that He will always help us see the best in others, give us the courage to let them know and to show us what is needed to push them to reach their potential. All can be seen as encouragement. "Whoever seeks good finds favor, but evil comes to one who searches for it." -Proverbs 11:27 (Matthew 5:6). Seek the good in your spouse, family, friends, strangers and even your enemies. You will find it. We tend to find what our mind is fixed on. We have so many people who look for the worst in each other and who like to discourage themselves. Look at how to build one another up. Sometimes this may mean pointing out a weakness someone may have *lovingly* in order to strengthen them, but it should always be out of encouragement to build one another up.

"For, "Whoever would love life and see good days must keep their tongue from evil and their lips from deceitful speech." -1 Peter 3:10.

"All kinds of animals, birds, reptiles, and sea creatures are being tamed and have been tamed by mankind, but no human being can tame the tongue. It is a restless evil, full of deadly poison. Ships are large, but driven by a very small rudder, and it is the same with our body and tongue. Just like a spark can start a fire, so one evil word can light your whole life on fire. Use your tongue to praise God and to encourage human beings who are made in God's likeness. You cannot have praise and cursing in one mouth. Clean and dirty water cannot come from the same well. An apple tree cannot bear pears." -James 3:3-12.

You cannot claim Jesus and yet not keep a tight rein on your tongue. (See James 1:26). "The goal of this command is love which comes from a pure heart and a good conscience and a sincere faith. Some have departed from these and have turned to meaningless talk." -1 Timothy 1:5-6. The tongue has more power than we understand. You can start a fire with one evil word, or you can light your life on fire. I have completely been guilty of running my mouth when I am not supposed to, and I can attest that this is true. It is convicting to think God is saying we cannot curse and praise out of the same mouth, as your words come from the same heart. We will all mess up and say things we do not mean. This is where grace comes in. However, the general outflow of what you say to and about others will show where your heart is. We praise and encourage others not because we are all perfect, as we all make mistakes, but every person is made in God's likeness.

"The tongue has the power of life and death, and those who love it will eat its fruit." -Proverbs 18:21 (1 Corinthians 14:7-10). "The soothing tongue is a tree of life, but a perverse tongue crushes the spirit." -Proverbs 15:4. One time, I had a patient say, "Your words have given me life. Your encouragement picked me up when I felt I had no hope. No hope for my physical injury, and no hope for my spiritual life." Our words literally are life, this is not a cliché. One of my patients was feeling suicidal, and words are what made them want to stay. Take advantage of this power. "Anxiety weighs down the heart, but a kind word cheers it up." - Proverbs 12:25. Everyone has anxiety. There is a difference between our general anxiety and those who have a disorder, but either way you can never go wrong with a kind word to cheer someone up. Our culture is so anxiety ridden, the least we can do is help everyone out. I know it can be hard to talk to others. What do you say? How do you say it? When do you say it? The best thing to do is to ask who knows them best. Our Sovereign Lord has given us well-instructed words to know what to say to those who need it most (Isaiah 50:4). "The words of the reckless pierce like swords, but the tongue of the wise brings healing." -Proverbs 12:18. When you use your words to bring life, you can literally heal others! "The mouth of the righteous is a fountain of life." -Proverbs 10:11.

"Make a tree good and its fruit will be good or make a tree bad and its fruit will be bad, for a tree is recognized by its fruit. You brood of vipers, how can you who are evil say anything good? For the mouth speaks what the heart is full of. A good man brings good things out of the good stored up in him, and an evil man brings evil things out of the evil stored up in him. But I tell you that everyone will have to give account on the day of judgment for every empty word they have spoken. For by your words, you will be acquitted, and by your words you will be condemned." -Matthew 12:33-37.

Wow. Judgment for every empty word I have spoken. All I can say is thank you Lord for grace. I have way too many to count. The realization I want us to take from this is how important our words are. Grace will always cover where you fall short, but out of love our desire should be to get our hearts right with God for the right words to flow out. "Jesus called the crowd to him and said, "Listen and understand. What goes into someone's mouth does not defile them, but what comes out of their mouth, that is what defiles them." -Matthew 15:10-11.

"Don't you see that whatever enters the mouth goes into the stomach and then out of the body? But the things that come out of a person's mouth come from the heart, and these defile them. For out of the heart come evil thoughts—murder, adultery, sexual immorality, theft, false testimony, slander. These are what defile a person; but eating with unwashed hands does not defile them." -Matthew 15:17-20.

As an occupational therapist, our clinic can get very busy. Helping patients with everything from the upper back, shoulder, elbow, wrist, hand, fingers, orthotics, helping emotionally, psychologically and on top of that completing the notes to go with each session. Some ask if it is so busy it burns me out. Even though some days I am more tired than others, it really helps when your attitude is "I cannot believe I get the opportunity to serve God's people and Him each day through this career." Same with my sports and coaching. People ask about the burnout, but really, I cannot believe I get the opportunity to have a healthy body to play and to work with such awesome athletes. Same with church. Instead of "Do we have to go to church?" How about, "I get to go to church to praise and learn about an incredible God and build the community he has for me!" Let me tell you, this does not come naturally. For anyone. No matter what anyone tells you. You need to make a conscious effort to feel this way each day, and eventually it will become a healthy habit. God puts in us enthusiasm and passion when the world takes it away.

God is in the most mundane tasks in our lives just as much as he is in the miracles. Never lose motivation because you feel God is asleep. We cannot even begin to comprehend how much God is involved in each of our lives. We need to trust Him, and He will show us what He can do. "So, I reflected on all this and concluded that the righteous and the wise and what they do are in God's hands." -Ecclesiastes 9:1. Many times, as people, we want to be shown to trust or to find motivation. We often live our lives putting the least amount of effort forward. Either just getting by day by day or letting ourselves get distracted by the little things. I do not want you to get to a point in your life where you are sad you did not put more effort in. The beauty is, no matter your age, God will start working with your effort and enthusiasm *today*.

"See to it, brothers and sisters, that none of you has a sinful, unbelieving heart that turns away from the living God. But encourage one another daily, as long as is it called "Today," so that none of you may be hardened by sin's deceitfulness." -Hebrews 3:12-13. To live in encouragement for ourselves, this requires encouraging others. Encouragement helps keep our hearts from being hardened and lead astray by sin. How? When we lift others, we focus on our strengths in

Christ. Sin naturally will make us feel weak and powerless, as there is no power in our weakness alone. Your power comes from Christ using our weakness. How do we discover our strengths? Many times, it comes from the encouragement of others. "And let us consider how we may spur one another on toward love and good deeds, not giving up meeting together, as some are in the habit of doing, but encouraging one another- and all the more you see the Day approaching." - Hebrews 10:24-25. "Assemble to listen and learn to fear the Lord your God and follow his law carefully." -Deuteronomy 31:12. Encouraging others helps us be encouraged. Encouraging others requires meeting together consistently. How can we encourage one another if we do not know them? How can we encourage one another if we do not meet? Many argue they do not see the need to go to church as they are saved by salvation alone, which may be true, but how can we encourage each other as the body of Christ if we never attend? We need to have friends and family who can call us out in love and encouragement to build us right back up to tackle whatever it is God has called us to do and how to use the gifts we have been given.

God did not listen to Balaam and turned the curse into a blessing, because he loves you. God turns curses into blessings! (See Deuteronomy 23:5 and Nehemiah 13:2). "I the Lord have rebuilt what was destroyed and have replanted what was desolate. I the Lord have spoken, and I will do it." -Ezekiel 36:36. How we can stay enthusiastic, and passionate and encourage others is not pretending everything is okay, but having confidence God can take the curses, the wrongs, and the desolate lands in our lives and make them for good. "You will be blessed when you come in and blessed when you go out. The Lord will grant that the enemies who rise up against you will be defeated before you. They will come at you from one direction but flee from you in seven." -Deuteronomy 28:6-7 (Deuteronomy 28:1-5 and Deuteronomy 28:8). Even though we are truthful to others that there will always be trials and sun-scorched lands, He will always be there to guide us to clear waters. He will never fail. "The Lord will guide you always; he will satisfy your needs in a sun-scorched land and will strengthen your frame. You will be like a well-watered garden, like a spring whose waters never fail." -Isaiah 58:11.

"Then all the peoples on earth will see that you are called by the name of the Lord, and they will fear you. The Lord will grant you abundant prosperity—in the fruit of your womb, the young of your livestock and the crops of your ground—in the land he swore to your ancestors to give you. The Lord will open the Heavens, the storehouse of his bounty, to send rain on your land in season and to bless all the work of your hands. You will lend to many nations but will borrow from none." - Deuteronomy 28:10-12.

God desires to bless the work of our hands and the passion we put into life. "But as for you be strong and do not give up, for your work will be rewarded." -2 Chronicles 15:7. God promises if we do what He commands us, walking in obedience, He will be with us just like He was with David (See 1 Kings 11:38 and 2 Kings 18:5-7). David and Hezekiah had great success because the Lord was with them. (See 1 Samuel 18:14).

"Praise God in the Heavens, praise him all his Heavenly hosts and angels, praise him all creation including the stars, the mountains, the animals, kings, princes and all nations, young and old, men and women, for we were all made this command, praise him forever as his decree will never pass away. His name alone is exalted. He raised up a horn for his people, the praise of his faithful servants, people close to his heart. Praise the Lord." -Psalm 148:1-14.

"...but people are tested by their praise." -Proverbs 27:21. It is hard to be passionate, have perseverance and be enthusiastic when we are struggling in life. Sometimes I really feel resistant because I feel like God is 'testing" me to see how I will react when I feel defeated and hopeless. I realized God is not a God who purposefully wants to see us suffer, but instead wants to see how much He has changed our hearts and where our focus is when we suffer. If our focus is on the cross, we will remain enthusiastic as we cannot help but praise, *with* the tears and heart break that are *still there* and still painful to say the least, as we understand our lives are short, and the mission God has us on is to keep others encouraged, which will lead to encouragement for ourselves.

"They preached the gospel in that city and won a large number of disciples. Then they returned to Lystra, Iconium and Antioch, strengthening the disciples and encouraging them to remain true to the faith. "We must go through many hardships to enter the kingdom of God," they said. Paul and Barnabas appointed elders for them in each church and, with prayer and fasting, committed them to the Lord, in whom they had put their trust." -Acts 14:21-23.

"We who are strong ought to bear with the failings of the weak and not to please ourselves. Each of us should please our neighbors for their good, to build them up. For even Christ did not please himself but, as it is written: "The insults of those who insult you have fallen on me." For everything that was written in the past was written to teach us, so that through the endurance taught in the Scriptures and the encouragement they provide we might have hope. May the God who gives endurance and encouragement give you the same attitude of mind toward each other that Christ Jesus had, so that with one mind and one voice you may glorify the God and Father of our Lord Jesus Christ." -Romans 15:1-6.

When we are patient with other's weaknesses, we are showing them encouragement even if they currently do not have the skills needed at school, work, sports, as a roommate, or as a spouse. Being patient means we have confidence they will eventually get it. God provides us with scripture to provide encouragement which leads to hope. When we have hope, we find endurance to continue forward, knowing there will be an end to the hardship. God has a purpose during it, and God desires to pour His goodness out on relationships when we encourage one another. God loves when we pursue to build up others, as they are in His image. As a parent, do you not love when your children have friends or a significant other in their life that builds them up? How much more does God love it! "The Lord detests the way of the wicked, but he loves those who pursue righteousness." -Proverbs 15:9.

Need motivation? "Where there is not revelation, people cast off restraint; but blessed is the one who heeds wisdom's instruction." -Proverbs 29:18. Motivation will follow if you have goals. "So, whether you eat or drink or whatever you do, do it all for the glory of God." -1 Corinthians 10:31. I find myself unmotivated when I feel what I am doing has no purpose. When we realize every single thing, we do in life could bring God glory, you will notice you get more motivated to do something as simple as doing the dishes, or working hard for that class you could care less about in high school or college. "Excel in your gifts from the spirit to build up the church." -1 Corinthians 14:12. You can find motivation by realizing your efforts can help others. You may only be looking at the direct effects, like how is trying hard in a class, that has nothing to do with my major, going to help someone else? God is big and is doing so much every second of the day, more than we realize. You never know how your gifts and efforts are going to benefit others and yourself. Your motivation can come realizing the everyday decision you make, the effort you put in, makes a difference.

"Complete your work so your willingness to do it will be matched." -2 Corinthians 8:11. "Be eager to help and your enthusiasm will stir most to action, just like those in Corinth did for the Macedonians." -2 Corinthians 9:2 (2 Corinthians 8:19).

"Finally, brothers and sisters, rejoice! Strive for full restoration, encourage one another, be of one mind, live in peace. And the God of love and peace will be with you. Greet one another with a holy kiss. All God's people here send their greetings. May the grace of the Lord Jesus Christ, and the love of God, and the fellowship of the Holy Spirit be with you all." -2 Corinthians 13:11-14.

We are supposed to be eager to help and show enthusiasm, which will lead to completeness through our actions to follow. "Therefore encourage one another and build each other up, just as in fact you are already doing." -1 Thessalonians 5:11. Encouraging others is a command, and it can be hard when we do not even feel encouraged ourselves. The beauty is even when we do not want to encourage or feel encouraged, it is no longer us that needs the power to do it but Christ who lives in us! To find motivation, enthusiasm, encouragement, dedication and passion, the only way we can have it consistently without it running out is to realize it comes from Christ inside of us. If we try to find it from only ourselves and situations in life, it will vary as much as life does.

"I have been crucified with Christ and I no longer live, but Christ lives in me. The life I now live in the body, I live by faith in the Son of God, who loved me and gave himself for me. I do not set aside the grace of God, for if righteousness could be gained through the law, Christ died for nothing!" -Galatians 2:20-21.

It is no longer I who lives, but Christ lives in me. How exciting to think the God of the universe, Jesus, lives in us! There is nothing we cannot do through Him!

"To them God has chosen to make known among the Gentiles the glorious riches of this mystery, which is Christ in you, the hope of glory. He is the one we proclaim, admonishing and teaching everyone with all wisdom, so that we may present everyone fully mature in Christ. To this end I strenuously contend with all the energy Christ so powerfully works in me." -Colossians 1:27-29.

Energy and enthusiasm are power. We were all created with different personalities and by no means am I saying we should all be spazzing out all the time (even though for some people that energy truly is a gift!). However, within each personality you can tell when there is a sense of enthusiasm and passion in what they love and do.

"May our Lord Jesus Christ himself and God our Father, who loved us and by his grace gave us eternal encouragement and good hope, encourage your hearts and strengthen you in every good deed and word." -2 Thessalonians 2:16-17 (Romans 15:13). Jesus provides us with all we need. Need more energy, it's yours! "Make your goal to encourage others in heart and unite them in love to complete their understanding to understand Jesus in whom all treasures of wisdom and knowledge come. People will give you fine-sounding arguments, and you will not believe them as you stay disciplined and firm in the faith of Christ." -Colossians 2:2-5.

"These, then, are the things you should teach. Encourage and rebuke with all authority." -Titus 2:15. How can encouragement go with rebuking? We can help others, sharing advice in an encouraging way. People in our lives will be more likely to respond to your rebukes if you try to say it lovingly and with encouragement that you know they can do it. When I encourage patients, I see objectively better measurements. As a therapist, when I correct a patient on an exercise they are doing wrong, I notice a difference if I simply critique or say it in a way that even though they are performing it incorrectly, I know they will be able to perform it with the proper technique, ultimately helping them recover quicker.

"So, I will always remind you of these things, even though you know them and are firmly established in the truth you now have. I think it is right to refresh your memory as long as I live in the tent of this body, because I know that I will soon put it aside, as our Lord Jesus Christ has made clear to me. And I will make every effort to see that after my departure you will always be able to remember these things." -2 Peter 1:12-15.

We can all use more encouragement. It is amazing how quickly we can all get down on ourselves. One day we can wake up super confident, and the next wonder if it is worth it. Never underestimate constant reminders of encouragement. You might think if you do it too much, it may not seem genuine. Pray God helps you come across genuine, as well as to find ways in others' lives to encourage them. You will find it, and with help, you will be able to encourage others in the ways they need whether they need more assertive encouragement to pick themselves up by the bootstraps, or gentler if they have suffered a significant loss. You will find the discernment if you ask for it.

I know your deeds, that you are neither cold nor hot. I wish you were either one or the other! So, because you are lukewarm—neither hot nor cold—I am about to spit you out of my mouth." -Revelation 3:15-16. It is easy to become lukewarm in life. To get comfortable and just cruise along. God wants so much more for you. He wants you to be enthusiastic and passionate about Him, leading you to be about life, others, yourself, your home, your pets, and experiences that will naturally motivate you and lead you to encourage others. We see a lot of carpal tunnel releases at my clinic, and I made the mistake of calling it a routine procedure. One of my surgeons rightly corrected me, saying there is never a routine procedure. Another example is with fundamentals in athletics. Ask any great athlete, as they will tell you there is no routine to excel in their sport, and they must be "hot" each practice to prepare for the game. We should feel the same way in life. We can be enthusiastic about our relationship with God, the life He has given us, the people He has given us, and the talents and experiences He has provided, or we can act like it is just another mundane day. The choice is yours, and I hope you choose to let your heart catch the fire and get excited when Monday comes around. Regardless of what you do, if you have enthusiasm doing it, it will be purposefully pre-designed to be worth it. "He performs wonders that cannot be fathomed, miracles that cannot be counted." -Job 5:9. "Praise be to the Lord, for he showed me the wonders of his love." -Psalm 31:21.

"What, then, shall we say in response to these things? If God is for us, who can be against us." -Romans 8:31. "Therefore, in the present case, I advise you: Leave these men alone! Let them go! For if their purpose or activity is of human origin, it will fail. But if it is from God, you will not be able to stop these men; you will only find yourselves fighting against God." -Acts 5:38-39. "It is the Sovereign Lord who helps me. Who will condemn me? -Isaiah 50:9. If this does not give you enthusiasm, I do not know what will. If you go into your day with God's vision and consider His desires, you can bet your tasks and service is going to be of origin from Him. God who can do all things is with you and for you every single day, working for your good and for His purpose. His purpose for you is better than your greatest dreams!

Be A Witness

"I can do all things through Christ who strengthens me." -Philippians 4:13

I can *witness the best news* through Christ who strengthens me.

Has someone questioned your faith? If there is no God, where do others find their purpose? Without God, who is to say what is right and wrong? When you realize He died to save you for eternity, you would be crazy about Him too. People will often ask you or wonder why or where your joy comes from. People sometimes think Christians are crazy, but what I think is crazy is not falling madly in love with a God who sent his only Son to die for you to have eternal life. I think it is crazy to not think about the afterlife or eternal life when the evidence is clear it exists. I think it is crazy to pretend there is no God when the evidence is clear. Even crazier, not to love this God! This earth is passing away and to live for this world that is temporary is not logical, loving a God and preparing for eternity is. History is recorded.

"Many of the Samaritans from that town believed in him because of the woman's testimony, 'He told me everything I ever did.' So, when the Samaritans came to him, they urged him to stay with them, and he stayed two days. And because of his words many more became believers. They said to the woman, We no longer believe just because of what you said; now we have heard for ourselves, and we know that this man really is the Savior of the world." -John 4:39-42.

"We are supposed to imitate the earlier churches in Judea in Jesus, knowing we will suffer the same things the churches suffered from the Jews." -1 Thessalonians 2:14.

"Blessed are those who are persecuted because of righteousness, for theirs is the kingdom of Heaven. Blessed are you when people insult you, persecute you and falsely say all kinds of evil against you because of me. Rejoice and be glad, because great is your reward in Heaven for in the same way they persecuted the prophets who were before you. You are the salt of the earth." - Matthew 5:10-13 (Luke 6:22-23.

You are the salt of the earth. Have you ever had food without salt? What happens when you add it? It brings a whole new meaning to the food you are eating! The same with how we share Jesus through our actions and words. If we end up being persecuted for sharing Him, we are to rejoice, not because we enjoy persecution, but we are honored to be experiencing what Jesus and the prophets before us did.

"But how is it to your credit if you receive a beating for doing wrong and endure it? But if you suffer for doing good and you endure it, this is commendable before God. To this you were called, because Christ suffered for you, leaving you an example, that you should follow in his steps. We can find peace knowing God sees. "He committed no sin, and no deceit was found in his mouth." When they hurled their insults at him, he did not retaliate; when he suffered, he made no threats. Instead, he entrusted himself to him who judges justly." -1 Peter 2:20-23 (1 Peter 3:13-14).

Jesus did not retaliate, not because what was happening to Him was right, but He trusted the Father so much and knew of His justice. "The apostles left the Sanhedrin, rejoicing because they had been counted worthy of suffering disgrace for the Name. Day after day, in the temple courts and from house to house, they never stopped teaching and proclaiming the good news that Jesus is the Messiah." -Acts 5:41-42.

"Jesus said this to indicate the kind of death by which Peter would glorify God. Then he said to him, "Follow me!" -John 21:19. Jesus literally told Peter how he would die, which is not recorded specifically in the Bible but if history is correct, it was crucifixion on a cross like Jesus...but upside down. Yet, he still picked up his cross to follow Him. I have struggled for so long to understand how, and how scary. The only answer I could come up with, that my brain does not always understand like my heart does, is that Jesus is worth it. It sounds cliché, many say it, but He is worth the cost, even if the cost is everything. Love makes you do some crazy things.

"Dear friends, do not be surprised at the fiery ordeal that has come on you to test you, as though something strange were happening to you. But rejoice in as much as you participate in the sufferings of Christ, so that you may be overjoyed when his glory is revealed. If you are insulted because of the name of Christ, you are blessed, for the Spirit of glory and of God rests on you. If you suffer, it should not as a murderer or thief or any other kind of criminal, or even as a meddler." -1 Peter 4:12-15 (Philippians 1:29-30).

I am surprised every time something bad happens to me, are you? Literally, every single time even though scripture is clear we are not to be surprised at the fiery ordeals that we experience. We are to rejoice knowing when we partake in the suffering, we will always partake in the joy.

"Also, seek the peace and prosperity of the city to which I have carried you into exile. Pray to the Lord for it, because if it prospers, you too will prosper." - Jeremiah 29:7. As believers, who runs our country affects us, and we need to try our best to vote for candidates we feel follow God. This is challenging I know, because as humans we are all flawed including our candidates. I wanted to provide some guidelines to help. God is pro-Israel "In righteousness you will be established: Tyranny will be far from you; you will have nothing to fear. Terror will be far removed; it will not come near you." -Isaiah 54:14. Israel is singled out as the nation of God's inheritance. Anyone who tries to move Jerusalem will injure themselves. (See 1 Kings 8:53, Zechariah 12:3, Deuteronomy 33:29 and Psalm 33:12) 1 Thessalonians 4:10-12 says we should each work hard if able and not to be dependent on anyone. If you do not get into your Bible, you'll go with what sounds good instead of what is biblical and true.

"Let everyone be subject to the governing authorities, for there is no authority except that which God has established. The authorities that exist have been established by God. Consequently, whoever rebels against the authority is rebelling against what God has instituted, and those who do so will bring judgement on themselves. For rulers hold no terror for those who do right, but for those who do wring. Do you want to be free from fear of the one in authority? Then do what is right and you will be commended. For the one in authority is God's servant for your good. But if you do wrong, be afraid, for rulers do not bear the sword for no reason. They are God's servants, agents of wrath to bring punishment on the wrongdoer. Therefore, it is necessary to submit to the authorities, not only because of possible punishment but also as a matter of conscience." -Romans 13:1-7 (Titus 3:1).

Every single leader could not be established if it were not for God. It does not mean every leader is following what God wants, but God can use them, even their evil for His purpose and good. They will still be punished if they do not find Christ after they die, however God is sovereign and is never surprised by an election. "Have confidence in your leaders and submit to their authority, because they keep watch over you as those who must give an account. Do this so that their work will be a joy, not a burden, for that would be no benefit to you." -Hebrews 13:17.

"Submit yourselves for the Lord's sake to every human authority: whether to the emperor, as the supreme authority, or to governors, who are sent by him to punish those who do wrong and to commend those who do right. For it is God's will that by doing good you should silence the ignorant talk of foolish people." -1 Peter 2:13-15.

We are to submit to all governing authorities unless they ask us to deny the word of God or disobey God. Peter was in a similar situation. The apostles were brought in and made to appear before the Sanhedrin to be questioned by the high priest.

"We gave you strict orders not to teach in this name," he said. "Yet you have filled Jerusalem with your teaching and are determined to make us guilty of this man's blood." Peter and the other apostles replied: "We must obey God rather than human beings! The God of our ancestors raised Jesus from the dead—whom you killed by hanging him on a cross. God exalted him to his own right hand as Prince and Savior that he might bring Israel to repentance and forgive their sins. We are witnesses of these things, and so is the Holy Spirit, whom God has given to those who obey him." -Acts 5:27-32.

Peter was clear his obedience is first to God, then to governing authorities. Notice he did not threaten the governing authorities or disrespect them (even though they may have read him speaking truth as disrespect). He replied to them truthfully,

343

which can be looked at as submission instead of running from them in rebellion.

"Whoever acknowledges me before others, I will acknowledge before my Father in Heaven. But whoever disowns me before others, I will disown before my Father in Heaven." -Matthew 10:32-33 (Luke 12:8-9, Luke 9:26, Mark 8:38 and Hosea 6:3). "By removing eternal risk, Christ calls his people to continual temporal risk", John Piper. Even though taking temporary risks daily to let Christ shine in your life may feel like a constant battle from the criticism of others, we need to care more about what God thinks and His truth. I want to point out it can be scary to think of times in our life when we may have denied Christ, whether in His morals, truth, or Him himself. Remember, Peter denied Him, too, and found grace. His faith wavered but was never diminished, and neither will yours. Jesus loved Peter and used Him regardless of his waver in faith.

"Peter asked, "Lord, why can't I follow you now? I will lay down my life for you." Then Jesus answered, "Will you really lay down your life for me? Very truly I tell you, before the rooster crows, you will disown me three times!" -John 13:37-38 (Matthew 26:34 and Luke 22:34).

"Peter replied, "Man, I don't know what you're talking about!" Just as he was speaking, the rooster crowed. The Lord turned and looked straight at Peter. Then Peter remembered the word the Lord had spoken to him: "Before the rooster crows today, you will disown me three times." And he went outside and wept bitterly." -Luke 22:60-62 (Matthew 26:74-75).

There is always grace, the difference is repentance. After Peter denied Jesus, he found the courage and confidence to be bold when speaking to others about the gospel. Being bold does not mean shouting and forcing Jesus on others, but lovingly sharing your hope and faith, and being bold when asked. Since our eternity is secured in Christ, we never need to worry about the outcome.

"When you are brought before synagogues, rulers and authorities, do not worry about how you will defend yourselves or what you will say, for the Holy Spirit will teach you at that time what you should say." -Luke 12:11-12. I know the biggest question I receive is what to say and how to say it. The good news is we are never alone, as the Holy Spirit will guide us and pick us up even when we feel we mess up. When telling others about Jesus, you want to make sure this person realizes you have a sincere love for them and care for them. Once they understand your motives are genuine, scripture is all that is needed since this is God directly talking to them. Ask others if they want to know for sure they are going to Heaven or if they have doubts. Only God can change hearts, but we are His ambassadors and His vessels. "We are therefore Christ's ambassadors, as though God were making his appeal through us. We implore you on Christ's behalf: Be reconciled to God." -2 Corinthians 5:20. For we are co-workers in God's service; you are God's field, God's building." -1 Corinthians 3:9 (Philippians 4:3). Paul says when we are all in the same cause of the gospel, we are co-workers whose names are in the book of life, as he talked about the women and Clement.

I have always felt the need to defend God, however I have realized God does not need defending. We can be so confident that the word of God is truth, there is no need to feel anxious about being wrong or how we word things. Takes off the pressure I had continually placed on myself! "The one who calls you is faithful, and he will do it." -1 Thessalonians 5:24 (Psalm 33:4). "He has made everything beautiful in its time. He has also set eternity on the human heart; yet no one can fathom what God has done from the beginning to end." -Ecclesiastes 3:11. Not everything is beautiful, but in God's perfect timing he can make the hardest times in our lives beautiful even though it isn't in the heart wrenching moments. Many ask about those who have never heard, but God is telling us he has placed eternity, or thinking about life after death, on the human mind. Jesus is the only way to Heaven, and he is saying no one is with excuse. However, our God is just. If someone desires to seek Him, He will find them. "You will seek me and find me when you seek me with all your heart." -Jeremiah 29:13.

"...but those who seek the Lord lack no good thing." -Psalm 34:10. The middle east is one of the fastest growing areas for faith in Christ. This would not make sense to most individuals as Christ is not encouraged in these areas, however these people are searching out for their purpose. God will not leave them. "But if from there you seek the Lord your God, you will find him if you seek him with all your heart and with all your soul. Take hold of my words with all your heart." -Proverbs 4:4. Part of seeking with all your heart is taking His words with all your heart. When you are in distress and all these things have happened to you, then in later days you will return to the Lord your God and obey Him. For the Lord your God is a merciful God; He will not abandon or destroy you or forget the covenant with your ancestors, which He confirmed to them by oath." -Deuteronomy 4:29-31 (Deuteronomy 28:9).

"I love those who love me, and those who seek me find me. With me are riches and honor, enduring wealth, and prosperity. My fruit is better than fine gold; what I yield surpasses choice silver. I walk in the way of righteousness, along the paths of justice, bestowing a rich inheritance on those who love me and making their treasuries full. "The LORD brought me forth as the first of his works, before his deeds of old; I was formed long ages ago, at the very beginning, when the world came to be. When there were no watery depths, I was given birth, when there were no springs overflowing with water; before the mountains were settled in place, before the hills, I was given birth, before he made the world or its fields or any of the dust of the earth. I was there when he set the Heavens in place, when he marked out the horizon on the face of the deep, when he established the clouds above and fixed securely the fountains of the deep, when he gave the sea its boundary so the waters would not overstep his command, and when he marked out the foundations of the earth. Then I was constantly at his side. I was filled with delight day after day, rejoicing always in his presence, rejoicing in his whole world and delighting in mankind. "Now then, my children, listen to me; blessed are those who keep my ways. Listen to my instruction and be wise; do not disregard it. Blessed are those who listen to me, watching daily at my doors, waiting at my doorway. For those who find me find life and receive favor from the LORD. But those who fail to find me harm themselves; all who hate me love death." -Proverbs 8:17-36.

God desires to be good to you, His child, and once you accept Him, He will always favor you. Keep His ways, listen for Him and wait for Him. If someone rejects God, and His son Jesus, they may not realize, but they are going in the direction of death since He is life himself.

"For the message of the cross is foolishness to those who are perishing, but to us who are being saved it is the power of God." -1 Corinthians 1:18. Regardless of what you believe, just imagine for a second you need a Savior for everything wrong you have done in your life to receive the gift of eternal life. Do you see why believers and Christians get so excited over the cross, seeing it as the very power of God? "The person without the Spirit does not accept the things that come from the Spirit of God but considers them foolishness and cannot understand them because they are discerned only through the Spirit." -1 Corinthians 2:14. My cousin at Stanford has started Veritas forum where discussions are held with different beliefs. Books are reviewed from Biologists where there is an invitation to see science and biblical faith coincide with each other as they present an evolutionary understanding of God's creation. Defense of Christianity is based on rational argumentation known as apologetics. Many Christians may not agree with apologetics as they think it is taking away from faith when it is quite the opposite. Faith is trusting in God without seeing, while also realizing he is a very rational God and is made evident in all the creation we do see.

"But in your hearts revere Christ as Lord. Always be prepared to give an answer to everyone who asks you to give the reason for the hope that you have. But do this with gentleness and respect, keeping a clear conscience, so that those who speak maliciously against your good behavior in Christ may be ashamed of their slander." -1 Peter 3:15-16.

Always be prepared to give an answer for the hope you have. When you share the hope and tell others about Christ, truth says to do so with gentleness and respect, keeping a clear conscious by letting your character reflect that of Christ. No one is saved through rational arguments; however, God is rational as He is the truth. I absolutely love science. In my career as an occupational therapist, our focus is on the science of the human body, mind, and spirit. I see God in the cadavers, in my patients each day and in the law that come with science. We discovered science as people, we did not invent science. God created our minds to think through these logical sciences. I remember learning the phrase "Biogenesis" in graduate school. This word means "life comes from life (physics)." The only explanation that we are alive and were created, is someone had to create us. Life can only come from life; it is a scientific principle. Also, if there is no God, there is no reason to life or right or wrong. To say science proves no evidence of God, means you are saying life that and ultimately science, have no meaning.

Even Paul made a point to say he did not stir up crowds intentionally, but simply proclaimed and worshiped God and made clear what the law says. He strives to do what is right and speak the truth of God, while keeping his conscious clear before God and man. There is a balance, and God will help you find it.

"My accusers did not find me arguing with anyone at the temple or stirring up a crowd in the synagogues or anywhere else in the city. And they cannot prove to you the charges they are now making against me. However, I admit that I worship the God of our ancestors as a follower of the Way, which they call a sect. I believe everything that is in accordance with the Law and that is written in the Prophets, and I have the same hope in God as these men themselves have, that there will be a resurrection of both the righteous and the wicked. So, I strive always to keep my conscience clear before God and man." -Acts 24:12-16.

Even though we may disagree with someone does not mean we cannot love them. Jesus loved those who persecuted and disagreed with him. He even loves us even though we disobey Him when we have faith. Do not fall into the lie that you cannot love others and not agree with their lifestyles. It is the very essence of love when we see others harming themselves through the disease of sin and try to steer them away. As an occupational therapist, if I see something harming my patient, something they are doing wrong, I will tell them. Also, if I know how to treat a patient, I will not withhold this information from them. Why? Because I care for them. If all I cared about was offending them, I would not say anything so they think they are doing it right and would be temporarily "happy." Which one is displaying love?

"Then Jesus said to his disciples, "Whoever wants to be my disciple must deny themselves and take up their cross and follow me. For whoever wants to save their life will lose it, but whoever loses their life for me will find it. What good will it be for someone to gain the whole world, yet forfeit their soul? Or what can anyone give in exchange for their soul?" -Matthew 16:24-26 (Mark 8:34-37, Matthew 10:38-39, John 12:25, Luke 14:27, Luke 9:23-25, Psalm 62:11-12 and Luke 14:33, Matthew 4:21-22, Matthew 9:9).

God doesn't just want part of us. He asks for all of us. It is to our benefit to truly know our identity. We must leave our own selfishness. Matthew, James, and John left their lives and jobs immediately to follow Jesus. We must take up our crosses every single day. Jesus died for us, the least we can do is live for him. "Lord, I know that people's lives are not their own; it is not for them to direct their steps. Discipline me, Lord, but only in due measure- not in your anger..." -Jeremiah 10:23-24.

God can change anyone's hearts. Do not give up. Do not stop witnessing and do not stop praying. Many who find Christ say it is as if they are living in a black room and when they find salvation, the light comes on. The only problem is many of them do not realize they are in a dark room because it is all they know. Even though I have been a Christian my whole life, as I grow closer in my relationship with Jesus, I realize even my own light continues to shine brighter. Many people even despise Christians because of our joy. Remind them we are inviting them to the same joy. God is our coach, looking down here to see who is on the bench ready to go in to play! "Yet when you relied on the Lord, he delivered them into your hand. For the eyes of the Lord range throughout the earth to strengthen those whose hearts are fully committed to him." -2 Chronicles 16:8-9 (2 Chronicles 13:18 and Psalm 121:7-8).

In 2 Chronicles the people of Judah were victorious because they relied on God. If you say to God "Lord, use me in any way you can" He will! You are exactly what He is looking for. God searches for those who want to further His kingdom with the gifts and talents He has given them. "The Lord looks down from Heaven on all mankind to see if there are any who understand, any who seek God. All have turned away, all have become corrupt; there is no one who does good, not even one." -Psalm 14:2-3 (Psalm 53:2-3, Romans 3:9-12). "The eyes of the Lord are everywhere, keeping watch on the wicked and the good." -Proverbs 15:3. "The wrath of God is being revealed from Heaven against all the godlessness and wickedness of people, who suppress the truth by their wickedness, since what may be known about God is plain to them, because God has made it plain to them. For since the creation of the world God's invisible qualities—his eternal power and divine nature—have been clearly seen, being understood from what has been made, so that people are without excuse. For although they knew God, they neither glorified him as God nor gave thanks to him, but their thinking became futile, and their foolish hearts were darkened. Although they claimed to be wise, they became fools and exchanged the glory of the immortal God for images made to look like a mortal human being and birds and animals and reptiles. Therefore, God gave them over in the sinful desires of their hearts to sexual impurity for the degrading of their bodies with one another. They exchanged the truth about God for a lie and worshiped and served created things rather than the Creator—who is forever praised. Amen. Because of this, God gave them over to shameful lusts. Even their women exchanged natural sexual relations for unnatural ones. In the same way the men also abandoned natural relations with women and were inflamed with lust for one another. Men committed shameful acts with other men and received in themselves the due penalty for their error. Furthermore, just as they did not think it worthwhile to retain the knowledge of God, so God gave them over to a depraved mind, so that they do what ought not to be done. They have become filled with every kind of wickedness, evil, greed and depravity. They are full of envy, murder, strife, deceit, and malice. They are gossips, slanderers, God-haters, insolent, arrogant and boastful; they invent ways of doing evil; they disobey their parents; they have no understanding, no fidelity, no love, no mercy. Although they know God's righteous decree that those who do such things deserve death, they not only continue to do these very things but also approve of those who practice them." -Romans 1:18-32.

Someone may argue you cannot see God, so He cannot exist. The truth is clear. God has made himself plain to us and has been clearly seen in His invisible qualities in what has been made so we are all without excuse. We were made to worship, and we will worship something that is created instead of the creator if what we are worshiping is not Jesus. "The fool says in his heart, 'There is no God'." -Psalm 14:1 (Psalm 53:1). Even though we cannot see God, He makes the evidence clear He is here. "Your path led through the sea, your way through the mighty waters, though your footprints were not seen. You led your people like a flock by the hand of Moses and Aaron." -Psalm 77:19-20 (Isaiah 51:10). Not only is He clearly here, but you see that He clearly guides. "Lord, I have heard of your fame; I stand in awe of your deeds, Lord. Repeat them in our day, in our time make them known; in wrath remember mercy." -Habakkuk 3:2 (Joshua 9:9).

How does creation show the evidence of God? Think of the tree you look at, the sky. You did not make the tree or the sky. Who did? Even if there was a so-called "big bang," who created the big bang? "But ask the animals, they will teach you, or the birds in the sky; and they will tell you; or speak to the earth, and it will teach you, or let the fish in the sea inform you. Which of all these does not know that the hand of the Lord has done this? In his hand is the life of every creature and the breath of all mankind." -Job 12:7-10. "For the director of music. A psalm of David.

The Heavens declare the glory of God; the skies proclaim the work of his hands. Day after day they pour forth speech; night after night they reveal knowledge. They have no speech; they use no words; no sound is heard from them. Yet their voice goes out into all the earth, their words to the ends of the world. In the heavens God has pitched a tent for the sun." -Psalm 19:1-4 (Habakkuk 2:14, Psalm 57:9-10, Psalm 108:4, Psalm 89:1-2, Psalm 57:9-10 and Psalm 108:4). God is seeking you. Every creation, He is welcoming you to a relationship with him. We are without excuse because we know very well, we cannot create the sun, the flowers which are all considered intelligent design. We would be denying our common sense if we were to say those things were not created when we cannot recreate them.

"Give thanks to the Lord, for he is good; his love endures forever. Let the redeemed of the Lord tell their story—those he redeemed from the hand of the foe," -Psalm 107:1-2 (Psalm 66:16). There are many controversies on whether we are to share Jesus' love with others, if it is appropriate if it will offend. Those of us who are redeemed are to tell of our testimony! "I do not hide your righteousness in my heart; I speak of your faithfulness and your saving help. I do not conceal your love and your faithfulness from the greater assembly." -Psalm 40:10 (1 Corinthians 9:16 and Psalm 119:46). What Jesus whispers to us, more often than not, can have a positive impact on others. Part of the reason I encourage you to not hold it in because it is amazing the encouragement you can bring to another, and to yourself when you share the good news. "What I tell you in the dark, speak in the daylight; what is whispered in your ear, proclaim from the roofs." -Matthew 10:27. "The Lord announces the word and women who proclaim it are mighty." -Psalm 68:11.

"But he said, "I must proclaim the good news of the kingdom of God to the other towns also, because that is why I was sent." -Luke 4:43. Jesus says He was sent for the very purpose to proclaim the good news of the gospel, why He came and of God's love. We are supposed to imitate Jesus. He is our example. There is a way to share, a timing, a tone, and a genuine care you should have for the person you share, but if Jesus' very desire and a part of your purpose for being here is to share with others the same security you have for eternity, you bet He will guide you in how to do it and when. "Jesus went through all the towns and villages, teaching in their synagogues, proclaiming the good news of the kingdom and healing every disease and sickness." -Matthew 9:35 (Luke 5:20-26, Matthew 9:2-8 and Mark 2:6-

12). "The blind receive sight, the lame walk, those who have leprosy are cleansed, the deaf hear, the dead are raised, and the good news is proclaimed to the poor." -Matthew 11:5 (Luke 7:21-22).

As for me, I will always have hope; I will praise you more and more. My mouth will tell of your righteous deeds, of your saving acts all day long— though I know not how to relate them all. I will come and proclaim your mighty acts, Sovereign Lord; I will proclaim your righteous deeds, yours alone. Since my youth, God, you have taught me, and to this day I declare your marvelous deeds." -Psalm 71:14-17 (Psalm 145:10-13). Though we have not personally experienced every miracle such as the sea parting or seeing the dead raised to life, we know these miracles to be true and have seen miracles in our own life. One being we were dead in our transgressions, and the dead being raised to life in the sense of our purpose and eternal destiny. "He commanded us to preach to the people and to testify that he is the one whom God appointed as judge of the living and the dead. All the prophets testify about him that everyone who believes in him receives forgiveness of sins through his name." -Acts 10:42-43. We were literally dead in our transgressions. When we are born our spirit is dead. Therefore, everyone in this world is looking for something or someone to fulfill them, to awaken that spirit when the only thing is Jesus. You will be fulfilled when you find Him. Your flesh and human nature continue, you will make mistakes and still have moments of weakness where you feel lonely, less than and struggle, but your foundation and ultimate being will always have purpose and meaning when alive in Him.

"Light in a messenger's eyes brings joy to the heart, and good news gives health to the bones." -Proverbs 15:30. You bring joy and bring healing when you share the good news. What more would you want to share with others?! "Then I heard the voice of the Lord saying, "Whom shall I send? And who will go for us?" And I said, "Here am I. Send me!" -Isaiah 6:8 (1 Samuel 3:10. 1 Samuel 3:10).

'You are my witnesses,' declares the Lord, 'and my servant whom I have chosen, so that you may know and believe me and understand that I am he. Before me no god was formed, nor will there be one after me. I, even I, am the Lord, and apart from me there is no savior.'" -Isaiah 43:10-11.

We should tell God, here I am, send me! Tell Him his servant is listening. You can have confidence you have been specifically chosen by God, and as His child He has equipped you to talk about your Father in a way you would talk about someone in your life you love and admire. You can be confident, just as God sent Jesus, Jesus is sending us. As the Father has sent me, I am sending you. (See John 20:2). "One night the Lord spoke to Paul in a vision: "Do not be afraid; keep on speaking, do not be silent. For I am with you, and no one is going to attack and harm you, because I have many people in this city." -Acts 18:9-10.

"The Spirit of the Sovereign Lord is on me, because the Lord has anointed me to proclaim good news to the poor. He has sent me to bind up the brokenhearted, to proclaim freedom for the captives and release from darkness for the prisoners, to proclaim the year of the Lord's favor and the day of vengeance of our God, to comfort all who mourn." -Isaiah 61:1-2.

When we share the good news, we bind up the brokenhearted, free the captives and comfort all who mourn. We are free in Christ. Free to admit we need help and cannot do this life on our own, bringing us fulfillment in this life and purpose from Him! The enemy may want you to think people living in sin look free, but what they're not telling you is they are enslaved. We are free in Christ because even when we mess up, we know His blood covers us. We are free in Christ because we know God's laws are good for us and produce the best for us. I love the example of walking by someone in authority and you have nothing to worry about, you are free! Now picture walking by authority with drugs hanging out of your pockets. Not a fun way to live.

"Their descendants will be known among the nations and their offspring among the peoples. All who see them will acknowledge that they are a people the Lord has blessed." -Isaiah 61:9. "But if I say, "I will not mention his word or speak anymore in his name," his word is in my heart like a fire, a fire shut up in my bones. I am weary of holding it in; indeed, I cannot." -Jeremiah 20:9. Part of sharing Jesus is the love is burning inside of you it is hard to hold it in. "remember this: Whoever turns a sinner from the error of their way will save them from death and cover over a multitude of sins." -James 5:20. The motivation is your genuine love for others. Knowing God can use you to share them, to save them from death covering over every short coming. "Then I will teach transgressors your ways, so that sinners will turn back to you." -Psalm 51:13. "True instruction was in his mouth and nothing false was found on his lips. He walked with me in peace and uprightness and turned many from sin." -Malachi 2:6.

"If anyone, then, knows the good they ought to do and doesn't do it, it is sin for them." -James 4:17 (Ezekiel 33:4-9 and Ezekiel 3:18-19). In Ezekiel 33:4-9 and 3:18-19 it talks about if someone does not listen to the warning themselves, it is their own fault but if the "watchman" sees the sword coming but does not blow the horn to warn others, the watchman is held accountable. God warned Ezekiel and is warning us if we do not help or share the warning from him to help others from their sinful ways that will cause them harm, we will be held accountable. However, if we do warn them and even if they do not listen, there will be a reward.

Three men in Babylon, Shadrach, Meshach and Abendnego, paid no attention to the King Nebuchadnezzar as he commanded the province to serve his gods or his image of gold (See Daniel 3:12). King Nebuchadnezzar told them if they do not worship the idol of gold, they will be thrown into the blazing furnace. He asked, "What god can rescue you then?!" -Daniel 3:15 (Daniel 3:5-6). Yet, they declared their God they serve will deliver them from the King's hand but even if he doesn't, they want the king to know they will not serve his gods or worship the image of gold (See Daniel 3:17-18). They were thrown into the blazing furnace.

The king made the furnace so hot that the flames of the fire killed the soldiers who took up Shadrach, Meshach and Abednego. In amazement the king asked, "Weren't there three men that we tied up and threw into the fire?" "Look! I see four men and the fourth looks like a son of the gods." Nebuchadnezzar then shouted, "Shadrach, Meshach and Abednego, servants of the Most High God, come out! They saw that the fire had not harmed their bodies, nor was a hair of their heads singed. Then Nebuchadnezzar said, "Praise be to the God of Shadrach, Meshach and Abednego, who has sent his angel and rescued his servants! They trusted in him and defied the king's command and were willing to give up their lives rather than serve or worship any god except their own God, for no other god can save in this way." Then the king promoted Shadrach, Meshach and Abednego in the province of Babylon, and made a decree no one was allowed to talk wrongly against their God. (See Daniel 3:21-30).

Shadrach, Meshach and Abednego show king Nebuchadnezzar and all of Babylon God's power by remaining faithful to God to the point that even if they were to be burnt up by the fire, it was not worth it to disown God. God remained faithful through their obedience and made good sharing His power with all of Babylon, and now all of us today who read the story. Just imagine what God can do through our faithfulness. In life you will walk through the fire, but not be burned even when you feel the heat. There will always be another in the fire standing next to you no matter what you face.

Daniel did the same when faced with persecution. Daniel was set over the entire kingdom over all the administrators and satraps because of his exceptional qualities. The administrators and satraps became jealous and wanted to try to charge him of breaking the law in some way but found no corruption because he was trustworthy. They decided for him to break the law, it had to involve the law of his God. The royal administrators, prefects, satraps, advisers, and governors all agreed the king should issue a decree that anyone who prays to any god or human being except himself shall be thrown into the lions' den. The king put the decree in writing and said it cannot be repealed. When Daniel learned the decree was published, he continued to go in his room three times a day on his knees and prayed, giving thanks to God, just like before.

The royal administrators, prefects, satraps, advisers, and governors found Daniel praying and asking God for help. They went to the king and said, "Did you not publish a decree that anyone who prays to any god or human being except to you would be thrown into the lions' den?" This distressed the king who wanted to rescue Daniel. Daniel was thrown into the lion's den, but the king said, "May your God, whom you serve continually, rescue you!" A stone was placed over the den. The king could not eat or sleep.

First thing in the morning, he got up and went to the lion's den. He called to Daniel "Daniel, servant of the living God, has your God, whom you serve continually, been able to rescue you from the lions?" Daniel answered, "My God sent His angel, and He shut the mouths of the lions. They have not hurt me, because I was found innocent in his sight." The king was overjoyed and gave orders to lift him out of the den. There was no wound on him because he trusted God. King Darius wrote to the entire earth issuing a decree that in every part of the kingdom people must fear and reverence the God of Daniel, for he is the living God that ensures forever. His kingdom and dominion will never end. He rescues and saves, performing signs and wonders in the Heavens and on the earth. He has rescued Daniel from the mouth of the lions! (See Daniel 6:3-5, Daniel 6:7, Daniel 6:9-12, Daniel 6:14, Daniel 6:16-23, Daniel 6:25-28 and Daniel 7:18).

Daniel also did not care about the consequences but continued to pray to God. As a result of His obedience, God used Him to change the heart of King Darius and the entire earth. He used Him to display His power and faithfulness to Daniel. Even though we cannot guarantee the outcome of our obedience, God is faithful. Even if His faithfulness is not deliverance in what we think should be every single problem we go through, it will be greater than we can imagine.

Obedience takes faith, but you realize having faith is the only way to live to get the best catch of your life. "When he had finished speaking, he said to Simon, "Put out into deep water, and let down the nets for a catch." Simon answered, "Master, we've worked hard all night and haven't caught anything. But because you say so, I will let down the nets." When they had done so, they caught such many fish that their nets began to break. So, they signaled their partners in the other boat to come and help them, and they came and filled both boats so full that they began to sink. When Simon Peter saw this, he fell at Jesus' knees and said, "Go away from me, Lord; I am a sinful man!" For he and all his companions were astonished at the catch of fish they had taken, and so were James and John, the sons of Zebedee, Simon's partners. Then Jesus said to Simon, "Don't be afraid; from now on you will fish for people." So, they pulled their boats up on shore, left everything and followed him." -Luke 5:4-11 (Matthew 4:19, Mark 1:17). Peter realized who Jesus was and could not even believe He was in His presence. They left the fish, as they were more intrigued with who created the fish and knew exactly where they were. Even when God will bless you for your faithfulness, you will be in more love with Him and not focus as much on your blessings. You will be more interested in others than in the fish or accomplishments themselves when you realize the purpose of your life, and why you were created.

"I am sending you out like sheep among wolves. Therefore, be as shrewd as snakes and as innocent as doves." -Matthew 10:16. We are supposed to stay innocent in the world, but have wisdom and discernment, being in the world, understanding it but not conforming. Loving everyone in the world but being careful not to blatantly disobey or do something God would not approve. "Brothers and sisters, stop thinking like children. In regard to evil be infants, but in your thinking, be adults." -1 Corinthians 14:20. When it comes to evil, be aware of what it is and who brings it to be in order to be equipped against it, but do not become consumed or have your mind fixated on it. "Do not suppose that I have come to bring peace to the earth. I did not come to bring peace, but a sword." -Matthew 10:34.

"Then Jesus came to them and said, "All authority in Heaven and on earth has been given to me. Therefore, go and make disciples of all nations, baptizing them in the name of the Father and of the Son and of the Holy Spirit, and teaching them to obey everything I have commanded you. And surely, I am with you always, to the very end of the age."' -Matthew 28:18-20.

"He said to them, "Go into all the world and preach the gospel to all creation. Whoever believes and is baptized will be saved, but whoever does not believe will be condemned. And these signs will accompany those who believe: In my name they will drive out demons; they will speak in new tongues; they will pick up snakes with their hands; and when they drink deadly poison, it will not hurt them at all; they will place their hands on sick people, and they will get well." After the Lord Jesus had spoken to them, he was taken up into Heaven and he sat at the right hand of God. Then the disciples went out and preached everywhere, and the Lord worked with them and confirmed his word by the signs that accompanied it." -Mark 16:15-20.

The ultimate purpose of our lives is to make disciples and to teach others God's commands. How we each go about doing it is an individual journey of following the Holy Spirits prompting. We can go forth with confidence knowing Jesus our coach and leader has authority over all of Heaven and Earth. He is right next to us, living in us to help us achieve our purposes.

"I have given you authority to trample on snakes and scorpions and to overcome all the power of the enemy; nothing will harm you. However, do not rejoice that the spirits submit to you, but rejoice that your names are written in Heaven." -Luke 10:19-20. Even if God works out the supernatural in situations in our lives, He reminds us that real joy does not come from the miracle, from the catch of large fish themselves but ultimately these things are being accompanied in our lives due to our salvation, and our love for the one who has given it to us.

Peter replied, "Repent and be baptized, every one of you, in the name of Jesus Christ for the forgiveness of your sins. And you will receive the gift of the Holy Spirit. The promise is for you and your children and for all who are far off—for all whom the Lord our God will call." With many other words he warned them; and he pleaded with them, "Save yourselves from this corrupt generation." Those who accepted his message were baptized, and about three thousand were added to their number that day." -Acts 2:38-41.

Baptism is an action you do to display your inward faith in Christ, as you have already been spirit baptized to receive salvation.

In Acts 9:31 it shares how the church is strengthened, full of peace and growing due to Saul speaking boldly, encouraged from the Holy Spirit. "Paul entered the synagogue and spoke boldly there for three months, arguing persuasively about the kingdom of God." -Acts 19:8.

"Then the high priest and all his associates, who were members of the party of the Sadducees, were filled with jealousy. They arrested the apostles and put them in the public jail. But during the night an angel of the Lord opened the doors of the jail and brought them out. "Go, stand in the temple courts," he said, "and tell the people all about this new life." -Acts 5:17-20.

When we speak truth, it brings strength, peace, and growth which everyone is searching for. In Acts 13:45 it shares that the Jews were jealous of Paul and contradict what he said. When people disagree with the truth, sometimes it can become more personal toward you, and they may say things about you that are not true. Even if others do not always respond lovingly to our words and if the consequences ever become as far as prison, God had Paul's back and He will have yours. God works as much in a prison, as in a grocery store, as in a school as much on a softball diamond. He is omnipotent and cannot be shut out.

In Acts 30-36 it shares that they tried to kill Paul and when the Roman commander in chief asked what he had done, the crowd was shouting different reasons, but ultimately just say to "get rid of him!" Jesus was in the same situation. The authorities and citizens could not find a reason to persecute Jesus or Paul, and instead of being rational they simply decided to crucify Jesus and get rid of Paul. This is proof of the constant spiritual warfare we all face, as the enemy had them convinced even though there is no logical, "worldly" reason to get rid of them, they had an urge to do so. We also should not be surprised at persecution that may seem completely irrational.

"Paul, an apostle of Christ Jesus by the will of God." -2 Corinthians 1:1 (Ephesians 1:1, Colossians 1:1, and 2 Timothy 1:1). God can, and will, use absolutely anyone. He wants to use you. God even specifically called Saul, who became Paul who is mentioned throughout this book as he wrote many of the letters in the New Testament, who persecuted those who loved Jesus.

"Lord," Ananias answered, "I have heard many reports about this man and all the harm he has done to your holy people in Jerusalem. And he has come here with authority from the chief priests to arrest all who call on your name." But the Lord said to Ananias, "Go! This man is my chosen instrument to proclaim my name to the Gentiles and their kings and to the people of Israel." -Acts 9:13-15.

"All those who heard him were astonished and asked, "Isn't he the man who raised havoc in Jerusalem among those who call on this name? And hasn't he come here to take them as prisoners to the chief priests?" Yet Saul grew more and more powerful and baffled the Jews living in Damascus by proving that Jesus is the Messiah." -Acts 9:21-22.

Paul persecuted the church, yet God specifically chose Him as his instrument. It is just like Jesus to pick someone and change their heart when Paul not only just chose to deny Him but chose to persecute others who accepted Him. For this very reason, I refuse to believe someone cannot be changed, ever. Even if my so-called common sense and unfortunate sometimes bitterness can arise, I pray for God to soften my heart, realizing anyone, absolutely anyone, can come to know Jesus and become new. I would not be surprised if this is one of the reasons God chose Paul, to show us not only can those who have completely lost their way and have tried to hurt others can be saved, but they can be used for his Glory, His purpose bringing their life purpose instead of what could seem to be a nuisance to society in the world's eyes.

"He stood beside me and said, 'Brother Saul, receive your sight!' And at that very moment I was able to see him. "Then he said: 'The God of our ancestors has chosen you to know his will and to see the Righteous One and to hear words from his mouth. [15] You will be his witness to all people of what you have seen and heard. [16] And now what are you waiting for? Get up, be baptized, and wash your sins away, calling on his name.' "When I returned to Jerusalem and was praying at the temple, I fell into a trance[18] and saw the Lord speaking to me. 'Quick!' he said. 'Leave Jerusalem immediately, because the people here will not accept your testimony about me.' 'Lord,' I replied, 'these people know that I went from one synagogue to another to imprison and beat those who believe in you." -Acts 22:13-19 (Acts 22:3-12, Acts 8:3, Acts 9:1-12, Acts 9:16, and Acts 9:17-20).

I love how Paul is asked "What are you waiting for?!" God is saying the same to each of us every morning. What are you waiting for? What is keeping you from going boldly in the direction of your purpose?

"They only heard the report: 'The man who formerly persecuted us is now preaching the faith he once tried to destroy.' And they praised God because of me." -Galatians 1:23-24. God used Paul's initial rebellion against Him, as Saul, and used his transformation to bring others to Himself. Our God is incredible like that! He can use the absolute, most horrible situations and acts in our lives or in the lives of those who affect us and use it for our good, and His glory, which is the purpose of our lives!

In Acts 14:19-20 it shares how Paul was stoned to the point they thought he was dead, but after the disciples gathered around him, he got up. We can never underestimate the power of facing the challenges in life together, and how much it strengthens us. "As they stretched him out to flog him, Paul said to the centurion standing there, "Is it legal for you to flog a Roman citizen who hasn't even been found guilty?" -Acts 22:25. "Paul looked straight at the Sanhedrin and said, "My brothers, I have fulfilled my duty to God in all good conscience to this day." -Acts 23:1. Even if you are accused unjustly, it will not phase you as long as your conscious is clear where your heart has been to serve God.

"'It is concerning the resurrection of the dead that I am on trial before you today." -Acts 24:21 (Acts 24:24-25). Also, Acts 25:3-5 talks about how they wanted to kill Paul. They wanted to kill him, ultimately because of the disputes over the resurrection of the dead. "When Paul came in the Jews who had come down from Jerusalem stood around him. They brought many serious charges against him, but they could not prove them. Then Paul made his defense: "I have done nothing wrong against the Jewish law or against the temple or against Caesar." -Acts 25:7-8 (Acts 23:9). "Paul answered: "I am now standing before Caesar's court, where I ought to be tried. I have not done any wrong to the Jews, as you yourself know very well. If, however, I am guilty of doing anything deserving death, I do not refuse to die." -Acts 25:10-11. Just like Jesus, the court could also not prove Paul did anything wrong to deserve death or even any punishment. The incredible thing is, just like Jesus, Paul also did not refuse the death penalty, even if it was going to come on him unjustly. The reason is, when you have such an accurate perspective in what God sees and thinks about you, and that is your foundation of your confidence and truth, understanding the end goal, circumstances in life, even to the point of death...unjustly, miraculously will not overcome you. They will affect you of course, as we should all want justice, but we know true justice is not administered until the end, and even though we should still desire it now, we know He who is just, will ultimately overcome.

"I found he had done nothing deserving of death, but because he made his appeal to the Emperor, I decided to send him to Rome. But I have nothing definite to write to His Majesty about him. Therefore, I have brought him before all of you, and especially before you, King Agrippa, so that as a result of this investigation I may have something to write. For I think it is unreasonable to send a prisoner on to Rome without specifying the charges against him." -Acts 25:25-27.

"Then Agrippa said to Paul, 'You have permission to speak for yourself.' So, Paul motioned with his hand and began his defense: "King Agrippa, I consider myself fortunate to stand before you today as I make my defense against all the accusations of the Jews, and especially so because you are well acquainted with all the Jewish customs and controversies. Therefore, I beg you to listen to me patiently. "The Jewish people all know the way I have lived ever since I was a child, from the beginning of my life in my own country, and in Jerusalem. They have known me for a long time and can testify, if they are willing, that I conformed to the strictest sect of our religion, living as a Pharisee. And now it is because of my hope in what God has promised our ancestors that I am on trial today. This is the promise our twelve tribes are hoping to see fulfilled as they earnestly serve God day and night. King Agrippa, it is because of this hope that these Jews are accusing me. Why should any of you consider it incredible that God raises the dead? "I too was convinced that I ought to do all that was possible to oppose the name of Jesus of Nazareth. And that is just what I did in Jerusalem. On the authority of the chief priests, I put many of the Lord's people in prison, and when they were put to death, I cast my vote against them. Many a time I went from one synagogue to another to have them punished, and I tried to force them to blaspheme. I was so obsessed with persecuting them that I even hunted them down in foreign cities. "On one of these journeys I was going to Damascus with the authority and commission of the chief priests. About noon, King Agrippa, as I was on the road, I saw a light from Heaven, brighter than the sun, blazing around me and my companions. We all fell to the ground, and I heard a voice saying to me in Aramaic,[a] 'Saul, Saul, why do you persecute me? It is hard for you to kick against the goads.' "Then I asked, 'Who are you, Lord? I am Jesus, whom you are persecuting,' the Lord replied. 16 'Now get up and stand on your feet. I have appeared to you to appoint you as a servant and as a witness of what you have seen and will see of me. I will rescue you from your own people and from the Gentiles. I am sending you to them to open their eyes and turn them from darkness to light, and from the power of Satan to God, so that they may receive forgiveness of sins and a place among those who are sanctified by faith in me.' "So then, King Agrippa, I was not disobedient to the vision from Heaven. First to those in Damascus, then to those in Jerusalem and in all Judea, and then to the Gentiles, I preached that they should repent and turn to God and demonstrate their repentance by their deeds. That is why some Jews seized me in the temple courts and tried to kill me. But God has helped me to this very day; so, I stand here and testify to small and great alike. I am saying nothing beyond what the prophets and Moses said would happen— that the Messiah would suffer and, as the first to rise from the dead, would bring the message of light to his own people and to the Gentiles." At this point Festus interrupted Paul's defense. "You are out of your mind, Paul!" he shouted. "Your great learning is driving you insane." "I am not insane, most excellent Festus," Paul replied. "What I am saying is true and reasonable. The king is familiar with these things, and I can speak freely to him. I am convinced that none of this has escaped his notice, because it was not done in a corner. King Agrippa, do you believe the prophets? I know you do." Then Agrippa said to Paul, "Do you think that in such a short time you can persuade me to be a Christian?" Paul replied, "Short time or long—I pray to God that not only you but all who are listening to me today may become what I am, except for these chains." The king rose, and with him, the governor and Bernice and those sitting with them. After they left the room, they began saying to one another, "This man is not doing anything that deserves death or imprisonment." -Acts 26:1-31.

Even though Paul was unfairly put on trial, he still respected King Agrippa, even to the point of saying he was honored to be in his presence. Even if we do not agree with our bosses, President, government, or those who rule over us, God has still put them into power and they are in His image meaning we should still have a sense of respect for them, even though we are not to idolize them. Paul was on trial for God, to proclaim Jesus. He admits he persecuted Christians but realized why is it crazy to think that God raises the dead?! He is God! Paul was called to share the good news to turn darkness to light and to turn people from Satan to God. Paul says we are to demonstrate our repentance from our deeds. God continued to help Paul through the persecution.

When Festus said Paul was insane, Paul responded he is not insane, and ended calling him "most excellent Festus." Notice the courage Paul takes to stand with the truth but continues to respect. I know this can sound sarcastic if you respond this way when others are refuting you, but you and God knows your heart. I really think it goes back to your tone. The perfect example of how we are to respond first with the words God wants, but also with the tone and demeanor He wants. King Agrippa asked Paul if he thought he could really convince him to be a Christian in such a short time, and Paul responds saying time does not matter. They realized what Paul was doing did not deserve death or imprisonment, and I'm sure Paul's tone and respect while sharing the truth helped them realize he genuinely cared for them and knew what he spoke was true. Pray God may open a door for our message and to proclaim it clearly. "Be wise how you act toward outsiders, making the most of all opportunities. Let your conversations be full of graces so you can answer anyone and everyone." -Colossians 4:3-6. We are to love everyone no matter what they believe genuinely, with a genuine care for them. Talk with them full of grace, understanding God's genuine love for them too, and we are to team up with God wanting them to be a part of the family. " For they themselves report what kind of reception you gave us. They tell how you turned to God from idols to serve the living and true God, and to wait for his Son from Heaven, whom he raised from the dead—Jesus, who rescues us from the coming wrath." -1 Thessalonians 1:9-10.

"He witnessed to them from morning till evening, explaining about the kingdom of God, and from the Law of Moses and from the Prophets he tried to persuade them about Jesus. Some were convinced by what he said, but others would not believe. They disagreed among themselves and began to leave after Paul had made this final statement: "The Holy Spirit spoke the truth to your ancestors when he said through Isaiah the prophet: "'Go to this people and say, "You will be ever hearing but never understanding; you will be ever seeing but never perceiving." For this people's heart has become calloused; they hardly hear with their ears, and they have closed their eyes. Otherwise, they might see with their eyes, hear with their ears, understand with their hearts, and turn, and I would heal them.' "Therefore, I want you to know that God's salvation has been sent to the Gentiles, and they will listen!" For two whole years Paul stayed there in his own rented house and welcomed all who came to see him. He proclaimed the kingdom of God and taught about the Lord Jesus Christ—with all boldness and without hindrance!" -Acts 28:23-31.

When persuading about Jesus, it is important to include the law of Moses as well as the gospel, as many try to separate them, but they complete one another. Jesus fulfilled the law for us, he did not eliminate it. The Holy Spirit will guide you. I hope no one's heart becomes calloused. How does a heart become calloused? Just like hands with lifting, hitting in softball or playing guitar. The more we lift, play guitar, and swing the bat, the more calloused our hands get. If someone continues to reject the truth and love of Jesus, their hearts become calloused. It is possible for the callous to be softened, as anything is possible with God, but I hope it does not get to this point. As I have seen callouses removed in the upper extremity clinic where I work, and it can be painful. Boldness will come from your confidence, which you can have only in God.

"How then, can they call on the one they have not believed in? And how can they believe in the one of whom they have not heard? And how can they hear without someone preaching to them? And how can anyone preach unless they are sent? As it is written: "How beautiful are the feet of those who bring good news!"

364

But not all the Israelites accepted the good news. For Isaiah says, "Lord, who has believed our message?" Consequently, faith comes from hearing the message, and the message is heard through the word of Christ. But I ask: Did they not hear? Of course, they did: "Their voice has gone out into all the hearth, their words to the ends of the world." -Romans 10:14-18 (Romans 15:19-21).

"And Isaiah boldly says, "I was found by those who did not seek me; I revealed myself to those who did not ask for me." -Romans 10:20 (Isaiah 52:7). Jesus is proclaimed throughout the entire earth, to the ends of the world. Everyone will hear the name of Jesus, and who they decide He is, is up to them. The gospel is bearing fruit and growing throughout the whole world. (See Colossians 1:6, 2 Corinthians 4:15, Acts 12:24, and Thessalonians 1:8).

"I will not venture to speak of anything except what Christ has accomplished through me in leading the Gentiles to obey God by what I have said and done." -Romans 15:18. Paul says the chains he is in has served to advance the gospel for Christ, and because of these chains his brothers and sister have become confident in the Lord and dare more to proclaim the gospel without fear. (See Philippians 1:12-14). When they saw Paul in prison but was innocent, for speaking of Christ, but feeling it was worth and he was still content, this ignited a spark in others to share in the same boldness. Anytime you are afraid about evangelizing, just imagine when you get to Heaven, and you see someone there because God was able to use you!

Paul suffered in Philippi but with God's help they dared to talk about the gospel in the face of strong opposition. (See 1 Thessalonians 1:1-2). "Until I come, devote to the public reading of scripture, to preaching and teaching." -1 Timothy 4:13.

"Therefore, since we are surrounded by such a great cloud of witnesses, let us throw off everything that hinders and the sin that so easily entangles. And let us run with perseverance the race marked out for us, fixing our eyes on Jesus, the pioneer and perfecter of faith. For the joy set before him he endured the cross, scorning its shame, and sat down at the right hand of the throne of God. Consider him who endured such opposition from sinners, so that you will not grow weary and lose heart." -Hebrews 12:1-3.

Sin looks good at first and can easily entangle us. We are to run with perseverance, as we know life will continue to knock us down but keep getting back up. When we get up, you look up. Look up to the origin and perfecter of what our faith is set on. He endured the worst of this life, the crucifixion, and was able to do so focusing on us, the Father and the joy set before Him after He suffered great trauma. We must consider Him who endured the worst opposition, so that we do not get weary or lose heart.

In the end, an angel will have the eternal gospel to proclaim to the earth, and he will say in a loud voice to Fear God, worship Him and give His glory, the one who created the Heavens and earth because His judgment has come. Another angel proclaims, "Fallen is Babylon the Great, the adulterous with all the nations." - Revelation 14:6-8. There will be a judgment in the end, and the goal of each one of us is to team up with God to make sure we can help as many people as possible not reach it.

"Israel is a scattered flock that lions have chased away. The first to devour them was the king of Assyria; the last to crush their bones was Nebuchadnezzar king of Babylon." Therefore, this is what the Lord Almighty, the God of Israel, says: "I will punish the king of Babylon and his land as I punished the king of Assyria." -Jeremiah 50:17-18 (Micah 5:5).

God will have justice on His final enemies, and we do not want anyone to be a part of His wrath, but to be with us forever in Heaven.

But how? How can we truly talk to others about the gospel? Especially when it seems it is being persecuted left and right, with people trying to get it out of schools, hospitals, and society. God is so much more powerful than we realize and cannot be stopped by human beings trying to keep Him out. A patient and I were once talking about forgiveness as she was very bitter toward a relationship in her life where she had been badly hurt. I told her that only through Jesus can I forgive. I explained about the story of the adulterous woman, where Jesus says to not stone her as she is forgiven, however because He loves her, He tells her she needs to turn from her sinful ways. My patient said she wanted to convert. We can never underestimate the power of developing relationships with others, and how much conversations in how we live can lead to the opportunity to share the gospel.

People will see the gospel in how you live, leaving your legacy that could affect them for eternity. Some may ask why you would want someone to change from their religion. We know Jesus is the way, truth and life, the only way to Heaven. If you need to explain it to someone in simple terms, you can even say you saw they were not finding joy in theirs.

"But before all this, they will seize you and persecute you. They will hand you over to synagogues and put you in prison, and you will be brought before kings and governors, and all on account of my name. 13 And so you will bear testimony to me. 14 But make up your mind not to worry beforehand how you will defend yourselves. 15 For I will give you words and wisdom that none of your adversaries will be able to resist or contradict." -Luke 21:12-15.

"But not a hair of your head will perish. Stand firm, and you will win life." -Luke 21:18-19 (15:18-25 and John 16:1-3). When you become a believer, know you will be persecuted in some way, shape or form, but know it will be worth it. God's Word is the ultimate defense for our lives. It is the undeniable truth that embodies pure love, which is what everyone is looking for. Stand firm, and you will win life. As it is, you do not belong to the world, but I have chosen you out of the world. (See John 15:19).

"You, however, know all about my teaching, my way of life, my purpose, faith, patience, love, endurance, persecutions, sufferings—what kinds of things happened to me in Antioch, Iconium and Lystra, the persecutions I endured. Yet the Lord rescued me from all of them. In fact, everyone who wants to live a godly life in Christ Jesus will be persecuted, while evildoers and impostors will go from bad to worse, deceiving and being deceived." -2 Timothy 3:10-13.

"No one who wants to become a public figure act in secret. Since you are doing these things, show yourself to the world." -John 7:4. Go out into the world with confidence to evangelize and witness for Jesus, knowing He is right next to you, guiding you, every step of the way!

Healing & Serving

"I can do all things through Christ who strengthens me." -Philippians 4:13

I can *make it through school and excel at my career* through Christ who strengthens me.

"Now no shrub had yet appeared on the earth and no plant had yet sprung up, for the Lord God had not sent rain on the earth and there was no one to work the ground..." -Genesis 2:5. Part of the purpose of creation, of you and I, was to work. Just the word "work" makes many of us cringe, just like the word "Monday" does. What if I told you, before sin we were supposed to work, and enjoy it?! "So, I saw that there is nothing better for a person than to enjoy their work, because that is their lot." -Ecclesiastes 3:22. The fall is what created turmoil within our work, and why it is now impossible to find a job that will not have some aspect of hardship to it. However, God has designed an intentional purpose in us in order to accomplish the career He calls us to. We are going to define career as I define occupations in my career as an occupational therapist and certified hand therapist. Occupations mean whatever you are purposed and called to do, as well as what you enjoy doing. This can be a wide range such as a full-time job, part time job, being a volunteer, missionary, stay at home parent, or student.

When you are in high school, it is so hard to know what you want to do for the rest of your life. My advice is to job shadow. This is what led me to my calling to be an occupational therapist. I shadowed a physical therapist and loved it, however I always struggled because I wanted to help people physically, psychologically/mentally, emotionally, nutritionally, and spiritually. What career could possibly do all of this? All these aspects are in the occupational therapy framework. Occupational therapy looks at bio-psycho-social needs of individuals. An occupational therapist helps others of all ages return to their occupations using scientific research and evidence-based practice for physical and mental health while remaining client-centered. An occupation is not only your job; it is anything anyone finds meaningful.

OT works with people mentally, physically, developmentally, emotionally with any diagnosis or symptoms which stops people from living out their everyday life. We want people to live satisfying lives. All ages. OT is a passion to help others achieve their full potential, to work toward their goals mentally and physically. OT helps others overcome challenges that restrict them and utilize their strengths. Minds and hands change the world. When someone has a hand injury, people do not realize how much this can affect their personal life. We look at people as multi-factorial. The term "occupational therapy" can encompass a wide range of activities, from sports to music to schoolwork for children with autism, and even basic tasks like showering for some people. For those struggling with depression, occupational therapy may involve finding the motivation to take care of their family and social life.

We work in outpatient clinics, hospitals, schools, nursing homes/skilled nursing facilities, community health facilities, with sport teams, home care, pediatric clinics, anywhere. We work with diagnoses ranging from shoulder injuries, hand injuries, psychological, musculoskeletal, neuroscience, upper extremity injuries, cardiovascular, special needs, cancer, or any other diagnoses you can think of. We also make custom-made splints and casts. We are your ultimate encouragers and life coaches. The theme for OTs is helping others live life to the fullest.

"You will not have to fight this battle. Take up your positions; stand firm and see the deliverance the Lord will give you, Judah and Jerusalem. Do not be afraid; do not be discouraged. Go out to face them tomorrow, and the Lord will be with you." -2 Chronicles 20:17. I had an overwhelming fear come over me almost every day of graduate school. I also had an overwhelming peace when I realized God was on my side. If you are struggling in school or feel you are not good enough, my advice is to pray this prayer. "Lord, I have the desire to be an occupational therapist/certified hand therapist (for me) in order to help your people. If it be your will, please help me in this time." When you are after a career to help His people, He is on your side. Does this mean you do not study? I also played collegiate volleyball. Does this mean I do not practice and expect to win games? Absolutely not. Do your best, but realize it is God who will provide, and that He has placed the dream and desire to work hard on your heart in the first place. "The horse is made ready for the day of battle, but victory rests with the Lord." -Proverbs 21:31. Prepare, work hard, have confidence in Him and watch God work!

I was not the top of my class, but I knew I would put in the work and study to accomplish my goals and dreams. Others may have more talent than you, but there is never an excuse for anyone to work harder. However, it was God which helped me pass every neuroscience exam, even when I thought it was hopeless. I used this philosophy as an athlete, and in graduate school. Also, find the purpose in every single class even when in your own eyes it may not seem significant. God has you taking a certain course for a reason.

My first semester of graduate school I struggled. I cried because my life seemed to only consist of studying, and all the studying I did never felt like enough. It was the night before our anatomy and physiology final, and we had just finished our fourth exam which took me all the time leading up to this point to study for. This was going to be one of the hardest exams in grad school, not only the content but the cadavers and lab. I felt hopeless. I went by our bluff to cry, pray and cry some more. One of the girls in my class came up and asked me, "Will this affect your eternal salvation?" The hope and peace which transcends understanding came over me.

This same amazing colleague of mine was in my statistical research scientific inquiry class. We went to a tutoring session together, and during the session the instructor talked about a research equation equaling two zeros instead of one. My friend asked, "Why does it matter if it is two zeros or one, since they equal the same?" The instructor replied jokingly, "Why do you matter?" Her reply was, "I matter to Jesus!" Even though the instructor was joking, it hit me. People in my life who have either said I am not good enough or have brought me down do not speak the truth. Only God does that. I needed to have the same confidence as her when talking about Jesus and myself, and after that, I did! The coolest thing was after, our professor started a PowerPoint for the class and the first thing the slide said was, "You matter to Jesus, and you matter to me no matter what the answer of any equation is in your life!"

Once I was working with a pediatric patient who would tell me "I already do it best so let me do it!" I was so frustrated because I knew exactly how to help him and treat him, and he would not let me. I thought how could he refuse my help, but then I was convicted. This is exactly how I am with God in my own life. So many times, I am telling God I know best, and how frustrated he must be!

"Whatever you do, work at it with all your heart, as if you are working for the Lord, not for human masters, since you know that you will receive an inheritance from the Lord as a reward. It is the Lord Christ you are serving." - Colossians 3:23-24. It makes such a difference in the work environment when you enjoy working with your supervisors, bosses and doctors, but what do you do if it's not enjoyable? You work with the same work ethic, understanding our jobs have been designed by God, and for God. He has gifted you with your talents and abilities, and when you work as if you are working for Him and not human masters, you are serving someone who will not change or treat you unfairly. You are working for someone who can provide you with the motivation you need to perform your job at your best. "So, Bezalel, Oholiab and every skilled person to whom the Lord has given skill and ability to know how to carry out all the work of constructing the sanctuary are to do the work just as the Lord has commanded." -Exodus 36:1 (Exodus 35:35).

"Slaves, obey your earthly masters with respect and fear, and with sincerity of heart, just as you would obey Christ. Obey them not only to win their favor when their eye is on you, but as slaves of Christ, doing the will of God from your heart. Serve wholeheartedly, as if you were serving the Lord, not people, because you know that the Lord will reward each one for whatever good they do, whether they are slave or free." -Ephesians 6:5-8.

We are to serve wholeheartedly, putting our best foot forward each day. "Teach slaves to be subject to their masters in everything, to try to please them, not to talk back to them, and not to steal from them, but to show that they can be fully trusted, so that in every way they will make the teaching about God our Savior attractive." -Titus 2:9-10. When we respect our bosses, supervisors, and doctors, we are in an essence showing them Christ.

"Anyone who has been stealing must steal no longer, but must work, doing something useful with their own hands, that they may have something to share with those in need." -Ephesians 4:28. God has designed each of us to work, and to work hard. Another motivation we should have in wanting to work is how we will share with others, and our families.

"Do not work for food that spoils, but for food that endures to eternal life, which the Son of Man will give you. For on him God the Father has placed his seal of approval." Then they asked him, "What must we do to do the works God requires?" Jesus answered, "The work of God is this: to believe in the one he has sent." -John 6:27-29.

When we have the mentality that our job will have eternal outcomes, it makes it a lot more exciting than thinking it is just to put food on the table that is here one day and eaten the next. "Therefore, my dear brothers and sisters, stand firm. Let nothing move you. Always give yourselves fully to the work of the Lord because you know that your labor in the Lord is not in vain." -1 Corinthians 15:58. You know that when you work for God, fruit will be produced in some way shape or form, and on

His timing.

"You know that the household of Stephanas were the first converts in Achaia, and they have devoted themselves to the service of the Lord's people. I urge you, brothers, and sisters, to submit to such people and to everyone who joins in the work and labors at it. I was glad when Stephanas, Fortunatus and Achaicus arrived, because they have supplied what was lacking from you. For they refreshed my spirit and yours also. Such men deserve recognition." -1 Corinthians 16:15-18.

Devoting your work to God, means devoting yourself to the people in your work, regardless of how you feel about them. You can supply what is lacking from one another, as a team. When we help one another at work, it provides refreshment and increased productivity.

"Whatever your hand finds to do, do it with all your might." -Ecclesiastes 9:10. I love my job at the clinic I am at. God tells us to put our entire heart into everything we do. I call this passion! Passion is a choice and God commands us to have it. I know it can be difficult because sometimes we are called to do things we may not want to. Find something you love, and you will find the passion. He knows it is needed to do the best we can in life. God's handprints are all over it! First off, it is very hard as a new graduate to get a job in the upper extremity setting. Our surgeons and therapists are incredible and experienced. One of our surgeons even did my great grandpa's carpal tunnel release when he was young! Today, I am proud to say I am one of his occupational therapists.

After I finished my course, lab, and clinical work at Concordia University Wisconsin, I went to the UW hospital at the University of Wisconsin Madison. Both CUW and UW prepared me, and I cannot begin to express how grateful I am. CUW's mission statement was helping mind, body and spirit while keeping Jesus at the center. Once I graduated, I felt on top of the world but soon was discouraged when people said they did not feel I had enough experience. I decided to call all the certified hand therapists in the state of Wisconsin to get tips on how to get into the field as a new graduate, even if they did not have openings. I ended up calling someone who is now the president of the American Society of Hand Therapy who said, "Hey, we are having someone retire, come and interview!" I went through multiple interviews including interviews with the supervisor of therapy, supervisor of the clinic and surgeons. During this process I was told by my supervisor, the clinic instructor, I had a friend at Madison who did her clinicals at hand to shoulder specialists of Wisconsin! She gave a great reference. Out of all the supervisors I could have had, what are the chances of that! Again, coincidence? No, God! He knew. Did you know that there is no word for coincidence in the Hebrew language? The Hebrews believed that ALL things were of God. Alright, I was then offered the job but needed to pass my boards next. Right when I think I am in the clear, another mountain rises in front of me. I continued to study and before I knew it, God lead me through once again. I passed!

God has worked in crazy ways once I became a therapist, and I am just getting started. Once I was treating a woman with dementia. I was making her a splint, and she was so scared. They brought her in from her nursing home, and you could tell she was unaware of where she was. She was nonverbal for a while, but then saw my cross necklace. She instantly relaxed and pointed to her own. Jesus brings peace no matter what circumstance we are in. I had another individual who I saw frequently for a thumb injury, and he started asking me more and more questions about faith. I prayed God would help me tell him whatever he needed to hear our last session. He did not show up for our last session. I was really bummed. Then, I received a call from the same patient later stating he woke up with a different break in his arm! What! How does that happen? I was sad about the individual being injured again; however, it was amazing the talks we had after. Another time I was grocery shopping, and a man turned around and saw me in the store. He then yelled, "You healed my hand!" 2 Kings 5:1 and 2 Kings 5:14-15 talk about a commander of the army of the King of Aram named Maamam who had leprosy. Through him the Lord gave victory. He dipped in the Jordan seven times and his skin was brand new, leading them to believe in the one true God.

We all want someone who will not give up on us. I had a friend in my program who was struggling, as I was. I promised her I would study with her until she passed our neuroscience course, even knowing I was not guaranteed to pass. I saw her potential when she didn't. More importantly, God sees our potential. Be that person. Everyone has potential and if you haven't noticed, it's sometimes harder to find it in ourselves than other people. She went into the final with tears, thinking there was no hope. Later that week she called me to thank me, but more importantly to thank God she passed! Be the person to remind others you will not let them fail, and they will not fail with God at their side!

As a therapist, one of the hardest parts of my job is putting people through pain when it is necessary for them to get better. However, I do it because I know the result will be worth it for them. Stretching leads to growth, but it can be painful. Sometimes people make the best advances when they are uncomfortable, I notice not only physically, but mentally. One population I worked with that shattered my heart was women who'd had breast cancer and need mastectomies. As women, we relate our breasts as part of who we are, and it was so heart breaking to see these women mourn this loss of their body. We must do scar work where they were removed, and we had to break "cords" from the lymph nodes that had died off under the armpits to increase their shoulder range of motion. Breaking of the cords was so painful, you could hear the snapping however, once they were released, they were shocked at their increased range. Every job will have its heart breaks and difficulties, but God will continue to show you His glory and miracles daily when you ask Him and look for them. You can be God's light in others darkness, no matter what setting you are in or what population you work with.

No matter what your degree and no matter what you do, you are the one for the job because God has called you to it. There is no difference between God and the secular world. We try to separate the two, but God is so powerful He uses all! Even when you make mistakes. I had two patients by the same name one time. One was a young guy and the other an older guy. I read the bio of the younger and sat down with the older. I asked him if his injury came from him tackling someone, and he laughed uncontrollably. He said no but half his deltoid was shot off! I had another lady once, who came in pointing at me saying I did not make her splint right. It took everything in me not to cry. My supervisor took me aside, saying how one time someone said to her "I want to talk to your supervisor" when she was making a splint. She said, "I am the supervisor." Even when we make mistakes, you are the one for the job.

My cousin felt God calling him to astrophysics to combine his love for science, the gospel, knowledge, and theology. Once he graduated, he felt God calling him to be a professor, but felt it would be a long shot compared to him going into research.

He was not the first author of any research, struggled to get his PHD and did not do a post doc which most professors do. He prayed. He felt God's calling was clear one night. He was accepted as a professor at MSOE. He said how this exemplified God's faithfulness even in his doubt. He stated, "he who created me for a purpose knows me better than I know myself, understands that purpose better than I do, and is even willing to step on and correct me when I've gotten confused on who I am and what I'm made to do. If God is for us, who can be against us? No one. Not even our own confusion! Thanks be to God!" No matter what walk of life you take, if you walk with Jesus, it will be amazing.

I wanted to share some of my anatomy and physiology knowledge of the human body I learned in graduate school and as an occupational therapist to show you how undeniably amazing God made us. First, our DNA, the molecule of heredity. The Human Genome Project even shows there is one biological human race. Also, our entire body is made of laminin which is a cross shaped protein making up the basis of our cells. The cross holds everything in life together.

"The Son is the image of the invisible God, the firstborn over all creation. For in him all things were created: things in Heaven and on earth, visible and invisible, whether thrones or powers or rulers or authorities; all things have been created through him and for him. He is before all things, and in him all things hold together. And he is the head of the body, the church; he is the beginning and the first born from among the dead, so that in everything he might have the supremacy. For God was pleased to have all his fullness dwell in him, and through him to reconcile to himself all things, whether things on earth or things in Heaven, by making peace through his blood, shed on the cross. Once you were alienated from God and were enemies in your minds because of your evil behavior. But now he has reconciled you by Christ's physical body through death to present you holy in his sight, without blemish and free from accusation— if you continue in your faith, established and firm, and do not move from the hope held out in the gospel. This is the gospel that you heard and that has been proclaimed to every creature under Heaven, and of which I, Paul, have become a servant." - Colossians 1:15-23.

Everything has been created through Jesus, and for Jesus. Because of Him, we have our purpose for now and in eternity. We are reconciled with God and can continue being established and firm in our faith.

We were created for God; God was not created for us.

"But as surely as God is faithful, our message to you is not "Yes" and "No." For the Son of God, Jesus Christ, who was preached among you by us—by me and Silas and Timothy—was not "Yes" and "No," but in him it has always been "Yes." For no matter how many promises God has made, they are "Yes" in Christ. And so, through him the "Amen" is spoken by us to the glory of God. Now it is God who makes both us and you stand firm in Christ. He anointed us, set his seal of ownership on us, and put his Spirit in our hearts as a deposit, guaranteeing what is to come." -2 Corinthians 1:18-22.

In Christ, our purpose is always "yes." He has sealed His ownership on us that cannot be taken away, placing the Holy Spirit in our hearts, who will guide us in our jobs, and every day of our lives.

"...yet for us there is but one God, the Father, from whom all things came and for whom we live; and there is but one Lord, Jesus Christ, through whom all things came and through whom we live." -1 Corinthians 8:6. Jesus is not only the Savior of the universe, but the purpose of the universe. Also, one of our surgeons told me the X, Y chromosomes for men would have thought to be less than the X, X for women, but it is not. Did you know our heart creates so much friction it could kill us without the pericardial sac? Did you know it is controlled by a small nerve called the Vagus nerve? We are a miracle each and every day. Speaking of purpose and being a miracle, think of birth! For my pediatric class, we had to come up with a list of each day from the day of conception, what changes occur for the baby and the mother and let me tell you how much can go wrong, but here you are, reading this book. You are a miracle.

I am a strong believer in you can do anything you put your mind to due to neuroplasticity allowing the phrase "practice makes perfect." Same with if we do not practice, the neural connections begin to prune. What we experience and more importantly, how we choose to live our lives have scientific and psychological effects on us. It is not just a saying, but science. When we live a life pleasing to God, our connections grow. When we use drugs, alcohol or other stimulants or depressors which have strong effects on our brain, our neural connections are affected. How about our eyes? Did you know we see the opposite of how our vision is processed in the brain? Our nerves flip along the tract. We also have muscles which attach to our eyes holding them in the perfect position so we can see. Now let's talk sports. My athletes out there, have you heard of adrenaline? We create adrenaline so the heart can pump the amount of blood needed to compete without having to communicate as much with the brain.

Time for my specialty and passion. As you know, I am an upper extremity/certified hand therapist at Hand to Shoulder Specialist of Wisconsin. The upper extremity is my "wheelhouse." Did you know seven muscles control just your index finger? Yep, your lumbrical, dorsal and volar interossei, flexor digitorum profundos, flexor digitorum superficialis (or sublimis) extensor indicis and extensor digitorum communis all control that one finger. The nerves that help control these muscles are the median, ulnar, and radial nerves, which break into further branches called the posterior and anterior interosseous nerves, which all come from the brachial plexus, which come off the spinal cord. It is even thought when Jesus was crucified, during crucifixions, the nails in the wrist severed the median nerve, causing excruciating pain initially. I am not telling you this information to confuse you or try to make you love what I do, but I want you to realize this is not an accident! How could all these connections accidentally happen to work so you can move and feel your upper extremity?! Not only this, but God cared so much about the detail He made Grayson's and Cleland's ligaments to hold your skin in place during the finger's movement. Also, extensor digitorum communis is a muscle with a tendon to all your fingers except the thumb usually. In some people, it is missing in your pinky, but want to know what God thought of? A separate muscle called your extensor digiti minimi, and even if this muscle is affected and can't function, a connection called your juncture tendinum can help your ring finger extend your small finger! Yet, people still think God doesn't care about the details! That is harder to believe than an all-knowing God who designed you. Oh, and the nerves break into digital ulnar and radial sides in your fingertips, just to throw in one more piece of information for you. "You were shown these things so that you might know that the Lord is God; besides him there is no other." -Deuteronomy 4:35. Even though this verse is referring to the miracles God performed out of Egypt, our body is also a miracle! "Do not be afraid, but let your hands be strong." -Zechariah 8:13.

Jesus is the ultimate healer, the great physician.

"Jesus went through Galilee, teaching in their synagogues, proclaiming the good news of the kingdom, and healing every disease and sickness among the people. News about him spread all over Syria, and people brought to him all who were ill with various diseases, those suffering severe pain, the demon-possessed, those having seizures, and the paralyzed; and he healed them." - Matthew 4:23-24 (Matthew 8:14-17, Matthew 1:20-34 and Luke 4:38-40).

"Great crowds came to him, bringing the lame, the blind, the crippled, the mute and many others, and laid them at his feet; and he healed them. The people were amazed when they saw the mute speaking, the crippled made well, the lame walking and the blind seeing. And they praised the God of Israel." -Matthew 15:30-31 (Matthew 14:35-36, Mark 6:55-56, Luke 6:18-19, Luke 9:11, Mark 7:37 and Luke 13:10-13). Specific examples include: Peter and John helped heal a man, and Peter asked those around "Why do you stare at us in amazement as if this was by our own power that we made this man walk? This is from God!" (See Acts 3:11-13, Acts 3:6-10, Acts 3:16, Acts 14:8-10 and John 5:14-15).

"They had Peter and John brought before them and began to question them: "By what power or what name did you do this?" Then Peter, filled with the Holy Spirit, said to them: "Rulers and elders of the people! If we are being called to account today for an act of kindness shown to a man who was lame and are being asked how he was healed, then know this, you and all the people of Israel: It is by the name of Jesus Christ of Nazareth, whom you crucified but whom God raised from the dead, that this man stands before you healed." -Acts 4:7-10.

"God did extraordinary miracles through Paul, so that even handkerchiefs and aprons that had touched him were taken to the sick, and their illnesses were cured, and the evil spirits left them." -Acts 19:11-12.

I was attending a seminar for my church where we were talking about confidence. One of the ladies shared that she feels like the small finger in the big picture of life, indicating she is not very confident in who she is. I could not help but speak up. I told her the small finger (otherwise known as the pinky) is one of the most important fingers of the hand! It is the most important for grip strength. I told her when I have patients who are unable to use their small finger due to a fracture, nerve impairment or dislocation, their entire function is messed up to say the least. This shows how important we each are, but how Satan makes us have a distorted view of ourselves. Even my upper extremity surgeons I work for share how complicated our finger extensor mechanism is. Even atheist scientists have admitted it is near impossible to have the upper extremity move in just the right way for use. You are the small finger, in other words, the most important and have a purpose in this life!

I had a patient with a bad fracture of her small finger. We went through some intense and trying therapy. Once she was discharged, she said," Who knew a broken finger would turn out to bring so much joy." I cried. This is the definition of how the Lord works. Sure, could God take away our free will, take away all the evil and make us all robots? Sure. What is more powerful. God forcing us to be good, or making good out of the evil and painful circumstances of our lives? I am not saying I enjoy seeing my patients hurt, nor do I wish this upon anyone. I am sure if you asked my patient if she would like to get hurt again, she would say no. This is just to show God's will and faithfulness is beyond what we can expect or imagine when hope seems lost. "All this, David said, 'have in writing as a result of the Lord's hand on me, and he enabled me to understand all the details of the plan.'" -1 Chronicles 28:19.

"...the wise heart will know the proper time and procedure." -Ecclesiastes 8:5. I think of our protocols we must follow from our doctors once our patients have surgery. There are guidelines, however we do have to use our clinical reasoning to know when to slow down or speed up a protocol, based on our doctors' orders and the progress of the patient. "My son Solomon, the one whom God has chosen, is young and inexperienced. The task is great, because this palatial structure is not for man but for the Lord God." -1 Chronicles 29:1. When we inquire on the Lord how to do our job, He gives us the proper time and procedures, as He knows the people you are working with and cares about them even more than you do. Even though experience is important, we all must be a beginner at some point which is unsettling, but it is relieving and brings courage to know God sees your beginning and will provide for you when you inquire of Him. Part of His way of providing is to bring mentors and those with experience into your life. "...by paying attention to the wise they get knowledge." -Proverbs 21:11. I cannot tell you how much watching and listening to my surgeons and therapists has increased my wisdom and knowledge very quickly, and I recommend you do the same in your line of work. "In everything that he undertook in the service of God's temple and in obedience to the law and the commands, he sought his God and worked wholeheartedly. And so, he prospered." -2 Chronicles 31:2. He sought God as a priority in prayer. When prayer is a priority, everything else falls into place. "The shepherds are senseless and do not inquire of the Lord, so they do not prosper, and all their flock is scattered." -Jeremiah 10:21.

"To God belong wisdom and power; counsel and understanding are his." -Job 12:13 Whether people with wisdom realize it or not, God created the laws and the universe, and all wisdom belongs to Him. He wants to share it with you and wants you to ask of Him. In my field, I understand God is the true healer. He mends the fractures, He provides sensation, He heals all wounds, and He produces strength. He uses our team to do so, and I am so grateful for all the incredibly gifted and wise coworkers, colleagues, therapists, surgeons, and bosses I have the honor to work with every day. "...mend its fractures." -Psalm 60:2. "They have hands, but cannot feel, feet, but cannot walk." -Psalm 115:7. "Praise be to the Lord my Rock, who trains my hands for war, my fingers for battle. He is my loving God and my fortress, my stronghold and my deliverer, my shield, in whom I take refuge, who subdues peoples under me." -Psalm 144:1-2. There are scriptures in Isaiah 1:6 and Proverbs 25:29 that talk about wound care and saying taking care of a wound is like singing songs to a heavy heart in proverbs. "They dress the wound of my people as though it were not serious." -Jeremiah 6:14. "Is there no balm in Gilead? Is there no physician there? Why then is there no healing for the wound of my people?" -Jeremiah 8:22. "But I will restore you to health and heal your wounds," declares the Lord." -Jeremiah 30:17.

"Son of man, I have broken the arm of Pharaoh king of Egypt. It has not been bound up to be healed or put in a splint so that it may become strong enough to hold a sword. -Ezekiel 30:21. Part of our job is to fabricate custom-made orthotics, otherwise known as splints. If people have a fracture that is "non-displaced," meaning there is a fracture, but the bone is still aligned, they still need to wear their splint to protect the fracture while it is weak to prevent surgery or is becoming "displaced." God also provides us with "splints" in our lives when we are fractured and broken, to hold us together.

"I will attach tendons to you and make flesh come upon you and cover you with skin; I will put breath in you, and you will come to life. Then you will know that I am the Lord. So, I prophesied as I was commanded. And as I was prophesying, there was a noise, a rattling sound, and the bones came together, bone to bone. I looked, and tendons and flesh appeared on them, and skin covered them, but there was no breath in them." -Ezekiel 37:6-8.

"A man with leprosy came and knelt before him and said, "Lord, if you are willing, you can make me clean." Jesus reached out his hand and touched the man. "I am willing," he said. "Be clean!" Immediately he was cleansed of his leprosy." - Matthew 8:2-3 (Mark 1:40-42 and Luke 5:12-13). Even if the healing is not what we are picturing, God is always willing to help and heal us. "This was to fulfill what was spoken through the prophet Isaiah: 'He took up our infirmities and bore our diseases.'" -Matthew 8:17.

"He was not far from the house when the centurion sent friends to say to him: "Lord, don't trouble yourself, for I do not deserve to have you come under my roof. That is why I did not even consider myself worthy to come to you. But say the word, and my servant will be healed. For I myself am a man under authority, with soldiers under me. I tell this one, 'Go,' and he goes; and that one, 'Come,' and he comes. I say to my servant, 'Do this,' and he does it." When Jesus heard this, he was amazed at him, and turning to the crowd following him, he said, "I tell you, I have not found such great faith even in Israel." Then the men who had been sent returned to the house and found the servant well." -Luke 7:6-10 (Matthew 8:5-10).

It truly amazes me the number of healings performed when Jesus saw others had faith. It was in their humility, that faith came. Trying harder will not increase your faith, but admitting to God you see His power, know His power, and know He can do all things even though your own faith may struggle, He will honor you and consider this to be great faith. "Then Jesus said to the Centurion, "Go! Let it be done just as you believed it would." And the servant was healed at that moment." - Matthew 8:13 (Matthew 9:29 and Matthew 15:22). "The woman came and knelt before him. 'Lord, help me!' she said." -Matthew 15:25. "Then Jesus said to her, "Woman, you have great faith! Your request is granted." And her daughter was healed at that moment." -Matthew 15:28. Also, Luke 8:41-47 shares a story about the woman in the crowd who had been bleeding over years and touched Jesus in the crowd and was instantly healed. "Then he said to her, "Daughter, your faith has healed you. Go in peace." -Luke 8:48.

"A widow lost her only son, and when Jesus saw her, his heart went out to her and he said, 'Don't cry.' He told the young man to get up, and Jesus gave him back to his mother. They were filled with awe, praised God and they said God has come to help his people." -Luke 7:12-16 (Matthew 14:14). God desires to help you, truly. I am not God and cannot tell you exactly what that help will entail or that everything we want will come true, but what I can tell you is I know the heart of God and He desires to help His children. How that happens and what that means, is for each of us to ask of Him.

Ten men had leprosy and called to Jesus. Jesus told them to go show themselves to the priests. They were healed on the way. Only one, a Samaritan, came back to praise God, threw himself at Jesus' feet and thanked him. Jesus said, "weren't there ten of you?" Go, your faith made him well." -Luke 17:12-19. Gratefulness has a healing power of its own. It is not happy people who are grateful, but grateful people who are happy.

"Do everything without grumbling or arguing, so that you may become blameless and pure, "children of God without fault in a warped and crooked generation." Then you will shine among them like stars in the sky as you hold firmly to the word of life." -Philippians 2:14-16. Do everything without grumbling. When you can find joy and not grumble, whether in your work or in your life, you will shine. How do we learn to not grumble as we all know life gives us plenty to grumble about? Getting into the word of life! "You too, be patient and stand firm, because the Lord's coming is near. Don't grumble against one another, brothers, and sisters, or you will be judged. The Judge is standing at the door!" -James 5:8-9. We should value people more than anyone. Staying patient and standing firm are two more tactics to help decrease our grumbling.

You can look at the exercise sheet, but unless you perform those exercises, it won't do any good, as you still need the sheet to know what to do. Same with the Bible. You need to read to know what it says, but if you do not put it into use it won't do what it needs to in your life. When we are born, we have all the muscles we could ever have already, but they will not do us any good unless we work them.

Psychology is a huge part of what we do, and there are even parts of Medicare that will not cover us if we do not address patients from a personal perspective within the roles they play every day. Procedural touch and comforting touch have been proven to relieve anxiety. Patients can see how we care just by our touch, touching what can look "unattractive." Many of the miracles Jesus performed, and many of the miracles in the Bible in general were accompanied by the laying on of hands, or when praying for others. In Acts 6:4-6 they devoted themselves to prayer and they laid their hands on those they prayed for. Patient's stories tell their fears and past medical history. Just the touch from another human being can show how much you care, helping to build rapport with a patient to motivate them. I think the same can work for those in our lives as well. You can help the patient manage pain if you control their anxiety which is controlled by the endocrine system. Gate control theory is affected by the mind as well as physical stimulation. Coping skills, diaphragmatic breathing and engagement in purposeful activity can help in a similar fashion.

I tried to view my boards like a sport, get my adrenaline going once it's game time. I won't stop there. I was struggling to give God my time, as I am always supposed to do first. When I did, I came across a verse that said, "They have lost connection with the head, from whom the whole body, supported and held together by its ligaments and sinews, grows as God causes it to grow." -Colossians 2:19. I had to look up what a "sinew" was. It turns out it is another name for a tendon or ligament! Coincidence? I think not.

If you ever feel like you are not enough, remember God has you at your exact job, in your exact location, at this exact time for a reason. If you ever feel inadequate, He will provide. I had a patient who was five times my size. He was a shoulder patient, meaning I would have to perform treatment with his arm that was about as big as me. When I first saw him, I thought, I can't treat him, I could barely lift his arm! God knew so much more. He ended up healing well, glory to God, and he ended up sharing his incredible testimony with me about how God saved him from the streets to him becoming a pastor today. There is always a purpose, and at your job you will always have a purpose.

A Competitor's Heart

"I can do all things through Christ who strengthens me." -Philippians 4:13

I can *make this play and win* through Christ who strengthens me.

Sports are my passion. I grew up playing volleyball, basketball, and softball since I could walk. I did not only play for my schools growing up, including high school, but I also played the travel/club sector, leading me to play collegiate volleyball for Concordia University of Wisconsin and on the 23u Wisconsin lighting women's fast pitch softball team. I played for the University of Wisconsin's club girls volleyball team and coached during my clinicals in graduate school. My Dad was the head coach for softball growing up and has been inducted into the USA Hall of Fame. These years consisted of state and national tournaments all around the country. My best friends growing up were my teammates, my dad was my coach, and my mom, brother, and the rest of my family were my constant encouragement. My Grandpa played on a 50 and over men's fast pitch softball team until he was 70 years old. We have Packer and Badger season football tickets, and Badger basketball tickets. Oh, I also love Dance Revolution and randomly competed at my hometown's library and at our National Conference for Occupational Therapy. Do you see how much I love sports yet?!

I think some people struggle saying it is hard to be involved in sports and serve God. Even though there are challenges, I see sports to serve God and those around me. God gave us our bodies and lives in them, and we are to take care of them. "Do you not know that your bodies are temples of the Holy Spirit, who is in you, whom you have received from God? You are not your own; you were bought at a price. Therefore, honor God with your bodies." -1 Corinthians 6:19-20. Sports are an amazing way to exercise because you forget you are exercising in the first place. Even if not sports, you can do Zumba, run or plenty of other ways to stay active! Any accomplishment can give glory to God. "Lord, you established peace for us; all that we have accomplished you have done for us." -Isaiah 26:12.

Sports show you what it is like to build a community. Sports teach you never to give up, and that practice can beat talent. Giants can fall even when others do not believe in you. Being smaller in sports where size matters, it has shown me I can play up to higher levels even when my size says no. You must learn to take corrections from your coach. The only way I was able to compete in all my sports, do well in school, and give time to God and my loved ones was discipline.

Anxiety and fear do not come from God. Sports teach you to push back your fear. The second you play timidly or play not to lose instead of to win, you will not reach your full potential. Regardless of sports and in life, you will never reach your full potential without God, because He made you with your potential in the first place. It is literally impossible without Him. Trying to live life without Him is like trying to hit a ball without a bat. You can have all the natural talent in the world that He blessed you with when you were born, but you will never fulfill the incredible things He has in store for you in every aspect of your life until you commit to Him.

In softball, if you are swinging to not strike out instead of to get a hit, you will not hit the hardest or best you can. I relate this to how Jesus wants us to live. One time, I was up to bat against the best pitcher in the state for high school to make it to the state tournament. Mind you, she was also on my travel team, so she knows exactly which pitches are hardest for me to hit. I was fearful going up to the plate, then sunk my feet in, prayed and found confidence. I hit the ball barely fair in right field, helping us win the game. If I had went into the box fearful, not trusting in the abilities God has given me, this would not have happened. I signed up to run my first half marathon. I did not know what to expect, since I have always been an athlete in team sports. My Dad told me, "You are in good enough shape, you just need to pray and run." All it took were these words to give me a burst of confidence to finish. God does not call the qualified, He qualifies the called.

With sports, especially being a captain, comes great responsibility. To whom much is given, much is required. You show your teammates their value and that you believe in them. The Packers are a great testimony to faith. Are you scared to be a captain because you are afraid you will fail? Just like having faith or being a leader, it is not about failing. You will fail in your life. It is how you handle your failure. Most people will not even try. Give yourself credit for trying.

"No discipline seems pleasant at the time, but painful. Later, however, it produces a harvest of righteousness and peace for those who have been trained by it. Therefore, strengthen your feeble arms and weak knees. "Make level paths for your feet," so that the lame may not be disabled, but rather healed." -Hebrews 12:11-12.

To play sports, you need to fight fatigue. Train your brain just like you train your muscles. There are scans of the brain showing proof of different activity when you have faith. This is where grit and resilience come in. There is never an excuse for anyone to work harder than you. Therefore, I love defense in basketball. Even if you miss your shots on offense, you can always control how quick you get back on defense. I always strived for the MVP award but knew a lot of times it was out of my control. One award I knew I could always win was the hustle. This is always in your control. "Those who disregard discipline despise themselves, but the one who heeds correction gains understanding." -Proverbs 15:32 (Proverbs 15:10 and Hosea 4:14). As one of the greatest coaches of all time Vince Lombardi once said, "The difference between a successful person and others is not a lack of strength, not a lack of knowledge, but rather a lack of will."

Practice. I understand some people are gifted naturally in some areas more than others, but I am telling you, you can do anything you set your mind to with faith, passion, and practice. I have played sports since I was little and the neuroplasticity in my brain was able to easily help me develop these skills. However, now I play guitar. When I first started, many said that maybe I didn't have the talent. I knew, just like sports, if I practiced, I could get good enough to play in church, for Miss Wisconsin and for my friend's wedding. I prayed and practiced, and it happened. I knew this was a way I wanted to worship God.

One key is to return to fundamentals in our sports to become a great player. Your form needs to be correct before you can generate all your power in your swing, shot and serve. It goes the same for Jesus. I think those of us in Christ tend to think "I know this story already" and not realize we need to continually go back to the core of our relationship with Christ and be renewed daily as we are being infected by sin constantly throughout our day. Absolutely, keep growing in your relationship as in sports keep growing in your skills, but you will never continue to flourish unless you keep the fundamentals at hand. The thought of Jesus being crucified on that cross should always shock you, and never seem like old or repeated news. If it ever does, it is time to go back to the fundamentals.

"Have nothing to do with godless myths and old wives' tales; rather, train yourself to be godly. For physical training is of some value, but godliness has value for all things, holding promise for both the present life and the life to come. This is a trustworthy saying that deserves full acceptance. That is why we labor and strive, because we have put our hope in the living God, who is the Savior of all people, and especially of those who believe." -1 Timothy 4:7-10.

We never have to strive for God's approval and love. It is given to us unconditionally. However, we strive toward our goals with the motivation being His love, instead of having the burden that we "have to be good enough." Frankly, that will not motivate you but simply drain you. Once an NFL kicker was on the news, and they were basically asking him how he felt after missing the kick, losing one of the most important games. His answer is key. He said he plays football, but his identity is in Christ. I love sports, but they are not my identity, and they are not yours either. I am not saying this to upset you, but to give you hope. I also heard a player say they were benched for many years, but eventually when he became the lead quarterback, he realized God's timing was perfect.

Sports will come to an end and change as we get older. Our bodies either will not work the same, or someone better may come along. I have been there. It feels like my life is over at that time. I felt this way because my identity was not where it needed to be. Sports will teach you discipline, how to be a good teammate, how to compete at high levels, how to have courage, have confidence, and bring accomplishments through teamwork showing God's power. There is a slight chance we will become professional athletes, but a guarantee is we will all stand before Jesus. Just like working out and sports, the same concepts apply. You cannot be good or get in shape only doing it once a week. Same with your relationship with Jesus. If you only focus on Him on Sundays, you will not be in shape on His team.

What about those with disabilities? I have coached for the Special Olympics, and in general being an occupational therapist, I have tried to help those who struggle physically have the opportunity to play in the beautiful world of sports. Bethany Hamilton is an amazing example of not letting adversity stop her, as she lost one of her arms due to a shark attack, yet she continues to surf. I was also helping at try outs for my high school one year, and I saw there was a girl with one arm playing. Anything is possible when passion and discipline is there. However, what if you were in an accident leaving your body paralyzed? No matter what, you could not move any part of your body and could not play sports. Is your life over? As much as it would feel like it, no doubt, it would not be because sports only give you a temporary crown, but when our identity is in the eternal crown, it can never be taken away.

Just as staying active and eating healthy nutrition is important, so is rest. The struggle in trying to find the balance is real. God commands us to rest just like He commands us to work hard. God did not create us to go full speed all the time. Life will throw you curve balls. You will swing and miss but stay persistent. Be the one who does not give up, and you will reap the benefits. God will show you how to swing. Most importantly, glorify God. Tim Tebow wore John 3:16 on his face during a game, and millions heard the gospel. We stay in shape not for our glory, but His. We exercise to have the energy and stamina to serve Him.

We can pray for the "best body," to be the "best athlete," or be in the "best shape," but this is where free will come in. God will provide opportunities to help you take care of your body, but with free will He lets us make the choice. We cannot pour into others unless we feel energized ourselves. I have such a sweet tooth and struggle to always eat the best. Honey and sweets are okay in moderation and have their place, but if you have too much, you will get sick. "If you find honey, eat just enough- too much of it, and you will vomit." -Proverbs 25:16 (Proverbs 25:27). I know God has given us food to enjoy, and I pray about what He wants me to put into my body. I used to like very few vegetables, and the more I prayed the better it got. "...plants for people to cultivate-bringing forth food from the earth: wine that gladdens human hearts, oil to make their faces shine, and bread that sustains their hearts." -Psalm 104:14-15. "He gets hungry and loses his strength; he drinks no water and grows faint." -Isaiah 44:12. When playing sports, it is important you nourish your body and stay hydrated. Staying hydrated includes making sure to get enough electrolytes.

"My son, pay attention to what I say; turn your ear to my words. Do not let them out of your sight, keep them within your heart; for they are life to those who find them and health to one's whole body." -Proverbs 4:20-22. Ultimately, what brings health and nourishment to us is to listen and fear the Lord and shun evil. He says to keep His Word close to our heart, and it will bring healing to our entire body. He will provide guidance in how to care for our bodies once this is our priority. "...fear the Lord and shun evil. This will bring health to your body and nourishment to your bones." -Proverbs 3:7-8.

My collegiate volleyball coach asked us to write an essay about what motivates us. I wrote that what motivates me is the One who created me. God talks about controlling our minds. Motivation begins in the mind. When you realize God puts a goal and passion in your heart, and you know you serve a God who will help you to accomplish them, you cannot help to begin to feel motivation. This motivation carried me to study to become a CHT, in sports, in my job and in my relationships most importantly. God has not given us abilities for only ourselves, but to glorify Him and serve others. Every day since I was eight years old, I have worn the necklace with a basketball on one side, and the verse which is the theme of this book on the other. "I can do all things through Christ who strengthens me." - Philippians 4:13. God has had this book in mind since I bought the necklace when I was eight. This is where my motivation began to share your purpose with you.

When serving others, you will not be able to keep your motivation strong if you always think you are bettering them. If you humbly think, wow, I get to serve this individual, you will continue to stay motivated, even when people resist you. People want to know you are serving them because you value them, not because you pity them. We serve because we see the other person as valuable, and it is an honor to serve them.

Playing sports has been the perfect demonstration of God's will for our lives. God gives us "practice" through His Word so we will be ready to play! You cannot be on the team or play if you do not know what God asks of you. However, you also cannot score if you do not swing the bat, shoot, or serve! God already told you He will bring you home; the path you get there is up to your preparation and willingness to trust Him. If you focus on the entire game ahead of time, you will get overwhelmed. Focus on each play. I'm not saying not to prepare because any athlete will tell you how much you need to prepare for each individual play. God's plan for your life will pan out if you focus on obeying the Holy Spirit in each moment of your life. "Not to us, Lord, not to us but to your name be the glory, because of your love and faithfulness." -Psalm 115:1.

"Like a broken tooth or a lame foot is reliance on the unfaithful in a time of trouble." -Proverbs 25:19. I know all about broken teeth, as I have three from diving to catch a foul ball and running into the fence. All that mattered was that I caught the ball, right? My teeth are now stable due to the help of a dentist who is a great family friend of ours, but before the final cap my teeth were not stable, and neither are the unfaithful. If there are people on the team who try to gossip about other teammates, I know it can be very awkward to just stop the conversation. Always pray and ask God how to redirect these conversations in the positives about your teammates, and what skills you feel they add to the team either physically, mentally or as an encouragement. Your team is supposed to be like your family, and you want to stay faithful.

"If you have raced with men on foot and they have worn you out, how can you compete with horses?" -Jeremiah 12:5. You should always practice for the best competition. What good is it to practice for lower competition when you know you eventually will have to play the best? Progress can and should come in small steps, but the goal should always be how to push yourself to be the best and reach the potential of the God given talents and abilities you have been blessed with. Our bodies are not our own; they belong to God and should be treated as valuable and cared for. "Therefore, I urge you, brothers and sisters, in view of God's mercy, to offer your bodies as a living sacrifice, holy and pleasing to God—this is your true and proper worship." -Romans 12:1. You are God's temple, when you have Christ His Holy Spirit lives inside of you. "Don't you know that you yourselves are God's temple and that God's Spirit dwells in your midst? If anyone destroys God's temple, God will destroy that person; for God's temple is sacred, and you together are that temple." -1 Corinthians 3:16-17. You are sacred! "For we are the temple of the living God. As God has said: "I will live with them and walk among them, and I will be their God, and they will be my people." -2 Corinthians 6:16. "And in him you too are being built together to become a dwelling in which God lives by his Spirit." -Ephesians 2:22 (1 Peter 2:4-5).

Even though the Bible talks about competing, and that sports and physical training are of some value, the most important, and in the end the only eternal value is to receive the eternal crown.

"Do you not know that in a race all the runners run, but only one gets the prize? Run in such a way as to get the prize. Everyone who competes in the games goes into strict training. They do it to get a crown that will not last, but we do it to get a crown that will last forever. Therefore, I do not run like someone running aimlessly; I do not fight like a boxer beating the air. No, I strike a blow to my body and make it my slave so that after I have preached to others, I myself will not be disqualified for the prize." -1 Corinthians 9:24-27.

It seems like Paul and John were both competitive. "Both were running, but the other disciple outran Peter and reached the tomb first." -John 20:4. "Finally, the other disciple, who had reached the tomb first." -John 20:8. It is great to want to push yourself to be the best you can to win the competition, but the key is not to gloat over your opponent and still love on them, you know...once you beat them... "Do not gloat when your enemy falls; when they stumble, do not let your heart rejoice, or the Lord will see and disapprove." -Proverbs 24:17-18. In all seriousness, I love sports and love competing, but I cannot let it get in the way of the goal and achievement of life, to receive the eternal crown that I cannot achieve on my own or by any effort, but only by following the best coach, leading us to the ultimate victory of life for eternity.

"Whatever happens, conduct yourselves in a manner worthy of the gospel of Christ. Then, whether I come and see you or only hear about you in my absence, I will know that you stand firm in the one Spirit, striving together as one for the faith of the gospel without being frightened in any way by those who oppose you. This is a sign to them that they will be destroyed, but that you will be saved—and that by God." -Philippians 1:27-28.

When you play with a team, you are striving together for one common goal, one common championship uniting yourselves together and making it easy to form trustworthy relationships. We are to be the same way as believers. We are striving together toward one goal, one finish line, to get as many as we can with us, on our team, under the Super Bowl championship coach. When we stand together, we stand firm and resist the enemy.

"Join with me in suffering, like a good soldier of Christ Jesus. No one serving as a soldier gets entangled in civilian affairs, but rather tries to please his commanding officer. Similarly, anyone who competes as an athlete does not receive the victor's crown except by competing according to the rules. The hardworking farmer should be the first to receive a share of the crops. Reflect on what I am saying, for the Lord will give you insight into all this. Remember Jesus Christ, raised from the dead, descended from David. This is my gospel, for which I am suffering even to the point of being chained like a criminal. But God's word is not chained. Therefore, I endure everything for the sake of the elect, that they too may obtain the salvation that is in Christ Jesus, with eternal glory." -2 Timothy 2:3-10.

What I love the most is, sports taught me about sacrifice. Sports teaches you to be the teammate willing to lay down the bunt to get your teammate, even though your stats will show you got the out. When I was Libero for volleyball, I had to think about sacrifice. What hurt worse, when I hit the floor to dive and save a ball, or when the ball would hit the floor and my teammates would be let down? It helped me think of others before myself. Sports teaches us that yelling at the umps and refs do nothing when we do not get our way, even if we are completely justified. This teaches us self-control when were falsely accused. Some have made the argument God does not care about sports. God cares about the hairs on your head; He cares about sports and can and will continue to use them for His glory.

Prayer & Conversations

"I can do all things through Christ who strengthens me." -Philippians 4:13

I can *pray consistently and fervently* through Christ who strengthens me.

Why do we pray? Relationship. Just like you talk to your best friend, spouse, and family, God wants this relationship with you. Prayer is not meant to manipulate God. God has His will; God has His plan, but prayer gives us access to God in relationship. People say we can't prove prayer works, but you can't disprove it works, either. Believers all over the world are praying for not only other believers, but for the world! It is impossible to come into the presence of Jesus, our Holy good God, and not have your heart or attitude changed whether you consciously realize it or not. One thing I can guarantee is it is impossible to pray to our Almighty God and not have some part of you or your attitude changed.

"If in trouble, pray. If you're happy, sing praises. If you are sick, have the church elders pray over you and anoint you with oil in the name of the Lord. The prayer offered in faith will make the person well."-James 5:13-15. "Pray without ceasing..." -1 Thessalonians 5:17. Pray about everything, all the time. We should set aside times to pray and be in the presence of God. But never forget you can call upon the name of God anytime, anywhere. God is everywhere! Before you pray with someone, thank God for them. Some may think that God only cares about big things. He is your best friend! Your best friend cares about everything, all the details in your life. He is a personal God. I was praying God would help me to eat healthier to take care of the body He has blessed me with, and I was shocked at the results. This was also surrounded by gratefulness and thankfulness for being able to eat healthy, great-tasting meals.

"And pray in the Spirit on all occasions with all kinds of prayers and requests. With this in mind, be alert and always keep on praying for all the Lord's people. Pray also for me, that whenever I speak, words may be given me so that I will fearlessly make known the mystery of the gospel, for which I am an ambassador in chains. Pray that I may declare it fearlessly, as I should." - Ephesians 6:18-20.

Pray about everything. God is so much fun, personal, has the best sense of humor and cares. He already knows everything about you, so you can feel comfortable sharing anything with Him. Be alert and pray for others. Pray we are fearless and bold for Jesus. "The end of all things is near. Therefore, be alert and of sober mind so that you may pray." -1 Peter 4:7. Even though no one knows when the end will be other than God, we know each day that passes makes it closer. What are we supposed to do about it? Pray. "Devote yourselves to prayer, being watchful and thankful." -Colossians 4:2. Prayer should be something we are devoted to daily and with it, being watchful and thankful. Being alert and ready means being on the lookout for danger. Never paranoid as we know God is protecting us, but aware in order to pray as our defense as our head coach calls us to do for success.

"And the word of the Lord came to him: 'What are you doing here, Elijah?' He replied, 'I have been very zealous for the Lord God Almighty. The Israelites have rejected your covenant, torn down your altars, and put your prophets to death with the sword. I am the only one left, and now they are trying to kill me too." The Lord said, "Go out and stand on the mountain in the presence of the Lord, for the Lord is about to pass by.' Then a great and powerful wind tore the mountains apart and shattered the rocks before the Lord, but the Lord was not in the wind. After the wind there was an earthquake, but the Lord was not in the earthquake. After the earthquake came a fire, but the Lord was not in the fire. And after the fire came a gentle whisper." -1 Kings 19:9-12.

God is searching for you, desiring to talk to you. Elijah ran out of fear, as his very life was being threatened. God came to Him as a gentle whisper during the chaos. God continues to talk to us in a still small voice through the Holy Spirit. "The voice of the Lord is over the waters, the God of glory thunders, the Lord thunders over the mighty waters. The voice of the Lord is powerful; the voice of the Lord is majestic." - Psalm 29:3-4. "The voice of the Lord strikes with flashes of lightning. The voice of the Lord shakes the desert;" -Psalm 29:7-8. "...how faint the whisper we hear of him! Who can understand the thunder of his power?" -Job 26:14. In the quiet is where God is loudest. God's voice can still thunder and be gentle. We cannot place God in a box. He will speak to us in whatever way He wants, and whatever it takes to get our attention.

"In the past God spoke to our ancestors through the prophets at many times and in various ways, but in these last days he has spoken to us by his Son, whom he appointed heir of all things, and through whom also he made the universe. The Son is the radiance of God's glory and the exact representation of his being, sustaining all things by his powerful word. After he had provided purification for sins, he sat down at the right hand of the Majesty in Heaven." - Hebrews 1:1-3 (Romans 16:25-27, Revelation 22:6 and Acts 3:17-25).

We have been in the last days since Jesus has come. Also, God can use others to speak to you. In the past, He used the prophets as said. "This has all taken place that the writings of the prophets might be fulfilled." Then all the disciples deserted him and fled." -Matthew 26:56. Jesus was crucified just as the prophets predicted centuries before. Today, in the last days, He speaks to every human being through the miracle of Jesus. If lies ever creep in that cause doubt concerning God's love for you, or if you hear voices making you feel as if you do not have purpose or are hopeless, look to the cross because the message will always be the same, exposing the lies. God cares about your life more than you do, and desires to talk with and have a relationship with you. He will speak to you in whatever ways that will best benefit your relationship. In Acts 13:4 the Holy Spirit led them to Cyprus and even in Acts 16:6-7, it's fascinating how the Holy Spirit kept them from going to Asia. When they tried to enter Bithynia, the Spirit of Jesus wouldn't let them. The Holy Spirit is living in us and will guide us when we ask in prayer.

"What other nation is so great as to have their gods near them the way the Lord our God is near us whenever we pray to him?" -Deuteronomy 4:7. They once said "You know; God is right next to you when you pray to Him. You don't have to change your voice or act different." I love this perspective, as it is true when we talk to God. He already knows everything about us, and He is our friend. We should feel relaxed to talk to Him the same.

"But when you pray, go into your room, close the door and pray to your father, who is unseen. Then your Father, who sees what is done in secret, will reward you. And when you pray, do not keep on babbling like pagans, for they think they will be heard because of their many words. Do not be like them, for your father knows what you need before you ask him." -Matthew 6:6-8.

Jesus gives an example of why we are to pray with persistence and never give up. There was a widow that kept bugging a judge for justice even though this judge did not fear God or care what people thought. Even though the judge was not just in his way, he granted her request from her persistence. Will God not bring justice for His chosen ones who cry out day and night to him? Another example, Jesus is a friend who knocks on another friend's door at midnight for bread. Even if the friend doesn't want to get up and get him the bread, since it is the middle of the night, because of friendship, the friend will still do it because of your audacity. (See Luke 18:1-7 and Luke 11:5-8). Jesus explains how persistence in prayer is important. If the unfair judge granted the request, and the friend who did not care enough about the man to get up for him out of love, but obligation, how much more will our loving Father in Heaven listen to our requests?

"Ask, and it will be given you; search, and you will find; knock, and the door will be opened for you. For everyone who asks receives, and everyone who searches finds, and for everyone who knocks, the door will be opened. "Which of you, if your son asks for bread, will give him a stone? Or if he asks for a fish, will give him a snake? If you, then, though you are evil, know how to give good gifts to your children, how much more will your Father in Heaven give good gifts to those who ask him!" Matthew 7:7-11 (Luke 11:9-13). God is waiting for you to ask for help. Ask, knock and search. Jesus explains that it even us as humans know how to feed and care for our children, how much more will our perfect Father in Heaven grant us what He best desires for us?

"He who did not spare his own Son, but gave him up for us all—how will he not also, along with him, graciously give us all things?" -Romans 8:32. If God was willing to give up His only Son for you, how can you think He will not be here for you every minute of your life?! Even though you may feel weak and scared of life, God is the master at life and is protecting you. "Are not all angels ministering spirits sent to serve those who will inherit salvation?" -Hebrews 1:14. Literally part of the angel's job is to minister you! Just as David faced Goliath, I am sure when he looked at David, he thought nothing of Him. If He could have seen the image of God behind David, he would have cowered in fear. Think of this and think of who is behind you as you face this world head on. "Very truly I tell you, my Father will give you whatever you ask in my name. Until now you have not asked for anything in my name. Ask and you will receive, and your joy will be complete." -John 16:23-24 (John 14:13-14). "If you remain in me and my words remain in you, ask whatever you wish, and it will be done for you." -John 15:7. If two or more agree it will be done for where two or more gather in his name, God is with them." -Matthew 18:19-20. When we make requests in Jesus' name, let His words remain in us and make requests based on His words. God already knows what is on your heart, so you should ask whatever your deepest, truest desires and dreams are, then trust God does answer prayer and will accomplish what He feels is best for you.

"What causes fights and quarrels among you? Don't they come from your desires that battle within you? You desire but do not have, so you kill. You covet but you cannot get what you want, so you quarrel and fight. You do not have because you do not ask God. When you ask, you do not receive, because you ask with wrong motives, that you may spend what you get on your pleasures." -James 4:1-3.

You do not have because you do not ask of God. You do not receive because you ask with wrong motives. "I cried out to him with my mouth; his praise was on my tongue. If I had cherished sin in my heart, the Lord would not have listened." -Psalm 66:17-18. I really need a heart check sometimes when praying, hoping what I am asking for is with the right intentions, and not evil that sometimes come out of my worldly desires. In my own experience, when I pray before a big exam, game, hard conversation, things seem to go better. Let me emphasize, they do not go the way I plan or want always, however it's the best way since it is God's way.

"Have faith in God," Jesus answered. "Truly I tell you, if anyone says to this mountain, 'Go, throw yourself into the sea,' and does not doubt in their heart but believes that what they say will happen, it will be done for them. Therefore, I tell you, whatever you ask for in prayer, believe that you have received it, and it will be yours." -Mark 11:22-24 (Matthew 21:21-22).

"…what the righteous desire will be granted." -Proverbs 10:24 (Proverbs

11:23 and Proverbs 14:22). "This is the confidence we have in approaching God: that if we ask anything according to his will, he hears us. And if we know that he hears us—whatever we ask—we know that we have what we asked of him." -1 John 5:14-15. When we pray, God wants us to have confidence. We may waver in confidence of our situation, thinking there is simply no way it can work out, but He wants our faith and confidence in Him even when we are weak. If what we ask is in accordance with His will, He hears us and will grant it. If it is not in His will, we can be happy He did not grant it. My heart understands, but my mind does not. It all comes down to trust. We may think we are not trusting enough or have enough faith. If you have faith as small as a mustard seed, you can move mountains and the fact that you are coming to God in prayer is showing where your faith lies! The fact that you go to God in prayer shows you have already won the battle! "He moves mountains without their knowing it." -Job 9:5.

"If any of you lacks wisdom, you should ask God who gives generously to all without finding fault, and it will be given to you. But when you ask, you must believe and not doubt, because the one who doubts is like a wave of the sea, blown and tossed by the wind." -James 1:5-6 (Matthew 20:1-2, Matthew 20:9-15, Mark 10:31 and Matthew 19:30). "That person should not expect to receive anything from the Lord. Such a person is double-minded and unstable in all they do." -James 1:7-8. Are you confused? Lacking direction? Wondering what life is about, what your exact purpose is or what the next move should be in your life? How about something as simple as wondering what you should make for dinner today? When should I work out? When should I spend time with my family, friends, or others? What career should I choose? Which vacation should I go on? How many kids should we have? God cares about every single detail about your life and has the answer and keys to every single part of our lives. God is the most generous being, and He desires to share His wisdom; all you must do is ask! He wants you to ask with confidence in Him.

Prayer sometimes seems more complicated than it needs to be. It is simply conversation with God. Sometimes when we do not know how to pray, something as simple as telling the Lord, and saying to please lead the way, I love you, please help, thank you, or forgive me are all powerful in and of themselves!

I used to be afraid to pray in a group. I cared more about what others heard me say, than focusing on me talking to God. Ironically, I prayed about this specifically and eventually was able to only focus on God during prayers to be more genuine. I understand people who may have never prayed before need some guidance, because once you are comfortable, you can just talk to God about anything. Your prayers are valuable and priceless to God.

"Each one had a harp, and they were holding golden bowls full of incense, which are the prayers of God's people. And they sang a new song, saying: "You are worthy to take the scroll and to open its seals, because you were slain, and with your blood you purchased for God persons from every tribe and language and people and nation. You have made them to be a kingdom and priests to serve our God, and they will reign on the earth." -Revelation 5:8-10.

To start, it is good to pray, asking for forgiveness of your sins and confessing we are sinners. We should pray with thanksgiving and for others. Pray for guidance and for the desires of your heart. Pray with confidence and end saying the good Lord's will be done. I never liked to pray this when I finished, because I wanted my own will to be done. I have figured out God's will is always better than mine, and have recently been begging His will be done. Finally, always listen for His response as it is there. "…and that you may love the Lord your God, listen to His voice, and hold fast to Him. For the Lord is your life, and He will give you many years in the land He swore to give your fathers, Abraham, Isaac, and Jacob." -Deuteronomy 30:20. Prayer is a two-way conversation. Make sure after you talk, you listen too.

"I thank my God every time I remember you. In all my prayers for all of you, I always pray with joy because of your partnership in the gospel from the first day until now." -Philippians 1:3-5 (1 Thessalonians 1:20). Praying for others is so important, just as important as praying for yourself. Praying in thankfulness for others is where genuine love begins to form. Prayer is more effective than positive thinking. Positive thinking will only get you so far. Prayer is partnering with God! When others see you praying it can help be a reminder for them to pray too.

"As for me, far be it from me that I should sin against the Lord by failing to pray for you. And I will teach you the way that is good and right. But be sure to fear the Lord and serve him faithfully with all your heart; consider what great things he has done for you. Yet if you persist in doing evil, both you and your king will perish." -Samuel 12:23-25 (Micah 5:13).

Samuel goes as far as calling it a sin to fail to pray for others. Praying for others is so important, as you have no idea what the people you love are going through that they do not even talk about. We have no idea how powerful our prayers are and how God can use them to lift up someone else. When God answers prayers, He not only thinks about how the situation will affect you but also others. God thinks about every tiny little detail we do not even realize is happening under the surface. "Indeed, he was ill, and almost died. But God had mercy on him, and not on him only but also on me, to spare me sorrow upon sorrow." -Philippians 2:27. Want to help your struggling family, friends, and patients? Help comes from your prayer for them. "...join me in my struggle by praying to God for me." -Romans 15:30. "Therefore I want the men everywhere to pray, lifting up holy hands without anger or disputing." -1 Timothy 2:8. When we pray for others, it diminishes anger and disputes, building up our relationships and teamwork with others.

Pray first, act second. If you pray about it, I guarantee God is working on it. I can tell you there is no better feeling than when someone is praying for you. "Be joyful in hope, patient in affliction and faithful in prayer." -Romans 12:12 (Acts 1:14). Joyful in hope. We are not joyful because of what we are going through, but the hope God can produce through it. Staying faithful in prayer means to remain consistent, even if the length and attitude of your prayers vary. God knows you will waver, but through the wavering He wants you to stay faithful. Some days, it is a simple "help" or "thank you," and others you are talking to Him all day.

"So, your servant has found courage to pray this prayer to you. Sovereign Lord, you are God! Your covenant is trustworthy, and you have promised these good things to your servant. Now be pleased to bless the house of your servant, that it may continue forever in your sight; for you, Sovereign Lord, have spoken, and with your blessing the house of your servant will be blessed forever." -2 Samuel 7:27-29 (1 Chronicles 17:25-26).

Prayer takes courage because you are admitting you cannot do it on your own and thanking God for what you cannot provide for yourself. He is trustworthy and promises good to His servants.

God will listen when you seek Him. Elijah was human like us, and when he prayed earnestly for it not to rain, it didn't and when he prayed for the Heavens to give rain, it did (See James 5:17-18). I know if God had answered every prayer since I was little, my life would be pretty messed up. Even if the answer is not what you want, He will answer your prayer when you trust in Him in deliverance. "Then Jehoahaz sought the Lord's favor, and the Lord listened to him." -2 Kings 13:4. "God delivered the Hagrites and all their allies into their hands because they cried out to him during the battle. He answered their prayers because they trusted in him." -1 Chronicles 5:20. In 2 Kings 7:17-20 Elijah prays to God to open eyes and to blind his enemies and God grants his request. Also, in 1 Kings 17:21-22 and 1 Kings 17:23-24, Elijah prayed for a boy's life to be returned to him, and He granted his request. Isaiah 38:4-8, 2 Chronicles 32:24 and 2 Kings 20:5 tells the story how God hears Hezekiah's prayer and sees his tears, bringing healing and adding to his life as he was so ill, he almost died and given deliverance from the King of Assyria. The Lord fulfills His promise.

"When I shut up the Heavens so that there is no rain, or command locusts to devour the land or send a plague among my people, if my people, who are called by my name, will humble themselves and pray and seek my face and turn from their wicked ways, then I will hear from Heaven, and I will forgive their sin and will heal their land." -2 Chronicles 7:13-14 (Deuteronomy 28:58-59).

God warns if we do not carefully follow the Bible, and do not revere His awesome and glorious name, there will be consequences. "...they never call on God. But there they are, overwhelmed with dread." -Psalm 53:4-5. "God hears the prayers of the righteous and the prayers of the upright pleases him, however his face is against those who do evil." -Proverbs 15:29 (1 Peter 3:12 and Proverbs 15:8). God says he called; they did not listen so when they called, I did not listen (See Zechariah 7:13). "He does not answer when people cry out because of the arrogance of the wicked. Indeed, God does not listen to their empty plea; How much less, then, will he listen when you say that you do not see him." -Job 35:12-14. The most dangerous thing anyone can do is to simply not come to God, to act like He does not exist and as if He is not complete and obviously seen in all of creation. The beautiful thing is, God always welcomes you back with open arms if you remember the story of the prodigal son. The key is you must run back. If anyone ignores His instruction God says their prayers are detestable (See Proverbs 28:9). God is always ready to pick you right back up, the key is reaching out for His hand instead of trying to do it on your own.

"In the morning he hears our voice as we ask our requests and wait expectantly." -Psalm 5:3.

God will answer when we call. (See Psalm 17:6, Psalm 86:7, Psalm 20:6, 2 Chronicles 30:27, 1 Kings 8:41-43, Psalm 120:1 and Psalm 119:1). "They were also to stand every morning to thank and praise the Lord. They were to do the same thing in the evening." -1 Chronicles 23:30. Before we start our day, we should lay out all our requests for Him who hears us. We are to wait *expectantly*. God loves when we wait expectantly because it shows we trust Him in faith. We know we never wait in vain, because He is near to all who call on Him, fulfilling the desires of all who fear Him. "The Lord is near to all who call on him, to all who call on him in truth. He fulfills the desires of those who fear him; he hears their cry and saves them. The Lord watches over all who love him, but all the wicked he will destroy." - Psalm 145:18-20 (Psalm 66:19-20 and Psalm 4:3). "...We do not make requests because we think we are worthy but because we know he is full of mercy." -Daniel 9:18. He will save us and watch over all who love Him. He fulfills the desires of all who fear Him. Anyone can tell you this does not mean you get whatever you pray for, but God sees the heart and desire behind what you are asking for, and the desire will be fulfilled even if we do not get exactly what we ask for.

God told Daniel "not to be afraid since he has set his mind to gain understanding and humbled himself before the Lord, God heard his words." (See Daniel 10:12 and 2 Chronicles 33:12-13). God does the same for Manasseh when he humbles himself. Amos called on our Sovereign Lord to forgive Jacob, as he is so small, he wouldn't survive his judgment by fire as it dried up the great deep and devoured the land, and the Lord listened. (See Amos 7:2-6) God hears us when we humble ourselves before Him, and if we are coming to Him chances are you have humbled yourself, otherwise you would not approach God in the first place thinking you can do life on your own. When you ask of wisdom, God will set your mind to understand.

Do you feel like you have been persistent in prayer, praying with confidence and trust in God, yet nothing seems to happen or change? Habakkuk had a similar situation. "How long, Lord, must I call for help, but you do not listen? Or cry out to you, "Violence!" but you do not save?" -Habakkuk 1:1. He says how long God; must I call for help but it seems like you are not listening?! God responds. "Look at the nations and watch- and be utterly amazed. For I am going to do something in your days that you would not believe, even if you were told." -Habakkuk 1:5 (Acts 13:41). God says we will all be amazed. Even if God laid out the map of our lives and the world, just like the prophets told the people, just like Jesus told the disciples how He was going to be crucified, and even though we have parts of the map through the revelation, we as human beings cannot fully comprehend how short life is and how much purpose our lives are going to impact eternity. When we trust in God, how amazing it will be and can be now. Even though I am just like anyone else that I do not understand, I choose to trust and be fully confident throughout my life, until the end when we enter eternity or if Jesus comes back first. We are going to be utterly amazed at how God has worked in every little detail, using every single prayer as a part of His ultimate will that He has set in place since the beginning of time.

"This, then, is how you should pray: "'Our Father in Heaven, hallowed be your name, your kingdom come, your will be done, on earth as it is in Heaven. Give us today our daily bread. And forgive us our debts, as we also have forgiven our debtors. And lead us not into temptation but deliver us from the evil one.' For if you forgive other people when they sin against you, your Heavenly Father will also forgive you." -Matthew 6:9-14 (Luke 11:1-4).

Jesus teaches us to pray to our God who is in Heaven, and that His name should be honored, respected, as He is a Holy, perfect God. We are to pray for His kingdom to come as when is prophesized to happen in the end. Even though His will already has this happening, we access this power when we pray. We ask for Jesus to give us our daily bread, which references back to Matthew 4:4, where we are told we do not live on bread alone, but every word from God. We ask for His forgiveness, just as we forgive those who sin against us. I think we say this without understanding what we are saying. When we pray how Jesus taught us, we are *forgiving everyone who has wronged us*. We continue for prayers to strengthen us against Satan, the enemy who wants to destroy everything God has created including you and me. Prayer helps us not to fall into temptation as we are not stronger than the enemy, but God is, and prayer links us to His power. Jesus also tells the disciples in the garden to pray so they do not fall into temptation since the spirit is willing, but the flesh is weak, according to Matthew 26:41.

"Jesus got up early while it was still dark, left the house to a solitary place to pray." -Mark 1:35. "He went to the mountainside to pray and spend the entire night talking to God." -Luke 6:12. "Even when crowds began gathering around him to heal their sickness, he often went to lonely places to pray." -Luke 5:15-16. Jesus would get up early to pray in a solitary place, would spend the entire night talking to God and even when surrounded by many others He was loving on and taking care of, He still went to lonely places to pray. We usually look at being lonely as a negative, but those times when we are alone are the best times to spend with God. There is a difference between feeling lonely and being alone. Think of all the people the Holy Spirit used to write the Bible while they were alone. God has a greater purpose for their loneliness. We still need our community; however, do not underestimate the purpose when God has you alone. I find we are more beneficial and have deeper, more intimate relationships and can supply the needs of others in our lives and love them better, the more we have alone and intimate time with God. God knows and loves people more than anyone, including those in your life you want to love on. Who better to spend time with? You can surround yourself with everyone and have everyone love you, but if you don't have God, you will always feel lonely. When we are lonely, we tend to make decisions we usually wouldn't to get others to notice us, whether it's how we dress or how we act. There will be no better, satisfying, and unfailing relationship than the one who created you. Set times alone with Him just like you would family or friends, and the more you get you will not be able to get enough.

In Acts 9:33-42, Peter heals a paralyzed man in Jesus' name, turning others to the Lord. Peter got on his knees and prayed and brought back to life the disciple, Tabitha. He told her to get up, and he took her by the hand, helping her to her feet increasing their belief in Jesus. In Acts 28:7-9 Paul healed the sickness of an entire island through prayer. While Peter was in prison, the church was praying for him. The night before Herod brought him to trial, an angel of the Lord came freeing him of his chains (See Acts 12:5-7). Peter said he knew without a doubt the Lord sent the angel to rescue him. Peter came to the house of Mary, and they couldn't believe it, they thought it had to be an angel. (See Acts 12:11-16) Prayer is power. Prayer is talking to the One with the most power, who when it is His will for His good purposes, can give you access to this power. Never doubt what God can do.

Jesus offered prayers and petitions of cries and tears to the only one who could save Him from death, and He was heard because of His submission. He learned obedience through His suffering and once made perfect, He is our salvation for eternal life and was designated by God to be high priest in the order of Melchizedek. (See Hebrews 5:7-10). Some may argue God did not "answer" Jesus' prayer when He asked God if there could be any other way to save humanity other than His crucifixion. Even though Jesus asked, He submitted to God's will, as He *wanted* God's will, and desired to save me, you, and the world. When we pray so desperately wanting God to take away the pain, He hears, He cares, and He answers, but when we are aligned with His will, we will want what He wants through the hard emotions, resistance and tears that come with it. It is a matter of aligning our hearts with God even when our minds and emotions are not. God will eventually align them when we are with persistence in the word.

It is sad that people use the word "coincidence" when it is answered prayer. One time my mom gave someone $30.00 exactly, and the person said they prayed for this exact amount. Coincidence? No, answered prayer. One time I prayed for help with finances. I went grocery shopping and as I was checking out someone gave me a coupon for free peanut butter and 10% off. Coincidence? No, answered prayer. Another time I was out to eat, and a server stopped by my table and said she would pack me a brand-new salad, at no charge! Then, a global pandemic hit, cutting my hours for work. God, what happened? You were helping me financially even though I was the one who made the poor choices, so why go backwards and have me work less hours? Right after I received the news and was working less hours, I received the news that I got a raise. I did not think I would get one until I passed my Certified Hand Therapy boards. Also, my friend was sending me gift cards, toiletry items and even sent me coffee money, without even knowing I was struggling. Then, I was given a Starbucks gift card for $15.00, and I ordered a tall almond milk honey latte, egg wrap and blueberry oatmeal. Have you ever ordered these items together? Guess how much they were? $15.00. Even. Coincidence? No, answered prayer. There is no such thing as coincidence. I am always making sure everyone is aware that prayer is not a magic trick. When you tithe, will you receive the exact amount of money back or more? Not necessarily. However, I also do not think we give God enough credit when it comes to what people claim are coincidences in life, but we know they are miracles and answered prayers.

Prayer, how can we hear God? You must experience and practice it. We all should have a place of prayer, on top of just talking to Him anywhere and everywhere.

"You of this generation, consider the Word of the Lord: Have I been a desert to Israel or a land of great darkness? Why do my people say, "We are free to roam; we will come to you no more"? Does a young woman forget her jewelry, a bride her wedding ornaments? Yet my people have forgotten me, days without number." -Jeremiah 2:31-32.

Prayer grows us because we are with the Lord even though it doesn't bring salvation. Prayer contributes to our spiritual strength. It makes us consistent and reliable with God. People of prayer are generally reliable. They have their priorities straight.

When I have so much work, the only way I can do it is to first spend time in prayer and pray about the task I am about to set forth to accomplish. If you make prayer a priority, everything else falls into place. Pray for many people specifically. No plan will help you if prayer is not a priority. Praise relates to prayer life. Praise is not only experiencing God, but it's God releasing something from the Heavenly of His presence and power. The closer you get to God the more you see. The higher you are the more you see. Prayer brings us closer to God.

"The Lord would speak to Moses' face to face, as one speaks to a friend." -Exodus 33:11. God is our friend. I hope I do not make it seem as if prayer must be a chore or obligation. I know our human nature can be distracted by the things of this world instead of talking to the creator who supplies and creates all things. Sometimes we need discipline and then the relationship builds with it. Even with my advice of having a room to pray, setting times to pray, what to pray, etc., please listen to me. The ultimate purpose is the relationship and just falling in love, talking, and being with God.

"Why do you complain to him that he responds to no one's words? For God does speak-now one way, now another- though no one perceives it. In a dream, in a vision of the night, when deep sleep falls on people as they slumber in their beds, he may speak in their ears and terrify them with warnings, to turn them from wrongdoing and keep them from pride." -Job 33:13-17.

I have never heard the audible voice of God, but I hear Him. God talks to us through His Word directly. Blessed are those you choose and bring near to live in your courts! God answers prayer is such ways that when we are overwhelmed by sin, He forgives. He answers us with righteous and awesome deeds. God is the hope of all the ends of the earth who formed the mountains and stilled the roaring seas. The whole earth is filled with the awe of His wonders calling songs of joy. He cares for the land as He waters it, producing grain. (See Psalm 65:2-10).

Sometimes we are in so much pain, we do not know what to say. "In the same way, the Spirit helps us in our weakness. We do not know what we ought to pray for, but the Spirit himself intercedes for us through wordless groans." -Romans 8:26. There have been times when the pain is so deep, you do not know what to pray and you just cry. God cares and loves you so much. He is not looking for you to be an expert on how to communicate what you are feeling. Sometimes what we are experiencing is so deep, there really are not words to explain it. God knows. His spirit will intercede for you when you do not know what to say, but still have the request for help. The concept of prayer is to just come to Jesus. That is all that matters.

Speaking of prayer, here is mine for you.

Jesus, I pray that what is read through this book, you use for this person's greater good. I pray they will not remember my name at the end, but yours. I pray they will see how much you love them. I thank you Lord for creating this individual and all the details you put into the greatness of who they are. Help them live this life for you, and I pray they find salvation through you to be with you in eternity. Help them see no matter their past, you have a plan for their future far greater than what they can imagine. Wrap your loving and strong arms around them, helping them feel your presence. Help them live each day with enthusiasm and passion pursuing their dreams, knowing they have purpose and can do all things through you who strengthens them! Amen!

Parenting & Family

"I can do all things through Christ who strengthens me." -Philippians 4:13

I can *be the parent my child needs* through Christ who strengthens me.

"In the beginning you laid the foundations of the earth, and the Heavens are the work of your hands. They will perish, but you remain; they will all wear out like a garment. Like clothing you will change them, and they will be discarded. But you remain the same, and your years will never end. The children of your servants will live in your presence; their descendants will be established before you." -Psalm 102:25-28 (Psalm 90:1-2 and Hebrews 1:10-12).

Being a parent is the most important job in the world, and no amount of training can prepare you for it. I mean the world looks at you as overseeing another human being that has a mind and will of their own! The definition of challenging. Even though parenting will be a journey of constant prayer, seeking counsel from others and learning, we can be grateful there are guidelines to help us along the way. Then Manoah prayed to the Lord, "Pardon your servant, Lord. I beg you to let the man of God you sent to us come again to teach us how to bring up the boy who is to be born." -Judges 13:8. Manoah asked how to bring up Samson, as he realized like most parents do that this is a hard task, and we all need guidance! "All your children will be taught by the Lord, and great will be their peace." -Isaiah 54:13.

"Jesus gave them this answer: 'Very truly I tell you, the Son can do nothing by himself; he can do only what he sees his Father doing, because whatever the Father does the Son also does. For the Father loves the Son and shows him all he does." -John 5:19-20 (John 5:21-30). Did you know we all have mirror neurons that guide us to imitate and behave what we see? We begin to develop so many of our neurons, even right after we are born. Even Jesus Himself made a reference that He only does what He sees His Father doing, our God. It is so important you begin to guide your children. "Start children off on the way they should go, and even when they are old, they will not turn from it." -Proverbs 22:6. Maybe you feel your parents or Father were not the best example, but God still asks us to honor them and him. If you feel He asked or has done things you do not think God would desire you to do, God is also our Father, and should be all our examples as well. "If the part of the dough offered as first fruits is holy, then the whole batch is holy; if the root is holy, so are the branches." -Romans 11:16.

"Love the Lord your God with all your heart and with all your soul and with all your strength. These commandments that I give you today are to be on your hearts. Impress them on your children. Talk about them when you sit at home and when you walk along the road, when you lie down and when you get up. Tie them as symbols on your hands and bind them on your foreheads. Write them on the doorframes of your houses and on your gates." -Deuteronomy 6:5-9 (Proverbs 7:2-3).

Kids learn by example. I learned to help others, handle my own finances, pray, study, work, exercise, and tithe because I saw my parents doing it. You will never be able to do it all, so please know loving God as a parent is the best example you can set for your child. I feel I can better trust God because I have seen my parents do it. Who do kids generally look up to and learn from more than anyone? Their parents! Who are they always watching? Their parents. How do they swear at such a young age when our words accidentally slip from us when they are around? Their ... You get the point. One time I was helping my little cousin bake cookies and told her not to eat the sprinkles while we were decorating. She looked at me and said, "But you're doing it?" Wow, she was right. I didn't even realize it, but what I realized quickly is how much children watch, learn, and behave like we do. We are to impress the commandments of God on our hearts, and on our children's hearts. Talking about God, His love and commandments is supposed to be a regular conversation at home, when you go for walks, before you go to bed and when you get up in the morning. Scripture should be in your home. Another example of how they are affected not only by the people but by words around them.

"Only be careful and watch yourselves closely so that you do not forget the things your eyes have seen or let them fade from your heart as long as you live. Teach them to your children and to their children after them. Remember the day you stood before the Lord your God at Horeb, when he said to me, "Assemble the people before me to hear my word so that they may learn to revere me as long as they live in the land and may teach them to their children." -Deuteronomy 4:9-10.

"Keep God's commands so you may enjoy a long life resulting in your children and their children fearing God." -Deuteronomy 6:2.

"One generation commends your works to another; they tell of your mighty acts. They speak of the glorious splendor of your majesty- and I will meditate on your wonderful works. They tell of the power of your awesome works- and I will proclaim your great deeds. They celebrate your abundant goodness and joyfully sing of your righteousness." -Psalm 145:4-7.

As parents, we are to tell our kids about the mighty acts God has done throughout His word and in our own lives to encourage them. If your son asks, "What is the meaning of the commands the Lord has given you?" In Deuteronomy, it says God commands we "obey and to fear Him so we may prosper. (See Deuteronomy 6:24). If our children ask what is the purpose of the commands God has given us, then why are they important? The word says God gives us the commands so we may prosper, because He wants you to thrive!

"For everyone belongs to me, the parent as well as the child- both alike belong to me. The one who sins is the one who will die." -Ezekiel 18:4. Our kids are God's, not our own but they are an incredible gift from him! "When they see their children, the work of my hands, they will keep my name holy; they will acknowledge the holiness of the Holy One of Jacob and will stand in awe of the God of Israel." -Isaiah 29:23 (Hebrews 2:13 and Isaiah 8:18). "Children come from God and are a reward from him comparing such as arrows in the hand of a warrior, blessed if you have many." -Psalm 127:3-5. He knows what is best for them, and we need to trust Him. I know this is so hard, because there is evil everywhere. However, God is everywhere too! "Who can hide in secret places so that I cannot see them?" declares the Lord. "Do I not fill Heaven and earth?" -Jeremiah 23:24. My parents said it was not easy, but they trust and are able to let me bloom because they know Jesus is on my side. Remember God loves your child more than you do. Think of how much you love your children! That is more love than we can fathom! Parents feel the pressure to be perfect for their children, and I want you to know you do not need to be perfect to inspire your kids. Your child needs to see a parent depending on God. Everyone who heard this wondered about it, asking, "'What then is this child going to be?' For the Lord's hand was with him." -Luke 1:66. "The Lord's hand was with them, and a great number of people believed and turned to the Lord." - Acts 11:21.

"...But as for me and my household, we will serve the Lord." -Joshua 24:15. If you are a parent, it is your responsibility to do your best to lead your children to Jesus and live a Godly life. We are all busy. I know it can be time-consuming, but what is more important than your children? I love the story when Jesus was at Martha's and Mary was at His feet listening. Martha was taking care of all the preparations and asked Jesus to make her help. Jesus said you are worried about so many things when all you need to focus on is me (See Luke 10:38-42). When questioning priorities, I think of what is eternal. One of the best prayers is asking God how to prioritize your time, as there is absolutely nothing wrong with taking care of your home, and there are other places in scripture God says it is good and important to stay busy taking care of our homes (See Titus 2:5). It is a matter of what the priority is for us to do from God in that moment. If we are always cleaning our homes with no time for Jesus or family, that is different than making cleaning your home apart of your priorities in general.

The only "things" which will last forever are people, God's word and God himself. However, it is impossible to keep your kids from evil in this broken world. The best thing you can do is equip them to be a light in the world and not giving into the evil. Jesus is the difference. No matter if your child does chores growing up, no matter if you pay for them growing up, no matter if they go to public or private, Jesus is the difference. Parents will say "spoiled" kids will not grow up working hard. Well, I am here to tell you, my parents helped me so much growing up. They provided, I appreciated. I mean, I was spanked and disciplined, but they paid for me to do club sports, paid for my schooling other than my loan I had to take out for graduate school (which was still a lot of money), and bought me a car and guess what? I went to school to work hard in school for good grades and to get my master's to become a certified hand therapist. I worked hard at sports. I desired to go to church. I wanted to respect my parents. We did not have curfews or controlled spied screen time. You know why? Jesus. I am by no means saying parents should not control these aspects or have differing opinions on it. My point is, that all parenting can be respected if Jesus is the difference. My brother and I still had our times where we got into trouble (me more than him), but my point being we went back to our foundation. I also know people who did many chores growing up, worked a lot and did not go to school, or even those who did. They did not want to work as hard or were not as appreciative because Jesus was not their motivation. "How can a young person stay on the path of purity? By living according to your word." -Psalm 119:9. You can't child-proof the world, but you can world-proof your child! My Mom and Dad have both been extremely influential in my life. My mom stayed home to take care of us and our home while my dad worked a full-time job as a commodities trader on the Board of Trade. The commonality of how they influenced me even with different jobs, was Jesus.

"Unless the LORD builds the house, the builders labor in vain. Unless the Lord watches over the city, the guards stand watch in vain." -Psalm 127:1. If your family is not centered on Jesus, pain will affect the home. There is no perfect family out there, just like there is no perfect human being other than Jesus. Many times, families lash out at each other because of hidden pains or unsaid issues which only create more hurt. The first step is identifying the hurt and admitting our sins. Genuine apologies go a long way. The beauty is if we let Him, God can make good from painful circumstances in our family. Not because our pain is not severe but because He is just that powerful. I admire how much my parents found joy in everything growing up. My mom would love to clean, telling us it was because she knew she had a family God blessed her with to clean after. Dad found joy in the business of working on the Board of Trade and coaching, saying he was blessed to have the ability to coach his children and take care of His family.

It is so important at a young age that we explain to children that Jesus is their best friend. Relationships will come and go since they are young, and that includes some bullying. Elisha was bullied and called a "badly" then God had a bear come and attack his oppressors (See 2 Kings 2:23-24). When our children have confidence that God is their best friend, they will be less likely to feel lonely and understand their value and worth even when others do not. We all know this world can be cruel, and it seems like no matter how popular we are in school, someone will always have something to say. The words will hurt our children, just like they can still hurt us as adults, even if we do not always admit it. My turning point was when I realized what Jesus says about me is true, that He designed how I am supposed to look, regardless of what others think about my talent, skills, or looks. Even with gossip and rumors. It is so easy to get inside our own heads, thinking what others say is true. Teach them what Jesus has to say because sometimes children do not even see what their parents say as the truth. I love that my mom thinks I am beautiful, but deep-down children sometimes feel parents are supposed to say that. Your words of encouragement impact your child, do not think otherwise. But just imagine telling your child the King of the universe hand-picked their eyes, nose, cheeks, and smile. That is something to take pride in!

It is so easy to brag when your child has an accomplishment, but it is important to always give the glory back to God. Dad's reminders are: 'Work hard. Give Glory to God. Be thankful for your skill set. You are champions for Jesus! Hard work and humility go hand in hand. Remember to serve. It is not all about you but the people you help. Stay grounded and stay humbled in Jesus! He is the tie that binds! I have no doubt! I pray you stop worrying about the things that don't matter. Give it to God! God has put you where you are, not only to be successful, but to help others. God has great plans, His plans, and that is all that matters. I love you and your brother more than you know." Out of all my dad's encouragement, nothing will comfort your child more than telling them God has perfect plans for their life, and with God all things are possible. My dad has always been my coach. No one has ever pushed me harder, told me to be quieter (even when the entire team is talking, I get yelled at), and yet has seen the most potential in me. If it were not for him and my mom, I would not be the student, athlete, therapist, or disciple I am today. He has instilled a passion and work ethic in me for school, sports, work, people, life, and God. He did not become this father by chance, but by choice of God.

A prayer he sent me and my brother before we left for college read this, "Dear Lord, my emotions are mixed. On one hand, I feel life's mission has been accomplished. On the other hand, I'm feeling a little sad about missing our kids already. Please remove my worry. Go with them Lord, as they head into the world. Bless them, protect them and keep them close to you. Do not let the world derail their faith or steal their optimism. Help me continue to keep praying for them, because they will always be my children even though they are on their own. I commit them into your hands God. In Jesus name, amen." I thought this was a great prayer to share for all the parents struggling when their children leave for college, as the heartache can be unbearable, I can imagine. Pray for your children. This is the best thing you can do. You will not have all the answers; none of us do, but God does!

My mom once said: "Great kids do not just happen. They are molded from birth with the Lord's guidance. Thank you, Lord, for letting us as parents have the opportunity to guide your children. Better comes from our Father. Continue to work hard, stay dedicated and motivated. Love you and your brother so much." My favorite quote from my mom has to be one time when I asked her, "Are you eating alone?" She said, "No, I'm having Taco Bell with Jesus." As hilarious as this sounds, we really are never alone, even at Taco Bell. I admire her confidence in the Lord, and it is something I strive for daily. I was always embarrassed to ever be alone until she introduced me to this mentality.

I have always been competitive in sports like my dad. I knew he would be proud if we placed at nationals for our travel softball team and if I played sports in college. I ended up playing volleyball. I also always had the dream to be prom queen like my mom and knew she would be so proud of me if I was. Well, the day came when I was crowned prom queen, just like her! I was beaming. However, I was surprised when both of my parents were proud, but I did not get the fulfillment from them that I was looking for. They told me these accomplishments did not make them proud or make them love me more or less. They already love me because I am their child. God looks at us the same, did you know that? I get this false mentality all the time I can make God "proud" of me, or worse, that I can disappoint Him if I do not do enough or be enough. God's love for you can never change no matter what you do because you are His child. He already loved you the moment you conceived in the womb as much as He will love you the day you die, with or without all your accomplishments.

I have friends and family who have dealt with infertility and miscarriages. I have talked with them to get an understanding of the intense pain, heartache and what brings them comfort in the difficult time. It is so hard because there is conflict in what brings some people comfort, but others hurt. Some people take comfort in knowing it will happen in God's time. Others experience grief when their heart is hurting. Some said the best thing is just to know others are hurting with them and praying for them. Check in with your friends and family to see how they are doing. Scripture references how God is the Giver and Taker of life, and the grief and prayer that were to follow. "The angel of the Lord appeared to her and said, 'You are barren and childless, but you are going to become pregnant and give birth to a son.'" -Judges 13:3. "He settles the childless woman in her home as a happy mother of children. Praise the Lord." -Psalm 113:9.

"So, Boaz took Ruth, and she became his wife. When he made love to her, the Lord enabled her to conceive, and she gave birth to a son. The women said to Naomi: "Praise be to the Lord, who this day has not left you without a guardian-redeemer. May he become famous throughout Israel! He will renew your life and sustain you in your old age. For your daughter-in-law, who loves you and who is better to you than seven sons, has given him birth." Then Naomi took the child in her arms and cared for him. The women living there said, "Naomi has a son!" And they named him Obed. He was the father of Jesse, the father of David." -Ruth 4:13-17.

God closed Hannah's womb. In deep anguish Hannah prayed to God weeping bitterly making a vow if He gave her a son, she will give him back all the days of her life. (See 1 Samuel 1:10-11). "Eli answered, "'Go in peace, and may the God of Israel grant you what you have asked of him.' She said, 'May your servant find favor in your eyes.' Then she went her way and ate something, and her face was no longer downcast. Early the next morning they arose and worshipped before the Lord and then went back to their home at Ramah. Elkanah made love to his wife Hannah, and the Lord remembered her. So, in the course of time Hannah became pregnant and gave birth to a son. She named him Samuel, saying, "Because I asked the Lord for him." -1 Samuel 1:17-20.

"I prayed for this child, and the Lord has granted me what I asked of him. So now I give him to the Lord. For his whole life he will be given over to the Lord." And he worshiped the Lord there." -1 Samuel 1:27-28. Elizabeth says the same in Luke 1:25 about John.

"Then Hannah prayed and said: "My heart rejoices in the Lord; in the Lord my horn is lifted high. My mouth boasts over my enemies, for I delight in your deliverance. "There is no one holy like the Lord; there is no one besides you; there is no Rock like our God. "Do not keep talking so proudly or let your mouth speak such arrogance, for the Lord is a God who knows, and by him deeds are weighed. "The bows of the warriors are broken, but those who stumbled are armed with strength. Those who were full hire themselves out for food, but those who were hungry are hungry no more. She who was barren has borne seven children, but she who has had many sons' pines away. "The Lord brings death and makes alive; he brings down to the grave and raises up. The Lord sends poverty and wealth; he humbles, and he exalts. He raises the poor from the dust and lifts the needy from the ash heap; he seats them with princes and has them inherit a throne of honor. "For the foundations of the earth are the Lord's; on them he has set the world. He will guard the feet of his faithful servants, but the wicked will be silenced in the place of darkness." -1 Samuel 2:1-9.

The stature and favor with the Lord and people. (See 1 Samuel 2:21 and 1 Samuel 2:26). The Lord was gracious to Hannah with three sons and two daughters, one being Samuel who grew up in. (See 2 Samuel 13:10-12)

"Both of them were righteous in the sight of God, observing all the Lord's commands and decrees blamelessly. But they were childless because Elizabeth was not able to conceive, and they were both very old." -Luke 1:6-7 (Luke 1:5).

"But the angel said to him: "Do not be afraid, Zechariah; your prayer has been heard. Your wife Elizabeth will bear you a son, and you are to call him John. He will be a joy and delight to you, and many will rejoice because of his birth, for he will be great in the sight of the Lord." -Luke 1:13-14 (Luke 1:8-12 and Luke 1:15-16).

"...to make ready a people prepared for the Lord." -Luke 1:17. However, in Luke 1:18-20 Zechariah doubted because of their age, and the angel made him silent due to his unbelief until John was born in Luke 1:63-65.

We look at those in the Bible and realize there is hope for all of us. Even those who made the greatest impact on the world from their faith in God, made the worst mistakes which lead to pain in their families. 2 Samuel 13:14 talks about David's daughter and son which unfortunately is a story about rape. Absolutely devastating. I say this so you know you are not alone if you feel the weight of the broken world affecting your family. God wants to help, and every single family has brokenness they have either worked through or are working through. Do not be fooled from outward appearances. "...but the house of the righteous stands firm." -Proverbs 12:7. "The Lord's curse is on the house of the wicked, but he blesses the home of the righteous." -Proverbs 3:33 (1 Chronicles 13:14 and 2 Samuel 23:5). The verse in 1 Chronicles 13:14 gives a specific example about how this was true for Obed-Edom. The Lord blessed his household and everything he had because the ark of God was in their household. We will never have it together, so the key is we are only righteous in Christ, and making the broken home centered on Christ to bring restoration and reconciliation within relationships in the family. From youth until today until we are old, we will never see the righteous forsaken and their children will be a blessing. (See Psalm 37:25-26).

He commands us to tell the next generation, our children, the praiseworthy deeds of the Lord in His power, the wonders He has done for Jacob and Israel so they can tell their children and put their trust in God, not forgetting his deeds or commands. (See Psalm 78:4-7). Every time I confided to my friend, Claire, who is about 10 years younger, with something I was worried about, her immediate response was to trust God. There is never anxiousness in her voice, and always peace that whatever happens, He will take care of. Whatever happens, He will turn for His glory. Whatever happens, will be His perfect will. I admire that there is no hesitancy whenever I come to her. You can tell she genuinely cares about me and what I am struggling with, but where the peace comes from is regardless of my situations, is her complete trust in God's omnipotence. No matter what the world has to say, it does not phase her. I have been working on responding the same way while our nation faces political turmoil and as the world continues to fall away from the ways of God.

"Blessed are those who fear the Lord, who find great delight in his commands. Their children will be mighty in the land; the generation of the upright will be blessed." -Psalm 112:1-2. "Whoever fears the Lord has a secure fortress, and for their children it will be a refuge." -Proverbs 14:2. Even though children still must make their own choices and parents cannot receive salvation for their children, it comes down to whether we fear the Lord or not. That stance will still have a direct effect on our children.

"Blessed are all who fear the Lord, who walk in obedience to him. You will eat the fruit of your labor; blessings and prosperity will be yours. Your wife will be like a fruitful vine within your house; your children will be like olive shoots around your table. Yes, this will be the blessing for the man who fears the Lord." -Psalm 128:1-4.

Your entire family is affected whether you fear the Lord or not, as this fear will directly impact how you live.

"Then our sons in their youth will be like well-nurtured plants, and our daughters will be like pillars carved to adorn a palace. Our barns will be filled with every kind of provision. Our sheep will increase by thousands, by tens of thousands in our fields; our oxen will draw heavy loads. There will be no breaching of walls, no going into captivity, no cry of distress in our streets. Blessed is the people of whom this is true; blessed is the people whose God is the Lord." -Psalm 144:12-15.

"A good person leaves an inheritance for their children's children, but a sinner's wealth is stored up for the righteous." -Proverbs 13:22. "Those who do not provide for their relatives, especially their own household, is worse than an unbeliever." -1 Timothy 5:7-8. God even provides financial guidance for families. He advises us as parents to provide for our own family directly in the household, as well as to leave an inheritance for grandchildren.

"If you spare your children discipline, God compares this to hating your kids but if you love them you will discipline." -Proverbs 13:24 (Proverbs 19:18 and Proverbs 23:13-14). Discipline creates hope and the Bible even says it steers children from death itself. "Folly is bound up in the heart of a child, but the rod of

419

discipline will drive it far away." -Proverbs 22:15. Isn't it funny that it seems you don't have to teach kids to misbehave? Many studies have been performed to determine whether kids will cheat or not for a reward if they do not think anyone is watching them as opposed to someone watching them or telling them that God or their imaginary friend is. I think most would say 100% of the kids cheated when thinking no one was watching. "Discipline your children, and they will give you peace; they will bring you the delights you desire." -Proverbs 29:17. Parents sometimes seem to be scared to discipline their children, thinking it will ruin their relationship with them when it is the opposite. If you discipline sternly out of love, trying to steer them on the right path and not to satisfy your own anger, it leads to peace and life for your children and your whole family.

Help your parents out. They are under so much pressure to "control" you even when they ultimately have no means to. Tell them you are confident God is taking care of you, so they know you are okay, even when going through hard times. "A fool spurns a parent's discipline, but whoever heeds correction shows prudence." -Proverbs 15:5 (Proverbs 13:1). Do not reject your parent's discipline but pay close attention to correction to have self-control. "To have a fool for a child brings grief; there is no joy for the parent of a godless fool." -Proverbs 17:21. "A wise son brings joy to his father, but a foolish son brings grief to his mother." -Proverbs 10:1 (Proverbs 17:25 and Proverbs 23:22-25). "If someone curses their father or mother, their lamp will be snuffed out in pitch darkness." -Proverbs 20:20. Do not curse your parents. I know it gets hard when the anger is fuming, and emotions are high. Words may come to mind but do all you can not to curse them.

You are supposed to honor your father and mother, as this is the first commandment with a promise. "Children, obey your parents in the Lord and honor your mother and father which is the first commandment with a promise, so that it may go well with you, and you can enjoy a long life. Fathers, bring up your children in the training and instruction of the Lord." -Ephesians 6:1-4. Paul says just like a nursing mother cares for her children, so he loves those in Thessalonica. He was delighted to share the gospel and his life. He talks about his toil and hardship, working to not be a burden while he preached the gospel. He says he dealt with each of them like a father that deals with his children, encouraging, comforting, and urging to live lives worthy of God, who calls you into his kingdom and glory. (See 1

Thessalonians 2:7-12). If your parents ask you to do something Christ would not approve of, pray God to show you how you can still do what is right while wording it in a way to honor your parents.

"Instruction is given not to rebuke older men harshly but talk as if he is your father. Treat younger men as brothers, older women as mothers and younger women as sisters with purity. Give proper attention to widows making sure their family puts their religion to practice by caring for them to please God." -1 Timothy 5:1-4.

This encouragement addresses you like a father and his son. It says to the son, take the Lord's discipline seriously, do not lose heart when He rebukes you because He disciplines who He loves, who has Jesus. Embrace hardship as discipline. God is treating us as His children, and what children are not disciplined by their Father? If you don't have discipline, you are not truly His child. We respect our earthy Father for his discipline; how much more should we submit to our Father and live! Our father's discipline for a little while, but God disciplines us for our good to share in his holiness. (See Hebrews 12:5-10).

"Remember how the Lord your God led you all the way in the wilderness these forty years, to humble and test you in order to know what was in your heart, whether or not you would keep his commandments. He humbled you, causing you to hunger and then feeding you with manna, which neither you nor your ancestors had known, to teach you that man does not live on bread alone but on every word that comes from the mouth of the Lord. Your clothes did not wear out and your feet did not swell during these forty years. Know then in your heart that as a man disciplines his son, so the Lord your God disciplines you." -Deuteronomy 8:2-5.

"My son, do not despise the Lord's discipline, and do not resent his rebuke, because the Lord disciplines those he loves, as a father the son he delights in." -Proverbs 3:11-12 (Revelation 3:19). Just like parent's discipline children because they love them, the Lord does the same with us.

"Anyone who loves their father or mother more than me is not worthy of me; anyone who loves their son or daughter more than me is not worthy of me." - Matthew 10:37 (Malachi 1:6). "Someone told him, "Your mother and brothers are standing outside, wanting to see you." He replied, "My mother and brothers are those who hear God's word and put it into practice." -Luke 8:20-21 (Matthew 12:49-50, Mark 3:34-35, Mark 10:28-31, Luke 18:28-30, and Matthew 19:27-30). God is clear we are to love and care for our families. Then what do these verses mean? Jesus is making a point that even though our family is supposed to be our priority, He is supposed to come first. He also makes the point that even though they are our family by blood they will always have a special place in our hearts. Our church family is what will last for eternity, which hopefully our families by blood are a part of, too. Anyone who is a believer in the world is a part of the church family, and He wants us to recognize them as just that.

"The disciples asked Jesus who is the greatest in the Kingdom of Heaven? He called a child and said unless you become like little children, you will never enter the Kingdom of Heaven. You must take the lowly position of this child to be the greatest in Heaven. Whoever welcomes one such child in my name welcomes me. God says the children's angels always see God's face." -Matthew 18:1-5 (Mark 9:36-37, Luke 9:48, Matthew 18:6, Luke 17:1-2, Mark 9:42, Matthew 19:13-14, Mark 10:13-16, Luke 18:15-17, Matthew 20:16, Matthew 19:13-14, Mark 10:13-16, Luke 18:15-1, Matthew 18:10, Matthew 18:6, Luke 17:1-2 and Mark 9:42).

God gives a harsh warning to those who cause children to stumble. When trying to help children or youth in general, let them feel you embracing them without judgment. Let them know even if they are struggling, you are there to walk beside them and they are welcome to talk to you anytime. Children are considered the greatest in the Kingdom of God and should be treated as and reminded of this!

"Teach sounds doctrine, teach older man to be temperate, worthy of respect, self-controlled, sound in faith, love and endurance. Teach older women to be reverent in how they live with no slander, careful with addictions to wine and to teach what is good. They should teach younger women to love their husbands and children, self-control, pure, busy at home, kindness, to be subject to their husbands. Encourage younger men to be self-controlled. Set an example doing what is good, teaching and showing integrity, soundness of speech that cannot be condemned so those who oppose you are ashamed." -Titus 2:1-8.

The guide for older men is to be temperate, worthy of respect, self-controlled, sound in faith, love and endurance while mentoring younger men to do the same.

Women are to work on refraining from talking about others behind their backs to bring them down or have others look differently about them, to enjoy wine but not to become addicted, and to mentor younger women in love, work and to have self-control. We are to teach, mentor, and live in such a way that those who oppose those who live for Christ cannot truly find a reason why.

I want to elaborate more on why and how to not slander others. I have struggled in two ways with slander. One, the desire to talk about someone else to others when they have hurt you in order to change how others feel about them. This is wrong and I have quickly convicted myself of that, and two, the desire of wanting to be honest with others when they inquire about an individual. There have been times my heart is in the right place in the sense I truly do not want others to feel ill toward anyone who has wronged me, but if someone asks me specifically about my relationship with that individual, I do not want to lie and say it is great. It is not your responsibility, and I would argue it is wrong for you to share what could slander that person depending on who you are talking to. Pray for God's discernment if you truly need advice on how to handle a situation or relationship. I know I have been convicted and need to be more careful that even in my heart if I think I am being truthful, if I willfully know what I am saying will slander the person, I need to pray for more discernment from Christ instead of the automatic sense of needing to tell the truth. Do not lie. I am not encouraging you to lie, as it is just as much a sin to do so, but I do feel God will help you with how to word your situation or relationship in a way you can get the help you need without slander.

"I have no greater joy than this, to hear my children walking in the truth." -3 John 4 (2 John 1:4). As a parent, I cannot imagine a greater joy than knowing our kids are walking in the truth. Even though we cannot make the decision for them, we have so much of an influence in our guidance, example, and prayer. The good news is, regardless of the outcome in your day-to-day life of parenting, you never have to feel anxious because God is the builder of your home and family, and you, your home and family belong to Him. Pray and put it in His hands. I cannot wait to see the beautiful home and family He creates for His glory and goodness, and for your goodness, through all the mistakes and imperfections. Even if some in the family refuse to believe, you can keep Him in the home. You best believe He is present with His Holy Spirit inside of you, and never underestimate the power of a praying family member. With God in the home, it will be the best! "For every house is built by someone, but God is the builder of everything." -Hebrews 3:4. "Everything under Heaven belongs to me." -Job 41:11.

CONCLUSION

Revelation 1:3 says, "Blessed is the one who reads aloud the words of this prophecy, and blessed are those who hear it and take to heart what is written in it, because the time is near." Revelation 22:7 says "Look, I am coming soon! Blessed is the one who keeps the words of the prophecy written in this scroll". We do not know when Jesus is returning, but we know it is soon!

Romans 13:11-12 says "And do this, understanding the present time: The hour has already come for you to wake up from your slumber, because our salvation is nearer now than when we first believed. The night is nearly over; the day is almost here. So let us put aside the deeds of darkness and put on the armor of light."

We do not know the exact date, so what now? What about today?

2 Peter 3:11-18 says "Since everything will be destroyed in this way, what kind of people ought you to be? You ought to live holy and godly lives as you look forward to the day of God and speed its coming. That day will bring about the destruction of the Heavens by fire, and the elements will melt in the heat. But in keeping with his promise we are looking forward to a new Heaven and a new earth, where righteousness dwells. So then, dear friends, since you are looking

forward to this, make every effort to be found spotless, blameless and at peace with him. Bear in mind that our Lord's patience means salvation, just as our dear brother Paul also wrote you with the wisdom that God gave him. He writes the same way in all his letters, speaking in them of these matters. His letters contain some things that are hard to understand, which ignorant and unstable people distort, as they do the other Scriptures, to their own destruction. Therefore, dear friends, since you have been forewarned, be on your guard so that you may not be carried away by the error of the lawless and fall from your secure position. But grow in the grace and knowledge of our Lord and Savior Jesus Christ. To him be glory both now and forever! Amen."

2 Peter 1:3-11 says "His divine power has given us everything we need for a godly life through our knowledge of him who called us by his own glory and goodness. Through these he has given us his very great and precious promises, so that through them you may participate in the divine nature, having escaped the corruption in the world caused by evil desires. For this very reason, make every effort to add to your faith goodness; and to goodness, knowledge; and to knowledge, self-control; and to self-control, perseverance; and to perseverance, godliness; and to godliness, mutual affection; and to mutual affection, love. For if you possess these qualities in increasing measure, they will keep you from being ineffective and unproductive in your knowledge of our Lord Jesus Christ. But whoever does not have them is nearsighted and blind, forgetting that they have been cleansed from their past sins. Therefore, my brothers and sisters, make every effort to confirm your calling and election. For if you do these things, you will never stumble, and you will receive a rich welcome into the eternal kingdom of our Lord and Savior Jesus Christ".

Thank you, Jesus, for using me in ways I never could on my own. Thank you everyone for your prayers. Thank you to my amazing editors, Ashley, Aimee and my designer Sharon. You took all my thoughts, helped me organize them and made it into finished work. I know it was not an accident God needed each of us working on this when He did. I couldn't do it without you, and I can't thank you all enough for your obedience to Him.

I want you to know you can do all things through Him, everything. I pray at the end of my book you do not remember my name, but His. God made you. God is for you. Jesus loves you. And made you for an exact purpose. With God, all things are possible. Whatever mountain is in front of you, Jesus is the answer. I hope you choose Him. I promise it will be the best decision you have ever made in your life, and then after! For more, go to YoucanthroughChrist.com.

"I can do all things through Christ who strengthens me." Philippians 4:13

ABOUT THE AUTHOR

Lexi is the founder of You Can Through Christ, a ministry focused on promoting Christ and encouraging men and women to grow in their faith and love of our Savior. In addition, she works as an occupational therapist and a certified hand therapist for a group of top hand surgeons. Lexi enjoys sports, hiking, trying new recipes and sharing her love of Jesus with the world. More information about Lexi and You Can Through Christ ministries can be found at https://youcanthroughchrist.com/.

Made in the USA
Monee, IL
23 April 2025